SpringerBriefs in Modern Perspectives on Disability Research

This book series on disability research is a comprehensive collection of research on disability and related issues. The series is designed to promote interdisciplinary collaboration and exchange, bringing together scholars and practitioners from different fields to share their perspectives and insights. Disability research is an interdisciplinary field that examines the social, cultural, historical, and political dimensions of disability. It encompasses a wide range of topics, including disability rights, accessibility, assistive technologies, healthcare, education, employment, and social welfare. Disability research scholars employ a range of theoretical and methodological approaches to understand the experiences of people with disabilities, as well as the ways in which disability intersects with other social identities such as race, gender, sexuality, and class.

The series seeks to advance knowledge and understanding of disability by publishing rigorous, innovative, and relevant research. It aims to promote disability rights and social justice by highlighting the ways in which people with disabilities are marginalized and discriminated against in society, and advocating for greater social inclusion and accessibility. The series also seeks to inform policy and practice by disseminating research findings that can help to shape policy decisions and contribute to positive social change.

Dasari Nagasen • Sai Kiran S. S. Pindiprolu
Editors

Transforming Disability Studies

Inclusive Approaches and Emerging Trends

Springer

Editors
Dasari Nagasen
School of Pharmacy
Aditya University
Surampalem, Andhra Pradesh, India

Sai Kiran S. S. Pindiprolu
School of Pharmacy
Aditya University
Surampalem, Andhra Pradesh, India

ISSN 3004-9709 ISSN 3004-9717 (electronic)
SpringerBriefs in Modern Perspectives on Disability Research
ISBN 978-981-95-9003-2 ISBN 978-981-95-9004-9 (eBook)
https://doi.org/10.1007/978-981-95-9004-9

This Springer imprint is published by the registered company Springer Nature Singapore Pte Ltd.
The registered company address is: 152 Beach Road, #21-01/04 Gateway East, Singapore 189721, Singapore

Contents

About the Editors and Contributors

About the Editors

Dasari Nagasen is an academician and pharmaceutical researcher in the field of Pharmaceutical Sciences, with a focused specialization in nanomedicine, advanced drug delivery systems, cancer therapeutics, and translational research. He is currently pursuing his Ph.D. at Andhra University, Visakhapatnam, and holds a Master's degree in Pharmaceutics, with strong expertise in formulation development and nanocarrier-based therapeutics.

He has 10 years of teaching and research experience and is presently serving as an Assistant Professor at Aditya University, Andhra Pradesh, India.

Nagasen has authored and co-authored multiple research articles, review papers, and book chapters published by reputed international publishers and peer-reviewed journals. He is actively involved in manuscript reviewing and academic writing, contributing to the advancement of pharmaceutical and biomedical research.

In addition to his academic role, he is deeply committed to research mentoring, academic entrepreneurship, and capacity building for early-career researchers, particularly in resource-limited settings.

Sai Kiran S. S. Pindiprolu, M.Pharm., Ph.D. Dr. Sai Kiran Pindiprolu is an accomplished academician and researcher in the field of Pharmaceutical Sciences, with a strong specialization in pharmacology, nanomedicine, and cancer therapeutics. He earned his Ph.D. and M.Pharm. in Pharmacology from JSS Academy of Higher Education & Research, Mysuru.

He has over 8 years of teaching and research experience and is currently serving as an Assistant Professor at Aditya University. He is a SERB-TARE Fellow (2021–2024) and has successfully completed an SERB-funded research project worth ₹18.3 lakhs. He is also a recipient of ICMR Senior Research Fellowship.

Dr. Pindiprolu has published 50+ research articles in reputed SCI/SCIE journals with 1000+ citations (H-index: 20) and has authored multiple book chapters with leading international publishers. He holds four granted patents in the areas of nanomedicine and targeted drug delivery. His research contributions have been recognized with awards such as Best Inventor Award (2023) and Best Research Scholar Award (2019).

He serves as Associate Editor and Guest Editor for several international journals and is an active reviewer for leading publishers including Springer Nature, Elsevier, Wiley, and Taylor & Francis. His research interests focus on targeted drug delivery systems, cancer stem cells, breast cancer therapy, and nanotechnology-based therapeutics.

Contributors

Swetha Addanki Department of Pharmaceutical Analysis, Malla Reddy Pharmacy College, Hyderabad, India

Masa Amala Department of Pharmacology, Krishna University College of Pharmaceutical Science and Research, Machilipatnam, Krishna, Andhra Pradesh, India

Baliwada Aparna Department of Pharmaceutical Chemistry, Malla Reddy Pharmacy College, Maisammaguda, Hyderabad, India

B. Babu Department of Pharmaceutical Analysis, JSS College of Pharmacy, JSS Academy of Higher Education and Research, The Nilgiris, Ooty, Tamil Nadu, India

Ashwitha Balasani Department of Pharmacy Practice, Malla Reddy Pharmacy College, Maisammaguda, Hyderabad, India

Sarad Pawar Naik Bukke Department of Pharmaceutics & Pharmaceutical Technology, Kampala International University, Ishaka, Uganda

Sara Chandurwala JSS College of Pharmacy, JSS Academy of Higher Education and Research, Nilgiris, Ooty, Tamil Nadu, India

Bindu Dwarampudi Department of Pharmaceutical Chemistry, Sri Vasavi Institute of Pharmaceutical Sciences, Tadepalligudem, India

B. Gowramma Department of Pharmaceutical Chemistry, JSS College of Pharmacy, JSS Academy of Higher Education and Research, The Nilgiris, Ooty, Tamil Nadu, India

B. Hardha Department of Pharmaceutical Chemistry, JSS College of Pharmacy, JSS Academy of Higher Education and Research, The Nilgiris, Ooty, Tamil Nadu, India

S. Mahalakshmi Department of Pharmacology, Malla Reddy Pharmacy College, Hyderabad, India

Geeta Sai Mani Chemical biology Core, H.Lee Moffitt Cancer Center and Research Institute, Tampa, FL, USA

Kesari Lakshmi Manasa Department of Pharmaceutical Chemistry, Malla Reddy Pharmacy College, Hyderabad, India

Swathi Nalla Department of Pharmacology, Malla Reddy Pharmacy College, Hyderabad, India

Vemula Navya Department of Pharmacy, Malla Reddy Pharmacy College, Maisammaguda, Hyderabad, India

Amol S. Rakte Department of Pharmaceutics, Indrayani Vidya Mandir's, Krishnarao Bhegade Institute of Pharmaceutical Education and Research, Talegaon Dabhade, Tal-Maval, Pune, Maharashtra, India

Ammana Sathwika Reddy Department of Pharmacy Practice, Malla Reddy Pharmacy College, Maisammaguda, Hyderabad, India

Gantla Deemanth Reddy Department of Pharmacy Practice, Malla Reddy Pharmacy College, Maisammaguda, Hyderabad, India

Andhavarapu Santosh Central Drug Standard Control Organization, New Delhi, India

Saravanan Data Works, Waterford, Ireland

Aithagoni Sathwika Department of Pharmacy, Malla Reddy Pharmacy College, Maisammaguda, Hyderabad, India

Muskan Sharma Department of Pharmaceutical Chemistry, JSS College of Pharmacy, JSS Academy of Higher Education and Research, The Nilgiris, Ooty, Tamil Nadu, India

Gurugubelli Sowjanya Ratan Tata Innovations Hub (RTIH), Rajamahendravaram, Andhra Pradesh, India

Gannavarapu Kumara Swamy Department of Pharmacy Practice, Malla Reddy Pharmacy College, Maisammaguda, Hyderabad, India

Nayudu Teja Department of Pharmaceutics, JSS College of Pharmacy, JSS Academy of Higher Education and Research, The Nilgiris, Ooty, Tamil Nadu, India

G. Tulja Rani Department of Pharmaceutical Analysis, Malla Reddy Pharmacy College, Maisammaguda, Hyderabad, India

Sanga Vaishnavi Department of Pharmacy, Malla Reddy Pharmacy College, Maisammaguda, Hyderabad, India

About the Editors and Contributors

Chapter 1
Introduction to the Modern Disability Perspective

Kesari Lakshmi Manasa, Bindu Dwarampudi, Nayudu Teja, Geeta Sai Mani, Andhavarapu Santosh, and Masa Amala

Abstract The view of disability represents a serious paradigm shift of the traditional models of deficit-view to the current, more inclusive, rights-based and socially constructed vision of disability. The perception of disability used to be based mainly on the medical model relied on impairment identification, diagnosis, and rehabilitation intervention. Nevertheless, the modern thinking, which was shaped by the social, cultural, and human rights models, understands disability as the dynamic interaction between people with various abilities and barriers that are attitudinal, environmental, and institutional—that limits their full-scale participation in society. This chapter presents the development of the disability perspectives, with the social model of disability, the biopsychosocial model, and the United Nations Convention on the Rights of Persons with Disabilities (UNCRPD) being the major theoretical approaches mentioned. The focus is on the ideas of accessibility, inclusion, empowerment, and intersectionality, that are the main points of contemporary discussion and policy formulation. This chapter attempts to create an awareness of disability as

K. L. Manasa (✉)
Department of Pharmaceutical Chemistry, Malla Reddy Pharmacy College, Hyderabad, India

B. Dwarampudi
Department of Pharmaceutical Chemistry, Sri Vasavi Institute of Pharmaceutical Sciences, Tadepalligudem, India

N. Teja
Department of Pharmaceutics, JSS College of Pharmacy, JSS Academy of Higher Education and Research, The Nilgiris, Ooty, Tamil Nadu, India

G. S. Mani
Chemical biology Core, H.Lee Moffitt Cancer Center and Research Institute, Tampa, FL, USA

A. Santosh
Central Drug Standard Control Organization, New Delhi, India

M. Amala
Department of Pharmacology, Krishna University College of Pharmaceutical Science and Research, Machilipatnam, Krishna, Andhra Pradesh, India

D. Nagasen, S. K. S. S. Pindiprolu (eds.), *Transforming Disability Studies*, SpringerBriefs in Modern Perspectives on Disability Research,
https://doi.org/10.1007/978-981-95-9004-9_1

not a personal tragedy but a crucial aspect of human diversity that requires social justice, equity, and active citizenship to take place.

Keywords Disability · Biopsychosocial · Medical model · Charity model · Social model

1.1 Introduction

Disability is an umbrella term, that include impairments, activity limitations, as well as participation restrictions. Impairment is a problem with body functioning or structure, an activity limitation is a problem that a person experiences in carrying out a task or an action whereas a participation restriction is a problem that a person experiences participating in a life situation. Disability is thus a complex phenomenon since it is a blend of characteristics of his or her body and characteristics of the society in which he or she lives. The Convention on the rights of persons with disabilities (2006) adopted by United Nations is the first legally binding disability specific human rights convention, which has given two definitions of disability. The Convention Preamble states that Disability is an outcome of the interplay between the people with the impairments and the attitudinal and environmental factors that deny them the full and effective involvement in the society with others. Again it points out that Persons with disabilities include people who have a long-term physical impairment and also those with a mental, intellectual, or sensory impairment when put together with other barriers, such a person may be subjected to restraint in the full and effective exercise of the rights to engage with the rest of the society on a same status. Both the terms show a shift towards a social model of disability as opposed to a medical model of disability.

More than one billion, 16% of the world, are disabled and more prevalent in the developing countries. People living with disabilities have greater chances of having poor socioeconomic outcomes in the form of poor education, health outcomes, low employment levels, and poverty. Poverty may also lead to disability by increasing malnutrition, inadequate access to education and health care services, poor working conditions, poor environment pollution, and the lack of access to clean water and sanitation. Disability may also contribute to the increase of the risk of poverty, as they have no education, and therefore, they have limited employment opportunities, low income, and expensive disability. Some of the barriers to complete social and economic inclusion of persons with disabilities are the nonadaptability of means of communication, gaps in service delivery, the nonadaptability of assistive devices, technologies, and the inaccessibility of physical environments and transportation, discriminating prejudice and stigma of the society. Food insecure households have higher persons with disabilities because they are less likely to have economic resources as they are more affected by poverty and less likely to have employment as opposed to other households which have no persons with disabilities. When there is witnessing of humanitarian crisis and conflict, individuals with disabilities would be more likely to encounter violence, exploitation or abuse, and die two to four times more often.

Disability is a part of human experience, which involves the various interactions of people with the physical, social, and institutional environments. The perception of disability in the society has during centuries been defined within a medical and charity system in which the disabled persons were regarded as objects of care, curing, or recovery. Nevertheless, a radical reconsideration of this position has occurred in the twentieth and twenty-first centuries, and an alternative view of disability has emerged: it is the result of environmental and attitudinal constraints and not a deficiency of the person him/herself that is the cause of disability. In this chapter, the reader is presented with the development of the disability thinking, where the prevalent medical approach to the issue was substituted with the social and human rights approaches. It covers the most important theoretical frameworks, policy emergence, and movements across the world which have transformed disability as a question of equity and justice. Through this change, the chapter is set to give a background knowledge on the current discourse of disability, inclusion, and empowerment (Barnes & Mercer, 2018).

1.2 Historical Evolution of Disability Perspectives

1.2.1 Ancient and Medieval Views

Disability in most societies in the ancient times was perceived in terms of spirituality or morality. Weaknesses were usually linked to divine retribution, sin, Karma, fate or supernatural interference. Experiences such as reverence, tolerance, hiding, and stigmatization of individuals with a disability might be diverse in different cultures. In both Greek and Roman societies, physical perfection was highly valued; they marginalized people who had obvious deficiencies. In medieval Europe, disability was associated with religious images, and that at times, disabled people were treated as objects of charity.

1.2.2 Enlightenment and Early Medicalization

During the Enlightenment, there were growing efforts to define disability in scientific and pathological terms. Doctors tried to find biological causes of impairments that gave rise to medical model of disability. Disability was a subject of scientific learning and not spiritual interpretation. Nevertheless, this change also supported the idea of disabled individuals being in need of treatment, correction, or institutionalization.

1.2.3 Institutional Era (Eighteenth–Twentieth Century)

Disability policy in Europe, North America, and some parts of Asia was large-scale institutionalized. Individuals with disabilities were confined in asylum, special schools, and long-term care centers in many cases without familial and community attachment. This period reinforced the belief that disability was an individual issue managed through segregation. There were widespread institutional abuses, neglect, and human rights abuses.

1.2.4 Postwar Rehabilitation and the Rise of Therapies

Numerous soldiers came back to the country after World Wars I and II with injuries and disabilities. Governments spent much on the rehabilitation sciences, development of prosthetics, vocational training and therapeutic programs. This was still based on medical views but this was the period when the role of involvement in the economic life was acknowledged.

1.2.5 Disability Rights Movement (1960s–1990s)

Disability activists wanted to be treated as equal citizens inspired by the ideas of civil rights, feminist, and antiapartheid movements. The protests in the United States, the United Kingdom, and Australia and other places resulted in some fundamental changes to the legislation, education, and social attitudes. The accessibility, antidiscrimination legislation, deinstitutionalization, independent living, supported decision-making, community integration are the key demands (Charlton, 1998).

1.3 Traditional Models of Disability

Traditional disability models reflect previous models of understanding and reaction to disability, and are mostly dependent on medical, religious, and charity worldviews. Such models are inclined to put the problem of disability in the individual, and impairment is viewed as deficit, abnormality, condition to be cured, corrected, or given special care. Consequently, individuals with disabilities were commonly considered as being dependent, helpless, or even tragic individuals, and were segregated in either an institution, special school, or on a welfare system. The moral, charity, and medical model all are traditional approaches that follow mainly the diagnosis, treatment, and sympathy instead of autonomy, rights, and inclusion. Even as they led to new developments in the field of rehabilitation and medical care, they strengthened the stigma, discrimination, and marginalization by ignoring the influence of social, environmental, and structural factors. The importance of learning about these conventional models is that they underline the historical foundations of the attitudes of the society toward disability, and the contrast they develop can help to understand how modern, rights-based, and socially oriented approaches came into existence.

Traditional views were mostly based on biomedical or charitable assumptions.

1.3.1 Charity Model

The charity model is one of the first frames of reference for understanding disability. This model views persons with disabilities mainly as victims of unfortunate situations who are deserving of pity, kindness, and charitable support. As part of the charity model, disability is perceived as:

Personal disaster: Disability is framed as a misfortune that has occurred to a person.
A basis for dependency: Persons with disabilities are positioned as fundamentally dependent on the goodwill of others.
A condition worthy of pity: The appropriate social response is sympathy, not empowerment. The charity model exists in many forms in Indian society. Religious institutions often provide support to people with disabilities under their charitable activities. The media will often represent persons with disabilities as objects of inspiration or pity. Often fundraising campaigns use emotional appeals about the difficulty or suffering of persons with disabilities to encourage donations.

Limitations of the Charity Approach
Despite good intentions, the charity model is problematic in a number of ways:

Reinforces inequality: It perpetuates asymmetry in power between the "generous giver" and the "thankful recipient."
Undermines dignity: Framing the issue in terms of dependency undermines the dignity, worth, and agency of persons with disabilities.
Provides temporary fixes: Charities provide helpful supports, but address needs of the moment, not systemic barriers.
Does not hold to account: Giving is voluntary, not a right, and children and adults with disabilities are not necessarily entitled to the continued services of a given charity, given it is relying on the priorities of the contributors. Framing disability as a charitable matter focus on the generosity of donors rather than recognizing the rights of the disabled to full membership of society.

1.3.2 Medical Model

The concept of the "medical model of disability" has historically shaped the way disability is viewed by the public and professionals alike, and it views disability as a problem that needs fixing within a person's body by someone who is a medical doctor. Within the medical model, the disabled body is viewed as an entity requiring fixing. In this case, "typical abilities" are viewed as superior, and disabilities, whether physical or cognitive, are viewed as impairments that need to be removed often with assistance from an outside person. This is the framework that is still embedded in current health care and educational models, whereby an individual's impairment is considered to be the reason that they are unable to fully participate in society.

As an example, an individual who is using a wheelchair to get from place to place may want to access the entrance of a building that has stairs and no ramp. For the medical model, the wheelchair user's challenge with entering the building relates to their mobility impairment instead of the fact that the building entrance does not have a ramp. The medical model lays the burden of disability onto the individual who has the disability and concentrates on what is "wrong" with that person, instead of what is "wrong" with the situation, context, or environment.

Due to the medical model of disability, individuals with disabilities are likely to experience a sense of social exclusion, devaluation, and in most cases, are assumed to be completely incapacitated or they are simply pitiable. Living with a disability has been seen as the greatest drawback to many people not because of their physiques but the reaction of the society. The reaction of society starts with the unwelcome reception by social attitudes and opined social norms, not to mention the planned physical surroundings, which tend to be accommodating to others, but not to people with disabilities.

1.3.3 Moral Model or Religious Model

The moral model perceives disability as having some kind of meaning in regard to the morals, behavior, thoughts/thinking, etc. of a person (or family) and their karma. This is the case that in some ways the embodiments of the moral model may also involve the element of shame or stigma of disability especially when disability may be taken as a consequence of something bad or wrong at times the disability may be regarded to be a bad mark or bad doing of something to the victim. Instead, and depending on the view, disability can be a sign of honor, or a religion, or faith in the person—consider a religious person who has been chosen to exist with his disability since God has faith in him. The disability can also be positively viewed or a reminder of endured life struggle like stepping on a landmine or having polio. Overall, the moral model is a commonly portrayed perspective across the globe and media—such as movies that utilize a physical disability to show bad or evil/like nature, socially vs. media, what is evident and what the disabled person can accomplish or excel at, such as climbing El Capitan in Yosemite in a wheelchair.

1.3.4 Limitations of Traditional Model

Conventional concepts/models of disability-medical, charity, and moral models are constrained by an exclusive focus on the body and on the individual impairment, rather than seeing the social or environmental possibilities/factors that construct disability. These models cast disabled people in the role of passive recipient of care, treatment, or pity, accentuating dependency and alienation from the rest of society. Traditional concepts of disability promote the position of deficit, cure, and normalization, simultaneously maintaining barriers created by inaccessible infrastructures, fear, and/or discrimination, and regulations associated with policies of exclusion. The old paradigms of disability justified segregation in the institutional and special school setting (practice), used a policy of stigmatization instead of inclusive practices, and prevented the right, autonomy, and potential of people with disabilities. Traditional models of disability are restricted, disconnected from issues of participation and inclusion, and most importantly, not sufficiently pertinent to the structural changes necessary for participation and full integration into society (Degener, 2016).

1.4 Modern Models of Disability

Current models of disability signify a shift from the view of disability as an individual medical issue, towards a more complex interaction between individual characteristics and social structures. Current models go beyond the deficits of individuals and look at rights, engagement, and inclusion. Current models are not focused on impairments alone and talk about the significance of social attitudes, environmental access, cultural meaning, and policy systems in the lives of persons with disabilities. These models have been shaped by disability activism, a human rights perspective, and interdisciplinary scholarship, and posit that societal barriers (for instance, discrimination, inaccessibility, and controlling social institutions) create many of the problems faced by persons with disabilities, rather than the social conditions or bodies of persons with disabilities. Modern perspectives include: The Social Model, The Biopsychosocial Model, Human Rights Model, Cultural Model, and the Capabilities Approach. Together, current perspectives support the notions of empowerment, equality, and dignity and can define disability in the context of human diversity. In summary, together they are providing more holistic, inclusive, and justice perspectives for the area of policy, education, health care, and social development in contemporary societies.

1.4.1 Social Model of Disability

According to the social model, disability is merely one part of a person, just as race/ethnicity, gender, etc., is one part of a person. Disability is said to occur as a result of the unfit between the disabled individual and the (physical and social) environment. Disability is a difference in function, while a handicap is a barrier imposed by society. According to this view, therefore, the answer to the disabled is not to fix the disabled individual but to fix the environment or society. Negative stereotypes, discrimination, and oppression are barriers to environmental change and inclusion in society. Films that portray the social model of disability are more likely to depict disabled characters (as opposed to able-bodied) with each other forming connection, and growing without reliance on an able-bodied character. Other films depict disabled characters, more realistically, in the context of loving families, not "burdened" with the disability, as part of a society that is discriminatory, or as an activist to change laws.

The social model of disability dates back to the 1970s with the Union of the Physically impaired against segregation (UPIAS) of Great Britain. The social model marked a radical change in a medicalized model. This model differentiates impairment (physical, sensory, or cognitive difference) and disability. In this model, the issue is not that a person uses a wheelchair, but that buildings do not have ramps and public transport is not accessible. Likewise, it is not the impairment that marginalizes, but the societal structures that fail to honor human diversity.

The social model has played a key role in transforming the policies of the people, advocacy movements, and promoting the ideas of inclusive design. It also addresses agency, dignity, and participation and leaves behind the concept of dependency and deficiency. Critics, however, argue that the model does not emphasize sufficiently the lived experience of impairment e.g. pain or chronic illness which can also play a huge role in quality of life. However, the social model has and will be the basis of the present-day disability studies (Shakespeare, 2013).

1.4.2 The Biopsychosocial Model

As a response to the purely medical or social models, the more holistic explanation of disability is the biopsychosocial model which was popularized by The World Health Organization (WHO) under the name International Classification of Functioning, Disability and Health (ICF). Disability is viewed as a cost of biological, psychological, and social interactive matters. The biopsychosocial model recognizes the importance of medical treatment and rehabilitation, but also places attention on the environmental and social context of disability. The biopsychosocial emphasis on health and functioning provides a comprehensive view whereby improving societal inclusion and accessibility are equally valid to clinical treatment.

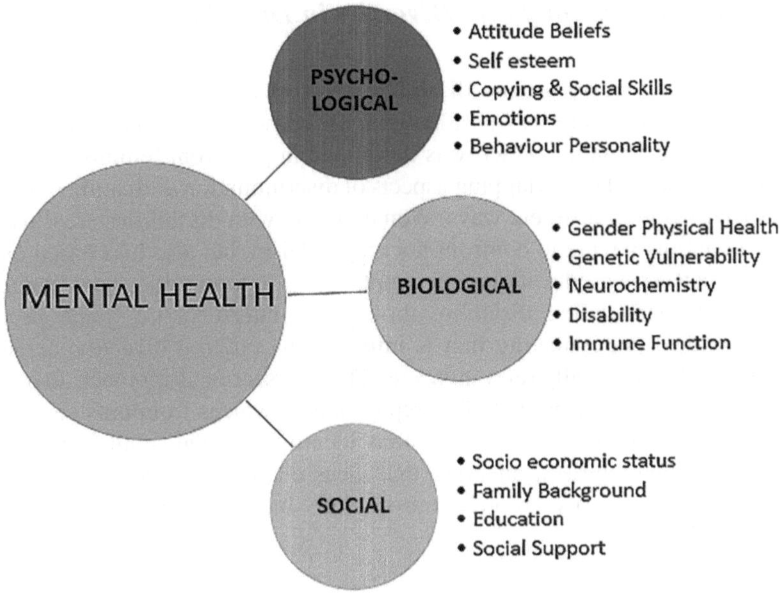

Fig. 1.1 Represents the Biopsychosocial Model of mental health

By recognizing biological, psychological, and social aspects of disability, the biopsychosocial model provides a bridge between theory and practice and became widely accepted in public health, occupational therapy and social work professions represented in Fig. 1.1.

1.4.3 The Human Rights Model of Disability

The latest and most influential model to the world is the human rights model. The model was created based on the concepts of equality, dignity, and autonomy in 2006, in the United Nations Convention on the Rights of Persons with Disabilities (UNCRPD). The Convention represented a significant acknowledgement that persons with disabilities are more than recipients of welfare; they are rights holders. The UNCRPD emphasizes participation, accessibility, and nondiscrimination as core principles, requiring states to lift barriers to full inclusion. The model also reframes disability as a changing condition influenced by the relationship between people and their environments. The rights perspective refocuses attention away from individual impairment and more toward societal obligation and ultimately universal design, inclusion in education, and equal opportunity employment.

1.4.4 Intersectionality and Diversity in Disability

Contemporary discourse around disability acknowledges that disability does not exist in a vacuum of other social identities like gender, race, class, and age. The notion of intersectionality, which was developed in part from feminist and critical race theories, views the overlapping aspects of discrimination as treating individuals to the social world in different ways. Women living with disabilities are illustrative of discrimination, having to confront not only ableism, but also bias based on gender, when accessing education and employment opportunities and navigating healthcare. Understanding disability through an intersectional frame promotes disability-related policymaking that is informed by cultural diversity, economic-inequality, and contextually relevant needs. The intersectional approach also widens the disability movement by including representative voices from outside disability communities or identities (e.g., indigenous identities, global-south countries, and neurodiverse communities), ensuring that ideas about the contemporary view of disability is necessarily representative and inclusive in a global sense (Nussbaum, 2006).

1.4.5 Education, Employment, and Social Inclusion

One of the most noticeable effects of disability under modernity occurred in inclusive education. The move from special education to inclusive education is based on the idea that all students should have the right to be educated in the general education system, with appropriate adaptations/alterations. An inclusive pedagogy, assistive technologies, and differentiation are now the accepted means of supporting different students with diverse needs. In the area of employment, modernity promotes equal opportunity, workplace accommodations, and affirmative action when hiring. In this modern view of disability, accessibility means much more than physical spaces, but also includes digital and attitudinal accessibility to enable each individual to use their skills and energy towards employment success. Social inclusion is also about encouraging participation within their communities, as well as social and cultural representation and accessibility.

1.4.6 Capabilities Approach

The Capabilities Approach of Amartya Sen, a renowned economist, and Martha C. Nussbaum, a renowned philosopher, is a normative approach that studies the capabilities of people in terms of what they can successfully do and be, rather than in terms of their resources, impairments, or economic outcomes. The capabilities approach also offers an additional point of interest in terms of disability, as the not only biomedical deficiencies or social impediments are considered, but also the question as to whether disabled individuals have the real freedom to live meaningful lives is addressed. Capabilities are substantive directions of choices are made in e.g. being educated, being part of community life, having access to work, safe bodily contact and cultural functions. The capabilities approach also further focuses on resources that can fall in the same category, but have varied requirements depending on the specific physical, social, or environmental conditions. Thus, equality should be beyond provision of resources. It entails fostering environments, facilitating technologies, accessible organizations, and personal accommodations to substantive freedom.

Nussbaum claims that human capabilities have ten prominent ones-life, bodily health, practical reason, control over the environment; and so on that should be granted to all human beings as justice. To individuals with disabilities, it will involve establishing a society centrally developed so as to eliminate the limiting influences and enable the growth and utilization of these strengths. This view is very consistent with the human rights approach to disability that emphasizes on the dignity, autonomy, and participation and has implications in the global disability policy, development programs, and inclusive education. Altogether, the capabilities approach offers a morally valid and holistic foundation of inclusion, diversity recognition, and structural barriers that affect people with disabilities.

1.4.7 From Awareness to Empowerment

The transition to a modern perspective of disability is not only an academic paradigm shift, it is a moral and social shift. The awareness campaigns, the advocacy groups, and social movements to explain the rights of those with disabilities have transformed the attitude of the society to a partnership rather than pity. Empowerment is now defined as the outcome when people with disabilities achieve more control of their lives, including about health care, education and community inclusion decisions. Technology has been a powerful enabling force as well. Digital access, assistive devices, and universal principles of design have enabled more independence and inclusion than has ever been possible in history. However, empowerment is more than physical access. It requires confronting long-standing and deep prejudices and re-culturing a stance of respect for difference (Oliver, 1990).

1.5 Global and Policy Perspectives

Disability became a global development issue in the last third of the twentieth century. Human rights agendas adopted by international organizations such as the WHO, UNICEF, and the UN started to reflect disability. This momentum peaked in 2006 with the UNCRPD, marking a shift to a rights-based model of disability.

While a modern perspective of disability is seen globally through the lens of the human rights agenda and sustainable development, the contents of the Sustainable Development Goals explicitly call for persons with disabilities to be included in education (Goal 4), employment (Goal 8), and the reduction of inequalities (Goal 10). Across the world, governments are increasingly passing domestic legislation in alignment with the UNCRPD, establishing standards for accessibility, antidiscrimination legislation, and social protection. However, significant differences between high-income and low-income countries exist. Stigma, lack of infrastructure and poverty continue to hinder the implementation of the modern perspective of disability in low-income countries. To ensure effective and successful implementation of the modern policy perspective of disability, intersectoral partnerships amongst government, civil society, academia, and persons with disabilities are essential (World Health Organization, 2001; World Health Organization and World Bank, 2011).

1.6 Current Challenges and Emerging Issues in Disability Studies and Disability Inclusion

Although there has been considerable advancement in policies, awareness, and rights-based frameworks, people with disabilities still encounter a range of ongoing and emerging issues. The greatest problem is between the law and the action. Although numerous nations have the disability rights laws in place, in line with the UN Convention on the Rights of Persons with Disabilities (UNCRPD), the obstacles, in terms of unavailable infrastructures, assistive technologies, and the social protection, are more extensive and enduring. Discrimination and stigma especially among the intellectually disabled, psychosocial, and those with invisible disabilities still limit the opportunities of people in terms of education, employment, and social participation. New and emerging issues are also reshaping the landscape of the disability inclusion. The rapid evolving technologies such as artificial intelligence, automation, and digital platform generate more opportunities and threats. Although technology has the potential to help people to be independent and more accessible, the issues of algorithmic discrimination, digital inequalities, and affordability continue to be a point of concern. Humanitarian crises and global warming affect disabled individuals in different ways and tend to unleash more harm on them during disasters since emergency planning and available shelters have not been developed properly (Rioux & Frazee, 2001). Besides this, demographic changes especially aging population are also raising the incidence of disability in all countries in the world and new models of care, city planning, and greater supports within the communities will be required. The growing awareness of mental health challenges in society supports the importance of considering insights into health that consider physical, psychological, and social health. As more attention is paid to disability identities and intersectional experiences, more emerging problems like gendered experiences of disability, economic inequity, and representation in the public life and media are a pressing matter of concern. To deal with the arising and persistent challenges, it will need to have a shared accountability and policymaking in which we will need to constantly review current and future manifestations of disability to make sure that we create a sense of belonging and dignity not only to disabled people but to all (Sen, 1999).

Future Directions in Disability Studies and Disability Inclusion
The discipline of disability studies and the inclusion concept are becoming regarded as the elements of human diversity and social justice in a more rewarding and promising contemporary context. Enlarged structures are progressively operationalizing intersectionality, universal design, and human rights in a fresh proactive view that encompasses inclusive, and not reactive, systems. One such proactive initiative involves meaningful development of inclusive policies involving persons with disabilities at every level of decision-making including, local, national, and global levels. Community-based systems of support, de-institutionalization, and public infrastructure that are accessible to all are still paramount. Increasingly, disability policies from every sector health, education, employment, urban planning, and digital innovation are integrating and incorporating strategies inclusive for all pursuits.

The future also rests upon exploiting technological innovation. Progress via assistive technologies, artificial intelligence, wearable devices, and smart environments can advance independence and participation. Nonetheless, the issues of affordability, equity, and ethical design will be needed to prevent further inequities. There is a need to make technology adhere to the creed of nothing about us without us and this should determine how technology is developed to develop solutions together with the disabled communities.

The other significant area of growth is to deepen research and evidence-base, and disability research is predominantly done through mixed-methods research, longitudinal research, and participatory research that incorporates the voices of persons with disabilities. Studies should create connections between disability and gender, caste, socioeconomic, aging, and mental health with increased awareness that disability is never an isolated phenomenon. This will involve the abandonment of impairment category to get into quality of life, well-being, and structural determinants of disability.

New demands of disability-inclusive disaster risk reduction and public health strategies will be determined by global and environmental issues such as climate change, displacement, pandemics, and humanitarian crises. The future requires the availability of early warning, the inclusion of the displaced communities in the evacuation and placement in shelters, and focus on the community social networks to create resilience. The final of the future directions will be a cultural transition towards inclusion that reorganizes the societal understanding of productivity, independence, and normalcy. Media representation and educational campaigns on inclusiveness and making people aware of it will be essential in altering the attitudes of people. Ultimately, it is hoped that dignity, equality, and access will be integrated into all systems and not merely allow persons with disabilities to engage, but thrive in the world in which they can enjoy the quality of life.

1.7 Conclusion

The modern view of disability transcends the narrow prisms of a medical diagnosis and welfare dependency. It views disability as multidimensional and social mediated so that it is not an issue to be fixed individually but to transform the system. Based on the principles of social justice, the contemporary perspective is that of equity, dignity, and participation of everybody. Since every society is dynamic, this perspective is one requirement which is beneficial not only to persons with disabilities, but to humanity as a whole. The acknowledgement of disability as a part of human diversity brings us one step closer to the achievement of a real inclusive world—world to the benefit of all, so that they can flourish, contribute, and belong.

References

Barnes, C., & Mercer, G. (2018). *Exploring disability*. Polity Press.

Charlton, J. I. (1998). *Nothing about us without us: Disability oppression and empowerment*. University of California Press.

Degener, T. (2016). Disability in a human rights context. *Laws, 5*(3).

Nussbaum, M. (2006). *Frontiers of justice: Disability, nationality, species membership*. Harvard University Press.

Oliver, M. (1990). *The politics of disablement*. Macmillan.

Rioux, M., & Frazee, C. (2001). The human rights paradigm. *Journal of Disability Policy Studies, 12*(2).

Sen, A. (1999). *Development as freedom*. Oxford University Press.

Shakespeare, T. (2013). *Disability rights and wrongs revisited*. Routledge.

United Nations. (2006). *Convention on the rights of persons with disabilities*.

World Health Organization. (2001). *International classification of functioning, disability and health (ICF)*.

World Health Organization & World Bank. (2011). *World report on disability*.

Chapter 2
Technological Advancements in Disability Support

Swathi Nalla, Swetha Addanki, Seelam Mahalakshmi, Nayudu Teja, and Sarad Pawar Naik Bukke

Abstract Technological advancements have redefined the landscape of disability support, shifting the focus from compensatory aids to empowerment, inclusion, and independent living. This chapter explores recent advancements in assistive technologies, digital platforms, and inclusive design that enhance accessibility for persons with disabilities. Key areas of discussion include mobility and communication aids, smart home integration, wearable devices, artificial intelligence (AI)-driven support tools, and virtual/augmented reality applications in education and rehabilitation. This chapter also examines how universal design principles and accessibility-driven policies are bridging the digital divide, fostering participation in social, educational, and professional spheres. Ethical considerations, affordability, and equity in access are critically analyzed to highlight persistent challenges. By showcasing both established tools and emerging trends, this chapter emphasizes the transformative role of technology in creating inclusive environments that promote dignity, autonomy, and meaningful engagement for individuals with disabilities.

Keywords Assistive technology • Inclusion • Accessibility • Artificial intelligence • Universal design • Rehabilitation • Disability support

---

S. Nalla (✉) · S. Mahalakshmi
Department of Pharmacology, Malla Reddy Pharmacy College, Hyderabad, India

S. Addanki
Pharmaceutical Analysis, Malla Reddy Pharmacy College, Hyderabad, India

N. Teja
Department of Pharmaceutics, JSS College of Pharmacy, JSS Academy of Higher Education and Research, The Nilgiris, Ooty, Tamil Nadu, India

S. P. N. Bukke
Department of Pharmaceutics & Pharmaceutical Technology, Kampala International University, Ishaka, Uganda

D. Nagasen, S. K. S. S. Pindiprolu (eds.), *Transforming Disability Studies*, SpringerBriefs in Modern Perspectives on Disability Research,
https://doi.org/10.1007/978-981-95-9004-9_2

2.1 Introduction

2.1.1 Evolution of Disability Support Systems

Traditionally, disability support systems used to be based on the medical and charity models that mostly perceived disability as something to be corrected, cured, or compensated. Early interventions were characterized by dependence where the disabled people were placed as passive recipients of an intervention and not active members of the society. The assistance provided in the first half of the twentieth century was concerned with simple physical aids, including crutches, manual wheelchairs, and artificial limbs, which were mainly restorative and functional.

The 2nd half of the twentieth century saw the paradigm shift where the social model of disability came into the limelight where disability was viewed as a result of social and environmental inefficiencies and not as a personal deficiency. Such a change promoted the focus on access, inclusion, and engagement. This was further strengthened by legislative milestones like the Americans with Disabilities Act (ADA, 1990) and the United Nations Convention on the Rights of Persons with Disabilities (UNCRPD, 2006).

The interaction of digitalization, the smaller scale of the equipment, and the rate of technological innovation in the past few decades has turned disability support to not an assistive one but an empowering one. With the development of digital technologies, smart devices, and artificial intelligence, people with disabilities now have equal access to education, employment, healthcare, and socialization on the level never before achieved. The development of the mechanical aid to the intelligent interactive systems is such a transformative process, dependence to independence, isolation to inclusion (Tomasello et al., 2024).

2.1.2 Technology as a Tool for Empowerment and Inclusion

Technology is not a supportive mechanism as it is today but rather a potent equalizer that acts as a bridge between the ability and opportunity. The creation of assistive and adaptive technologies, including screen readers and speech synthesizers, or more advanced prosthetics and brain–computer interfaces, has transformed the notion of the inclusion in the twenty-first century.

Technological Empowerment Is Implemented in Several Areas

Disability educational empowerment can be achieved through the use of accession digital learning platforms and open-ended e-content that will enable learners with disability to participate in mainstream education.

Economic empowerment is facilitated through digital workspaces, remote employment technologies, and adaptive interfaces that enable equal access to the workforce.

Social empowerment is created by the interaction, self-expression, and advocacy technologies created because of communication technologies.

In addition, new technologies like AI-driven accessibility applications, IoT-based smart environments, and virtual/augmented reality applications are contributing to even greater degrees of autonomy. Such technologies are not only eliminating barriers, but also transforming engagement to fit the individual tastes, skills, and demands of individuals.

Nevertheless, equal access is also essential in the process of empowerment. The positive aspects of technology can also be attained upon meeting the problems of affordability, usability, and awareness. Inclusive design, participatory innovation, and user-centered development will see to it that persons with disabilities do not merely have beneficiary role in technological change; but they are co-creators as well (Sharma, 2023).

2.1.3 Objectives and Scope

The main objective is about how technology can transform accessibility, inclusion, and independence among persons with disabilities. It not only analyzes the traditional and new assistive technologies available but also explains how digital revolution is transforming the social, educational, and work experience of the differently abled people.

The main points of this chapter are:

1. To follow the development of the disability support system, focused on the traditional assistive devices to intelligent, adaptive technologies.
2. To examine how technological innovation can enhance inclusion, empowerment, and independence.
3. To talk about the use of modern technologies like artificial intelligence, virtual space, and the Internet of Things in assisting people with disabilities.
4. To emphasize the significance of universal design, ethical implications, and policies based on accessibility as the means of closing the digital divide.
5. To find out difficulties, constraints, and prospects of the sustainable and fair adoption of technology.

This chapter has an interdisciplinary approach where it uses the perspectives of rehabilitation sciences, computer technology, design, and social inclusion policy. It aims to offer a comprehensive explanation on how the technological progress can bring about a world in which diversity, dignity, and autonomy may be valued by all people by exploring practical examples, ethical issues, and policy frameworks.

2.1.4 Traditional Approaches to Disability Support

Until recently in human history, the paradigms used in disability support have been medical and charitable with the main emphasis on care, cure, and protection instead of empowerment or participation. The medical model of disability saw disability as an individual loss or illness that needed clinical care. As a result, it turned to rehabilitation, institutionalization, and caregiver dependency instead of acceptance and inclusion in society.

Historically, charitable institutions, religious organizations, and philanthropic agencies were in the center of the provision of aids and services. Though the intentions of such efforts were good, they tended to promulgate paternalistic approaches and regarded persons with disabilities as an object of sympathy and not of rights. Physical aids like walking sticks, hearing trumpets, and manual wheelchairs were created with mitigation in mind more than facilitation.

In the mid-twentieth century, the world started moving towards the understanding of disability as a social and environmental problem. Social model of disability put forward the concept of focusing on physical, attitudinal, and institutional barriers rather than impairment as the real causes of the exclusion. Yet, in spite of the theoretical advancement, the implementation of inclusive principles into practice was rather restricted by the technological, economical, and policy factors. The initial assistive devices were effective but were not flexible, customizable and cost-effective to expand their influence on independent living (Langtree, 2025).

2.1.5 Technological Transformation and Independent Living

With the development of digital technology at the end of the 20th and beginning of the twenty-first centuries, a new age of disability assistance began, an era of independence, autonomy, and empowerment. The advent of technology has transformed the meaning of assistive support as passive aid to the proactive enablement of the users to play bigger roles in routine affairs of life.

Assistive devices were transformed with the introduction of microprocessors, sensors, and intelligent control systems. Power-assisted wheelchairs with navigation; myoelectric, neuro-controlled prosthetic limbs; the development of communication tools beyond the previously rudimentary symbol boards by speech-generating devices and augmentative and alternative communication (AAC) applications all came because of mobility aids.

Independent living has not only been extended to physical mobility, but also to access to information, education, employment, and community life. The use of technologies like screen readers, voice-to-text converters, smart home automation, and wearable devices has helped to bridge functional gaps and allow users to engage well with their surroundings. Efforts to bring Internet of Things (IoT) and Artificial

Intelligence (AI) together have led to another level of autonomy, where smart responses of systems to user needs are based on context-aware systems.

Additionally, the inclination towards user-centered design will see to it that technologies will be not only practical, but also reflect the lived experiences of persons with disabilities. This has given rise to a culture of self-determination in which people are given the power to define and control their support systems instead of being passive consumers of care (Sweeting et al., 2024).

2.1.6 Social and Psychological Impact of Digital Inclusion

The digital revolution has enhanced functional autonomy; however, it has had far-reaching effects on the social and psychological aspects of disability. The availability of digital tools and online spaces provides people with disabilities with the opportunity to communicate, learn, and participate in community life meaningfully to improve their self-esteem, identity, and social belonging.

Online communities, social media tools, and online advocacy organizations enable the persons with disabilities to experience, connect, and engage in the worldwide discussion of accessibility and inclusion. This online presence disrupts the stereotypes, creates awareness, and builds empathy in the wider society. It has also played a role in the increased acknowledgment of disability as a form of diversity as opposed to deficiency since it is now possible to self-represent oneself and what he or she goes through online.

Psychologically, technology leads to the development of self-efficacy and agency that diminishes the need to depend on the caregiver and increase the agency to control daily activities. Adaptive technologies and available learning tools have boosted the educational achievement and employability, which directly relates to emotional well-being and financial independence.

Nevertheless, the positive side of digital inclusion is not universal. Access to assistive technologies remains under the influence of digital inequality due to the socioeconomic status, level of technological literacy, and the lack of infrastructure. In addition, excessive technology usage in the absence of proper human support can create social isolation in some situations. Therefore, the trick is to come up with a balanced approach to one in which digital inclusion is an addition to human connection and engagement in community life, not a substitute (Tripathi et al., 2024).

2.2 Recent Developments in Assistive Technologies

The last 20 years have seen a dramatic change in the sphere of assistive technology due to the technological advancement that occurred. The move towards simple mechanical aids to computerized, technologically centralized systems has expanded the area of assistance that can be given to persons with disabilities. These developments do not only improve physical functioning but also increase education, work, and socialization opportunities. The subsections below present important areas of the recent development.

2.2.1 *Mobility Aids and Smart Wheelchairs*

The mobility technologies have grown into complex systems, which combine the sensors, robotics, and navigational technologies out of a basic mechanical equipment. The current smart wheelchairs come with obstacle detector systems and GPS coordinates and voice or gesture control systems, allowing people to travel safely and autonomously on different surfaces.

Exoskeletons, which are powered and robotic, are also transforming the mobility of people with spinal cord injury or muscular impairments. These exoskeletons are based on electromechanical actuators and real-time motion feedback that enable ambulation and rehabilitation. Moreover, light metals like carbon fiber and adaptive suspension systems have enhanced comfort and usability.

Mobility has been augmented by the combination of Internet of Things (IoT) and the artificial intelligence (AI) which, in turn, has rendered it more responsive. An example is the use of AI in wheelchairs, which can adjust speed, route, and braking based on environmental factors and also have connectivity functions that enable caregivers to control and help the wheelchair remotely. All the innovations mentioned result in enhancing the autonomy, safety, and social inclusiveness of mobility-impaired people (Manzoor & Vimarlund, 2018).

2.2.2 *Communication and Speech Assistance Tools*

Communication technologies have changed radically in the case of speech or language impaired persons. The early symbol boards and mechanical typewriters have led to more complex Augmentative and Alternative Communication (AAC) systems which employ speech synthesis, text prediction, and voice output.

Currently, AAC tools use eye tracking systems, touch screens, and neural input hardware allowing users with extreme physical disabilities to interact. Programs like Proloquo2Go, Talkitt, and Voiceitt can be customized on vocabulary, tone, and speech rhythm to suit the personality and situation.

Combination with mainstream technologies—smartphones can now have speech-to-text capabilities, video call captions can be served in real-time, and AI-based translation applications have made communication more inclusive. Such technologies not only expand the expressive capacity, but also contribute to educational involvement and professional interaction, breaking the barriers of communication that have existed for a long time (Tsatsou, 2019).

2.2.3 *Cognitive and Sensory Support Devices*

Cognitive and sensory-assistive technologies cater to individuals with learning disabilities, memory deficits, or sensory impairments. Cognitive aids, such as reminder apps, digital calendars, and adaptive learning platforms, provide structured routines and task management support for people with conditions like autism spectrum disorder, ADHD, or dementia.

For the visually impaired, tools like screen readers (JAWS, NVDA), Braille displays, and wearable smart glasses translate visual information into auditory or tactile formats. Similarly, AI-based hearing aids with noise filtering, directional microphones, and wireless connectivity significantly enhance sound clarity for the hearing-impaired.

Emerging technologies like haptic feedback systems, smart canes, and sensory substitution devices further expand access to environmental information, thereby promoting confidence, and spatial awareness. These innovations bridge cognitive and sensory gaps, fostering both functional independence and social inclusion (Mattern, 2025).

2.2.4 *Adaptive and Environmental Control Systems*

The availability of adaptive and environmental control technology enables persons with physical disability to use their environment in a natural way. The ability to control lighting, temperature, doors, and appliances using smart home systems (which are driven by Internet of Things (IoT)) is available via voice command, smartphone, and/or motion sensor.

Compact, cost-effective, and configurable Environmental Control Units (ECU's) give users the opportunity to easily manage their home environment. The integration of ECU's with products like Amazon Alexa, Google Assistant, and Apple Home Kit, have brought the concept of accessibility into the mainstream, and offer an intuitive means of interacting with these systems.

Automated doors, accessible kiosks, and adaptable elevators in public spaces increase mobility and usability. These adaptive environments represent the implementation of Universal Design Principles in the real world and demonstrate that built spaces can be designed to accommodate people with differing abilities without the necessity of modifying those spaces after they have been constructed (Giansanti & Pirrera, 2025).

2.3 Artificial Intelligence and Emerging Digital Tools

The rapid development of artificial intelligence (AI) is creating an entirely new level of assistance for people with disabilities. Through the ability of systems to adapt, anticipate, and react to the unique needs of each individual, AI is turning the non-adaptive assistive tools we have all used for years into dynamic, intelligent aids. AI technology is providing a new model for accessibility and inclusion across numerous industries and areas including communications, navigation, and more.

Accessibility and Inclusion Through AI Technology

AI technology has been at the center of the evolution of accessibility solutions. Technologies like Microsoft's Seeing AI, Google's Lookout, and Be My Eyes utilize computer vision to provide users who are blind or visually impaired with real-time descriptions of what they see, read aloud what is written, and identify objects they encounter.

In addition to describing visual content, AI utilizes natural language processing (NLP) to enhance comprehension of written text through real-time translation, summarization, and contextualized reading support. AI can also be utilized to provide automated captions, lip-reading support, and sign language recognition to facilitate communication by individuals who are deaf or hard-of-hearing in educational, entertainment, and employment environments.

Additionally, the data analysis provided through AI in health and physical rehabilitation allows healthcare providers to monitor patient or client progress, tailor their exercise routine to meet specific needs, and provide early warning signs that may indicate a complication is developing, thus enabling them to better serve the unique needs of their patients or clients and improve outcomes.

2.3.1 *Personalized Support through Machine Learning*

A subdivision of AI is Machine Learning (ML), which is derived to enable assistive systems to learn and evolve as users use the system. ML algorithms learn interaction patterns, including speech rhythm or typing style or motion, to customize interfaces and feedback.

As an illustration, adaptive keyboards memorize common words to enhance text prediction, whereas AI-powered wheelchairs change control sensitivity depending on the usage rates. Likewise, cognitive support services apply ML algorithms to identify variations in attention or mood and issue reminders or therapeutic interventions, respectively.

Such a degree of individuality leads to the comfort, efficiency, and independence of the user, as well as adapts technology to the preferences and abilities of the individual.

2.3.2 Virtual Assistants, Predictive Text, and Automation

The mainstream accessibility is due to the increasing ubiquity of virtual assistants such as Siri, Alexa, and Google Assistant. These systems also support voice usage in accessing information, communication, and control of the environment which reduces use of manual input.

Automated correction systems and predictive text algorithms are software that makes communication easy to users with dyslexia, motor impairments, or limited literacy. Automation also spreads to smart homes, cars, and offices where intelligent systems react to voice, gesture, or context.

The intelligent ecosystems such as these are the intersection of universal design and automation in creating environments in which accessibility is not an appendix, but an inherent part.

2.3.3 The AI Disability Services Ethical Dynamics

Although the opportunities presented by AI are immense, it presents ethical issues, social issues, and policy concerns. The problems related to the privacy of data, algorithmic bias, and transparency need to be approached with care not to cause exclusion or abuse. As an example, the biased datasets may cause the misunderstanding of the speech or gestures of people with unusual patterns, which contradicts the aim of accessibility.

In addition, there is the risk of autonomy and informed consent due to the excessive use of digital surveillance as a method of health or behavior monitoring. To implement AI-based systems ethically, it is crucial to make them transparent, accountable, and they should be developed through collaboration with persons with disabilities.

The emergence and implementation of AI in disability services should be developed and implemented through a rights-based approach, which should be based on the principles of dignity, participation, and equity. This has made technology to be a source of empowerment and not control (Elsahar et al., 2019).

2.4 Wearable Technology and Smart Environments

Wearable technology and smart environmental systems have been converging, and this has transformed the way persons with disabilities interact with their environment. These innovations are not limited to help but promote autonomy, safety, and social inclusion through offering real-time feedback, monitoring, and environmental adaptation control. They are a combination of a paradigm shift of reactive care model to proactive and predictive support systems.

2.4.1 Health Wearables and Monitors

Smartwear devices like smartwatches, fitness trackers, biosensors, and adaptive prosthetics are very important in the process of monitoring body physiological parameters and improving daily functionality. In the case of people with disabilities, they are equipped with a device that follows the vital signs (heart rate, oxygen saturation, and mobility patterns), detects falls, and notifies the caregiver or medical professional in case of an emergency.

Most recent advances have involved prosthetic limbs with built-in sensors that are able to provide haptic feedback, allowing the user to feel pressure or touch. Smart gloves can be used to perform hand movement rehabilitation, and the devices based on electromyography (EMG) can help people with neuromuscular conditions by converting muscle activities into digital responses.

By integrating AI, these devices can examine the trends and anticipate possible health events and facilitate early intervention and preventive care. An example of these applications is that, in epileptic patients, EEG bracelets can predict seizures, and in patients with heart disorders, smart bracelets can detect irregular heartbeats and alert healthcare providers in real-time.

Essentially, assistive wearables are not only restorative but also safety promoting, confidence promoting and self-managing, decreasing dependency and enhancing general quality of life.

2.4.2 Smart Homes and Internet of Things (IoT) Implementation

The Internet of Things (IoT) has turned the home setting into a system of intelligent devices that interact with each other without any inconvenience. In the case of individuals with disabilities, smart home systems provided by IoT can be more controllable, accessible, and convenient by using voice commands, mobile apps, or gesture recognition systems.

Common examples include

Intelligent lighting and thermostat that will automatically control the light or air conditioning depending on the user or the sensor of a person.

Doors, curtains, and appliances controlled using voice with virtual assistant systems such as Alexa or Google Assistant.

Emergency notifications and safety sensors that indicate smoke or gas leaks, or falls and directly call the emergency services.

It is not only the convenience behind IoT-based homes, but rather an adaptive environment, which learns based on routine of the user. In the long run, the system will be able to predict the requirements, e.g. by adjusting the bed to the position to alleviate pressure or to adjust the kitchen to allow accessibility. These innovations explain how the concept of universal design combine with technology to come up with living spaces that are inclusive, efficient, and dignified.

2.4.3 Context-Sensitive and Adaptive Living Systems

Another important development in assistive living has been the development of context-aware systems—environments which understand situational data (time, location, the activity of the user, and physiological data) and offer dynamic support.

As an example, an intelligent home can sense when a user with mobility issues tries to rise and turn on the lights, open the doors, or alert a caregiver in case instability can be detected. Equally, intelligent wearables have the ability to be linked with the home systems to turn off or turn on the temperature or lights, or play loud music depending on the level of stress or fatigue the user is experiencing.

The systems can integrate AI with IoT and sensor networks to provide adaptive ecosystems that can develop continuously based on user requirements. In addition to comfort, the innovations will enhance safety, individualization, and empowerment, which is a major step towards sustainable and independent living of persons with disabilities (Szabó et al., 2023).

2.5 Virtual and Augmented Reality in Education and Rehabilitation

The technology of Virtual Reality (VR) and Augmented Reality (AR) has allowed creating new opportunities in the sphere of education, treatment, and rehabilitation of people with disabilities (it was mentioned in Table 2.1). These technologies enable learning, motor training, cognitive rehabilitation, and development of social skills in a manner that cannot be replicated by traditional methods because they involve the creation of immersive and interactive environments.

Table 2.1 It represents VR/AR tools for learning and skill development

VR/AR Learning and Skill Development Tools	Purpose	Provide students with various needs with an opportunity to access, engage in learning, and experience with multisensory interactive tools
	Technology	AR (Augmented Reality): Superimposes virtual information on physical spaces VR (Virtual Reality): It involves immersion of the users into entirely simulated controlled environments
	Applications in Education	Learner with Learning Disabilities/Autism: Visual and kinesthetic learning support through adaptive simulations VR Classrooms: Provide stress-free and anxiety-free spaces AR Visually Impaired: Translates text into audio or sub-tactile feedback 3D Modeling Tools: This allows the student with motor disabilities to be able to interact with virtual objects to understand concepts better
	Influence on Learning	Fosters interactive, inclusive, and self-directed learning. Fills the gap between accessibility and conventional pedagogy.

2.5.1 VR/AR Tools for Learning and Skill Development

2.5.2 Immersive Rehabilitation and Cognitive Therapy

VR and AR are newly known as effective tools of physical and cognitive recovery in the process of rehabilitation. Physical therapy programs based on VR allow with the help of gamified exercises to encourage patients to practice repetitive movement training—an important part of poststroke/injury recovery.

In the same fashion, AR-based rehabilitation systems provide visual feedback in the form of real-time corrective posture or gait, and VR simulated environments provide individuals with traumatic brain injury, anxiety, or post-traumatic stress disorder with a simulation of real-world situations.

These experience-based platforms enable therapists to track the progress accurately, dynamically change the level of difficulty, and develop an engaging therapy experience that enhances compliance. The added features of biofeedback sensors to determine physiological responses in real time also facilitate the measurement and modification of therapy (García-Peñalvo & Franco-Martín, 2019).

2.5.3 Successful Implementation Case Studies

Multiple practical cases emphasize the revolutionary nature of VR and AR in assisting with disabilities:

Rehabilitation Robotics (Lokomat System, Switzerland): A VR-based robotic gait trainer is a device that is applied in spinal cord and stroke rehabilitation and improves walking patterns and motivation.

Floreo (USA): VR-based program of social skills training among children with autism, which enables them to practice their interaction safety and in a controlled environment.

MindMotiontm (UK): It is a VR application which offers individualized neuro-rehabilitation workouts to upper-limb-deficient patients.

AR-based Navigational Applications: Applied by visually deprived people as a tool to allow them to get real-time audio guidance on safe navigation.

These case studies show that immersive technologies are able not only to improve the results of recovery, but also develop autonomy, engagement, and confidence, which are part of a holistic well-being and inclusion (Chemnad & Othman, 2024).

2.6 Universal Design and Digital Accessibility

The real value of technological innovation is only attained when it is beneficial to everybody in a fair manner. Universal design and digital accessibility can be very important in the context of disability support, as they make technology not only inclusive but deliberate instead of an adaptation. When combined, these principles can make digital tools and spaces the source of independence, participation, and equality.

2.6.1 The Tenets of Universal and Inclusive Design

Universal Design (UD) is an architectural/design theory, which seeks to design products and environments that can be used by everyone, to the maximum degree, without any other adaptation or specialized design. UD is about inclusion and is coined by architect Ronald Mace as promoting inclusion not by modifying but proactively.

Universal Design has seven major principles broadly accepted in the discussion of accessibility, namely:

1. Equal Use—The design is practical and can be sold to individuals of varied abilities.
2. Flexibility in Use—Supports a great variety of preferences and abilities.

3. Simple and Intuitive Use—Not complex to use, irrespective of the user experience and literacy level.
4. Perceptible Information—Expresses well using various sensory modalities (visual, auditory, and tactile).
5. Tolerance of error—Reduces risks and nonintended behavior.
6. Low physical effort—Can be effectively and comfortably utilized.
7. Approach and Use Size and Space—This is sufficient space whether in mobility or in posture.

In the digital age, these principles go beyond architecture to include software, websites, applications, and virtual worlds. Inclusive design focuses on the diversity of users, specific to cognition, sensory, and physical differences. Inclusive design is a sustainable way of inclusion, unlike accessibility retrofitting, which makes products accessible after they have been developed.

2.6.2 Accessible Software, Websites, and Interfaces

Digital Accessibility is the ability of a product, service or entity to be usable by everyone including people with disabilities using accessible information and communication technology (ICT). As digital instruction, work and even medical practice continue to increase, equalized software and web design represent a key slice of the tech equity pie.

Technical and functional requirements for accessible digital content are established by global standards, the WCAG 2.1 from W3C (Web Content Accessibility Guidelines of the World Wide Web Consortium).

These include provisions for:

Image alt descriptions to help the visually impaired, Use keyboard navigation for mouse users, For visual clarity color contrast ratios, Captions and Transcripts for Audio/Video Content, Mobile-friendly design for use on tablets and assistive devices.

Accessibility testing tools and audits are part of software development lifecycles to provide compliance and user-centric quality assurance. Furthermore, mobile apps are including voice commands, gesture recognition, and artificial intelligence-driven personalization that can make interfaces tailor to the unique user aesthetics.

2.6.3 Integration of Accessibility Standards in Product Development

The successful incorporation of accessibility requirements in product development requires multidisciplinary cooperation among engineers, designers, people with disabilities, and end-users. Including people with disabilities in user research and usability testing helps keep products based in reality.

Integrating your product development pipelines with accessibility toolkits, checklists and design frameworks (like Microsoft Inclusive Design Toolkit and Apple's Accessibility Guidelines) brings consistency of action and accountability. Accessibility Automated testing can validate accessibility, just as all types of quality.

Furthermore, many organizations now adopt the "Accessibility by Default" principle, embedding inclusive considerations from prototype to production. This approach not only broadens market reach but also aligns with corporate social responsibility (CSR) and sustainable development goals (SDG 10: Reduced Inequalities). The outcome is technology that is not only compliant but consciously inclusive, contributing to dignity, usability, and independence for all users.

2.7 Policy, Ethics, and Equity in Technology Access

As tech is part of our daily routine, we have to think about the right, wrong, and social issues that come with it. We cannot have access and inclusion on our own; we need strong policies, fair standards, and ethical leadership that protect the rights and dignity of people with disabilities.

2.7.1 Policies Based on Access and Global Projects

More and more, global policy plans have seen the link between human rights and digital access. The United Nations Convention on the Rights of Persons with Disabilities (UNCRPD), especially Articles 9 and 21, says member states must make sure people can access the Internet and other communication tools and should follow universal design principles.

Projects at the international and national levels that push for these goals include:

UNESCO's Inclusive ICTs in Education Policy Guidelines—calling for accessible educational software and hardware.

World Health Organization's Global Report on Assistive Technology (GReAT)—providing information on fair access to assistive products.

Accessible India Campaign (Sugamya Bharat Abhiyan)—improving accessible infrastructure and ICT in India.

European Accessibility Act (2025)—creating consistent standards for access across the EU.

These plans call on governments and companies to buy and sell in ways that follow the principles of access for all, and are in favor of accessible innovations. There is more focus now on digital access as a right, not a special treatment.

2.7.2 *Ethical Concerns: Privacy, Consent, and Data Security*

The use of technology in disability support often involves personal health data, behavioral monitoring, and continuous tracking, raising significant ethical concerns around privacy, consent, and data security.

Wearable devices, AI-driven assistive systems, and smart home technologies collect vast amounts of sensitive information, from medical records to daily routines. Without stringent data governance frameworks, this information is vulnerable to misuse, breaches, or discriminatory profiling (The Hindu, 2025).

Ethical technology development mandates:

Informed consent and transparency about data collection and use.

User control over personal data and storage duration.

Robust cybersecurity measures to prevent unauthorized access.

Algorithmic accountability to ensure AI decisions remain unbiased and explainable.

Furthermore, ethical design requires respecting user autonomy technologies should empower rather than monitor or control. The balance between safety and privacy is delicate, demanding continuous evaluation through ethical review boards and participatory oversight mechanisms (Moon et al., 2019).

2.7.3 *Addressing Affordability and the Digital Divide*

Even with all the good work that has been done, we are still far away from making technologies that help disabled people available for all. This gap we have in getting enough people to use digital tools is what we call the digital divide.

Getting the right kind of assistive devices is not easy. The cost is high, local production is limited, the devices are often not covered by insurance, and very often, people are not aware of the assistive devices that could help them. This is especially true in low- and middle-income countries. To close the digital divide, we need to do these things:

Public–private partnerships (PPPs) to make and deliver devices at a lower price.

Open-source assistive technology to reduce the costs and help with new ideas.

Capacity-building programs that increase digital literacy for persons with disabilities.

Policy-driven mechanisms to include assistive technology into funding, health, and education budgets.

Getting equitable access to technology is not just the right thing to do; it is very important for socio-economic reasons. Inclusive access helps people participate more, be more productive, and be more part of the wider community, and ensure that no one is left behind in this age of digital transformation (Thangavel et al., 2025).

2.8 Challenges and Future Prospects

Even with major advances in technology to help people with disabilities, many problems still prevent full use of solutions that are inclusive and empowering. Knowing these problems and fixing them before they occur is necessary to keep moving forward (Morris, 2024).

2.8.1 Barriers in Implementation and User Adoption

Many things make it hard for assistive technology to be used effectively:

High Costs and Affordability: Machines with advanced features, like AI-powered artificial limbs or smart wheelchairs, are still too expensive for most people to buy, particularly in poor nations.

Technological Complexity: High-tech machines may need technical skill or long training, which makes them hard to use for people who do not know much about computers.

Infrastructure Limitations: Poor internet access, inconsistent electricity, and lack of support services make it hard to use technology in small towns or rural areas.

Cultural and Social Barriers: Stigma, wrong ideas about disability, and not much knowledge in families or caregivers can lower use of technology.

Fixing these problems needs designs that are inclusive, cheap to make, and work with communities that will use them, so that the technology is not only there, but easy to use and accepted socially (Reddy, 2025).

2.8.2 The Role of Education and Awareness

Getting people to use technology and getting the most use out of it needs education and awareness:

Digital Literacy Training: Teaching people with disabilities how to use assistive technology will give them more independence and self-confidence.

Caregiver and Professional Education: Teachers, therapists, and doctors on how to guide and support people with assistive tools will make sure the technology is used well.

Public Awareness Campaigns: Teaching people about what technology can do will make the use of stigma less likely and will encourage society to support the use of assistive tools.

Educational programs need to be sensitive to where they are, easy to access, and really happen, so that there is a system where innovation is balanced with human ability and social acceptance (Hocoma, n.d.).

2.8.3 *Future Trends: AI Convergence, Robotics, and Neurotechnology*

Newer technologies mean more change for help with disability:

AI Convergence: Putting AI into wearable tech, smart homes, and rehab tools will make help that is based on what will happen, what should happen, and what fits the person. This help will be on the person's terms.

Robotics: Better prostheses, exoskeletons, and helper robots will make it easier to move, be strong, and be free, with a special focus on people who have very bad physical problems (Fiveable, 2024).

Neurotechnology: Brain–computer interfaces (BCIs) and neural prostheses might help go back to talking, moving, and sensing, and make up for what was thought impossible before.

The tomorrow of help with disability will need new ideas from many fields, mixing tech, design, morals, and rules to make what is not only able to work but also will work for all, do good, and last (Lee & Xie, 2024).

2.9 Conclusion

Technology ideas have truly changed an area of help with disability, but it is no longer on just make-do, but about power, inclusion, and independence. Using assistive devices, AI, wearable settings, VR/AR objects, and universal design rules, the world is starting to make places where people with disability can do things fully, safely, and with what they are used to.

2.9.1 *Summary of Key Insights*

Disability support went from medical and charity ways to support ones to the ways that can help or support by way of social support and technology. The devices used to help mobility, talking, thinking, and to the senses are being improved upon by devices with AI, IoT, and ones that make the use of more than one sense. To make sure that devices work in all areas, the ideas of universal use and digital ease have been adopted. The ideas of policy directions and just use are still needed to give all people access to the use of devices.

2.9.2 *Moving Forward to a Way of Use that Is Comfortable for All*

The joining of the new ways of use and the rights related to them, with ones that include all people, has shown how one can reach a world where everyone is included. The ways of use should be made affordable, able to be used by all means, and to use things that will last. These use ideas should be used by all people with disabilities and it does not matter where they live or how much they make.

2.9.3 *Dignity, Independence, and Equal Use*

In the end, the use of support devices should be used as a way to help and not take away the power of human ability. When the use of these devices focus on respecting the lives of others, their ability to work or be independent, and their chance to be part of social life, then they will be able for persons with disabilities to fully take part in all parts of education, work, and social life. Moving beyond easy use and to the whole idea of being equal, independent, and active in life.

References

Americans with Disabilities Act of 1990, 42 U.S.C. § 12101 et seq. (1990).

Chemnad, K., & Othman, A. (2024, February 16). Digital accessibility in the era of artificial intelligence - Bibliometric analysis and systematic review. *Frontiers in Artificial Intelligence, 7*, 1349668. https://doi.org/10.3389/frai.2024.1349668

Elsahar, Y., Hu, S., Bouazza-Marouf, K., Kerr, D., & Mansor, A. (2019). Augmentative and alternative communication (AAC) advances: A review of configurations for individuals with a speech disability. *Sensors, 19*(8), 1911. https://doi.org/10.3390/s19081911

Fiveable. (2024, August 1). *Equity in access to technology – Intro to Engineering*. https://fiveable.me/key-terms/introduction-engineering/equity-in-access-to-technology

García-Peñalvo, F. J., & Franco-Martín, M. (2019, November 11). Sensor technologies for caring people with disabilities. *Sensors (Basel), 19*(22), 4914. https://doi.org/10.3390/s19224914

Giansanti, D., & Pirrera, A. (2025). Integrating AI and assistive technologies in healthcare: Insights from a narrative review of reviews. *Healthcare, 13*(5), 556. https://doi.org/10.3390/healthcare13050556

Hocoma. (n.d.). *Lokomat – robotic gait training for rehabilitation.*

Langtree, I. C. (2025, April 23). *Models of disability: Types and definitions.* Disabled World. https://www.disabled-world.com/definitions/disability-models.php

Lee, H., & Xie, I. (2024). *Disability, accessibility, and universal design.* Elsevier. https://doi.org/10.1016/B978-0-323-95689-5.00139

Manzoor, M., & Vimarlund, V. (2018). Digital technologies for social inclusion of individuals with disabilities. *Health and Technology, 8*(5), 377–390. https://doi.org/10.1007/s12553-018-0239-1

Mattern, R. (2025, January 20). *Trends shaping assistive technology for 2025 and beyond.* Assistive Technology Blog. https://assistivetechnologyblog.com/trends-2025

Moon, N. W., Baker, P. M. A., & Goughnour, K. (2019). Designing wearable technologies for users with disabilities: Accessibility, usability, and connectivity factors. *Journal of Rehabilitation and Assistive Technologies Engineering, 6*, 2055668319862137. https://doi.org/10.1177/2055668319862137

Morris, F. (2024). Universal Design and assistive digital technologies: Enhancing inclusion of persons with disabilities. In H. S. Dunn, M. Ragnedda, M. L. Ruiu, & L. Robinson (Eds.), *The Palgrave handbook of everyday digital life.* Palgrave Macmillan. https://doi.org/10.1007/978-3-031-30438-5_16

Reddy, K. J. (2025). Technological innovations in rehabilitation: Virtual reality. In *Innovations in Neurocognitive Rehabilitation.* Springer. https://doi.org/10.1007/978-3-031-88117-6_4

Sharma, R. (2023). Role of technology in empowering women: A pathway to inclusive development. *Journal of Education and Society, 19*(4). https://doi.org/10.52783/jes.8623

Sweeting, A., Warncken, K. A., & Patel, M. (2024). The role of assistive technology in enabling older adults to achieve independent living: Past and future. *Journal of Medical Internet Research, 26.* https://doi.org/10.2196/58846

Szabó, P., Ara, J., Halmosi, B., Sik-Lanyi, C., & Guzsvinecz, T. (2023). Technologies designed to assist individuals with cognitive impairments. *Sustainability, 15*(18), 13490. https://doi.org/10.3390/su151813490

Thangavel, S., Sharmila, K., & Sufina, K. (2025). Revolutionizing education through augmented reality (AR) and virtual reality (VR): Innovations, challenges and future prospects. *Asian Journal of Interdisciplinary Research, 8*(1), 1–28. https://doi.org/10.54392/ajir2511

The Hindu. (2025, October 14). *How AI has revolutionised the world of assistive devices to aid persons with disabilities.* The Hindu.

Tomasello, L., Trunfio, A., Ranno, M., & Zitelli, G. (2024). The evolution of the concept of disability: Social and educational inclusion. *American Journal of Clinical and Medical Research, 2024*, 670. https://doi.org/10.47991/2835-9496/AJCMR-164

Tripathi, S., Rana, D. P., & Sircar, S. (2024, July–December). Smart interiors for aging adults: Integrating technology for independent living. *International Journal of Housing and Human Settlement Planning, 10*(2). https://doi.org/10.37628/IJHHSP

Tsatsou, P. (2019). Digital inclusion of people with disabilities: A qualitative study of intra-disability diversity in the digital realm. *Behaviour & Information Technology, 39*(5), 1–16. https://doi.org/10.1080/0144929X.2019.1636136

United Nations. (2006, December 13). Convention on the Rights of Persons with Disabilities. Retrieved from https://www.un.org/disabilities/documents/convention/convoptprot-e.pdf

Chapter 3
Policy Reforms and Legal Frameworks in Disability Rights

Swetha Addanki, Swathi Nalla, Mahalakshmi Seelam, and Teja Nayudu

Abstract Disability Studies has undergone a significant transformation and is no longer traditional, medical, and charity-related aspects toward rights-based and inclusive approach. This change places more emphasis on empowerment, respect, and active participation of people with disabilities as complete members of the society. The attempts to facilitate inclusion in the areas of education, employment, health, and the administration have changed the perspective of social accessibility and justice drastically in the society. These changes are in tandem with principles of international human rights. Significant legislative interventions, in particular, the introduction of the United Nations Convention on the Rights of Persons with Disabilities (UNCRPD) and the creation of analogous national regulations, have played a key role in introducing regulations concerning equal access, antidiscrimination, inclusive education, and comprehensive social support. However, the actual progress in the world remains restrained by achieving a successful implementation of the policies, maintaining effective oversight and addressing the intersectionality problems faced by people who are at the cross-section of multiple marginalized groups in the overall population of disabled people. Disability Studies is expanding its boundaries with new developments such as the use of assistive technologies, access to digital information, community-based projects, and the involvement of the community in the policy-making process. This paper, offers critical examination of how the rights of people with disabilities have advanced over the years and achieved milestones and failures on a legislative and policy level. It emphasizes the necessity of continuous reform, cooperation between different stakeholders, and the need to implement context-related strategies to have a more inclusive and sustainable future.

S. Addanki (✉)
Department of Pharmaceutical Analysis, Malla Reddy Pharmacy College, Hyderabad, India

S. Nalla · M. Seelam
Department of Pharmacology, Malla Reddy Pharmacy College, Hyderabad, India

T. Nayudu
Department of Pharmaceutics, JSS College of Pharmacy, JSS Academy of Higher Education and Research, The Nilgiris, Ooty, Tamil Nadu, India

D. Nagasen, S. K. S. S. Pindiprolu (eds.), *Transforming Disability Studies*, SpringerBriefs in Modern Perspectives on Disability Research,
https://doi.org/10.1007/978-981-95-9004-9_3

Keywords Disability studies · Paradigm shift · Rights-based approach · Inclusion · Accessibility · Social justice · Human rights · Policy reform · Legal frameworks · UNCRPD · Inclusive Education · Nondiscrimination · Social protection · Assistive technologies · Digital inclusion · Community-driven models · Participatory policymaking · Intersectionality · Marginalized Groups · Multistakeholder Collaboration · Sustainable future

3.1 Introduction

3.1.1 Context and Justification

The disability was often equated with the inability to work, and therefore, in the past, disabled people were regarded as belonging to the group of the deserving poor. The United Nations (UN) General Assembly passed the resolution, the UN Standard Rules on the Equalisation of Opportunities of Persons with Disabilities in the year 1993 through resolution 48/96. This is a resolution that covers key issues like human rights, education, vocational training, and physical environment, medical acre, transport, and information access by people with disabilities.

UNCRPD was adopted with the adoption of the Optional Protocol in 2006 and opened to signature in 2007. UNCRPD is a framework used to advise governments on the way to meet international standards to align with existing policies, legislation, and programs.

The convention on the Rights of Persons with Disabilities (CRPD) is an international benchmark in the acknowledgement and advancement of the rights of the disabled individuals throughout the world. In signing this treaty, countries declare definite legal obligations to improve and safeguard these rights on their territory. Effective progress in the Convention requires a practical intervention of governments so that people with disabilities, as well as their supporters, can perceive positive differences in their everyday lives. Specifically, Article 4 provides a set of expectations in which every participating nation is obligated to balance its laws and policies with the stipulations provided in the CRPD (United Nations, 2006).

3.1.2 Transformative Milestones in Advancing Disability Rights

Article 1 states that the CRPD shall facilitate, safeguard, and guarantee that all human rights as well as fundamental freedoms are fully and equally enjoyed by all persons with disabilities and that the inherent dignity of the persons with disabilities is also respected. Article 3 presents a set of fundamental values that govern the ways in which countries are supposed to update or even develop their national laws

(Shumba & Moodley, 2018). These principles are foundations of everything considered about the Convention and have a uniform application throughout the various articles of the Convention.

A rights-based and inclusive approach to disability is grounded in respect for the dignity, autonomy, and informed choices of every individual, while firmly upholding the principles of equality and nondiscrimination. It recognizes the importance of enabling active participation in work, community life, and social relationships, thereby countering exclusion and dependency. Central to this perspective is the understanding of disability as an inherent and valuable aspect of human diversity rather than a limitation to be corrected. Ensuring genuine equality requires the removal of physical, social, and institutional barriers so that all individuals can access opportunities on an equal footing. This approach also emphasizes gender equity, acknowledging the distinct and often compounded challenges faced by women and girls with disabilities. Moreover, it affirms the evolving capacities of children with disabilities, supporting their growing ability to express their views, claim their rights, and participate meaningfully in decisions that affect their lives (Degener, 2016).

Social model of disability too recognizes the significance of rights and has frequently been linked to the rights based approach to disability compared to the needs based or welfare approach to disability policy (Finkelstein, 2007). One key milestone was the realization of economic, social and cultural rights in 2012 that allowed the United Nations to complete the circle of the prescriptive rules that the United Nations intended with the designation of the Universal Declaration of Human Rights. The CRPD is an excellent illustration of the indivisibility and interdependence of the two categories of human rights. Article 12 (3) CRPD addresses the support provided to disabled persons in order to exercise their legal ability (Degener & Koster-Dreese, 1995).

The active participation of organizations like the United Nations, national governments and international funding organizations is influential in formation of proliferating networks which deal with the issues of race, gender, and disability in diversified cultural systems.

Despite the disability rights movement being a small percentage of Americans with disabilities, the supporters have been able to champion the claims of the entire community. During its early years of establishment in the 1970s, the movement pursued the policy goals of other civil rights movements particularly at the federal front to seek political and legal changes. The results have been mixed over the last ten years, despite the disability rights activists working together in greater coalitions to fight cuts in social spending and criticize conservative methods of civil rights.

The disability advocacy groups have tirelessly, and in many cases, unnoticed, to achieve equal rights and opportunities to about 43 million Americans with disabilities in the past twenty-five years. The enactment of a historic legislation on July 26, 1990, signed by President Bush, was a milestone to the disabled community. This act was geared towards making the transition process easier and making sure that organizations are able to meet its requirements effectively (Gesellschaft für Technische Zusammenarbeit (GTZ), 2006).

3.1.3 Concept of Disability and Social Inclusion

Traditionally, disability was mostly seen as a personal tragedy, which was the subject of treatment, shelter, and compassion. Previously, the provision of support was usually done by organizations like asylum, almshouse, religious or philanthropic groups, which usually led to the segregation of the disabled in the mainstream society. The concept of social inclusion presupposes numerous dimensions and usually refers to the engagement in a diverse sphere of human organization, government, expression, and control of resources altogether is the hidden framework that predetermines the collective action and defines the direction of the societal development. A study on global social dynamics by the United Nations defines that social inclusion is undertaken as a process of ensuring that all individuals, irrespective of the origin or circumstances, have equitable access to the full aspects of society by increasing opportunities, access to resources, voice, and respect of rights (Khaled & Dijkzeul, 2025).

Persons with disabilities experience much less participation in education, economic activities and politics than their nondisabled counterparts do. They also experience reduced health outcomes and poverty levels. These issues are caused by, and lead to the fact that Persons with disabilities have continued to feel systemically excluded as they have continuous difficulties in accessing fundamental facilities such as healthcare, education, employment, and transportation-facilities that are generally more accessible to the general population. At the international level, the World Report on Disability published by the World Health Organization states that in low and middle-income countries, about 80 percent of persons with disabilities live, which is why the overlap between disability and socioeconomic deprivation is rather high. In spite of the benefits linked to social inclusion, studies on low-income, and middle-income countries have shown that persons with disabilities often face widespread exclusion, stigmatization, discrimination, and possibly violence. The powerful avenue towards nurturing inclusion is to formulate the strategies that are based on the values and practices as suggested in the CBR model by World Health Organization (Bright & Kuper, 2018).

3.2 Historical Perspective on Disability Policy

3.2.1 Early Welfare-Based Approaches

The welfare and charitable philosophies had the most impact on the policy of disability. These views that had developed in the 19th and early 20th centuries were influenced by the modern social, religious, and economic perceptions of people with disabilities. Industrialization and urbanization resulted in the growing conspicuity of poverty and dependency which inspired governments and charitable groups to initiate welfare programs. As the welfare state grew in the middle of the twentieth century, the disability benefits became part of the larger social security programs, such as pension, health insurance, and social assistance programs. Although these measures were important in offering the much-needed financial assistance, they still made people with disabilities look like beneficiaries of the welfare and not an individual deserving of rights and participation. Disability policy continued to have the primary goal of compassionate assistance, in preference to empowerment or inclusion (Walker et al., 2021).

3.2.2 *Transition to Rights-Based Perspectives*

The charity-related welfare schemes became more condemned by disability activists at the end of the twentieth century. Their efforts led to a paradigm shift in the social model of disability and motivated global policies of human rights and inclusion, including the adoption of the United Nation's Convention on the Rights of those with Disabilities in 2006, changed the attention to care and protection to rights, inclusion, and equality (Percy, 1993).

Era	Approach	Main characteristics	Policy focus
Nineteenth century	Charity/poor relief	Philanthropic, moral obligation	Custodial care
Early twentieth century	Medical-rehabilitation	Disability as medical issue	Cure, rehabilitation
Mid twentieth century	Welfare-state	Social protection, benefits	Economic security
Late twentieth century onwards	Rights-based	Social inclusion, empowerment	Equality, accessibility

3.2.3 *Global Milestones in Disability Legislation*

Legal frameworks have been developed across all the countries investigated to avoid discrimination and many of them contain a direct protection of persons with disabilities as well as guarantee their integration into the labor force. Peru is an excellent example of protecting equal working opportunities of handicapped persons. Its Anti-Discrimination Law represents a powerful attitude to noninclusion in the labor field. Costa Rica collaborated with the United Nations Development Programme (UNDP) to develop critical frameworks targeted at increasing job prospects for people with disabilities, including the National Disability Policy 2011–2021, the Labour Code, and the National Labour Inclusion Plan. Mexico also demonstrates effective practices in this area. Mexico has enhanced protections against discrimination for persons with disabilities through the 2019 reforms to the Federal Labour Law and the earlier General Law for the Inclusion of People with Disabilities enacted in 2011 (Austin & Bentham, 2019).

3.3 International Legal Frameworks

3.3.1 *The United Nations Convention on the Rights of Persons with Disabilities*

The UNCRPD and its Optional Protocol in 2006, and the documents were made available to states for signatures the following year. Rather than being a mere policy instrument, the Convention serves as a worldwide reference point, encouraging states to reconsider and improve their legal and administrative systems to reflect modern disability-rights ideas. It embodies a global commitment to creating societies in which people with disabilities are treated as equal contributors in social and economic progress. The Convention asks States to vigorously defend and cultivate the basic rights by means of legislative and programmatic transformation. This is a prerequisite of Article 4 that obligates countries to change and harmonize their internal rules of law in accordance with the norms of the Convention (United Nations, 2007).

3.3.2 *Role of WHO, ILO, and Other International Bodies*

Global organizations have created a significant impact in transforming the landscape of international law in the period of modern history. They have not only been acting on the parameters of existing legal restrictions but also have contributed to the creation of new legal norms and institution of international governance. Such organizations take their rise through administrative power and then go back to be the creators to illustrates their norm-creating capacity. The United Nations Charter have played a part in constructing the international legal system as has the continued presence of the UN-affiliated and other multilateral organizations. The past century has seen the growth of implementation of numerous norms in international law by the various organizations, alongside the redefinition of the international bodies through which the legal regimes are created, communicated, and transformed (Helfer, 2006).

3.3.3 *Comparative Analysis of International Models*

The internationalization of the study of disabilities has taken a variety of conceptual models based on the varieties of perceiving disability. The perspective of Medical model operated in Europe and North America regarding disability is, a problem that is prevalent in the individual, is brought about by disease and it focuses on diagnosing, treating, and rehabilitating the individual with the intention of either curing or normalizing the individual. This model was criticized because it overlooked the social and environmental barriers.

The Social model emerged in the United Kingdom and emerged around the disability rights movement, which claims that impairment does not cause disability; instead, society creates barriers through inaccessible environments, discrimination, and marginalization, which result in disability. The model also transfers the blame to the society rather than to the individual and encourages access, inclusion, and equality (Priestley, 2005).

The Biopsychosocial model is another health model which is proposed by the world health organization in the form of international classification of functioning, disability, and health (ICF) and is a combination of both medical and social approaches. It describes disability as the product of interplay of health, psychological, and environmental factors.

The Human rights model is formalized by UNCRPD which regards disability as a human right and social issue. It focuses on dignity, autonomy, equality, and non-discrimination whereby persons living with disabilities are viewed as rights-holders and governments as duty-bearers.

Policymakers and stakeholders must prioritize capacity building, harmonization of standards, and the development of flexible models of governance to counter the multiple changes of fast changing environment and interdependence global. Such an inclusive approach is essential in the creation of powerful regulatory frameworks that are efficient in both defending the national and international interests (Barnes & Mercer, 2005).

3.4 National Policy and Legislative Reforms

3.4.1 Constitutional Provisions and Fundamental Rights

Gender discrimination is likely to be more effective in treating individuals unfairly based on their governance frameworks. International bodies enforce adherence to law and introduce context-specific skills of controlling local objectives whereas multilateral entities establish universal standards of regulations, encourage international cooperation, and focus on the interests that do not limit the geographical location. Consequently, constitutions, domestic laws, and treaties have been drafted in a bid to fight these injustices.

Gender equality is among the issues that were acknowledged by the framers of the Constitution and was included in the legal framework of the Constitution as one of the pillars of the legal system that led to further legislations and principles that promote equal rights (Schriner et al., 1995).

Specific Disability Rights Standards

Although based on broad human rights principles, the CRPD advances these standards by providing governments with particular guidance on how to protect the rights of individuals with disabilities (Dyzenhaus et al. 2001). The Convention outlines these rights in various parts, and each is thoroughly stated (Table 3.1).

Table 3.1 Overview of Key Articles and Associated Rights under the UNCRPD Framework

Article No.	Right/principle	Key focus/description
Article 5	Equality and nondiscrimination	Upholds equal legal status for individuals and mandates that no person be treated unfairly or excluded due to disability
Article 10	Entitlement to the inherent preservation of human life	Emphasizes the fundamental value of human life and requires states to protect and defend the lives of people with disabilities to the same extent as everyone else
Article 12	Guaranteeing that all individuals are treated as persons before the law and possess the right to make and enforce decisions affecting their lives	Affirms the equal legal standing of persons with disabilities and requires states to provide the support systems needed for them to make and act on decisions
Article 14	Guarantee of individual liberty and protection from unlawful restraint or harm	Disability may not be used as a basis for unlawful arrest, detention, or limitation of personal liberty
Article 15	Torture is strictly prohibited, as is any action that causes extreme suffering, humiliation, or dehumanization	Mandates complete protection of persons with disabilities from torture or any form of abusive or degrading treatment
Article 16	Shielding individuals from violence, abuse, and exploitation	Governments must take proactive and responsive efforts to prevent and address all forms of exploitation, violence, and abuse
Article 17	Respect for the Integrity of the Person	Emphasizes the duty to honor and preserve the bodily and psychological wholeness of individuals with disabilities, free from intrusion or harm
Article 18	Freedom of Movement and Nationality	Confirms the right to nationality, unrestricted movement, and the provision of valid identity papers
Article 19	Upholding the autonomy of individuals to shape their daily lives while being socially connected and supported within the broader community	Upholds the notion that everyone should be able to govern their own lives and be integrated into the fabric of communal life, with enough support and resources to facilitate this autonomy
Article 21	Right to express thoughts, hold opinions, and access information	Promotes accessible formats and technologies to enable communication and expression
Article 22	Respect for Privacy	Protects personal, health, and family information from arbitrary or unlawful interference
Article 23	Safeguarding the integrity of family relationships and the privacy of the home	Secures equal opportunities in marriage and family life and ensures that reproductive choices are respected and protected
Article 24	Right to Education	Promotes inclusive education of all levels and lifelong learning

(continued)

Table 3.1 (continued)

Article No.	Right/principle	Key focus/description
Article 25	Assurance that individuals are entitled to conditions and services necessary to maintain physical and psychological health	Upholds the principle that healthcare systems must be inclusive, economically accessible, and sensitive to the medical and support needs of persons with disabilities
Article 27	Recognize that all persons have the right to seek, choose, and maintain work as valuable members of the labor force	Promotes equal opportunity, fair wages, and safe, accessible workplaces for persons with disabilities
Article 28	Affirms that individuals are entitled to adequate living conditions, including housing, food, and basic necessities, along with social protection programs to safeguard their welfare	Supports the right to basic living necessities such as food, housing, clothes, and the social safety nets that are necessary to human dignity
Article 29	A capability to participate in political processes and public affairs	Enables participation in elections, eligibility for public positions, and involvement in governmental matters
Article 30	Allows persons to attend cultural events and participate in leisure, recreational, and sports activities	Guarantees that individuals have the same opportunities to obtain cultural resources, engage in leisure and recreational pursuits, and take part in sporting events

3.4.2 Key National Legislations

Legislations on disability have been developed to advocate a rights-based, inclusive, and nondiscriminatory approach which, instead of the charity and medical models, advocates social justice and human rights. Universal Declaration of Human rights (UDHR) which was introduced in 1948 provided the basis of development of disability rights by stating that all human beings are born free and equal in dignity and rights. The strong legal foundation of inclusive development comes in the form of the international covenant of Economic, Social and Cultural Rights which guarantee persons with disabilities these rights regardless of their disabilities. In 1993, governments on the right to equal opportunities in fields like education, jobs, access, and social inclusion. The inclusion of persons with disabilities in the global development agendas is supported by sustainable Development Goals of SDGs in 2015 that have a guiding principle of Leave No One Behind (Lawson, 2008).

3.4.3 Policy Initiatives and Government Schemes

The policy initiatives concerning disability are mainly instituted by intergovernmental organizations, which include the United Nations (UN), WHO, UNESCO, and the World Bank. These programs encourage a rights, inclusive, and sustainable disability development strategy. The UNCRPD assists governments to develop inclusive laws and schemes associated with education, employment, health, accessibility, political participation, and social protection. WHO Global Disability Action Plan (2014–2021) Introduced by the WHO, this plan of action is focused on better health and quality of life of persons with disabilities, the increased strength of rehabilitation services and the strengthening of disability-inclusive health systems (World Health Organization, 2020).

3.5 Institutional and Administrative Framework

3.5.1 Central and State Disability Commissions

The international laws that regulate disability rights comprise international laws such as UNCRPD, 2006. It provides international norms that govern the protection, promotion, and inclusion of persons with disabilities and directs member states to devise and intensify local and sub-national systems including Central and State Disability Commissions. As a way of checking on these standards, the UN Committee on the Rights of Persons with Disabilities reviews reports sent by governments and gives recommendations on how to better the governance of areas with disability. This framework is assisted by international bodies like the WHO, UNCRPD and UNICEF which provide policy advice on matters relating to health, employment, education, and social inclusion. Therefore, it is through international agencies that bestow the normative and control system that shapes and drives the operations of the Central and State Disability Commissions at the national and state levels (United Nations, 1948).

3.5.2 Role of Nongovernmental Organizations

NGOs are very instrumental in the advocacy, safeguarding and enhancing the rights of the disabled. International NGOs also promote disability rights by engaging in the process of policy formulation and implementation of the UNCRPD policies and by making sure that the voices of persons with disabilities are heard at international level. They also collaborate with UN organs, governments, and other stakeholders to check the abuse of human rights and makes states answerable on their promises. Another activity that NGOs undertake is awareness creation, research, capacity building, inclusive education and employment, community-based rehabilitation and international cooperation and knowledge dissemination. International NGOs empower the global disability rights movement through advocacy and service provision, as well as monitoring activities which in turn contribute towards the social inclusion, equality, and empowerment of persons with disabilities globally (Meyers, 2016).

3.5.3 Public–Private Partnerships in Disability Empowerment

The ILO advocates inclusive employment which is enforced in the form of Vocational Rehabilitation and Employment to peoples with disability. Such programs promote equal employment, skill enhancement, and working conditions. UNESCO promotes inclusive education with policies that are in line with Education for all and Sustainable Development Goal 4 to ensure access to high-quality education by learners with disabilities via teacher training, curriculum adaptation, and accessible learning environments. The world bank promotes the inclusion of disability by offering social protection programs, inclusive infrastructural programs, educational reforms as well as data collection programs (Dunay et al., 2016).

3.6 Judicial Interventions and Case Laws

3.6.1 Landmark Judgments in Disability Rights

Several landmark legal and policy initiatives have played a transformative role in advancing social justice, equality, and human welfare across different periods. The Civil Rights Act of 1964 in the United States marked a decisive break from institutionalized racial segregation by prohibiting discrimination in education, employment, and public accommodations, thereby laying a legal foundation for equal citizenship. Earlier, the New Deal reforms introduced between 1933 and 1939 reshaped the relationship between the state and society by responding to the economic crisis of the Great Depression through social welfare programs such as Social Security, strengthened labor protections, and expanded governmental responsibility for economic stability. At the global level, the Universal Declaration of Human Rights adopted in 1948 established a shared framework of fundamental rights and freedoms that profoundly influenced national constitutions and domestic legislation worldwide. Parallel struggles for political equality were reflected in women's suffrage laws enacted across several countries in the early twentieth century, including the Nineteenth Amendment in the United States and the Representation of the People Acts in the United Kingdom, which secured women's voting rights and expanded democratic participation. More recently, the Affordable Care Act of 2010 represented a significant shift in health policy by extending insurance coverage, regulating insurance practices, and protecting individuals with pre-existing conditions, substantially reducing the number of uninsured people and strengthening access to healthcare (United Nations, 1993).

3.6.2 Judiciary Role in Policy Enforcement

The judiciary also guarantees the Constitution through its ability to ensure that constitutional laws and policies that are enacted by the legislature and exercised by the executive are in line with the constitutional principles and safeguard fundamental rights. Judiciary serve as a checkpoint to lawlessness and violations and through judicial review, they invalidate policies that abuse the constitution (Government of India, 2006, 2016). The citizens have been empowered by Public Interest Litigations to question wrongful acts of the government and thus fostering transparency and accountability. It is important to note that the judiciary has played a major role in identifying and implementing the Right to Education as a fundamental right thus enhancing social equity and economic development (Grant, 2010).

3.6.3 Emerging Trends in Legal Interpretation

Legal interpretation refers to the manner in which judges, legal practitioners, and scholars derive meaning from statutes, constitutional provisions, and other legal texts in order to apply them to real-world situations. In recent years, this process has evolved beyond a narrow or literal reading of legal language, with greater emphasis placed on understanding the broader purpose and social context of legislation. Rather than focusing solely on the words used, courts increasingly seek to identify the intent of the law and the conditions under which it operates. Alongside this purposive and contextual method, constitutional principles and human rights considerations now play a central role in judicial reasoning. Legal provisions are frequently interpreted in harmony with fundamental rights and constitutional values, ensuring that the application of law advances fairness, equality, and respect for human dignity. This rights-oriented approach reflects a growing judicial commitment to aligning legal outcomes with the core ideals upon which constitutional democracies are founded (Patel & Vyas, 2023).

3.7 Contemporary Policy Reforms

3.7.1 Inclusive Education and Employment Policies

Inclusive schools are incredibly useful in the reduction of bias, creation of friendly environments, formation of an increasingly inclusive society and opening education to all. The social justification includes educating all children together and also to contribute to the change in the attitude toward diversity and helps establish the basis of equity and equality, but, furthermore, it is justified by the economic factors (Mojtahedi et al., 2023).

The WHO points at disability people who significantly underrepresented in the labor market compared to their nondisabled counterparts and experienced higher unemployment rates and more barriers at work. Current work methods in the labor market usually anticipate that individuals with disabilities should find their ways out of these obstacles and solve them by themselves, as opposed to organizations being proactive and assume leadership (World Health Organization, 2011). The Equality Act and Disability Discrimination Act that were introduced into the legislation in 2010 and 1995 is predisposed to working with employers responding to accessibility when it is asked directly, instead of taking proactive, broad-based strategies. Consequently, the emphasis is frequently placed on the disabled people in an unequal way and thus, it may lead to ignoring the capabilities of the individuals, experience, and contribution done by disabled individuals to the workforce (Opertti et al., 2014).

3.7.2 Accessibility and Universal Design Standards

Countries participated in UNCRPD required to incorporate the concepts of accessibility, and Universal Design on a legislative, infrastructural, educational, workforce, and technological levels. The accessible physical and digital environments are being designed by the international standards such as the ISO 21542:2021 and the U.S. ADA Standards of Accessible Design, which offer specific guidelines to the governments. Modern urban development policies focus on barrier-free design, convenient transportation, and open spaces that are accessible to all users and smart city projects are progressively integrating Universal Design in urban planning to assist all users to move easily. Universal design learning is increasingly being implemented in the education sector where it is being used to develop adaptable and inclusive learning experiences (Black et al., 2015).

3.7.3 Social Security, Health, and Rehabilitation Reforms

The reforms on social security are aimed at securing income, social protection, disability pensions, employment benefits, and poverty reduction to enhance self-sufficiency in living and social inclusion. Health reforms also focus on equal access to both affordable and quality healthcare services, early diagnosis and treatment, preventive care and nondiscriminatory health policies, as stipulated in the article 25 of the UNCRPD (Council of Europe, 2003). Rehabilitation reforms favor holistic habilitation and rehabilitation services such as medical, psychological, vocational, as well as community-based rehabilitation so that persons with disabilities can attain maximum independence and contribution to the society (Article 26). These international reforms invite the member states to build in disability-inclusive policies in the national systems, change charity-based approach to a rights-based approach as well as the dignity, equality, and full participation of persons with disabilities in the global system (Sabatier & Mazmanian, 1979).

3.8 Challenges and Future Directions

3.8.1 Policy Implementation and Monitoring Issues

Implementing the policy is the process through which the administrative structures, administrative institutions, and concerned stakeholders actualize the policy decisions by converting the directives into tangible actions and outcomes. On the contrary, policy monitoring entails continuous and systematic collection, analysis, and reporting of information to determine the effectiveness of a policy and to gauge its progress towards the desired goals. Combining these processes together is what will guarantee that the intent of policy is achieved in practice and that its effectiveness is regularly checked and refined.

Policy implementation and oversight are frequently challenged by a range of structural and contextual obstacles that limit their effectiveness. Administrative and bureaucratic inefficiencies often slow decision-making and weaken coordination among implementing agencies, while limited financial, human, and technical resources further constrain the translation of policy goals into practice. Ambiguity in policy objectives can create confusion among stakeholders, leading to inconsistent execution and diluted outcomes. These difficulties are commonly compounded by political interference and instability, which may disrupt continuity and shift priorities, as well as by socio-cultural barriers that reduce acceptance or compliance at the community level. In addition to implementation challenges, policy monitoring, and evaluation systems often remain underdeveloped. Weak data collection and management frameworks hinder evidence-based assessment, while inadequate institutional mechanisms and the absence of clear performance indicators make it difficult to measure progress or impact. Limited public participation in evaluation processes further reduces transparency and accountability, ultimately affecting the sustainability and credibility of policy interventions (Brynard, 2000).

3.8.2 Disability Mainstreaming and Cross-Sectoral Integration

The mainstreaming of disability and cross-sectoral integration is a milestone to the attainment of comprehensive, inclusive development. Instead of disability being seen as a distinct welfare issue, mainstreaming has brought the inclusion of disability in all aspects of policy-making, planning, and implementation in order to ensure that individuals with disabilities have equal opportunities and could fully engage in all spheres of society, including social, economic, cultural, or political. This practice is strongly connected with such global initiatives as UNCRPD and the 2030 Agenda of Sustainable Development, which prioritize the idea of leaving no one behind. Mainstreaming disability implies the consideration of disability thoughtfully in all the policies, programs, and activities, both in its design and evaluation (Mabbett, 2018). Disability affects many areas of life, including education, employment, health, housing, transportation, communication, and governance, therefore, the piecemeal solutions are not sufficient. Integration between the sectors, however, requires all the fields to take the initiative of finding out and breaking the barriers that do not allow genuine inclusion (Mitra, 2018).

3.8.3 Future Strategies for Inclusive Development

Inclusive development is a concept that refers to a style of development that ensures equitable participation and mutual benefits of all groups in the population, particularly those who have traditionally been prevented because of their gender, disabilities, ethnicity, and financial disadvantages. This framework does not only emphasize economic progress, but social equity, observance of human rights, and sustainability in the long-run in its quest of the holistic well-being of the society.

Future strategies include

Inclusive development requires a multidimensional approach that integrates economic, social, technological, and institutional strategies to ensure equitable participation for all sections of society. Economic inclusion can be strengthened through policies that promote broad-based growth, enhance skill development, expand employment opportunities, and ensure access to formal financial systems. Social inclusion depends on the adoption of inclusive curricula and the principles of universal design for learning, which recognize diverse learning needs and create supportive educational environments for every learner. Technological inclusion is equally vital and involves expanding access to affordable internet services, fostering digital literacy, and providing assistive technologies to empower marginalized communities. At the governance and institutional level, inclusion is realized by actively engaging citizens, civil society organizations, and underrepresented groups in policy formulation through consultations, social audits, and transparent e-governance mechanisms, thereby reinforcing accountability and participatory decision-making.

3.9 Conclusion

The exploitation of disability rights policies and legal frameworks shows that there was a major shift in the world and in the national level in the changing paradigm of approaches is less focused on charity and welfare, towards rights-based and inclusive model of development. This change is demonstrated through historical patterns, legislative changes, judicial activism, and institutional attitudes, where the society is currently embracing the growing definition of disability as inherent to human rights, equality and the social justice.

On the global level, dignity, autonomy, and active participation have been determined as the principles through such tools as the UNCRPD. These pillars have been strengthened by major organizations like the WHO, ILO, and other international bodies using international standards, common data frameworks, and coordinated support and urging countries to design their own systems to accommodate wider ideas of accessibility and inclusion.

In countries, the push to empower and access equality has been spearheaded by constitutional protection, extensive legislations and direct policy initiatives. However, some of the current challenges such as inadequate execution, disjointed institutions, and constrained resource distributions continue to hamper the maximum achievement of rights. The courts have led, in particular, not only enforcing the values of the constitution, but also interpreting disability protections according to jurisprudential changes in the prospective of human rights.

The recent shifts in policy and legislative changes highlight a high tendency to become more inclusive, laying stress on accessibility and universal design in the fields of education, employment, health, and social net services. These developments are an indication of actual momentum in the direction of creating a society where everyone can take part, yet actual inclusive development will take long-term dedication: by encompassing the topic of disability in all policy sectors, establishing a functioning oversight system, and making disability inclusion on a priority level.

To move forward, future directions should be on strengthening the institutional capacity, to use innovation and technology in enhancing access, and participatory governance that engages people with disability in meaningful decision-making. The policy frameworks should be informed using sound data, entrench universal design principles, and they must be designed through collaboration between governments and civil organizations as well as the private sector.

Finally, disability rights progress cannot be made only through the legal texts; it requires a solid political push, greater awareness of the population, and moral responsibility. Real inclusion will involve transforming the governance systems, development, and practices of communities to ensure that all people irrespective of their abilities are empowered to participate and contribute fully to society. It is only in the light of such an all-inclusive and concerted change that the demand of the call of nothing about us without us can be transformed into a reality.

References

Austin, J. L., & Bentham, J. (2019). *The theory of legislation*. Cambridge University Press.

Barnes, C., & Mercer, G. (Eds.). (2005). *The social model of disability*. Disability Press.

Black, R. D., Weinberg, L. A., & Brodwin, M. G. (2015). Universal design for learning and instruction: Perspectives of students with disabilities in higher education. *Exceptionality Education International, 25*(2).

Bright, T., & Kuper, H. (2018). A systematic review of access to general healthcare services for people with disabilities in low and middle income countries. *International Journal of Environmental Research and Public Health, 15*(9), 1879.

Brynard, P. A. (2000). Policy implementation. In F. Cloete & H. Wissink (Eds.), *Improving public policy* (pp. 165–179). Van Schaik Publishers.

Council of Europe (Ed.). (2003). *Rehabilitation and integration of people with disabilities: Policy and legislation* (7th ed.). Council of Europe Publishing.

Degener, T. (2016). Disability in a human rights context. *Laws, 5*(3), 35. https://doi.org/10.3390/laws5030035

Degener, T., & Koster-Dreese, Y. (1995). *Human rights and disabled persons: Essays and relevant human rights instruments*. Martinus Nijhoff.

Dunay, A., Sharma, A., & Illés, C. B. (2016). Disability and employment: An overview on the role of education and educators. In *Asian conference on education 2016 proceedings*. International Academic Forum. http://papers.iafor.org

Dyzenhaus, D., Hunt, M., & Taggart, M. (2001). The principle of legality in administrative law: International trends. *Oxford Journal of Legal Studies, 21*(1), 129–156.

Finkelstein, V. (2007). *The social model of disability and the disability movement*.

Gesellschaft für Technische Zusammenarbeit (GTZ). (2006). *Disability and development: A contribution to promoting the interests of persons with disabilities in German development cooperation*. German Development Cooperation.

Government of India. (2016). The Rights of Persons with Disabilities Act, 2016 and National Policy for Persons with Disabilities, 2006. Government of India.

Grant, J. P. (2010). Subjects of international law. In *International law essentials*. Dundee University Press.

Helfer, L. R. (2006). Understanding change in international organizations: Globalization and innovation in the ILO. *Vanderbilt Law Review, 59*(3), 649–726.

Khaled, A. F., & Dijkzeul, D. (2025). *Advancing disability-inclusive humanitarian programming and coordination in South Sudan*.

Lawson, A. (2008). *Disability and equality law in Britain: The role of reasonable adjustment*. Hart Publishing.

Mabbett, D. (2018). Disability and development: Integrating disability in sustainable development goals. *Disability & Society, 33*(7), 1057–1077.

Meyers, S. (2016). NGO-ization and human rights law: The CRPD's civil society mandate. *Laws, 5*(2), 21.

Mitra, S. (2018). Disability, health and human development. *World Development, 104*, 1–14.

Mojtahedi, M. C., Mikkola, R., & Saxén, N. (2023, April). Advancing rights and inclusion of persons with disabilities in humanitarian action: A donor perspective. *International Review of the Red Cross, 105*(922), 416–433.

Opertti, R., Walker, Z., & Zhang, Y. (2014). Inclusive education: From targeting groups and schools to achieving quality education as the core of EFA. In L. Florian (Ed.), *The SAGE handbook of special education* (2nd ed., pp. 149–170). SAGE.

Patel, R., & Vyas, R. (2023). The role of judiciary in enforcing the right to education in India. *International Journal of Indian Psychòlogy, 11*(3), 4923–4931. https://doi.org/10.25215/1103.463

Percy, S. L. (1993). Challenges and dilemmas in implementing disability rights policies. *Journal of Disability Policy Studies, 4*, 41–63.

Priestley, M. (2005). The social model of disability and European social policy. In C. Barnes & G. Mercer (Eds.), The social model of disability: Europe and the majority world (pp. 19–34). Disability Press.
Sabatier, P. A., & Mazmanian, D. A. (1979). The conditions of effective implementation: A guide to accomplishing policy objectives. *Policy Analysis, 5*(4), 481–504.
Schriner, K. F., Rumrill, P., & Parlin, R. (1995). Rethinking disability policy: Equity in the ADA era and the meaning of specialized services for people with disabilities. *Journal of Health and Human Services Administration, 17*(4), 478–500.
Shumba, T. W., & Moodley, I. (2018). Review of policy and legislative framework for disability services in Namibia. *South African Journal of Physiotherapy, 74*(1), 399. https://doi.org/10.4102/sajp.v74i1.399
United Nations. (1948). *Universal declaration of human rights*. United Nations General Assembly. https://www.un.org/en/about-us/universal-declaration-of-human-rights
United Nations. (1993). *Standard rules on the equalization of opportunities for persons with disabilities*. United Nations General Assembly.
United Nations. (2006). *Convention on the rights of persons with disabilities and optional protocol*. United Nations. https://www.un.org/disabilities/documents/convention/convoptprot-e.pdf
United Nations. (2007). *Convention on the rights of persons with disabilities (UN-CRPD)*. https://social.desa.un.org/issues/disability/crpd/convention-on-the-rights-of-persons-with-disabilities-crpd
Walker, C. C., Druckman, A., & Jackson, T. (2021). Welfare systems without economic growth: A review of the challenges and next steps for the field. *Ecological Economics, 186*, 107066.
World Health Organization. (2011). *World report on disability [Internet]*. WHO. http://www.who.int/disabilities/world_report/2011/report.pdf
World Health Organization. (2020). *WHO policy on disability*. WHO.

Chapter 4
Inclusive Education: Bridging Gaps in Learning

B. Hardha, B. Gowramma, Muskan Sharma, B. Babu, and Nayudu Teja

Abstract The objective of comprehensive curriculum is to eliminate cognitive and emotional obstacles that prohibit pupils with different requirements from fully participating during school. It includes equality and fairness, giving opportunities for all learners to achieve their goals despite their background, ability, or gender. The legal duties, philosophical roots, and concrete measures for ensuring current inclusive policies will all be covered within this chapter. It emphasizes the crucial importance of educational alteration, faculty ownership, and related budgets in transforming ideas into real valuable instruction, particularly in places that have inadequate resources. Technologies include collaboration in instruction, Universal Design for Learning (UDL), and the adoption of digital resources which encourage flexibility and are highly student-focused. In addition to assisting students who have challenges, these techniques enhance cooperation, increase outcomes, and build understanding among learners of all abilities through instances and cases from throughout the world. The section additionally shows how enduring growth calls for tackling existing barriers such as engrained biases, insufficient education of teachers, and structural shortcomings. In addition, it is believed that closing colleges and universities necessitates the formation of an equitable ecosystem that is in keeping with the Sustainable Development Goals rather than essentially altering outdated mechanisms. It emphasizes even more the importance of creating an environment

B. Hardha (✉) · B. Gowramma · M. Sharma
Department of Pharmaceutical Chemistry, JSS College of Pharmacy, JSS Academy of Higher Education and Research, The Nilgiris, Ooty, Tamil Nadu, India
e-mail: gowrammab@jssuni.edu.in

B. Babu
Department of Pharmaceutical Analysis, JSS College of Pharmacy, JSS Academy of Higher Education and Research, The Nilgiris, Ooty, Tamil Nadu, India
e-mail: babu@jssuni.edu.in

N. Teja
Department of Pharmaceutics, JSS College of Pharmacy, JSS Academy of Higher Education and Research, The Nilgiris, Ooty, Tamil Nadu, India

D. Nagasen, S. K. S. S. Pindiprolu (eds.), *Transforming Disability Studies*, SpringerBriefs in Modern Perspectives on Disability Research,
https://doi.org/10.1007/978-981-95-9004-9_4

for learning that comprehends inclusion, reduces disparity, and qualifies the coming generations for making a balanced contribution to life.

Keywords Inclusive Education • Educational Equity • Universal Design for Learning (UDL) • Stakeholder Collaboration

4.1 Introduction

Whatever their intellectual capacity, age, socioeconomic background, cultural or physical attributes, or language proficiency, an equitable education ensures that all learners are given an outstanding education in an identical environment. It is based on the belief that responsive teaching practices, fairness, and motivation help all learners achieve their full potential. In addition to grouping students together, it guarantees a fair and high-quality education in which involvement and acceptance are valued. This inclusive education is a basic human right which includes the principles of social justice by recognizing diversity as a strength rather than a weakness. Instead of segregating students as lacking, it ultimately encourages learning spaces which are adaptable, teaching strategies which are flexible, and a curriculum which is responsible. All across the world, education systems differ due to health, economic, cultural, and social barriers. To rectify these, accessible education should be based on individual needs and ensure equality for all by giving the same opportunities and resources. For example, a child with low vision needs assistive technology; on the other hand, a student from a disadvantaged family may require financial or social support. By the way, equal education helps everyone to succeed. If this is not done, gaps in education will exist, resulting in disadvantage and exclusion. Removing limits based on gender, income, and disability will promote holistic growth, fairness, and inclusion. Both moral and practical drivers promote growth in the world today. With globalization, migration, social change, and technology, classrooms are diversifying at an increasing rate. Educational institutions provide not only skills in academics but also tolerance, empathy, and cooperation to prepare children for the future. In this way, accessible classrooms will project an inclusive society that celebrates preparing children for the future and for success.

4.2 The Development and Progression of Accessible Education

The evolution of inclusive education illustrates the role of learning, equality, and society's growing awareness of human rights. It was noted that during the 19th and 20th centuries disabled students were removed from schools and were placed in separate institutions meant for disabled students. Although this type of segregation offers customized instruction, it results in reduced social interaction and may negatively affect students with disabilities, even though the schools do provide individualized teaching. At that time, education was largely considered a privilege reserved for able-bodied children, while marginalized groups frequently lacked access to formal schooling. Worldwide efforts that redefine learning as an equal opportunity as opposed to a special privilege caused an enormous shift in the latter half of the twentieth century. A major turning point was the signing in 1948 of the Universal Declaration of Human Rights, which formally recognized learning as an inherent right and laid the foundation for global systems. In the past few years, education has played a crucial role in the development of an individual to ensure and encourage equity in society.

The important role of schooling adapted to the unique needs of learners with intellectual disabilities was recognized (1971). The year 1981 was declared as the United Nations Year of Disabled Persons to raise consciousness of equality, diversity, and a requirement for change in structure on a global basis. Collectively, these courses showed the failings of institutionalized learning and stressed the need for inclusive mainstream education that emphasizes diversity, preserves justice, and provides the same opportunities to all students.

The worldwide pledge to guarantee every child, especially children with limitations, an opportunity for fundamental schooling was reiterated at the United Nations Conference on Education for All (1990, Jomtien, Thailand). The symposium demonstrated that integrated education supports continuous growth of society by emphasizing that free education is a financial and social need as well as a moral duty. The states that schools are needed to ensure equal opportunities for all learners regardless of their language, economic, and cultural status And also adds that they should undergo critical alterations including preparation by teachers, study syllabus, and availability of resources (Abdullah et al., 2023; Table 4.1).

India's recent developments in accessible education have been in response to its unique societal setting while remaining current with global developments. In earlier times, children from excluded communities or individuals who had disabilities had little to no opportunity for educational opportunities; children had a tendency to take part in private education initiatives, specialized organizations, or private courses, most of which were both substandard and difficult to get hold of. The National Policy on Education (1986), which established instruction as an essential component and championed equal learning opportunities for all students, constituted an important change by encouraging the transfer of pupils with unique requirements into conventional schools. Building around these foundations, programs like the District Primary Education Programme (DPEP, 1990s) helped to make improvements in infrastructure, teacher training, and promotional projects to widen access, diminish gaps, and promote integration.

These initiatives were strengthened even more by the Sarva Shiksha Abhiyan (Bajpai, 2018), which utilized information centers, accessible resources for learning, and child-oriented classes to concentrate on those who are less fortunate, such as girls, minority communities, and young people with disability. The Right of

Table 4.1 Evolutionary landmarks of accessible education in global and Indian contexts

Year/period	Event/policy/declaration	Significance
1948	Universal Human Rights Declaration	Declared education a basic and inalienable right for all
1960s–1970s	Formation of special education institutions and early integration schemes (India)	Implemented specialized instruction for children with disabilities alongside initial steps toward mainstream inclusion
1971	UN statement on the rights of persons with intellectual disabilities	Affirmed that individuals with cognitive challenges are entitled to both education and inclusion in community life
1981	International year for persons with disabilities	Shined an international spotlight on the struggles of people with disabilities
1986	National Education Policy (India)	Facilitated the participation of children with disabilities in regular schooling wherever achievable
1990	World Conference on Education for All, Jomtien	Emphasized the vital necessity for all students to have easy access to education
1990s	District Primary Education Programme (DPEP) (India)	Directed efforts toward universal education, emphasizing the inclusion of children with disabilities
1994	UNESCO Salamanca statement	Recommended that schools adapt to the needs of all children, including those with varying abilities and learning challenges
2005	Sarva Shiksha Abhiyan (SSA) (India)	Supported universal access to primary education while fostering accessible learning spaces
2006	UN Convention on the Rights of Persons with Disabilities (UNCRPD)	Legally enforced the adoption of accessible schooling practices across primary, secondary, and higher education
2009	Right to Education (RTE) Act (India)	Guaranteed that all children between 6 and 14 years, including those with disabilities and from marginalized communities, receive free education
2015	Sustainable Development Goal 4 (SDG 4)	Required governments to deliver education that is accessible, equitable, and of quality to all learners by 2030
Recent years	Samagra Shiksha Abhiyan (India)	Strives to deliver accessible and fair education across primary, secondary, and higher education levels

Children to Free and Compulsory Education (RTE) Act, 2009, which required equitable possibilities for learning and equitable enrolment of pupils aged 6–15, was a monumental step. Earlier schemes, including the Samagra Shiksha Abhiyan, worked together through elementary, advanced, and continuing education for schools by focusing on adaptive technologies, building advancements, and instructor capacity development that allow instructors to efficiently implement accessibility practices. Despite these innovations, difficulties still remain. Many educational facilities remain influenced by a lack of funding, ineffective staff members, and deeply rooted cultural assumptions promoting bigotry and lowered hopes for students who are visually impaired or are in less fortunate circumstances. Accessibility is still an important concern, particularly for those from rural regions, and many educators say their students are unprepared to use relevant methods for instructing. Still, gradual improvements in recent decades demonstrate the increasing recognition of affordable education as a socioeconomic goal as well as an ethical obligation. India's accessible college system is further defined by governmental structures. Adequate measures for accessibility to education were implemented by the Persons with Disabilities (PWD) Act of 1995 and the broader Rights of Persons with Disabilities (RPWD) Act of 2016.

The National Education Policy emphasized the significance of equity, preparation for educators, and the application of technological resources to address a range of educational needs, while the provisions of the RTE Act (2009) enhanced these demands (Chawla, 2024). Overall, the above steps establish that authorities and organizations have ethical and contractual obligations in ensuring that no one is left out. The growth of accessible education throughout history demonstrates how including children with disabilities in ordinary lessons will not be enough to produce full inclusion. To develop educational settings that accept uniqueness as a benefit, a fundamental change must take place, incorporating school change, preparation of educators, involvement by the community, and regular evaluation. The two national policies such as the Right to Education Act (2009) and the National Education Policy (2020) and global structures like the Salamanca Statement (1994), share an identical vision: education systems need to evolve conceptually, academically, and in terms of culture in order to establish equal privilege and real engagement for all students (Lombardi, 2019; Winter, 2019). Based on nineteenth-century segregated schools to present inclusive systems, cases from both India and other cultures indicate the relevance of legislation, innovative approaches to learning, and a heightened social awareness of inclusion. Even though there are continual difficulties, the general tendency creates an effective foundation to support equal and permanent systems of learning that help everyone reach their potential.

4.3 Core Ideas and Objectives of Accessible Education

Everyone should have access to a top-notch education with a chance for growth as an individual, irrespective of their expertise, economic standing, spoken language, or background in culture. To ensure that educational facilities properly meet the specific needs of every student, approaches to instruction, syllabuses, evaluation methods, and systems of governance must all be completely changed rather than simply arranging every pupil in the same classroom. At a fundamental level, accessible education respects diversity and sees academic variations as strengths rather than shortcomings that enhance the educational experience. Education facilities become tiny representations of modern society as many skill levels, languages, and cultural traditions coexist, enabling cooperation, empathy, and continuous enrichment. An essential component of accessible education involves offering equitable opportunities which is strongly linked to promoting variety.

Providing everyone with equal access to schooling through tools, networks of support, and adaptation to each child's particular requirements—instead of treating all pupils equally—is what the concept of equity means. Learners enter education with a range of histories, abilities, and obstacles; some have physical obstacles, ailments, or social hurdles arguing for individualized methods to promote success. For example, pupils with eye problems may use Braille characters or highlighting software, and students with difficulties with hearing may need help with spoken language or dubbed information. Also, low-income pupils may be able to maintain their involvement through financial assistance, complimentary supplies for school, or meal programs. By overcoming these differences through assistive devices, flexible assessments, and extra support, accessible education ensures every student has the same opportunity to excel. Fairness needs to be stretched past the classroom to include extracurricular engagement, leadership positions, and social interactions in order to encourage kids to develop self-worth, drive, and courage. In this sense, affordable education is both a classroom breakthrough and a form of social justice, enabling impoverished pupils to reach their highest potential. An additional essential concept is removing obstacles to learning and full engagement. Access is restricted by psychological, attitude, and logistical obstacles unless they are consciously abolished. Practical obstacles such as the lack of stairs or staircases or tactile signals disadvantage students with mobility or sensory disabilities. Specific learning styles receive priority over other methods when coaching is inflexible and standardized. For example, memorizing words by heart might disregard creativity or experiential learners and discriminate against adolescents from language minorities.

Since they could decrease pupil participation and trust in themselves due to low expectations or prejudices of classmates, educators, or friends, attitude barriers can be equally detrimental even though they are less noticeable. Such problems demand structural remedies, such as the Universal Design for Learning (UDL), which delivers a range of methods of instruction and appraisal techniques and Individualized Education Plans (IEPs), offering specific support. Increased inclusion is helped by flexible evaluation processes, teacher preparation, and peer mentoring. By slowly eliminating barriers, classrooms develop places where all pupils are understood, motivated, and set up to succeed. A separate goal of accessible instruction is promoting the overall development of students. It stimulates spiritual, social, emotional, and physical growth in addition to studies.

Engaging with people from different backgrounds and ability sets promotes the development of empathy, versatility, resilience, and teamwork. Children who work with fellow pupils who have challenges, for instance, often acquire compassion and traits of leadership, while those who have special needs acquire independence as well as social abilities. Students are able to take part in their studies if they are placed in accepting and supporting learning environments which promote interpersonal skills, taking chances, and recovery after failure. Furthermore, affordable learning equips students with the values and expertise required in numerous sectors, social responsibility, and fruitful international interaction, nurtures personal growth, and makes them caring and environmentally conscientious citizens. The thoughts of appreciating plurality, nurturing justice, abolishing constraints, and advancing wholehearted growth all have been connected. Celebrating differences require impartiality; obstacles to growth may not coexist in equity; and full growth requires both acceptance and consideration of variances.

When combined, it comprises the fundamentals of affordable education, influencing teaching methods, institution procedures, and politics. In order to accomplish those objectives, teamwork among teachers, managers, politicians, individuals, and the general public is essential. Instructors may serve as a benchmark for accessibility behaviors through the application of safe instructional settings and specific instruction. Managers and policymakers must offer the appropriate system, training, representation in courts, and funds. Communities and family members play an important part in establishing attainable beliefs beyond school walls.

The main objectives of open schooling are to provide everybody with a chance to excel in education, eliminate disparities, promote a sense of society, and turn diversity into an incubator of innovation and creative thinking. It prepares children to live in a dependent world without empathy, obligation, and comprehension. In the end, accessible education is much more than just a teaching technique; it is a groundbreaking principle based on fairness, equity, and humanity. By embracing diversity, maintaining equity, removing barriers, and fostering holistic growth, it provides an environment of learning in which everybody may excel and make valuable contributions to humanity. Outside educational achievement, it strives to cultivate strong, caring people who can build warm and pleasant society.

4.4 Factors Limiting Access and Engagement in Learning

Equal education is essential to deliver fair and quality education. Few obstacles associated with this are organization, individual obstacles. If these hurdles are not eliminated, the goal of "education for all" may remain aspirational rather than realistic (Bhatia & Singh, 2021). One of the most significant and persisting problems is attitude. Individuals who appear as "different" face challenges, discrimination, and stereotypes in classes, institutions of learning, and society broadly. These perceptions have become prevalent between instructors, students, parents, and society at large, and they may affect a child's perceived approval, support, and desire for participating. For instance, as they are seen as incapable, educators frequently decrease standards or bar learners who have cognitive or physical disabilities from engaging in active learning. Children from marginalized social groups whether due to their caste, race, or minority status may encounter additional preconceptions about their skill set or motivation. These cultural obstacles not merely restrict enthusiasm but also trigger psychological stress, which reduces security and interest. When individuals absorb these prejudices and give up, perform poorly, or even drop out, the pattern of discrimination can remain.

To deal with such issues, community outreach efforts, educational material that stresses respect, compassion, and fairness, and educator education on inclusivity and awareness are all necessary. Education needs to create an environment that acknowledges the unique worth and potential of every learner (Ahmad, 2015; Oad, 2023; Johnsen, 2020). Economic and architectural obstacles may constitute major obstacles. Many schools, notably those in rural or impoverished communities, lack the tools required for instructing students with a wide range of needs. Physical accessibility difficulties, such as the dearth of ramps or elevators, extensive doorways, or wheelchair-friendly facilities, prevent students who have limitations in mobility from learning successfully and effectively. Lack of mode of transport options, especially for areas that are remote, further restricts access. Teachers' ability to satisfy each student's demands is hampered by congested classrooms, an educator shortfall, and a shortage of support facilities or specialized educational facilities. Structural problems might involve systematic planning defects related to how resources are distributed, zoning laws, and accessible architectural standards. In order to remove these barriers, specialized legislation and expenditures in accessible transit infrastructure and learning environments will be needed (Antil, 2014; Ari et al., 2022; Banerjee, 2014; Al-Hroub & Jouni, 2023; Kohout-Diaz, 2023).

Cognitive barriers are a substantial problem. Traditional instruction has been defined by rigid curricula, standardized testing, and consistent approaches to learning that overlook variability among learners.

Approaches that stress studying and high-pressure tests are helpful for some pupils but harmful for people with problems with learning. In particular, students with difficulties with reading, ADHD, or additional educational problems might find it tough to study in an ordinary school setting, though learners with multiple languages may need language support. Gaps in teacher preparation exacerbate these issues by making it difficult for lots of educators to provide unique training or apply accessible practices like sharing information.

Instructional hurdles must be tackled through flexible learning principles like Universal Design for Learning (UDL) and regular training to provide teachers with appropriate skills (Aiello & Pace, 2020). Equipment and constraints on resources contribute to making inclusion significantly more difficult. Assistive technology, such as keyboard readers, visual devices, hearing instruments, and compatible keys, is essential in fostering participation, but many schools lack access to them and the required training. The digital divide contributes to poverty, especially for struggling or remote regions where there is a lack of technologically sophisticated education facilities, electricity, and the World Wide Web. To remedy such issues, intensive educational and educational training and additional investment in technology are essential (Chakraborti-Ghosh, 2018; Kunwar & Adhikari, 2023; Nzuza, 2023). Social and economic hurdles are still a problem. Unemployment, youth labor, early marriage, displacement, and isolation prevent many children from entering or attending school. Families that are having challenges with finances can begin setting a lower value on higher education for girls or children who have special needs. Hidden expenses like clothing, educational materials, transportation, and ailments further restrict vulnerable pupils. Social and financial obstacles also have an impact on attendance and learning output since toddlers could show up at school starving or tired. To address those issues, comprehensive solutions including community gathering, health projects, monetary transfers with conditions, and endowments will be needed (Chaudhary, 2017; Das, 2013; De Bruin, 2019; Newman & Conway, 2017; Waisman et al., 2022; Forlin et al., 2011; Adesokan & Bojuwoye, 2023).

To sum everything up, there are many distinct but related challenges to accessible education. Cultural rules, educational technology, and economic and social issues can reinforce one another, particularly for students who experience multiple challenges. To defeat them, a broad and well-coordinated method will be needed. It is vital that teacher education, involvement in society, changing the curriculum, readily available spaces, technological assistance, flexible ways of teaching, and socioeconomic support work together. Stakeholders, including elected officials, school administrators, friends, neighbors, and learners, are needed to create surroundings that are inclusive, beneficial, and respectful to diversity. Quality education requires exhaustive strategies that handle interlinked difficulties in order to construct instructional environments where everybody is recognized, valued, and driven. Only by constant, coordinated actions can schools realize their commitment to "schooling for everybody," which calls for equal opportunities, meaningful involvement, and integrated growth for all pupils (Guleria, 2021; Jameel, 2011; Kaushik, 2016; Newman & Conway, 2017; Waisman et al., 2022; Kohama, 2012; Adesokan & Bojuwoye, 2023).

4.5 Techniques for Supporting Diverse Learners

Ensuring individual and the educational growth is essential to fill the gaps in achieving accessible education for learners with varied requirements. Also, it is understood that including more students in classrooms is not advisable in order to increase successful education, whereas teaching methods and learning resources should be effectively improved. Various learning styles and interest also help in achieving good quality education. Visual methods of teaching such as pictures and flow charts will help the students deepen their understanding. UDL offers methods for changing syllabus design which helps learners in getting quality education. These methods will help in providing equal education to reduce the obstacles (Hollings, 2021; Kavkler et al., 2015). These methods involve digital tools which are essential. Disabled students can also access various education tools without any problem. Also, the students can benefit from immediate feedback and address gaps in their knowledge. These tools should be used with proper preparation by tutors. Also, the tutors should focus on proper learning by making students essential for quality education. In addition to the adaptation of academics, individual learning plans are essential for learners who need help. Altering techniques and simplifying materials are some examples of adapting to academics. ILP introduces individualized learning practices to learners, mainly those with disabilities (Arnaiz-Sánchez et al., 2023; Memon & Memon, 2025). Above all, it is considered as filling the learning spaces.

These practices will change classrooms into a place where education is accessible to each and every one who aims to achieve quality education.

4.6 Role of Stakeholders in Accessible Education

Accessible education is not only based on one individual but the result of all who have to work together to produce a surrounding that supports all students. NGO, parents, tutors, and communities all should get involved in accessible education. Each and every one should make a unique contribution in ensuring that all the students, irrespective of their backgrounds, contribute to education (Barajas Motta et al., 2025; Kulkarni & Gathoo, 2017; Kumari et al., 2024; Hollings, 2021). Teachers serve as vital change agents and educational facilitators who support accessible education. In addition to their usual duty of teaching, teachers are in charge of creating learning environments that celebrate diversity and fit a range of abilities (Altaf et al., 2017). As change agents, learners battle prejudice, remove prejudice, and achieve equity in and out of the classroom. Effective access teaching needs regular professional growth, including classes on accessible pedagogy, sensitivity training, and exposure to a variety of educational modalities. Continued encouragement guarantees that every requirement of students is addressed with proficiency, imagination, and empathy but also allows educators to adapt to changing circumstances in the classroom. Because they play an essential function in spreading diverse views, parents and society are equally crucial. As crucial partners in the schooling of their kids, parents contribute priceless insights into their children's aspirations, challenges, and strengths. Teachers can effectively personalize activities and guidance once they acquire information.

When children get involved in teacher–parent associations, assist at school-related events, and get involved in governance processes, the relationship between the home and the educational institution is strengthened. Engagement in the community is vital for decreasing stigma and creating tolerance in addition to maintaining close familial connections and creating connections of support for schools. Local education efforts, donations, and neighborhood groups are essential for increasing inclusion, especially among children from impoverished or marginalized backgrounds. Social services including medical facilities, psychological professionals, and cultural programs promote inclusive policies and create a full support system that benefits every child by addressing concerns that impact education far beyond the learning environment (Limaye, 2016; Ketheeswaran, 2025; Madan & Sharma, 2013; Sari et al., 2025).

Management and administration at schools are equally important to the adoption of inclusive policies. Administrators, heads of schools, and staff members have a bearing on participation by the enforcement of rules, the distribution of funds, and the development of an educational environment which promotes variety and fairness. When teachers and administrators stipulate inclusion in their strategic plans, expenditures, and regulations, organizations show their dedication by offering structures for accountability that support long-term accessible practices. Administrators have a duty to provide people with access to specialized staff that include resource specialists, mental health professionals, and medical professionals, in furtherance of ensuring secure transport, steps, adaptive bathroom facilities, staircases, and other readily accessible facilities (Mahapatra, 2016; Serrano-Tamayo, 2021; Swargiary, 2024; Khadija, 2022). A further prerequisite for successful management is the development of mutually beneficial channels for those interested which encourage cooperative problem-solving and continuous assessment of accessible methods. If the head of the institution is actively involved in giving accessible education by ensuring creativity it will result in the betterment of society and the individual. Government is responsible and frames all the essential provisions, ethical and economical, which helps in creating accessible education. Government controls the financial support of educational facilities, the delivery of accessible educational materials, incorporating of accessible pedagogy into teacher education programs, and the availability of assistive technology for pupils with need. Nongovernmental organizations (NGOs) enhance government aid via offering specific help in districts with little funding or systemic inadequacies. NGOs often test out innovative community-based models that may eventually be complemented by funding from the government, in addition to conducting advocacy, support, physical medicine, job instruction, and remedial classes. In poorer and rural communities, NGOs often function as catalysts, raising profile, gathering resources, and enabling disadvantaged children and their families to fight for their right to receive an education (Genovesi et al., 2022).

Learners also serve as important participants in the advancement of equality. For accessible education to be effective, the peer culture within the school is just as important as structural and policy changes (Singal, 2020; Chimhenga, 2016). For instance, instructors, parents, and counselors have to collaborate together to effectively integrate students who have challenges and provide them with continuous encouragement within home and at classroom. Neighborhood involvement can impact regional policy setting, though organizations generally act as a connection between governmental authorities and people with limited opportunities. Government plans give validity and reliability, but execution requires engagement in individuals, households, and academics. Together they can be beneficial to all learning policy designs to ensure daily learning in the school space alongside outcomes for over a longer period of time.

4.7 Applied Studies and Evidence-Based Approaches

Substantial case reports and desirable practices will show how this accessible education can be implemented successfully with creativity, teamwork, and dedication. These models support information which is insightful about the tactics that will function well in different situations. Models of accessible education, which are successful for students with different disabilities, involve studying together in a common setting. For example, in Scandinavian nations classrooms have open learning areas, groups which are cooperative, and adjustable seating to allow students so that they can learn freely and participate equally. In order to meet each and every student's needs of learning, teachers or guides may employ formative assessments, peer mentoring, and unique and varied instruction. These models demonstrate how accessible classroom designs benefit all students, including those without disabilities, by creating an enhanced learning environment (Faragher et al., 2021). The participation of differently abled students in mainstream education is one of the main goals of inclusion. Strong frameworks for mainstreaming children with disabilities have been put in place in nations like Canada and Australia, thanks to resource support teachers, assistive technology, and individualized education plans (IEPs). In India, programs under the Samagra Shiksha Abhiyan and Sarva Shiksha Abhiyan (SSA) have prioritized accessible education by giving children with disabilities financial support, appliances, and other aids. Case studies show that students with disabilities can perform on a par with their peers when the right support systems are in place, such as Braille learning materials, sign language interpretation, or modified exams.

In villages and cities, there are also chances of gaps in ensuring equal education. Including economic educational chances, changing the syllabus according to everyone's needs, and adding persons for volunteering were introduced by NGOs in the villages in India. Newer teaching practices help in ensuring practical-based learning and high-quality education (Villa & Thousand, 2021). Also including early teaching and problem- and practical-based education helps in student quality learning.

Diverse learners now have more options thanks to technological advancements like virtual classrooms, gamified learning apps, and accessible online learning platforms. It has also been demonstrated that education practices that integrate the cultural experiences of students' linguistic and cultural backgrounds into the curriculum enhance learning outcomes and student engagement. These methods foster twenty-first-century abilities like empathy, critical thinking, and teamwork in addition to meeting a variety of needs. The case studies and best practices show that with careful preparation, sufficient funding, and consistent dedication, accessible education is possible (Mbua, 2023). They summarize that when all the organizations like institutions, national and international, governments, and other communities combine and collaborate to create learning environments for everyone, inclusion becomes a reality and not just a theoretical concept.

4.8 Challenges and Future Directions

Despite being progressive, the way to accessible education for everyone is fraught with obstacles and difficulties. Existing problem is the inconsistency within the existing policies and the practiced policies. Although international, national, and government organizations provide best practices and policies of frameworks that support inclusion, there is a minor alteration in the policies and the principles regarding effective and productive teaching methods. Few schools may not have enough resources available or the clarity required to put forth accessible education which may lead to inconsistency in accessibility in different regions. The need for training teachers and professional development is another existing problem. Apart from being the backbone of accessible classrooms, many teachers lack the training and knowledge that would help in handling the variety of learning essentials. The verified teaching approaches are essential to prepare for the traditional education programs which leave gaps in competencies like differentiated instruction, adaptation to curriculum, and assessment which is accessible to each and every one equally. It was noted that many educators felt difficulty in handling the learners with different capabilities, needs, and identities without professional development. Another problem is mobilizing resources that are sustainable. Consistent investment in teaching and learning resources, assistive technology, infrastructure, and specialized support is necessary for implementing accessible education. However, it is very challenging to guarantee sustainability due to financial constraints mainly in developing contexts. However, escalation is ultimately limited by inadequate funding due to short-term efforts and lack of private and public partnerships. Further developments in accessible education will encourage resolving the issues. Experiences in learning in accessible education can help each student in using technologies like AI and adaptive learning platforms. Digital inclusion is growing in vitality as one of the online platforms with options that further provide greater access to education to all learners including those with disabilities and in underserved regions. Further educator's cooperation, international networking, and other organizations which facilitate research exchange, models which are creative, and good practices result in a knowledgeable approach and more coordinated accessible education. The future of accessible education is bright, despite obstacles such as gaps in policy practice, poor preparation of teachers, and scarce resources that still help in progress.

4.9 Conclusion

Accessible education is a game changing technique that ensures equality and high-quality learning for everyone. The conclusions include that accessible education is based on "opportunity to all," with a focus on diversity and removing barriers to involvement. Throughout its existing and present approaches, accessible education has repeatedly been essential for social growth, promoting cognitive skills with the cooperation of people and other communities. By giving all the students good and productive learning, accessible education leads to learning opportunities. It also helps in addressing the gaps such as inaccessible infrastructure and lack of existing and essential resources. Accessible education promotes fairness, empathy, and equality worldwide, as well as is a social justice tool. Long-term dedication helps in closing the gaps in education through some innovative steps using creative tools and techniques which are needed in the future. Development in the near future includes global networking development, critical learning, practical-based learning,

AI-driven learning and teaching that is sensitive. As an end in itself, accessible education focuses on transforming the system of education in order to ensure and bring equity, encourage teamwork, and enable each and every student to reach their greatest potential. It is not just about integrating students into classrooms.

References

Abdullah, N. K., Hamzah, M. I., Yasin, M. H., Tahar, M. M., Rahman, J., Haron, Z., Wahab, M. Z., Razak, M. A., Zainurin, M. F., Kamarudzaman, N. H., & Jopri, S. (2023, January 1). Teacher's acceptance and readiness in implementing Zero Reject Policy (ZRP) in rural schools in Malaysia. *e-BANGI Journal, 20*(1).

Adesokan, A., & Bojuwoye, O. (2023). Teachers' perceived barriers to inclusive education. *ASEAN Journal of Community and Special Needs Education, 2*(2), 91–96.

Ahmad, F. K. (2015, January). Challenging exclusion: Issues and concerns in inclusive education in India. *Researchpaedia, 2*(1), 15–32.

Aiello, P., & Pace, E. M. (2020, June 30). Inclusive educational principles, policies, and practices in Italy. In *Oxford research encyclopedia of education*. Oxford University Press.

Al-Hroub, A., & Jouni, N. (2023, November 16). Historical and theoretical approaches to inclusive education. In *School inclusion in Lebanon: Integrating research on students with giftedness and learning disabilities into practice* (pp. 47–65). Springer.

Altaf, A., Kawish, A. B., & Anwar, I. (2017). Inclusive education in visually impaired children: Stakeholders perspective. *Rehabilitation Science, 2*(1), 16–20.

Antil, N. (2014). Inclusive education: Challenges and prospects in India. *IOSR Journal of Humanities And Social Science, 19*(9), 85–89.

Ari, R., Altinay, Z., Altinay, F., Dagli, G., & Ari, E. (2022, February 15). Sustainable management and policies: The roles of stakeholders in the practice of inclusive education in digital transformation. *Electronics, 11*(4), 585.

Arnaiz-Sánchez, P., De Haro-Rodríguez, R., Caballero, C. M., & Martínez-Abellán, R. (2023, January 31). Barriers to educational inclusion in initial teacher training. *Societies, 13*(2), 31.

Bajpai A. (2018). Child rights in India: Law, policy, and practice. Oxford University Press.

Banerjee, R. (2014). Towards inclusive education in India: Implementation of the convention on the rights of persons with disabilities. *TASH Connections, 40*(3), 9–13.

Barajas Motta, N., Chiappe, A., & Sáez Delgado, F. M. (2025). Bridging the gap: AI and teacher training for inclusive education 4.0. *Journal of Research in Special Educational Needs*.

Bhatia, R., & Singh, R. (2021). Inclusion: Historical perspectives, inclusive education and current status. *Ilkogretim Online, 20*(1), 8587–8605.

Chakraborti-Ghosh, S. (2018). Inclusive education in India: A developmental milestone from segregation to inclusion. *Journal of Educational System, 1*(1), 53–62.

Chaudhary, B. (2017). Challenges and opportunities for inclusive education in India. *Research Journal of Philosophy & Social Sciences, 43*(2), 23–30.

Chawla, B. (2024, August 13). Educational policies and their impact on equity and access. *International Journal of Innovations in Science, Engineering and Management*, 68–74.

Chimhenga, S. (2016). Stakeholders' attitudes towards inclusive education for students with learning disabilities: Perspectives of parents, teachers and students in secondary schools of Zimbabwe. *Global Journal of Advanced Research, 3*(6), 479–486.

Das, A. (2013, February 1). Inclusive education in India: Are the teachers prepared? *International Journal of Special Education*.

De Bruin, K. (2019, August 3). The impact of inclusive education reforms on students with disability: An international comparison. *International Journal of Inclusive Education, 23*(7–8), 811–826.

Faragher, R., Chen, M., Miranda, L., Poon, K., Rumiati, Chang, F. R., & Chen, H. (2021, March). Inclusive education in Asia: Insights from some country case studies. *Journal of Policy and Practice in Intellectual Disabilities, 18*(1), 23–35.

Forlin, C., Earle, C., Loreman, T., & Sharma, U. (2011, September 1). The sentiments, attitudes, and concerns about inclusive education revised (SACIE-R) scale for measuring pre-service teachers' perceptions about inclusion. *Exceptionality Education International, 21*(3).

Genovesi, E., Jakobsson, C., Nugent, L., Hanlon, C., & Hoekstra, R. A. (2022, October). Stakeholder experiences, attitudes and perspectives on inclusive education for children with developmental disabilities in sub-Saharan Africa: A systematic review of qualitative studies. *Autism, 26*(7), 1606–1625.

Guleria, M. N. (2021, February 18). Inclusive education: A roadmap for the qualitative transformation in education. *Information Technology in Industry, 9*(1), 42–48.

Hollings, S. (2021, December 20). Implementation barriers of inclusive education and their impact on stakeholders: A review of the literature. *International Journal of Childhood Education, 2*(1), 27–45.

Jameel, S. S. (2011). Disability in the context of higher education: Issues and concerns in India. *Electronic Journal for Inclusive Education, 2*(7), 3.

Johnsen, B. H. (2020). From historical roots to future perspectives towards inclusive education. In *Theory and methodology in international comparative classroom studies* (p. 18). Cappelen Damm Forskning.

Kaushik, N. (2016). Capacity building of teachers for inclusive education. *International Journal of Education and Applied Research, 6*(1), 89–92.

Kavkler, M., Babuder, M. K., & Magajna, L. (2015, March 31). Inclusive education for children with specific learning difficulties: Analysis of opportunities and barriers in inclusive education in Slovenia. *Center for Educational Policy Studies Journal, 5*(1), 31–52.

Ketheeswaran, K. (2025, April 4). Changes in Stakeholders' attitudes towards inclusive education practices. *Journal of Innovative Practices Education, 1*(1).

Khadija, H. (2022, July). Stakeholders in education. *The Annals of the University of Oradea. Economic Sciences, 31*(1), 425–435.

Kohama, A. (2012, June). *Inclusive education in India: A country in transition*. Unpublished Undergraduate Honours thesis, Department of International Studies, University of Oregon.

Kohout-Diaz, M. (2023, June). Inclusive education for all: Principles of a shared inclusive ethos. *European Journal of Education, 58*(2), 185–196.

Kulkarni, K. A., & Gathoo, V. S. (2017, August 22). Parent empowerment in early intervention programmes of children with hearing loss in Mumbai, India. *Disability, CBR & Inclusive Development, 28*(2), 45–58.

Kumari, M., Bika, S. L., & Bhesera, H. (2024, June 15). A systematic review on inclusive education research: Identifying concerns over children with disabilities. *Asian Journal of Education and Social Studies, 50*(7), 230–238.

Kunwar, R., & Adhikari, S. (2023, October). An exploration of the conceptualization, guiding principles, and theoretical perspectives of inclusive curriculum. *Journal of Contemporary Research in Social Sciences, 5*(1), 1–3.

Limaye, S. (2016). Factors influencing the accessibility of education for children with disabilities in India. *Global Education Review, 3*(3), 43–56.

Lombardi, M., Vandenbussche, H., Claes, C., Schalock, R. L., De Maeyer, J., & Vandevelde, S. (2019, September). The concept of quality of life as a framework for implementing the UNCRPD. *Journal of Policy and Practice in Intellectual Disabilities, 16*(3), 180–190.

Madan, A., & Sharma, N. (2013). Inclusive education for children with disabilities: Preparing schools to meet the challenge. *Electronic Journal for Inclusive Education, 3*(1), 4.

Mahapatra, S. K.. (2016). Accessibility and quality education of persons with disabilities in India: An open schooling perspective. In *Pan-Commonwealth Forum 2016 November*, Vol. 8, pp. 27–30.

Mbua, E. M. (2023). Inclusive education. *Principal Leadership, 7*(1), 1–25.

Memon, F. N., & Memon, S. N. (2025). Digital divide and equity in education: Bridging gaps to ensure inclusive learning. In *Impact of digitalization on education and social sustainability* (pp. 107–130). IGI Global.
Newman, I., & Conway, J. (2017). Busting the barriers to inclusive learning environments. *The Journal of Inclusive Practice in Further and Higher Education, 2017*, 30.
Nzuza, Z. D. (2023). Strategies for creating inclusive learning for learners experiencing barriers to learning. *REID (Research and Evaluation In Education), 9*(2), 2.
Oad, L. (2023, May 16). Journey of inclusive education exploring its evolution and future perspectives. *Spry Journal of Literature and Linguistics, 1*(1).
Sari, T. P., Septian, E., & Suhindarno, H. (2025, April 3). Stakeholders mapping analysis the implementation of inclusive education: in power and interest perspective. *Jurnal Noken: Ilmu-Ilmu Sosial, 11*(1), 19–34.
Serrano-Tamayo, L. J. (2021) Identification of stakeholders and practices of inclusive education. In *International conference on advances in teaching and learning in higher education, Dubai.*
Swargiary, K. (2024, August 1). *The role of stakeholders in education: Government, school leaders, teachers, staff, parents, community, and society towards students*. EdTech Research Association.
Villa, R., & Thousand, J. (2021, May 15). *The inclusive education checklist: A checklist of best practices*. National Professional Resources.
Waisman, T. C., Alba, L. A., & Green, S. A. (2022, April 1). Barriers to inclusive learning for autistic individuals. *Pediatrics, 149*(Supplement 4), e2020049437Q.
Winter, S. (2020, April 4). Inclusive and exclusive education for diverse learning needs. In Quality Education (pp. 451–463). Cham: Springer International Publishing.

Chapter 5
Mental Health and Disability

Gurugubelli Sowjanya, Baliwada Aparna, Nayudu Teja, Amol S. Rakte, Vemula Navya, Aithagoni Sathwika, and Sanga Vaishnavi

Abstract This chapter critically looks at this relation between mental health and disability which is very intricate and sometimes controversial. It makes mental health conditions, also known as psychosocial disabilities, squarely within the area of disability studies beyond traditional and medically dominant approaches. The chapter starts with the discussion of theoretical change of the medical model to the social and biopsychosocial models and the criticism that is transformative as provided by the Mad Studies movement. It examines the lived experience of psychosocial disability and deals with the problem of identity, stigma, and the politics of labeling. Much attention is devoted to intersectionality, the high co-occurrence of mental distress among the physically, sensory, and intellectually challenged, and neurodiversity paradigm. This chapter is an organized account of the systemic obstacles such as stigma, poverty, and coercive legal practices that manifest the disability multiplied. It in turn promotes inclusive, rights-based solutions including person-centered care, peer support, trauma-informed practices, and complete adherence to the UN Convention on the Rights of Persons with Disabilities (CRPD). Lastly, the chapter gives future directions, which include the participation of

G. Sowjanya (✉)
Ratan Tata Innovations Hub (RTIH), Rajamahendravaram, Andhra Pradesh, India

B. Aparna
Department of Pharmaceutical Chemistry, Malla Reddy Pharmacy College, Maisammaguda, Hyderabad, India

N. Teja
Department of Pharmaceutics, JSS College of Pharmacy, JSS Academy of Higher Education and Research, The Nilgiris, Ooty, Tamil Nadu, India

A. S. Rakte
Department of Pharmaceutics, Indrayani Vidya Mandir's, Krishnarao Bhegade Institute of Pharmaceutical Education and Research, Talegaon Dabhade, Tal-Maval, Pune, Maharashtra, India

V. Navya · A. Sathwika · S. Vaishnavi
Department of Pharmacy, Malla Reddy Pharmacy College, Maisammaguda, Hyderabad, India

D. Nagasen, S. K. S. S. Pindiprolu (eds.), *Transforming Disability Studies*, SpringerBriefs in Modern Perspectives on Disability Research,
https://doi.org/10.1007/978-981-95-9004-9_5

research, the integration of ethical technologies, and the decolonization of mental health practices. The general thesis is that an inclusive disability studies has to make mental health central to the latter, and not peripheral, but rather at its heart.

Keywords Mental Health · Psychosocial disability · Mad studies · Social model · CRPD · Stigma · Peer support · Intersectionality · Neurodiversity

5.1 Introduction: Entwined Realities

Historical views of mental health and disability have been viewed as separate domains of interest that are tackled through different systems, policies, and academic fields. However, in the life of man, they are deeply and irrevocably connected. It is impossible to discuss disability without considering the mental health aspect because human psychology does not want to exclude the psychological consequences of living in a world that is often inaccessible. On the other hand, to treat mental health and not think about the paradigm of disability is to run the risk of maintaining individualistic, pathologizing discourse, which ignores the social, political, and environmental context of distress. This chapter attempts to address this artificial split, in which there is a need to have an integrated grasp that both disciplines need.

5.1.1 Beyond the Binary: Rethinking Mental Health and Disability

Traditionally, the sense of disability could be perceived through a physical or sensory prism in the course of decades. When reflected upon at all, mental illnesses were usually regarded as a different type of illness that was managed in the specific field of psychiatry. This is a socially and clinically unsustainable dichotomy. The feeling of depression may occur in a person with a mobility impairment as a result of social isolation and systemic ableism. A person with a severe case of anxiety can be an individual who is highly disabling in terms of work, social, and full participation in the community life, hence he or she is disabled psychosocially. This is recognized by the World Health Organization through the International Classification of Functioning, Disability and Health (ICF) which characterizes disability as a dynamic kind of interaction among health conditions and contextual factors (both personal and environmental). This chapter works under the following understanding, that mental ailment may be one of the major causes of disability and that mental well-being is a very important determinant in the experience of any disability.

5.1.2 Chapter Overview and Objectives

This chapter aims to give a broad overview of the relation of mental health and disability in a social justice-based critical perspective. We shall pass through the theoretical terrain that has formed our knowledge, on the one hand, repressive medical to the other, social. We will glimpse into the experience of psychosocial disability, understand its overlapping with other disability, and deconstruct the systemic barriers that form and multiply distress. More importantly, the chapter will not end with criticism but rather spend much space on examining transformative and inclusive practices and policies that resonate with the disability rights slogan, which is—Nothing About Us Without Us. We intend to empower the reader with a subtle, evidence-based, and ethically consistent view that advocates the rights, dignity, and agency of people living at the intersection of mental health and disability.

5.2 Theoretical Frameworks: Locating Mental Health in Disability Studies

The way we frame a problem determines our approach to solving a problem. Those theoretical models which are applied to mental health and disability have an enormous implication on the life of people, as it impacts all aspects of clinical intervention as well as social policy.

5.2.1 The Medical Model: Pathologizing Distress

Medical model has been the leading paradigm to explain mental health in the past. In this context, mental illnesses are theorized as discrete internalized pathologies (disorders) or illnesses in the brain or mind of the individual. It is concerned with symptom recognition, diagnosis, and treatment (usually by medication and psychotherapy) in order to amend the supposed deficit which is deemed biological or psychological in nature. Although this model has been used to advance significant research in neuroscience and benefit many, it is highly constrained. It is inclined to overlook the social determinants of health, including poverty, trauma, discrimination, and social isolation, which are powerful agents of mental distress. By placing the problem only on the individual, the medical model may unintentionally create stigma, dehumanize human experience by turning a human into a list of symptoms, and powerless the individual through placing the person into a position of a passive receiver of expert knowledge.

5.2.2 *The Social Model: Unpacking Social and Environmental Barriers*

The social model of disability, which developed out of the disability rights movement, is important in establishing a distinction between impairment (a physical, sensory, or psychological difference) and disability (the social exclusion and barriers of people with impairments). The social model changes the question of What is wrong with you? when used in the context of mental health. to What is wrong with a society that disables you? Social stigma, discrimination, employers being closed off, lack of social support and fear are barriers rather than the symptoms of depression/psychosis. It is not the anxiety itself that impairs the person with the social anxiety, but the society that requires a person to be always extroverted and does not offer any room to express themselves in a less extroverted manner. This model is empowering because it puts the problem outside of the individual, making the personal tragedy a political right and access issue. Critics, however, claim that it has the capacity to lesser the very physical, embodied pain, and distress of impairment.

5.2.3 *The Biopsychosocial Model: An Integrative Approach*

Engel (1977) proposes the synthesis of the biopsychosocial model. It hypothesizes that health and disability can be best explained by complex interaction of biological (genetics, neurochemistry), psychological (thoughts, emotions, trauma history), and social (culture, family, and socioeconomic status) factors. In the case of a veteran with Post-Traumatic Stress Disorder (PTSD), e.g., the biopsychosocial model would involve his/her neurobiological reaction to stress (biological), his/her recollection of the traumatic experiences and his/her coping strategies (psychological), and the degree of social support and the acceptance of his/her experience by society (social). This system of holism is popular within the clinical practice since it offers a holistic intervention map. But as a disability studies lens, it jeopardizes the preservation of clinical power and can be appropriated to lip service to the social factors and still focus on medical solutions.

5.2.4 *The Mad Studies Movement: Challenging Epistemic Injustice*

A more radical opposition is that of the Mad Studies movement. Mad Studies is a trans-disciplinary discipline that originated in the activist and survivor knowledge of psychiatry and is fundamentally a challenge to the epistemology of psychiatry and even the definition of the terms sanity and madness. It challenges the authority of those who determine what is mentally normal and abnormal and points to how psychiatry has been and continues to be used to control women, racial minorities, and political dissidents. Scholars of mad Studies and activists reclaim the concept of mad as a political identity and make the knowledge based on lived experience of mental distress and on the mental health system central. They promote the alternatives to coercive psychiatry, insist on the end of involuntary treatment, and present the hearing of voices or other abnormal experiences as normal manifestations of human diversity, which should be perceived and learned to coexist. The movement is the most radical epistemological break of the medical model which enforced the opinion that the specialists on madness are mad people themselves (Beresford, 2019).

5.3 Mental Health Conditions as Disability: Legitimacy, Identity, and Experience

Even though their potential functional impossibility is obvious, mental health conditions do not receive the same legitimacy as physical disabilities. This chapter considers the definition of having a psychosocial disability.

5.3.1 The Lived Experience of "Psychosocial Disability"

The psychosocial disability is a term adopted to explain the experience of being disabled as a result of mental health condition that is on the rise. It focuses on how the person is mentally (psycho) and socially (social) oriented. The lived experience is associated with severe impediments to involvement in major spheres of existence: education, employment, civic engagement, and social relationships. Depression fatigue can as much disable a person as multiple sclerosis fatigue. Learning and attention can be impaired by the cognitive "brain fog" related to anxiety or drugs. This is further complicated by the fact that most mental health conditions tend to be unpredictable and thus planning or committing is not feasible and it can be misunderstood to be ineffective instead of an unstable disability that needs some flexible accommodations.

5.3.2 The Invisibility and Hypervisibility of Mental Distress

The psychosocial disability tends to work in a paradox of being visible. It is often an invisible disability; one might appear okay but inside, s/he is struggling with excruciating agony. This invisibility may result in incomprehension, substantiation, and reinforcement. The friends, family, and employers might not take the severity of the condition seriously, accusing that the person is malingering or work is not doing all that they can. On the other hand, the disability is hyper visible when symptoms are externally manifested—by the onset of a panic attack in a crowd, self-injurious behavior, or the signs and symptoms of psychosis. This is hypervisibility that can easily invoke fear, stigma, and social rejection. The person is no longer viewed as a human being but as a risk or a case and thus discrimination and even coercive intervention occur.

5.3.3 Identity and the Politics of Labeling: Patient, Consumer, Survivor?

The concept of identity that people associate themselves with in regard to their mental health experience is highly personal and politicized. The word patient presupposes a patient–clinician relationship characterized by clinical dominance and inactivity. Client or consumer implies a more market relationship, which is empowering but can also obscure power inequalities of care. Most especially the survivors of mental health system who have suffered manipulation or fallen prey to coercion in the mental system boast of the title of survivor. This phrase is a strong demonstration of resistance and strength towards a system, which is potentially destructive. The neurodiversity movement has proposed identity-first language (e.g. Autistic person) as an attempt to resist pathologizing the person-first language (person with autism). Likewise, other of the Mad movement recover identity-first language such as a Mad person. These decisions are not purely semantic but are concerned with questions of basic beliefs regarding the presence of a problem or belonging to a diverse minority group (Shakespeare, 2006).

5.4 Intersectional Complexities: Mental Health across the Disability Spectrum

The mental health experience does not take place within a vacuum. It overlaps with any other type of disability and forms distinct and compounded experiences that need sensitive and special understanding and attention.

5.4.1 The High Prevalence of Mental Health Conditions Among People with Physical/Sensory Disabilities

The literature always indicates that individuals with physical and sensory disabilities are more likely to have mental problems especially depression and anxiety compared to the general population. It is not an unavoidable outcome of impairment itself, but a combination of very many overlapping factors, including chronic social isolation, the presence of ableism and discrimination, the lack of significant work and social engagement, and constant emotional work navigating an inaccessible world. This is further compounded by the absence of easily available mental health services that would lead to a treatment gap to an already susceptible population.

5.4.2 Neurodiversity and Mental Health: Autism, ADHD, and Co-occurring Conditions

The neurodiversity paradigm does not present such conditions as autism, ADHD, dyslexia, and others as disorders to be treated, as the natural variations in human neurology. Still, being a neurotypical means living in a disabling world and results in high incidence of co-occurring mental illnesses. An example is autistic people who often face anxiety disorders, which are often caused by an incessant demand to hide their true selves and operate in overwhelming senses. People with ADHD usually experience rejection sensitive dysphoria and low self-esteem over a lifetime of being referred to as lazy in the world or disruptive. The acknowledgment of these mental health issues in the context of neurodiversity implies that one considers the social and environmental factors as the cause of anxiety and depression instead of thinking of anxiety or depression as independent, internalized pathology.

5.4.3 The Impact of Chronic Illness and Pain on Mental Wellbeing

Chronic diseases and chronic pain syndromes (e.g. fibromyalgia, Ehlers–Danos syndrome, multiple sclerosis) are at the border of physical and mental health. The uncompromising character of pain, tiredness, and erratic symptoms may cause deep mourning, loss of self, and mental distress. This is augmented by the medical gaslighting many individuals (as well as women) with unseen chronic conditions go through (when their symptoms are disbelieved as being in their head) and adds a level of psychological trauma. This forms a vicious circle where the mental distress can enhance the feeling of pain and the physical suffering increases the mental health crisis and requires the integrated care approach that takes care of both aspects at the same time (Oliver, 1990).

5.5 Systemic Barriers and Social Determinants

Psychosocial disabled persons encounter numerous barriers to the system that go well beyond the manifestations of the illness that are entrenched in social systems and policies.

5.5.1 Stigma and Discrimination: The Double Burden

One of the most important obstacles is stigma. It has several levels of operation:

Public Stigma: Negative stereotypes and biasile attitudes (e.g. fear, pity, blame) of the general population towards individuals with mental health conditions.

- ***Self-Stigma:*** Interpretation of the negative beliefs, which causes shame, low self-esteem, and unwillingness to seek help.
- ***Structural Stigma:*** The institutional, legislative, and policy-based discrimination system. This consists of discriminatory employment policies, unequal insurance benefits of mental health services and media pedagogies of associating mental illness with violence.

5.5.2 Poverty, Unemployment, and Social Exclusion

Mental health conditions and socioeconomic disadvantage have a high bidirectional relationship. Risk factors that predominately lead to the development of mental conditions include poverty, precarious housing, and food insecurity. On the other hand, a psychosocial disability may cause joblessness and underemployment because of stigmatization, inadequate workplace accommodations (e.g., flexible hours, serene environment, and disabling symptoms). This develops a vicious circle of poverty and suboptimal mental health that becomes hard to break. This isolation is further exacerbated by social exclusion, which constitutes the break of social networks and communal involvement and undermines the protective mechanisms that are essential to recovery and well-being.

5.5.3 Legal Capacity and Coercion: The Shadow of Guardianship and Involuntary Treatment

One of the most significant problems of human rights to people with psychosocial disabilities is a general refusal of recognition of their legal ability. Policies in most countries allow forced hospitalization and treatment, transcend the will and preferences of an individual, and implement guardianship or substituted decision-making systems. Although they may be generally approved as the best interests or necessity to be treated, these practices are the core infringement of the autonomy, bodily integrity, as well the right to equal recognition before the law as laid in the CRPD Art. 12. Coercion may lead to the long-term psychological damage and loss in faith in the support system and drive individuals out of seeking help when it is needed most (Bracken & Thomas, 2005).

5.6 Inclusive and Transformative Practices

To these challenges, there is an increase in a movement that promotes practices that are founded on respect, autonomy, and human rights.

5.6.1 Person-Centered and Recovery-Oriented Care

Person-based care changes the power-based of clinician to collaboration based. It puts emphasis on personal goals, values, and preferences of the individual. Recovery-oriented care does not view recovery as a cure or lack of symptoms but as a subjective process, a journey of living a meaningful, fulfilling, and hopeful life with constraints. This strategy aims at developing strengths, resilience, and community integration which is more or less in line with the social model of disability because it targets the life domains beyond the aspect of symptom management.

5.6.2 Peer Support and the Power of Lived Experience

Peer support refers to the giving of assistance and support to individuals who have encountered mental challenges by individuals, who have experienced the same situation. The practice, administered by Certified Peer Specialists or in peer-run organizations, has its own advantages: it eliminates isolation, offers credible role models of recovery and gives hope and a sense of community. Peer support disrupts the traditional hierarchical approach of services and demonstrates knowledge acquired through experience as being as important as the professional knowledge.

5.6.3 Trauma-Informed Approaches as a Standard

Considering the strong association between mental health complications and trauma, a trauma-informed intervention is necessary. This model acknowledges the prevalence of the traumatic experience and acknowledges the ways of getting better. It entails the acknowledgment of the prevalence of trauma, its signs and symptoms, retraumatization resistance, and incorporation of the knowledge on trauma to the policies and practices. A trauma-informed system involves all the organizational operations, including physical facilities and relationships with clients, being structured in terms of promoting safety, trust, and empowerment.

5.6.4 Community-Based Support and Deinstitutionalization

In line with the CRPD demand of inclusion of community (Article 19), the world is shifting towards massive, segregated psychiatric institutions to community-based support services. These services are assertive community treatment (ACT) teams, supported housing, psychosocial rehabilitation clubs and crisis respite centers. The idea is to support them in a natural setting of the person encouraging self-reliance and social integration. Effective deinstitutionalization, however, has to be properly funded and a community service network must be in place to avoid transinstitutionalization to homelessness or prisons.

5.7 Policy, Rights, and Advocacy

Systemic change requires robust legal frameworks and vigorous advocacy movements.

5.7.1 The UN Convention on the Rights of Persons with Disabilities (CRPD): A Paradigm Shift

CRPD, which was adopted in 2006, is a seismic alteration in the international law. It clearly brings psychosocial disabled persons under its scope and stipulates a shift of a medical-welfare paradigm to the paradigm of human rights. The major articles in mental health are:

Article 12: Equal recognition before the law, which means a replacement of substituted by supported decision-making.
Article 14: Liberty and security of person, which outlaws any deprivation of liberty in respect of disability.
Article 15: The right against torture and cruel, inhuman or degrading treatment, which opposes involuntary treatment.
Article 19: Living on your own and belonging to the community.
Article 25: The right to health, free, and informed consent.

5.7.2 Mental Health Law Reform: Aligning with the CRPD

The interpretation of the CRPD Committee is simple, the laws of mental health that allow involuntary treatment and replace decision-making are nonconformities. This has brought a world debate and a move towards a reform in the law. The nations have become challenged to establish the laws that will eliminate the element of coercion and instead, create the supported decision-making regimes, advance directives and access to voluntary and rights-based mental health services within the community. It is not easy and a controversial process, yet this is the direction that needs to be taken to harmonize the national laws with the human rights standards.

5.7.3 The Role of Disability and Mad Pride Activism

Policy change does not occur in empty space. It is propelled by the unyielding efforts of disability rights groups and Mad activist groups. The movements such as Mad Pride have been celebrating the mad identity and culture in an open manner where the stigma is challenged through the use of mass events and art. Psychiatric and survivor-run organizations promote legal capacity, end forced treatment, and redistribute institutional care into community-based care. Their motto, Nothing About Us Without Us, is a strong wish to be included in whatever decisions that will be made concerning their lives (Engel, 1977).

5.8 Future Directions in Research and Practice

To continue the transformative work, several key areas demand attention in the coming years.

5.8.1 Participatory Action Research: Nothing About Us Without Us

The future of the research in this sphere should be participatory. Participatory Action Research (PAR) is a research approach in which people with lived experience are not considered as subjects, but rather coresearchers throughout the research process; in terms of defining the questions and methodology, as well as data collection, results analysis, and publication of findings. This makes research relevant, ethical, and empowering to the community where the research is intended to serve, which disputes the exploitation of the marginalized groups of people historically in research.

5.8.2 Integrating Technology for Accessible Mental Health Support

Technology can provide hold onto future solutions of augmenting access to support. These also involve teletherapy, which can access individuals in isolated locations or individuals with mobility issues; mood tracking and mindfulness smartphone applications; and peer support groups on the internet. But, what is ethically important is access to digital information by individuals with different types of disabilities, data confidentiality, and avoiding the substitution of human relationships with technologies. Technology must be an empowering tool and not a new form of marginalization (United Nations, 2006).

5.8.3 Global Perspectives and Decolonizing Mental Health

The Western, Global North perspectives have dominated the disability studies and the practice of mental health. An important way forward in the future is to magnify global and Indigenous knowledge. This includes the local manifestations of distress and healing, the inapplicability of Western diagnostic labels, such as PTSD and depression, and analyzing the mental health effects of colonialism, racism, and economic exploitation. Decolonizing mental health refers to the establishment of space that accommodates other epistemologies and healing practices that were previously suppressed historically (World Health Organization, 2001).

5.9 Conclusion

Mental health being part and parcel of disability study is not some academic play-acting; rather a moral and practical necessity. This chapter has contended that stigma is perpetuated by the artificial division of mental and physical disability, service gaps are created, and the holistic nature of human experience is not reflected. Using the social model, Mad Studies, and the intersectionality as the critical lenses, we are able to deconstruct the systems that disable people with mental health conditions. We have also discovered that the issues are deep, including epistemic injustice and forceful measures as well as widespread social exclusion.

Nonetheless, the way forward is lightened with transformative practices that focus on the human rights and agency. A more just and inclusive society is provided by the assimilation of person-centered care, the legitimization of peer support, the establishment of trauma-informed systems, and the adherence to the ideals of the CRPD. Future of research and practice needs to be coconstructed with individuals of lived experience, and the above phrase Nothing about us without us should become a reality. But the bottom line is that disability studies need to evolve into a full embrace of mental illness and the ability to face our vulnerability as a whole and the ability to be resilient, strong, and able to change. It is concerned with creating the world where no one will be handicapped by stigma, exclusion, and lack of support, and the mind of each and every person will be appreciated as a component of the rich tapestry of human diversity.

References

Beresford, P. (2019). *Mad studies*. Routledge.
Bracken, P., & Thomas, P. (2005). *Postpsychiatry: Mental health in a postmodern world.*
Engel, G. L. (1977). The need for a new medical model: A challenge for biomedicine. *Science, 196*(4286), 129–136.
Oliver, M. (1990). *The politics of disablement.*
Shakespeare, T. (2006). *Disability rights and wrongs.*
United Nations. (2006). *Convention on the rights of persons with disabilities (CRPD).*
World Health Organization. (2001). *International classification of functioning, disability and health (ICF).*

Chapter 6
Disability Within Marginalized Communities

B. Babu, B. Gowramma, Nayudu Teja, Sara Chandurwala, and Saravanan

Abstract This chapter argues that a comprehensive understanding of disability is impossible without an intersectional analysis that centers the experiences of marginalized communities. Disability does not exist in a vacuum; it is profoundly shaped by other social categories such as race, class, gender, sexual orientation, and migration status. The chapter begins by establishing the theoretical framework of intersectionality, tracing its roots in Black feminist thought and explicating its critical application to disability studies. Through detailed case studies, it demonstrates how interlocking systems of oppression including racism, sexism, ableism, and economic injustice produce unique and compounded forms of disablement. The analysis then scrutinizes the systemic barriers embedded within judicial, healthcare, and social service institutions that disproportionately harm marginalized disabled people. In response, the chapter advocates for an inclusive praxis that prioritizes community-based participatory research, culturally responsive support, and solidarity across movements. It concludes with a forward-look-

B. Babu (✉)
Department of Pharmaceutical Analysis, JSS College of Pharmacy, JSS Academy of Higher Education and Research, Nilgiris, Ooty, Tamil Nadu, India
e-mail: babu@jssuni.edu.in

B. Gowramma
Department of Pharmaceutical Chemistry, JSS College of Pharmacy, JSS Academy of Higher Education and Research, Nilgiris, Ooty, Tamil Nadu, India

N. Teja
Department of Pharmaceutics, JSS College of Pharmacy, JSS Academy of Higher Education and Research, Nilgiris, Ooty, Tamil Nadu, India

S. Chandurwala
JSS College of Pharmacy, JSS Academy of Higher Education and Research, Nilgiris, Ooty, Tamil Nadu, India

Saravanan
Data Works, Waterford, Ireland

D. Nagasen, S. K. S. S. Pindiprolu (eds.), *Transforming Disability Studies*, SpringerBriefs in Modern Perspectives on Disability Research,
https://doi.org/10.1007/978-981-95-9004-9_6

ing discussion on the necessity of decolonizing disability studies, incorporating global and Indigenous perspectives, and reorienting policy and advocacy toward intersectional justice. The central thesis is that the transformation of disability studies hinges on its ability to confront and dismantle all intersecting forms of structural inequality.

Keywords Intersectionality · Marginalized Communities · Systemic Oppression · Ableism · Racism · Poverty · Cultural Humility · Decolonization · Participatory Research

6.1 Introduction: The Intersectional Imperative

Traditional disability scholarship and activism have often, albeit unintentionally, centered the experiences of a hypothetical "average" disabled person frequently imagined as white, male, and from the Global North. This limited focus renders invisible the complex realities of those who navigate disability alongside other marginalized identities. To truly transform disability studies, we must shift our gaze to the margins, where the interplay of multiple forms of oppression creates distinct and intensified experiences of disablement. This chapter posits that disability is not a monolithic experience but a heterogeneous one, deeply mediated by the prism of social location.

6.1.1 Moving beyond a Single-Axis Framework

A single-axis framework that analyzes only disability or only race or only gender is fundamentally inadequate. It fails to capture the lived reality of a low-income, disabled woman of color, for whom ableism, racism, and sexism are not separate, sequential encounters but a simultaneous, fused experience. Her access to diagnosis, the quality of healthcare she receives, her vulnerability to violence, and her barriers to employment and housing are all products of this intersection. Ignoring this complexity leads to policies and interventions that are, at best, ineffective and, at worst, actively harmful to those at the margins. This chapter moves beyond this reductive approach, embracing the messiness and richness of intersectional lived experience as the starting point for all analysis.

6.1.2 *Chapter Aims and Structure*

This chapter aims to deconstruct the myth of a universal disabled experience and illuminate the specific mechanisms through which marginalization compounds disability. We will first ground our analysis in the theoretical framework of intersectionality. Subsequently, we will explore a series of case studies that highlight the intersection of disability with race, gender, poverty, LGBTQIA+ identity, and refugee status. The chapter will then critically examine the systemic structures that perpetuate this intersectional disadvantage before proposing a path forward through inclusive research, ethical practice, and transformative policy advocacy. Our ultimate goal is to chart a course for a disability study that is not only inclusive in name but is fundamentally reconfigured by the knowledge and leadership of its most marginalized members (Crenshaw, 1989).

6.2 Theoretical Foundation: Intersectionality as an Analytical Lens

To understand disability within marginalized communities, we require a robust theoretical tool that can dissect the complexity of multiple, overlapping identities. Intersectionality provides this essential lens.

6.2.1 *The Genesis of Intersectionality: From Black Feminist Thought to Disability Studies*

The term "intersectionality" was coined by legal scholar Kimberlé Crenshaw in 1989 to describe the unique discrimination faced by Black women, whose experiences were not captured by frameworks that treated race and gender as mutually exclusive categories. Its intellectual roots, however, lie in decades of Black feminist thought, as articulated by figures like Sojourner Truth, Anna Julia Cooper, and the Combahee River Collective. They argued that their oppression was not divisible into "racism" plus "sexism" but was a unique synthesis of both.

Applying intersectionality to disability studies compels us to ask: Who is being left out of our current narratives of disability? It challenges the field to interrogate its own assumptions and to recognize that the social model of disability, while powerful, must be complicated by considering which social barriers are erected and for whom. A ramp addresses a physical barrier, but it does not address the racial profiling a disabled Black man might face when entering the building, or the linguistic exclusion a Deaf immigrant might experience once inside.

6.2.2 *Interlocking Systems of Oppression: Ableism, Racism, Sexism, and Classism*

Intersectionality views systems of oppression not as separate silos but as interlocking pillars upholding a structure of privilege and disadvantage. Ableism the system of assigning value to people based on their bodies and minds is deeply intertwined with racism, which does the same based on perceived racial difference.

For example, the historical classification of Black people as intellectually inferior was a fusion of racist and ableist ideologies used to justify slavery and segregation. Similarly, sexist stereotypes often portray women as emotionally unstable or physically fragile, which can lead to their genuine mental or physical health conditions being dismissed as "hysteria" or exaggeration a confluence of sexism and ableism. Economic class further compounds this; poverty can cause disability through poor healthcare, malnutrition, and dangerous work conditions, while disability can cause poverty through exclusion from the workforce and the high costs of care. These systems are mutually constitutive, reinforcing one another to create a matrix of domination.

6.2.3 *The Cumulative Impact: Rejecting Hierarchies of Oppression*

A key tenet of intersectionality is the rejection of hierarchies of oppression the futile debate over which form of discrimination is "worse." The focus instead is on the cumulative and often multiplicative impact of multiple marginalized identities. Research consistently shows that individuals at these intersections experience worse outcomes across a spectrum of indicators: health, education, employment, and contact with the criminal legal system. This cumulative burden, sometimes termed "weathering," leads to accelerated decline in health and well-being. Understanding this cumulative impact is crucial for developing effective support systems and policies that address the whole person, not just a single facet of their identity (Erevelles, 2011).

6.3 Case Studies in Intersectional Disablement

Theoretical concepts become tangible when examined through the lens of specific lived experiences. The following case studies illustrate the concrete manifestations of intersectional disablement.

6.3.1 *Race and Disability: The Legacy of Eugenics and Systemic Neglect*

The relationship between race and disability is historically fraught. The eugenics movement, which sought to "improve" the human gene pool, specifically targeted racial minorities, people with disabilities, and the poor for sterilization and institutionalization. This legacy continues in modern systemic biases. Children of color, particularly Black and Indigenous boys, are over-identified for disciplinary action in schools and under-identified for gifted programs, often being funneled into special education programs that are more about behavioral control than educational support. In healthcare, racial biases can lead to under-treatment of pain and misdiagnosis of conditions; for instance, Black patients are more likely to be diagnosed with schizophrenia and less likely to be diagnosed with mood disorders compared to white patients presenting with identical symptoms. This diagnostic overshadowing, where a person's race or disability leads clinicians to overlook other conditions, is a direct result of intersecting prejudices.

6.3.2 *Gender and Disability: Gendered Violence, Care, and Invisibility*

Disabled women, girls, and gender-nonconforming people face a heightened risk of gender-based violence. Perpetrators may target them assuming they are less likely to be believed or able to report the abuse. Support services, like shelters, are often physically inaccessible or their staff untrained to support disabled survivors. Conversely, women are overwhelmingly cast into the role of caregivers for disabled family members, a role that is socially devalued and economically unrewarded, impacting their own career prospects and mental health. Furthermore, disabled women's health needs, particularly regarding sexual and reproductive health, are often rendered invisible by a pervasive assumption of asexuality, leading to a denial of services like cervical cancer screenings or support for parenting.

6.3.3 *Poverty and Disability: The Cycle of Deprivation and Exclusion*

The link between poverty and disability is a vicious cycle. People living in poverty are at greater risk of acquiring a disability due to factors like inadequate healthcare, hazardous living conditions, and dangerous employment. Once a person has a disability, they face significant barriers to escaping poverty: attitudinal barriers in hiring, a lack of workplace accommodations, and social protection systems that trap them in poverty through meager benefits and complex bureaucracies. This "poverty-disability nexus" means that efforts to address disability without tackling economic inequality are doomed to fail, and vice-versa.

6.3.4 *LGBTQIA+ Communities and Disability: Navigating Dual Stigmatization*

LGBTQIA+ individuals with disabilities navigate dual stigmatization. They may face homophobia, transphobia, and biphobia within disability services and spaces, and simultaneously encounter ableism within LGBTQIA+ communities that often prioritize able-bodied, neurotypical ideals of beauty and desirability. This can lead to intense isolation. Accessing competent healthcare is a major challenge; a transgender disabled person may struggle to find a provider who is knowledgeable about both gender-affirming care and their specific disability. The stress of chronic minority status ("minority stress") can also exacerbate mental health conditions within this population.

6.3.5 *Refugees and Displaced Persons with Disabilities: Invisible in Crisis*

In situations of conflict, disaster, and displacement, people with disabilities are among the most vulnerable, yet they are consistently overlooked in humanitarian response. Refugee camps are rarely designed with accessibility in mind, making it difficult to access food distribution points, sanitation facilities, and healthcare. Emergency information is often not provided in accessible formats. Many lose essential assistive devices like wheelchairs or hearing aids during their flight. The trauma of displacement can also create new psychosocial disabilities. Despite making up an estimated 15% of any displaced population, people with disabilities remain largely invisible in the planning and execution of humanitarian aid, a stark example of intersectional exclusion (Mingus, 2011).

6.4 Systemic and Structural Barriers

The lived experiences of marginalized disabled people are not merely the result of individual prejudices but are produced and sustained by systemic and structural barriers. These are the policies, institutional practices, and cultural norms that are embedded in the fabric of society, creating a world that is inherently exclusionary for those at the intersections of multiple marginalized identities.

6.4.1 Discriminatory Design: How Systems Inherently Exclude

Systemic barriers are frequently embedded within institutions in ways that make exclusion appear routine rather than intentional, a phenomenon often described as being *discriminatory by design*. Many physical, legal, and social systems are developed around an implicit model of a "standard" citizen, typically assumed to be able-bodied, neurotypical, and socially dominant. As a result, public transport networks, built environments, and digital services often overlook diverse access needs, with missing ramps, audio cues, or captioning creating obstacles that are further compounded for disabled individuals from marginalized racial or linguistic backgrounds. In education, standardized assessments and inflexible curricula tend to reward limited learning styles, placing disabled learners and students from minoritized communities at a distinct disadvantage, while punitive disciplinary practices can channel Black and Brown disabled students away from schooling and into the justice system. Similar patterns are evident in economic structures, where workplace norms that prioritize extended working hours and intense social competition exclude many people with autism, chronic illness, or mental health conditions, especially when biased recruitment practices amplify existing inequalities.

6.4.2 The Justice System: From Victimization to Incarceration

For many disabled people who live at the margins of society, the justice system often functions less as a source of protection and more as a mechanism of structural harm, closely aligned with what disability justice advocates identify as the prison–industrial complex. Individuals with intellectual and psychosocial disabilities are disproportionately exposed to violence and victimization, yet they frequently face serious challenges when attempting to report crimes or pursue legal remedies, including poor disability awareness among law enforcement, communication barriers, and the misreading of disability-related behaviors as a lack of credibility. These difficulties are compounded by intersecting inequalities related to race, gender, and socioeconomic status, which place disabled women of color from economically disadvantaged backgrounds at particular risk of being denied justice. Simultaneously, disability itself is often treated as a criminal issue, with behaviors associated with mental distress or neurodivergence interpreted as disorderly or defiant. The dismantling of institutional psychiatric care in the absence of adequate community-based alternatives has further shifted people with psychosocial disabilities into prisons, effectively transforming carceral spaces into substitute mental health facilities. Once incarcerated, disabled individuals face elevated risks of mistreatment, prolonged isolation, and insufficient accommodations, reinforcing cycles of trauma, exclusion, and compounded disablement.

6.4.3 Healthcare Disparities: From Diagnosis to Treatment

Health care systems often mirror broader social hierarchies, producing unequal and harmful outcomes for disabled individuals who already occupy marginalized positions. A key mechanism through which this occurs is the tendency to interpret new symptoms through the lens of an existing disability or psychiatric label, resulting in serious conditions being overlooked or inadequately treated. This problem is intensified by the use of clinical decision tools that rely on embedded assumptions about race, which can distort assessments of disease severity and delay timely referral or intervention. When disability and racial marginalization intersect, the risks of error and neglect increase significantly. Barriers to care are further compounded by inaccessible health facilities, economic precarity, and the absence of culturally and linguistically responsive services. Together, these intersecting constraints contribute to delayed treatment, poorer long-term health management, and preventable illness and death among marginalized disabled populations (Schalk, 2017).

6.5 Toward an Inclusive Praxis: Centering Marginalized Voices

Recognizing these systemic failures necessitates a radical shift in how research and support services are conducted. An inclusive praxis theory put into practice requires ceding power and centering the leadership and knowledge of marginalized disabled people themselves.

6.5.1 Community-Based Participatory Research (CBPR) as an Ethical Model

Community-Based Participatory Research (CBPR) represents a collaborative research framework in which all stakeholders are actively and equitably engaged, with explicit recognition of the distinct knowledge and expertise each partner contributes. Within disability research, particularly in marginalized communities, this approach is not merely methodological but fundamentally ethical. CBPR operationalizes the principle of "Nothing About Us Without Us" by positioning community members as cocreators of knowledge rather than passive research participants; they are involved in shaping research questions, developing methods, generating and interpreting data, and sharing outcomes. This shared ownership ensures that research processes and outputs are contextually grounded, culturally responsive, and aligned with the community's most urgent needs. In contrast to extractive research traditions that have historically benefited institutions while offering little to marginalized groups, CBPR emphasizes capacity building, power sharing, and long-term relationship development. By addressing histories of mistrust and exploitation—particularly among communities of color and other minoritized groups CBPR fosters trust and enhances the sustainability of resulting interventions. For instance, a CBPR initiative examining housing insecurity among disabled LGBTQIA+ youth would be jointly led by members of that community, who might select participatory methods such as photovoice or oral histories to authentically capture lived experiences, generating insights and solutions that are far more meaningful and actionable than those derived from conventional survey-based research.

6.5.2 Culturally Responsive and Humble Support Practices

Service provision for marginalized populations requires a decisive shift away from uniform, one-size-fits-all approaches toward models that are culturally responsive and grounded in cultural humility. Cultural responsiveness emphasizes the development of informed understanding about diverse cultural groups and the adaptation of services to reflect this knowledge, including the use of multilingual and multiformat materials, sensitivity to culturally specific beliefs surrounding disability and help-seeking, and the recruitment of a diverse and representative workforce. Complementing this, cultural humility represents a deeper and ongoing commitment to critical self-reflection, requiring service providers to acknowledge and actively address power imbalances inherent in provider–client relationships. Rather than positioning themselves as sole experts, practitioners grounded in cultural humility recognize individuals and communities as authorities on their own lived experiences and cultural contexts. This approach encourages providers to remain open to learning, to question assumptions, and to engage collaboratively, thereby fostering more respectful, effective, and equitable service delivery.

6.5.3 Building Solidarity Across Movements

The struggle for the liberation of marginalized disabled people is fundamentally interconnected with the broader pursuit of justice for all oppressed communities, making sustained and meaningful cross-movement solidarity indispensable. Central to this approach is the Disability Justice framework, articulated by disabled queer and trans people of color, which advances a set of guiding principles such as intersectionality, collective sustainability, and cross-movement organizing. This framework calls on disability advocacy to actively align with struggles for racial justice, immigrant rights, and LGBTQIA+ liberation, while simultaneously urging these movements to embed disability justice within their own agendas rather than treating it as peripheral. Alongside this, mutual aid practices represent a tangible expression of solidarity, as communities collectively organize to meet shared needs in the absence or failure of institutional support. Often led by those most affected by systemic marginalization, mutual aid initiatives are grounded in reciprocity and shared responsibility, recognizing that all individuals have both needs and capacities. By providing resources such as food, accessible transportation, and peer-based support, these networks not only address immediate survival needs but also challenge structural inequities and reimagine care as a collective, justice-oriented practice.

6.6 Policy and Advocacy for Intersectional Justice

Transforming systems requires transforming policy. However, policies that are not explicitly designed with an intersectional lens will inevitably fail those at the margins.

6.6.1 Critiquing Universalist Policies: The Need for Targeted Interventions

Policies framed through a universalist lens, while ostensibly equitable, often reproduce inequality because they overlook the unequal starting positions and structural barriers experienced by different social groups. A universal benefit such as childcare support may appear inclusive in principle, yet it remains insufficient if childcare facilities are physically inaccessible or if staff lack the training required to support disabled children, thereby excluding disabled families in practice. An intersectional policy response would retain the universal benefit while pairing it with targeted investments in accessibility, workforce training, and additional financial support for low-income disabled parents. This logic underpins the concept of targeted universalism, which establishes a shared societal objective such as ensuring that all students complete secondary education while recognizing that distinct groups require differentiated pathways, resources, and interventions to achieve that goal. By aligning targeted strategies with universal aims, targeted universalism moves beyond one-size-fits-all policymaking and promotes outcomes that are substantively, rather than merely formally, equitable (Combahee River Collective, 1977).

6.6.2 Data Disaggregation and Making Marginalization Visible

The principle that "what gets counted counts" holds particular significance for advancing intersectional justice, as the persistent absence of disaggregated data continues to obscure the lived realities of marginalized disabled populations from policy and decision-making processes. When disability data are not examined alongside factors such as race, gender, income, and sexual orientation, structural inequalities remain hidden, limiting the ability of policymakers to identify and address compounded forms of disadvantage. For example, without intersectional data, disparities in employment outcomes between disabled women of color, white disabled men, and nondisabled women of color remain invisible, undermining the design of meaningful and effective equity interventions. At the same time, the collection and use of such data must be governed by strong ethical commitments. Data practices should be codeveloped with affected communities to ensure transparency, consent, and accountability, safeguarding against misuse while ensuring that data serves as a tool for empowerment and social transformation rather than surveillance or control.

6.6.3 Advocacy Led by and for Marginalized Disabled People

Advocacy attains its greatest effectiveness and legitimacy when it is driven by those who are most directly impacted by the issues at stake. Centering the leadership of marginalized disabled people requires the intentional redistribution of resources, funding, and visibility toward organizations that are created and led by these communities, as their work is grounded in accountability and lived reality. Such organizations consistently demonstrate deeper analytical insight and more innovative strategies because they emerge from direct experience rather than external interpretation. Equally important is the elevation of lived experience within policy and decision-making spaces. The knowledge produced through everyday encounters with structural barriers, exclusion, and resistance constitutes a critical form of expertise that must be recognized alongside, and often above, traditional professional authority. Prioritizing these voices challenges the dominance of perspectives rooted in privilege and ensures that policies and advocacy efforts are responsive, ethical, and aligned with the actual needs and aspirations of marginalized disabled communities.

6.7 Future Directions: Decolonizing Disability Studies

The final frontier for a truly inclusive disability studies is to decolonize the field itself, challenging its Western, Global North biases and opening itself to a plurality of worldviews.

6.7.1 Global Perspectives: Challenging Western Dominance

The social model of disability has been highly influential in challenging medicalized understandings of impairment, yet it emerged within particular historical and political conditions in the United Kingdom and the United States. When applied uncritically to contexts in the Global South, it risks reproducing forms of intellectual colonialism by overlooking vastly different social, economic, and geopolitical realities. In many regions, the most significant disabling forces may stem less from inaccessible infrastructure and more from armed conflict, food insecurity, environmental degradation, or austerity measures shaped by global economic governance. A decolonial approach to disability studies must therefore situate disability within these broader structural conditions and draw insight from local histories of resistance and survival. Equally important is the recognition of scholarship and activism from the Global South as generative sources of theory in their own right. Rather than treating these contexts as illustrative case studies filtered through Western frameworks, disability studies must actively engage with and learn from the conceptual contributions developed by scholars and communities who articulate disability in relation to poverty, colonial legacies, collective care, and community-based knowledge systems.

6.7.2 Indigenous Knowledge and Models of Disability

Many Indigenous knowledge systems offer profoundly different ways of understanding human variation and collective responsibility, presenting transformative alternatives to dominant Western medical and social models of disability. Rather than centering individualism—whether through an emphasis on "fixing" the person or solely removing individual barriers—Indigenous worldviews often foreground relationality and interdependence. Within these frameworks, difference is not framed as deficit or abnormality but understood as an integral and valued aspect of the community, with well-being arising from reciprocal relationships and shared responsibility. Decolonizing disability practice therefore requires attentiveness to these relational ethics and a willingness to learn from Indigenous perspectives that situate care within communal life. This also involves recognizing and respecting traditional healing practices, which frequently address physical, spiritual, emotional, and social dimensions of well-being as interconnected rather than separate. By valuing these holistic approaches alongside, rather than subordinating them to, Western biomedical paradigms, disability research and practice can move toward more inclusive, culturally grounded, and just forms of care.

6.7.3 The Role of Allyship and Accompliceship

For nondisabled individuals and those who hold relative privilege within the disability community, meaningful engagement requires a shift from symbolic or performative allyship toward the more demanding role of accompaniment. While allyship often remains at the level of verbal support or public affirmation, being an accomplice involves concrete action and a willingness to share risk in challenging oppressive structures. Accomplices actively leverage their privilege to disrupt inequitable systems, follow the leadership of those most marginalized, and commit resources, time, and influence even when doing so entails discomfort or personal cost. Crucially, this orientation is not a label to be adopted but an ongoing practice to be enacted. It requires sustained self-reflection, accountability, and a readiness to listen rather than dominate conversations, to work collectively rather than seek recognition, and to support marginalized voices in ways that center justice over visibility (Tuck & Yang, 2012).

6.8 Conclusion

This chapter has argued that centering marginalized communities is not a peripheral concern for disability studies but the very key to its transformation. An intersectional analysis reveals that the experience of disability is never solely about impairment but is always configured through the powerful forces of race, class, gender, sexuality, and nationality. The case studies of intersectional disablement demonstrate that systemic barriers are not generic; they are precisely engineered by interlocking systems of oppression to disproportionately impact those at the margins.

The path forward requires a fundamental reorientation of research, practice, and policy. We must abandon universalizing approaches in favor of targeted, context-specific interventions developed through community-based participatory research. Practitioners must embrace cultural humility, recognizing the limits of their own knowledge and prioritizing the expertise of lived experience. Advocacy must be led by those most affected, building solidarity across movements to challenge the interconnected structures of ableism, racism, patriarchy, and economic exploitation.

Ultimately, decolonizing disability studies and embracing intersectionality is an act of intellectual and ethical rigor. It demands that we listen to the voices we have historically silenced and allow those voices to reshape our theories, our practices, and our vision of justice. A disability study that truly transforms society must be one that fights for a world where no one is marginalized, in any way, for any reason.

References

Crenshaw, K. (1989). *Demarginalizing the intersection of race and sex.*
Erevelles, N. (2011). *Disability and difference in global contexts.*
Mingus, M. (2011). *Access intimacy: The missing link.*
Schalk, S. (2017). *Bodyminds reimagined: (Dis)ability, race, and gender in black women's speculative fiction.*
Tuck, E., & Yang, K. W. (2012). *Decolonization is not a metaphor.*

Chapter 7
Future Directions in Disability Research

Baliwada Aparna, G. Tulja Rani, Gannavarapu Kumara Swamy, Ammana Sathwika Reddy, Ashwitha Balasani, Gantla Deemanth Reddy, Gurugubelli Sowjanya, Amol S. Rakte, and Nayudu Teja

Abstract A growing global attention toward the rights of disabled citizens and their inclusion compels focused research that is correspondingly commensurate with the fast-evolving landscape of disability practices, technologies, and policies. Disability cannot be a singular concept; rather, it is an enormous, complex domain that includes a series of sectoral interests, varying diagnostic or impairment groups (spinal cord trauma, cerebral palsy, intellectual disability, or autism), and numerous life conditions (such as housing, education, employment, health, justice, and citizenship) (Shakespeare, 2015). Disability policy is no less expansive, branching over issues of the broader community, e.g., health, housing, and technology. Therefore, any effort at mapping this area and formulating a future research agenda must equally be comprehensive and of the community it is meant to serve (Llewellyn & Emerson, 2021).

B. Aparna (✉)
Department of Pharmaceutical Chemistry, Malla Reddy Pharmacy College, Maisammaguda, Hyderabad, India

G. Tulja Rani
Department of Pharmaceutical Analysis, Malla Reddy Pharmacy College, Maisammaguda, Hyderabad, India

G. K. Swamy · A. S. Reddy · A. Balasani · G. D. Reddy
Department of Pharmacy Practice, Malla Reddy Pharmacy College, Maisammaguda, Hyderabad, India

G. Sowjanya
Ratan Tata Innovations Hub (RTIH), Rajamahendravaram, Andhra Pradesh, India

A. S. Rakte
Department of Pharmaceutics, Indrayani Vidya Mandir's, Krishnarao Bhegade Institute of Pharmaceutical Education and Research,
Talegaon Dabhade, Tal-Maval, Pune, Maharashtra, India

N. Teja
Department of Pharmaceutics, JSS College of Pharmacy, JSS Academy of Higher Education and Research, The Nilgiris, Ooty, Tamil Nadu, India

D. Nagasen, S. K. S. S. Pindiprolu (eds.), *Transforming Disability Studies*, SpringerBriefs in Modern Perspectives on Disability Research,
https://doi.org/10.1007/978-981-95-9004-9_7

Keywords Inclusive Education · Educational Equity · Universal Design for Learning (UDL) · Stakeholder Collaboration

7.1 Introduction

A growing global attention toward the rights of disabled citizens and their inclusion compels focused research that is correspondingly commensurate with the fast-evolving landscape of disability practices, technologies, and policies. Disability cannot be a singular concept; rather, it is an enormous, complex domain that includes a series of sectoral interests, varying diagnostic or impairment groups (spinal cord trauma, cerebral palsy, intellectual disability, or autism), and numerous life conditions (such as housing, education, employment, health, justice, and citizenship) (Shakespeare, 2015). Disability policy is no less expansive, branching over issues of the broader community, e.g., health, housing, and technology. Therefore, any effort at mapping this area and formulating a future research agenda must equally be comprehensive and of the community it is meant to serve (Llewellyn & Emerson, 2021).

An essential element of modern disability research is its intersectionality. The experiences of disability intersect with multiple aspects of identity, especially among Aboriginal and Torres Strait Islander peoples in Australia, as well as within gender, ethnicity, and LGBTQI+ communities. Such intersections can produce compounded layers of disadvantage. Marginalized groups, especially women with disabilities, often face heightened barriers to progress in the labor market, limiting opportunities for inclusive growth. Workplace discrimination is acknowledged as a principal factor leading to social exclusion, creating a situation of intersecting discrimination based on both disability and gender. To effectively address this issue, it is essential to reduce and eliminate social discrimination and stigma while simultaneously promoting positive coping strategies to empower these demographic groups (Dueñas-Zambrana & Cruz-Morato, 2025). In recent decades, advancements in the field of disability have significantly progressed, driven by innovations in science, technology, and healthcare, as well as by international and interdisciplinary collaborations. Simultaneously, governmental and nongovernmental organizations, in conjunction with civil society, are vigorously advocating for awareness, sensitization, and inclusion of individuals with disabilities. To effectively harness this energy and inform future policies and practices, it is essential to regularly assess the existing research landscape to discern trends, pinpoint gaps, and recognize opportunities. This chapter addresses this need by conducting a concentrated analysis of research articles on disabilities published in India from 1945 to 2023, employing bibliometric methodologies and visualization tools to illuminate trends, collaboration patterns, and thematic evolution in the field (Borgohain et al., 2024). This chapter utilizes this methodological framework to present crucial information regarding advancements, focal points, and prospective developments in disability research on a broader scale. The findings are of considerable importance to a diverse array of stakeholders, including academics, policymakers, administrators, service providers, and funding organizations. Finally, this analysis is meant to facilitate evidence-informed decision-making that will guide inclusive future development in schooling, healthcare, social policy, and technology for the foreseeable future (Borgohain et al., 2024).

7.1.1 *Inclusive Research Methodologies*

Inclusive research processes usually emphasize the daily circumstances required to construct genuine inclusion as centering the users themselves as the core of the experience. Much can be learned about research focused on inclusive youth sport, which stipulates the definitive role of the coach as accommodating children with disabilities to flourish through the construction of the appropriate milieus. Such research illustrates that besides simply facilitating autonomy-support, the effectiveness of inclusion relies on the ability of a coach to facilitate social encounters and cultivate nonsports-specific competencies, among which self-confidence belongs (O'Rourke et al., 2025). Sport programming for children of differing abilities provides learning opportunities for children to engage and learn from each other, an activity which goes a long distance toward reducing stigma and stereotyping behaviors (Kamberidou et al., 2019).

While coaches are key to developing belongingness in these contexts (O'Rourke et al., 2025; Allan et al., 2023), participants warn coaches not to coerce friendships. The preferred method involves coaches providing children with a framework and the capacity to engage organically, employing sports as a shared, familiar experience, while allowing them autonomy in cultivating social relationships (Carroll & Allen, 2021). If coaches effectively cultivate an environment that fosters children's social skills, they may establish a genuine sense of belonging within the sport (O'Rourke et al., 2025). This work also uncovers significant obstacles rooted in perceived differences. Coaches and other support personnel, such as educators, frequently make the mistake of assuming that children with disabilities are less capable than their peers and, consequently, cannot be adequately challenged (O'Rourke et al., 2025).

This harmful assumption often relegates disabled children to the position of "assistant," thereby depriving them of essential skill development opportunities (Arbour-Nicitopoulos et al., 2018). An essential component of inclusive practice is that coaches provide all children with appropriately challenging activities that facilitate skill mastery, competence, and self-esteem (O'Rourke et al., 2025).

Moreover, peer social dynamics introduce an additional layer of complexity. Prejudice and stereotypical biases against disabled students can manifest as exclusionary practices, active hostility, and bullying. For children and adolescents, who often prioritize peer acceptance, this experience can be more detrimental than discrimination faced by adults. This observation underscores the coaches' multifaceted role, beyond technical aspects, in actively fostering a culture of respect and inclusion among peers (Fig. 7.1).

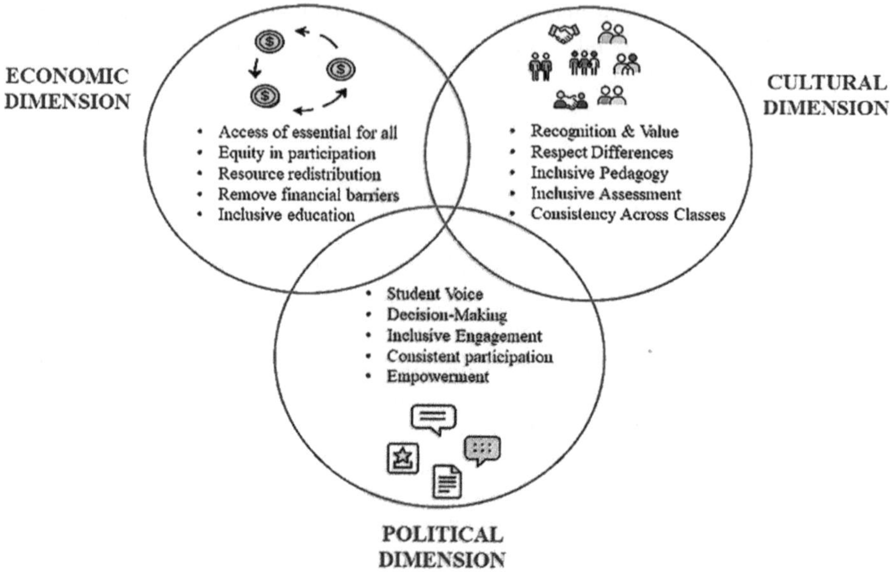

Fig. 7.1 A comprehensive review of the economic, cultural, and political dimensions of students with disabilities, emphasizing the distribution of resources, the acknowledgment and appreciation of differences, and the avenues available for students to express their opinions and influence school policies

7.2 Physical Infrastructural Facilities

7.2.1 Medical Facilities

Substantial barriers in healthcare for individuals with disabilities persist, including protracted waiting times and challenging interactions between patients and healthcare professionals. While the implementation of disability-responsive training for healthcare practitioners is crucial for improving patient satisfaction, it is inadequate by itself. A comprehensive strategy is necessary, combining enhanced training through sophisticated methodologies with inclusive institutional policies and structural reforms to tackle workforce disparities and the unequal allocation of facility-based services. Addressing these interrelated structural issues is crucial to substantially reduce unmet healthcare needs, thus improving the daily quality of life for individuals with disabilities (Rotarou et al., 2025).

7.2.2 Environmental Facilities

Environmental facilities are essential for ensuring the safety, autonomy, and social inclusion of individuals with disabilities, although their design and implementation are often shaped by prevailing economic conditions and temporal contexts. These facilities involve modifying both newly built and existing structures, communal spaces, and service environments to enable independent and secure use by individuals with diverse functional needs (Peters, 2022). Environmental accessibility includes multiple areas, such as public and workplace settings, requiring restaurants, offices, and other establishments to undertake structural alterations, redesign tasks, and provide sufficient staff training to effectively assist disabled employees (Hines et al., 2020). This includes housing and residential services, focusing on identifying and removing physical barriers in private living spaces by implementing measures such as installing accessible sanitation facilities, suitable flooring, adequate heating, and modifying doors, walls, and windows to accommodate individual requirements. To guarantee the importance of these initiatives, public infrastructure must comply with inclusive design standards and regulatory guidelines that improve usability for all individuals (Stone, 2019). The principal objective of accessibility standards and construction regulations is to ensure equitable access to the built environment, transportation systems, and information and communication services, thereby enabling individuals with disabilities to live independently and participate fully in social, economic, and civic activities (Al-Amrat & Khasawneh, 2022; Shater et al., 2023).

7.2.3 Educational Facilities

Countries must recognize the fundamental rights of children, youth, and adults with disabilities to equitable access to education at all levels, integrating inclusivity as a foundational principle of the educational system. Fulfilling this commitment necessitates several facilitating conditions, including the removal of physical obstacles in educational settings, the availability of support services like sign language interpretation, and unimpeded access to educational resources and support systems (Santos et al. 2019). An accessible educational institution must be constructed to guarantee barrier-free entry and utilization, facilitated by secure and navigable approach routes, clearly delineated access points, allocated parking, and well-maintained external ramps. Equal emphasis should be placed on internal accessibility by providing ramps, functional stairways, clearly marked entrances, and efficient signage, ensuring that all interior areas, including corridors, doors, restrooms, and classrooms, are designed to facilitate ease of movement and independent utilization. In addition to physical access, education is essential for promoting social participation and justice by tackling structural and institutional inequalities that lead to exclusion, a goal attainable solely through an equity-based approach. Inclusive education actualizes this principle by providing each learner with resources customized to their needs, facilitating their attainment of full potential within the educational setting (Sedláčková et al., 2025). Mainstream classrooms, although typically the most suitable environment, must be intentionally structured to support students with motor impairments, facilitating the effective utilization of assistive devices such as wheelchairs, canes, and crutches, while enabling movement, seating, and task execution with minimal challenges (Shater et al., 2023). Alongside physical adaptations, educational institutions require support from trained staff, accessible transportation, and suitable assistive technologies (ATs). An inclusive educational environment transcends classroom confines to include health services, commercial facilities, and transportation systems, all of which must be modified to guarantee full accessibility and meaningful participation for individuals with disabilities (Marongedza et al., 2023).

7.3 Noninfrastructural Facilities

7.3.1 Awareness Programs

A major area for future research is how to plan and carry out awareness campaigns that teach people with disabilities and the general public about their rights and responsibilities as citizens. These programs help a lot to spread information about legal rights, promote inclusivity, and raise people's awareness of their own rights. Awareness and educational programs should also focus on specific practical needs that are likely to have a direct effect on health and quality of life. For example, the growing number of people with developmental disabilities means that we need to do more to teach them about nutrition and health. Special programs that focus on hygiene, diet control, and preventing obesity are given priority because they can improve the health and nutrition of disabled people, especially those in institutions (Kim & Jeon, 2024).

7.3.2 Government Initiatives

Educational systems accommodating disabilities should be established through governmental initiatives, grounded in robust legislative frameworks of rights and accompanied by explicit provisions for accommodations. Principal actions encompass:

(a) **Enacting Comprehensive Legislation:** Formulate and implement stringent disability rights statutes that forbid discrimination across all aspects of life—including employment, housing, and public services—and ensure equitable access to education with requirements for accessibility and reasonable accommodation.
(b) **Implementing Educational Accommodations:** Educational systems must incorporate flexible curricula and assessment methods that address diverse learning styles, ensuring that all learners have equal opportunity to demonstrate their understanding and abilities. It is imperative to constantly provide appropriate accommodations during assessments, such as extended testing duration or alternative evaluation formats, to address individual requirements. Concurrently, administrative procedures must be streamlined to minimize bureaucratic impediments, enabling students to promptly access assistive devices and support services without unnecessary delays.

7.4 Technological Advancements and Disability

Assistive Technology (AT) encompasses a broad array of instruments, including durable medical equipment (DME), mobility aids like wheelchairs and walkers, prosthetic limbs, environmental control systems, and communication devices. The primary objective of AT is to enhance personal functional independence by simplifying navigation through environmental barriers, optimizing self-autonomy, and promoting participation in daily activities. Consequently, it optimizes opportunities for social integration, especially in higher education and employment. The use of these devices has increased markedly over the last twenty years, and this trend is expected to persist. AT achieves optimal success when it is appropriately aligned with the individual's personal needs, preferences, environment, and the capabilities of the device. When effectively implemented, AT possesses significant potential to foster individual independence, facilitate access to postsecondary education, and promote successful employment. Furthermore, for elderly individuals, suitable technology effectively compensates for diminished physical abilities and promotes positive mental outcomes in later life (Xiang et al., 2021). It is essential to create and implement technology-driven interventions that are attuned to the evolving capabilities, needs, and expectations of the expanding global population of elderly individuals. To fully harness the potential of these technological advancements, they must be accompanied by focused patient education, continuous monitoring initiatives, and progressive public health strategies. These measures signify a constructive advancement in enhancing the quality of life for the elderly through technological interventions (Su & Mejía, 2024).

7.4.1 AT and Higher Education

The absence or unavailability of AT constitutes a significant obstacle for college students with physical disabilities. Typical accommodations via AT encompass voice recognition systems, reading machines, FM systems, and text enlargement software. Among these, voice recognition and reading machines are notable for their adaptability, providing substantial assistance to students with diverse disabilities, including visual impairments, mobility challenges, and learning disabilities.

7.4.2 AT and Employment

AT has proven to be a highly effective component of vocational rehabilitation by enhancing employability and career development for individuals with disabilities (Noll et al., 2006). The benefits of implementing AT in the workplace are significant, leading to enhanced productivity, increased self-confidence, improved attendance, and greater paid work hours, thus serving as one of the most effective tools for disabled employees. The considerable importance attributed to it indicates that a lack of understanding regarding ATs may constitute one of the most significant barriers for the unemployed (Stumbo et al., 2009). However, the successful integration of AT in workplace environments requires collaborative and inclusive settings where various essential elements are present: individuals with disabilities, employers, and colleagues must engage actively in both decision-making phases (selection and execution); all participants must maintain constructive and proactive mindsets; service providers must deliver thorough guidance along with prompt follow-up to resolve any issues; and workplace settings must allow for some degree of flexibility regarding responsibilities (Stumbo et al., 2009).

7.4.3 Disability and Intersectionality

Intersectionality has emerged as a significant analytical instrument utilized across various disciplines, including the humanities, cultural studies, and social sciences, to elucidate intricate social and cultural dynamics (Barsch et al., 2020). Its utility lies in its capacity to uncover the complex nature of inequality and relationships of power, and therefore the possibility of an examination of the overlapping facets of social penalty (Krösche, 2025). It therefore becomes an ever-more necessary tool for use in education research and studies of disability with a view to the promotion of inclusive practice. It is, however, necessary to be extremely cautious in its application within disability research, for disability is a particular site in which surface-level interpretations of intersectionality are possible (Frederick & Shifrer, 2019). Both institutions and people may adopt practices of obscurity or minimization of elements of disability, implying that what seems to be an intersectional strategy actually works to reduce the perception of its unique penalties (Watermeyer, 2012). This has a habit of causing the forgetting of essential ones, including the well-established, though neglected, correlation between disability and socio-economic penalty (Chatzitheochari & Platt, 2019).

A core process within the maintenance of these intersectional disadvantages is stigma, defined as a social process of exclusion, rejection, and devaluation, depending on imbalances in social, political, and economic power. Stigmatization is expressed in various forms, including structural discrimination (evident in policies and institutional practices), interactional discrimination (occurring in daily social interactions), and stigma consciousness—a cultivated sense of shame and expectation of negative judgment that may lead individuals to hide their identities (Chatzitheochari & Butler-Rees, 2023). Ultimately, the experience of stigma extends beyond the existence of a disability and is intricately linked to an individual's perceived deviation from conventional standards of ability and behavior (Monk, 2022). The tangible effects of interrelated systems of authority and stigma are particularly evident in educational and professional environments. Empirical evidence indicates that individuals from low-income backgrounds, racially minoritized groups, and those with disabilities are significantly more prone to disruptions that can impede their education and career prospects. The confluence of these intersecting identities engenders an elevated risk. For example, individuals with disabilities are significantly more prone to such disruptions compared to their nondisabled counterparts, and this risk is exacerbated for those who are concurrently low-income and non-White. In certain circumstances, up to one in five individuals with intersecting identities encounter significant setbacks in their education or career.

7.4.4 Artificial Intelligence: A New Field for Intersectional Bias

- The exclusionary nature of common technological applications is intensified by algorithmic biases present in artificial intelligence (AI) frameworks. The former generally depend on databases that incorporate persistent linguistic and ableist biases, situating AI within socio-technical contexts that reinforce existing power structures instead of serving as universal tools (Heeks, 2022; Noble, 2020). Notwithstanding, advancements in machine learning, generative AI frameworks continue to replicate and exacerbate societal biases, especially against individuals facing multiple intersecting marginalities.

  Research on the collaborative creation of AI-generated images with individuals from diverse cultural and linguistic backgrounds exposes the inherent systemic constraints of AI in accurately representing various identities without reinforcing existing social stereotypes. AI systems frequently examine descriptive language within a framework of ingrained biases associated with gender, race, disability, age, and body mass. An AI is likely to associate a disabled female from a specific ethnic group with advanced age, even in the absence of age-related parameters in the query. This demonstrates the capability of AI visualization software to replicate prevalent social discourses that are often erroneous and based on stereotypes (Soldatic et al., 2025).

  Furthermore, AI systems frequently default to racial and cultural stereotypes, as evidenced by the inclination to prioritize lighter-skinned phenotypes as the archetypal representation of "Asian," thus marginalizing individuals from varied Asian backgrounds. Similarly, computer-generated images of women often conform to strict, hyper-feminized, and Western-centric standards of body representation, thereby revealing biases shaped by the intersection of whiteness and sexism (Sutko, 2020).

  To achieve precise representations, individuals with intersecting minority identities are often compelled to "over-specify" their characteristics, including detailed information for each aspect of their identity, in an effort to counteract the algorithm's inherent biases. This process imposes an emotional and psychological burden on end-users, who are compelled to perpetually engage and rectify biases embedded within the system. This situation highlights the urgent need for AI to incorporate diverse, intersectional identities from its inception, rather than expecting systematically marginalized individuals to advocate for their own accurate and inclusive representation (Konrad, 2021).

7.5 Future Research Directions and Considerations

The application of an intersectional framework has significantly enhanced the discourse on disability, and current scholarship uncovers numerous deficiencies and gaps that indicate a clear trajectory for future research initiatives. In advancing within this area, scholars are compelled to look beyond existing constraints and utilize richer, broader, and contextually cognizant research processes.

There is first of all an immediate need for increased accuracy in the classification of types of disabilities. A large percentage of current studies almost entirely concentrate on women who are physical disability experiencers, combine various impairments, or completely exclude the description of types of disabilities. Future studies should engage with a different range of impairments to explore unique circumstances. Inasmuch as there is prominent stigma still rife in many communities, there is a special need to study the experiences of people who have psycho-social disabilities and intellectual or learning disabilities to develop a richer understanding of unique challenges and possibilities (McConkey et al., 2016).

Second, while a few studies discuss the intersection of race, gender, and disability, future studies should explicitly discuss additional intersecting identities. This means exploring the lives of people with different sexuality dispositions, comparing challenges and motivations across different age groups, and exploring the interaction of additional roles, for example, caring for other family members, and a person's disability identity (Flores et al., 2021).

Third, there is a genuine need for geographic and cultural elements of the investigation to be considerably expanded. A majority of studies are centralized in the developed Western world and the United States. This narrow focus results in a narrow perception of the varying experience of people with disabilities worldwide. There is a genuine requirement for wide, worldwide studies in areas hitherto neglected, including Africa, Asia, Latin America, and the Middle East. Such studies should also account for ways in which national cultural values and different levels of socio-economic development create different challenges and forms of support compared to those of developed economies (Chan & Hutchings, 2023).

Fourth, further research should refine the study of systemic and environmental determinants. This necessitates transcending personal experience to analyze obstacles within significant institutions such as workplaces, educational establishments, and healthcare systems. It is essential to comprehend the perspectives of peers and colleagues that may either hinder or foster inclusivity and advancement. Investigations in this domain may enhance studies on the bullying and harassment of various minority groups, thereby underscoring the importance of specialized behavioral interventions and the advocacy of disability activists within organizations and communities (Chan & Hutchings, 2023). Ultimately, for this discipline to develop comprehensively, it is imperative that it is established on solid theoretical foundations. A significant deficiency in the current literature is the lack of explicit theoretical motivation in numerous studies (Collins & Chepp, 2013). Subsequent longitudinal and cross-national studies must be grounded in established theories—such as critical disability theory, social cognitive theory, or a more integrated intersectionality theory—to guarantee coherence and enhance the robustness and longevity of contributions to the discipline.

7.6 Emerging Areas of Disability Research

A significant emerging trend in disability studies is the shift toward methodological integration, which contests the prevailing qualitative–quantitative dichotomy of methodologies. While quantitative studies are crucial for assessing the prevalence of various issues and cross-validating extensive hypotheses, they frequently inadequately represent the intricate realities faced by individuals with disabilities. Qualitative studies, employing methods like in-depth interviews, provide an essential perspective on lived experiences, thereby elucidating whether progressive theories have influenced individuals outside advocacy networks to perceive themselves and their situations differently (O'Day & Killeen, 2002). This qualitative investigation is adept at revealing unexpected discoveries and elucidating the intricate relationships among impairment, societal perceptions, and institutional obstacles. Although AT is frequently regarded as a universal solution, qualitative studies reveal significant issues, such as prohibitive costs, insufficient training, and restrictive programs. Such studies indicate that issues like unemployment frequently embody a complex array of factors that are challenging to disentangle using quantitative evidence alone (O'Day & Killeen, 2002). Thus, the future trajectory of disability studies is not predicated on a debate of "quantitative versus qualitative," but rather on integrating the strengths to construct both a more comprehensive and precise framework for informing effective policy interventions (O'Day & Killeen, 2002). This methodological innovation is essential as the field increasingly prioritizes technology's role in enhancing accessibility and participation. Individuals with physical disabilities—a demographic exceeding two million in the United States, encompassing acquired, degenerative, and congenital impairments—face significant obstacles in accessing essential computing technology. Despite the plethora of alternative access modalities, such as speech recognition and eye-tracking, none of these individuals possess the appropriate solutions to facilitate their full engagement in education, work, and community life (Koch Fager et al. 2019; Cook et al., 2020).

Addressing this deficiency establishes a central theme for future endeavors, emphasizing inclusive research and development by involving individuals with disabilities in every stage of design and execution, rather than solely during the final testing phase. There are real options for enhancing the design and usability of existing AT, for instance, streamlining and strengthening eye-gaze systems, simplifying device integration, and reducing the cognitive load of complex access procedures (Koester et al., 2025). Highly innovative is the use of AI to develop innovative modes of access. Potential is high, but end-user involvement is critical. Areas of interest include the integration of large language models (LLMs) within systems of Augmentative and Alternative Communication (AAC) to allow for an efficient conversation, and the creation of user-friendly technology capable of dynamic adaptation to an individual's performance or fluctuating abilities over time (Koester et al., 2025; Koester & Mankowski, 2015). Third, scholarly study must move beyond technology of interest to the ecosystem serving it. There is a need to put focus on service delivery improvement. This implies investigating the performance of the assessment method, enhancing awareness among all the concerned stakeholders, and supporting users to vocalize their needs. Supporting practitioners to adopt good, user-friendly methods is essential, as well as providing continuous follow-up, because poor follow-up often leads to abandonment of technology (Konrad, 2021). Even if technology and service delivery are prominent, broader psychological, societal, and public policy challenges are pervasive and hinder universal inclusion and demand focus through continuous, rigorous study (Konrad et al., 2022).

7.7 Future Research Directions (Fig. 7.2)

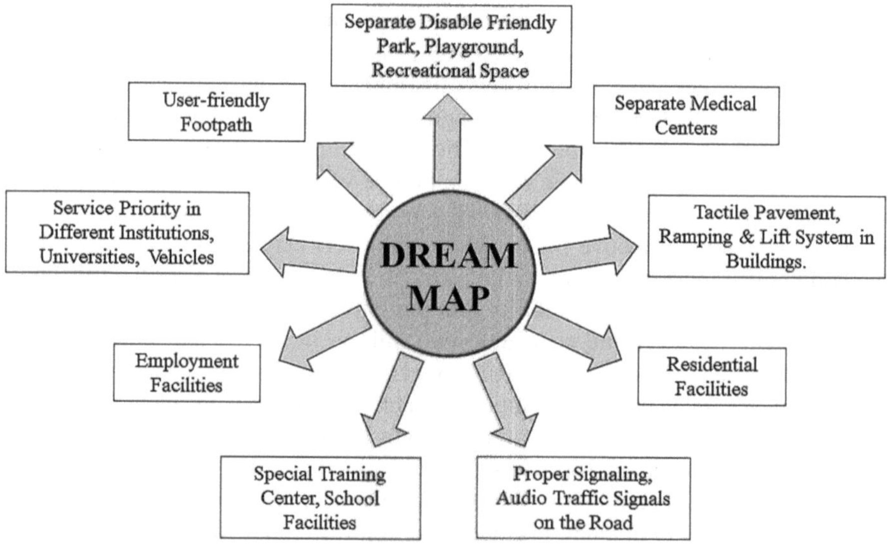

Fig. 7.2 Illustration of the required infrastructural, social, as well as service-based facilities needed for the overall involvement of citizens with disabilities

7.8 Future Directions for Inclusive Environment and Construction Facilities

Future disability research concerning the built environment must move beyond broad compliance to adopt more targeted and sophisticated approaches, addressing the nuanced barriers that persist despite existing regulations (Shahraki, 2021).

Key avenues for future research are:

Enlarge the Concept of Disability: Research should expand the focus beyond the conventional consideration of locomotor disabilities to the explicit consideration of the access barriers faced by those who live with intellectual, psychosocial, and cognitive disabilities (Shahraki, 2021; Alqahtani et al., 2025).

Implementation of Longitudinal and Comparative Methodologies: Longitudinal studies must be conducted to assess the enduring effects of newly enacted accessibility legislation. Furthermore, comparative research examining disparities between urban and rural contexts or among various cultural settings can elucidate context-specific challenges and optimal practices (Alqahtani et al., 2025).

Embracing User-Led Codesign: A key trend must be the adoption of user-focused codesign, where the full participation of disabled people is part of the research and designing process to ensure that solutions are based on their lived experiences (Alqahtani et al., 2025).

Surpassing Economic Viability: Research must overcome political viability obstacles by exploring affordable access pathways and innovative funding mechanisms, such as public–private partnerships, to ensure that access is both sustainable and integral to every construction project (Alqahtani et al., 2025).

7.9 e-Environments to Promote Inclusive Education

This previous big movement to digital learning brought into focus the role of e-learning among disabled learners as a pertinent future research area. Future research should be targeted to two significant trends. Future research on e-learning should give greater attention to its socio-psychological dimensions, recognizing that learning remains fundamentally relational even in digital environments. Rather than focusing solely on academic performance, studies should examine how virtual platforms can be intentionally designed to foster meaningful teacher–student interactions and peer connections that support learners' emotional well-being and intellectual development (Lipka et al., 2019). At the same time, accessibility must be treated as a foundational principle rather than an afterthought. Many existing digital learning systems are primarily developed for nondisabled users, creating exclusionary barriers. Embedding universal design for learning at the earliest stages of platform development can produce inherently flexible and inclusive systems, reducing the need for retrofitted accommodations, preventing emotional harm, and enabling equitable participation for all learners (Cataudella et al., 2021).

7.10 AI and Future Directions

While AI promises much to advance digital inclusion, the current use often brings further challenges to users with disabilities, making it a priority research agenda for the future. Primary focus needs to be placed on algorithmic bias, as AI technologies built based on nondiverse datasets could prove to reinforce current societal biases, most notably in particular fields. This challenge is compounded by the problems presented, albeit indirectly, through inaccessible interfaces and high demands on intelligence, where the very users the technology hopes to support will be isolated (Cataudella et al., 2023; Min, 2023). Moreover, the absence of transparency in behind-the-scenes AI decision-making, otherwise referred to as the "black box" issue, complicates the identification and contesting of unfair results (Tsamados et al., 2022). Excessive reliance on automation risks dehumanizing essential processes, such as recruitment (Nacheva, 2024). Therefore, forthcoming research on disability should guide the development of AI by establishing evidence-based methodologies that promote fairness, accessibility, and transparency, ensuring that technological advancements yield genuine and inclusive justice.

7.10.1 AI in Education

Integrating AI into education is a vital aspect of disabilities research, as it offers the potential to create more flexible, tailored, and inclusive learning environments. Although technologies like virtual reality and speech recognition offer significant potential to enhance student engagement and facilitate skill acquisition, realizing this potential presents several critical systemic challenges. Future research should concentrate on overcoming the barriers that hinder successful implementation. This encompasses a significant deficiency in teacher preparation, rendering educators unprepared to utilize AI effectively, alongside insufficient digital infrastructure in educational institutions (Alghamdi, 2022; Ayanwale et al., 2022; Alsolami, 2025; Garg & Sharma, 2020; Kharbat et al., 2020). In addition to these systemic issues, future research endeavors should prioritize the elements of AI technologies that are involved in their design. Generic platforms, currently prevalent, are inadequate; thus, research should inform the creation of culturally and linguistically customized AI programs that are both pedagogically beneficial and capable of addressing diverse learning requirements (Knox et al., 2019). The forthcoming research agenda must encompass both human and technological dimensions, examining methods to enhance support for educators while concurrently advancing the development of contextually appropriate and genuinely effective AI resources.

7.10.2 AI in Employment

The rapid advancement of AI creates a complex situation regarding the future employment of individuals with disabilities, offering opportunities via ATs while also posing significant risks of job displacement due to automation. A significant concern is that the impact of AI on unemployment is not uniformly distributed; research indicates that while the adoption of advanced AI may reduce unemployment rates for disabled individuals with secondary and tertiary education, it appears to have a negligible positive effect on those with only primary education, potentially worsening existing inequalities (Abid et al., 2024). Consequently, the primary future objective of disability research necessitates advancing beyond mere awareness of these issues to effectively enhance the role of AI in the labor market. The adoption of AI-based ATs, speech recognition systems, and adaptive mechanisms presents a significant opportunity to broaden access to employment by directly improving workplace accessibility and facilitating task execution (Alexiadou, 2022). This opportunity necessitates a proactive agenda led by inclusive policies and effective governance, including the implementation of AI-related protocols to mitigate bias in autonomous recruitment processes, promoting the adoption of accessible AI solutions among companies, and investing in dedicated skill-building programs. Future research must prioritize the development and evaluation of cohesive policy frameworks to ensure that AI advancement mitigates job displacement and fosters a more inclusive and equitable labor market for all individuals with disabilities (Cheatham & Randolph, 2022; Jetha et al., 2023; Fisher et al., 2024; Omri & Afi, 2025).

7.10.3 AI and Significant Technological Advancements

A significant future research emphasis on disability is the development of AI-driven systems that facilitate technological access for individuals with physical limitations. Innovative systems such as Windows Sphere employ AI to integrate gesture recognition, voice assistants, and adaptive interfaces, enabling individuals to interact with technology autonomously and seamlessly. The systems provide precise offline processing, addressing the issues associated with outdated assistive devices, alleviating fatigue, and establishing elevated standards for accessible computing (Sudharsanan et al., 2025). A prospective avenue is the amalgamation of AI and the Internet of Things (IoT) to create intelligent, responsive environments that improve autonomy and safety for individuals with disabilities. Deep networks can interpret sensor data to monitor daily activities, identify threats, and facilitate independent living. Advanced methodologies—such as ensemble systems incorporating graph convolutional networks (GCNs), long short-term memory (LSTM) networks, and convolutional autoencoders (CAEs)—can autonomously categorize activities and respond to varied user requirements. The enhancement of such systems to ensure effective and reliable support should be the focus of forthcoming research (Abokhoza &

Jahmani, 2023; Brik et al., 2021; Arasi et al., 2025). Ultimately, AI-based Robot Therapy (AIBRT) has the potential to revolutionize the lives of individuals, particularly children afflicted with autism spectrum disorder (ASD), ADHD, and learning disabilities. Socially assistive robots (SARs) utilizing machine learning, computer vision, and natural language processing can provide tailored, reliable, and engaging interactions to facilitate communication, emotional regulation, and social skills development. The systems employ sensors and AI-driven feedback to provide real-time assessments and enhanced treatment protocols. Integrating AIBRT into routine practice and mainstreaming it represents a crucial advancement in improving care for individuals with disabilities (Yahya et al., 2024).

7.11 Innovations in Apparel Industry: A New Approach

A crucial future focus for disability research is the technological advancement of the apparel industry to more effectively accommodate individuals with disabilities. Consequently, the primary future objective of disability research necessitates advancing beyond mere awareness of these challenges to effectively enhance the role of AI in the labor market. The implementation of AI-based ATs, speech recognition systems, and adaptive mechanisms presents a significant opportunity to broaden workplace accessibility and facilitate task execution. This opportunity necessitates a proactive agenda led by inclusive policies and effective governance, including the implementation of AI-related protocols to mitigate bias in autonomous recruitment processes, promoting the adoption of accessible AI solutions among companies, and investing in dedicated skill-building programs. By concentrating on these technological innovations, forthcoming research can direct the industry toward developing genuinely adaptive, trendsetting solutions that enhance daily living and promote increased social inclusion (Rana et al., 2024).

7.12 Conclusion

Inclusive research on disability is increasingly evolving toward a holistic, integrated, and visionary framework that recognizes the diverse experiences and intersecting challenges faced by individuals. Advancements over the past decade in inclusive methodologies, infrastructure, healthcare, education, and awareness initiatives demonstrate the necessity of eliminating stigma while endorsing rights-based policies and governmental programs. Simultaneously, emerging technologies such as intelligent environments, socially assistive robots, and AI-driven products may enhance individuals' independence, accessibility, and engagement. Innovations should be based on the principles of equality, transparency, and user-centricity to drive transformation. A notable prospective research avenue is enhancing quality of life (QoL) by promoting self-determination—the capacity to be the primary architect of one's own life. Research should investigate the impact of assistance on enhanced quality-of-life outcomes, as well as the support systems offered by families, schools, and communities that empower individuals with disabilities. Ultimately, future research on disability must achieve a balance between theoretical rigor and practical requirements, considering social policy, technological advancements, and cultural competence. By ensuring all sites are accessible—structural, technological, and social—we can empower individuals with disabilities to lead fully realized, independent lives.

References

Abid, M., Ben-Salha, O., Kanetaki, Z., & Sekrafi, H. (2024). Does the impact of artificial intelligence on unemployment among people with disabilities differ by educational level? A dynamic panel threshold approach. *IEEE Access, 12*, 131024–131034. https://doi.org/10.1109/ACCESS.2024.3456962

Abokhoza, R., & Jahmani, A. (2023). Towards retention in airline industry using neutrosophic DEMATEL method: Does social media marketing activities affect passengers' retention. *IJNS, 21*, 161–176. https://doi.org/10.54216/IJNS.210214

Al-Amrat, M. G. R., & Khasawneh, M. A. S. (2022). Students with special education disabilities' spatial skills. *Journal of Positive Psychology and Wellbeing, 6*, 3185–3194.

Alexiadou, E. A. (2022. [cited 2025 Sept 30]). Artificial intelligence in disability employment: Incorporating a human rights approach. In B. Custers & E. Fosch-Villaronga (Eds.), *Law and artificial intelligence [Internet]* (pp. 135–148). T.M.C. Asser Press. https://doi.org/10.1007/978-94-6265-523-2_7

Alghamdi, A. A. (2022). Digital transformation within Saudi education system: 2020 and beyond. *The Educational Review, USA, 6*, 419–425. https://doi.org/10.26855/er.2022.08.014

Allan, V., Gainforth, H., Turnnidge, J., Konoval, T., Côté, J., & Latimer-Cheung, A. (2023). Narrative as a learning tool for coaches of athletes with a disability: Using stories to translate research into practice. *Physical Education and Sport Pedagogy, 28*, 546–567. https://doi.org/10.1080/17408989.2021.2006619

Alqahtani, F. K., Sherif, M., Abdelhafeez, M., Ghanem, A., Shafaay, M. A., & Alkahtani, B. N. (2025. [cited 2025 Sept 30]). Enhancing accessibility for people with disabilities through upgrades in construction facilities in Saudi Arabia: A quantitative assessment. *Journal of Disability Research [Internet], 4*. https://doi.org/10.57197/JDR-2024-0114

Alsolami, A. S. (2025). The effectiveness of using artificial intelligence in improving academic skills of school-aged students with mild intellectual disabilities in Saudi Arabia. *Research in Developmental Disabilities, 156*, 104884. https://doi.org/10.1016/j.ridd.2024.104884

Arasi, M. A., AlEisa, H. N., Alneil, A. A., & Marzouk, R. (2025). Artificial intelligence-driven ensemble deep learning models for smart monitoring of indoor activities in IoT environment for people with disabilities. *Scientific Reports, 15*, 4337. https://doi.org/10.1038/s41598-025-88450-1

Arbour-Nicitopoulos, K. P., Grassmann, V., Orr, K., McPherson, A. C., Faulkner, G. E., & Wright, F. V. (2018). A scoping review of inclusive out-of-school time physical activity programs for children and youth with physical disabilities. *Adapted Physical Activity Quarterly, 35*, 111–138. https://doi.org/10.1123/apaq.2017-0012

Ayanwale, M. A., Sanusi, I. T., Adelana, O. P., Aruleba, K. D., & Oyelere, S. S. (2022). Teachers' readiness and intention to teach artificial intelligence in schools. *Computers and Education: Artificial Intelligence, 3*, 100099. https://doi.org/10.1016/j.caeai.2022.100099

Barsch, S., Degner, B., Kühberger, C., & Lücke, M. (Eds.). (2020. [cited 2025 Sept 29]). *Handbuch Diversität im Geschichtsunterricht [Internet]*. Wochenschau Verlag. https://doi.org/10.46499/1628

Borgohain, D. J., Bhardwaj, R. K., & Verma, M. K. (2024). Mapping the literature on the application of artificial intelligence in libraries (AAIL): A scientometric analysis. *LHT, 42*, 149–179. https://doi.org/10.1108/LHT-07-2022-0331

Brik, B., Esseghir, M., Merghem-Boulahia, L., & Snoussi, H. (2021). An IoT-based deep learning approach to analyse indoor thermal comfort of disabled people. *Building and Environment, 203*, 108056. https://doi.org/10.1016/j.buildenv.2021.108056

Carroll, M., & Allen, J. (2021). 'Zooming in' on the antecedents of youth sport coaches' autonomy-supportive and controlling interpersonal behaviours: A multimethod study. *International Journal of Sports Science & Coaching, 16*, 236–248. https://doi.org/10.1177/1747954120958621

Cataudella, S., Carta, S., Mascia, M. L., Masala, C., Petretto, D. R., & Penna, M. P. (2021). Psychological aspects of students with learning disabilities in E-environments: A mini review and future research directions. *Frontiers in Psychology, 11*, 611818. https://doi.org/10.3389/fpsyg.2020.611818

Chan, X. W., & Hutchings, K. (2023). Inequalities, barriers, intersectionality, and facilitators of careers of women with disabilities: Themes and future research agenda from a scoping review. *Frontiers in Psychology, 14*, 1104784. https://doi.org/10.3389/fpsyg.2023.1104784

Chatzitheochari, S., & Butler-Rees, A. (2023). Disability, social class and stigma: An intersectional analysis of disabled young people's school experiences. *Sociology, 57*, 1156–1174. https://doi.org/10.1177/00380385221133710

Chatzitheochari, S., & Platt, L. (2019). Disability differentials in educational attainment in England: Primary and secondary effects. *British Journal of Sociology, 70*, 502–525. https://doi.org/10.1111/1468-4446.12372

Cheatham, L. P., & Randolph, K. (2022). Education and employment transitions among young adults with disabilities: Comparisons by disability status, type and severity. *International Journal of Disability, Development and Education, 69*, 467–490. https://doi.org/10.1080/1034912X.2020.1722073

Collins, P. H., & Chepp, V. (2013. [cited 2025 Sept 29]). Intersectionality. In G. Waylen, K. Celis, J. Kantola, & S. L. Weldon (Eds.), *The Oxford handbook of gender and politics [Internet]* (1st ed., pp. 57–87). Oxford University Press. https://doi.org/10.1093/oxfordhb/9780199751457.013.0002

Cook, A. M., Polgar, J. M., & Encarnação, P. (2020. [cited 2025 Sept 30]). *Assistive technologies [Internet]*. Elsevier. https://doi.org/10.1016/C2016-0-02627-X

Dueñas-Zambrana, C., & Cruz-Morato, M. A. (2025. [cited 2025 Sept 29]). The integration of vulnerable populations for inclusive development: Study of disability and gender in Spain. In B. Casais (Ed.), *Integrated science to achieve sustainable development goals [Internet]* (pp. 185–198). Springer Nature Switzerland. https://doi.org/10.1007/978-3-031-88777-2_11

Fisher, S. L., Bonaccio, S., & Connelly, C. E. (2024). AI-based tools in selection: Considering the impact on applicants with disabilities. *Organizational Dynamics, 53*, 101036. https://doi.org/10.1016/j.orgdyn.2024.101036

Flores, L. Y., Settles, I., McGillen, G. G., & Davis, T. M. (2021). Critical contributions to scholarship on women and work: Celebrating 50 years of progress and looking ahead to a new decade. *Journal of Vocational Behavior, 126*, 103490. https://doi.org/10.1016/j.jvb.2020.103490

Frederick, A., & Shifrer, D. (2019). Race and disability: From analogy to intersectionality. *Sociology of Race and Ethnicity, 5*, 200–214. https://doi.org/10.1177/2332649218783480

Garg, S., & Sharma, S. (2020). Impact of artificial intelligence in special need education to promote inclusive pedagogy. *IJIET, 10*, 523–527. https://doi.org/10.18178/ijiet.2020.10.7.1418

Heeks, R. (2022). Digital inequality beyond the digital divide: Conceptualizing adverse digital incorporation in the global South. *Information Technology for Development, 28*, 688–704. https://doi.org/10.1080/02681102.2022.2068492

Hines, E. M., Moore, J. L., Mayes, R. D., Harris, P. C., Vega, D., Robinson, D. V., et al. (2020). Making student achievement a priority: The role of school counselors in turnaround schools. *Urban Education, 55*, 216–237. https://doi.org/10.1177/0042085916685761

Jetha, A., Bonaccio, S., Shamaee, A., Banks, C. G., Bültmann, U., Smith, P. M., et al. (2023). Divided in a digital economy: Understanding disability employment inequities stemming from the application of advanced workplace technologies. *SSM - Qualitative Research in Health, 3*, 100293. https://doi.org/10.1016/j.ssmqr.2023.100293

Kamberidou, I., Bonias, A., & Patsantaras, N. (2019. [cited 2025 Sept 29]). Sport as a means of inclusion and integration for 'those of us with disabilities'. *Zenodo*. https://doi.org/10.5281/ZENODO.3464696

Kharbat, F. F., Alshawabkeh, A., & Woolsey, M. L. (2020). Identifying gaps in using artificial intelligence to support students with intellectual disabilities from education and health perspectives. *AJIM, 73*, 101–128. https://doi.org/10.1108/AJIM-02-2020-0054

Kim, J., & Jeon, M.-S. (2024). Nutrition education programs necessary for social welfare facilities for persons with disabilities: A cross-sectional study. *Korean Journal of Community Nutrition, 29*, 1. https://doi.org/10.5720/kjcn.2024.29.1.1

Knox, J., Wang, Y., & Gallagher, M. (Eds.). (2019. [cited 2025 Sept 30]). *Artificial intelligence and inclusive education: Speculative futures and emerging practices [Internet]*. Springer Singapore. https://doi.org/10.1007/978-981-13-8161-4

Koch Fager, S., Fried-Oken, M., Jakobs, T., & Beukelman, D. R. (2019). New and emerging access technologies for adults with complex communication needs and severe motor impairments: State of the science. *Augmentative and Alternative Communication, 35*, 13–25. https://doi.org/10.1080/07434618.2018.1556730

Koester, H. H., & Mankowski, J. (2015). Automatic adjustment of keyboard settings can enhance typing. *Assistive Technology, 27*, 136–146. https://doi.org/10.1080/10400435.2014.997899

Koester, H., Koch Fager, S., Gormley, J., Jakobs, E., Johnsen, K., & Brumberg, J. (2025). Supporting effective alternative access for individuals with physical disabilities: State of the science, emerging technologies, and future research directions. *Augmentative and Alternative Communication, 41*, 304–317. https://doi.org/10.1080/07434618.2025.2499676

Konrad, A. M. (2021). Access fatigue: The rhetorical work of disability in everyday life. *College English, 83*, 179–199. https://doi.org/10.58680/ce202131093

Krösche, H. (2025. [cited 2025 Sept 29]). Intersectionality and dis/ability—A relationship determination from a history education perspective. In S. Barsch & F. Rein (Eds.), *Think! Historically [Internet]* (pp. 13–24). Universitätsverlag Kiel | Kiel University Publishing. https://doi.org/10.38072/2703-0784/p58

Lipka, O., Forkosh Baruch, A., & Meer, Y. (2019). Academic support model for post-secondary school students with learning disabilities: Student and instructor perceptions. *International Journal of Inclusive Education, 23*, 142–157. https://doi.org/10.1080/13603116.2018.1427151

Llewellyn, G., & Emerson, E. (2021 [cited 2025 Sept 29]). *Audit of disability research in Australia [Internet]* (p. 1397390). University of Melbourne. https://doi.org/10.26188/15153561.V1

Marongedza, L., Hlungwani, P. M., & Hove, P. (2023). Institutional constraints affecting secondary school student performance: A case study of rural communities in Zimbabwe. *Cogent Education, 10*, 2163552. https://doi.org/10.1080/2331186X.2022.2163552

McConkey, R., Kahonde, C., & McKenzie, J. (2016. [cited 2025 Sept 29]). Tackling stigma in developing countries: The key role of families. In K. Scior & S. Werner (Eds.), *Intellectual disability and stigma [Internet]* (pp. 179–194). Palgrave Macmillan UK. https://doi.org/10.1057/978-1-137-52499-7_12

Min, A. (2023). Artificial intelligence and bias: Challenges, implications, and remedies. *JOSR, 2*, 3808–3817. https://doi.org/10.55324/josr.v2i11.1477

Monk, E. P. (2022). Inequality without groups: Contemporary theories of categories, intersectional typicality, and the disaggregation of difference. *Sociological Theory, 40*, 3–27. https://doi.org/10.1177/07352751221076863

Nacheva, R. (2024. [cited 2025 Sept 30]). Hired by artificial intelligence: Digital inclusion practices for people with disabilities. *JUMP [Internet], 8*. https://doi.org/10.32674/66c03968

Noble, S. U. (2020. [cited 2025 Sept 29]). *Algorithms of oppression: How search engines reinforce racism [Internet]*. New York University Press. https://doi.org/10.18574/nyu/9781479833641.001.0001

Noll, A., Owens, L., Smith, R. O., & Schwanke, T. (2006). Survey of state vocational rehabilitation counselor roles and competencies in assistive technology. *WORK: A Journal of Prevention, Assessment & Rehabilitation, 27*, 413–419. https://doi.org/10.3233/WOR-2006-00587

O'Day, B., & Killeen, M. (2002). Research on the lives of persons with disabilities: The emerging importance of qualitative research methodologies. *Journal of Disability Policy Studies, 13*, 9–15. https://doi.org/10.1177/10442073020130010201

O'Rourke, R. H., Knibbe, T. J., McPherson, A. C., Faulkner, G. E., Wright, F. V., & Arbour-Nicitopoulos, K. P. (2025). Developing disability inclusive coaching principles within community recreational sport programming for children. *JSAMS Plus, 6*, 100109. https://doi.org/10.1016/j.jsampl.2025.100109

Omri, A., & Afi, H. (2025. [cited 2025 Sept 30]). Impact of artificial intelligence on employment of people with disabilities: The moderating role of governance quality. *Journal of Disability Research [Internet], 4*. https://doi.org/10.57197/JDR-2025-0007

Peters, S. J. (2022). The challenges of achieving equity within public school gifted and talented programs. *Gifted Child Quarterly, 66*, 82–94. https://doi.org/10.1177/00169862211002535

Rana, M. R. I., McBee-Black, K., & Swazan, I. S. (2024). Adaptive apparel for people with disabilities: A systematic literature review and future research agenda. *International Journal of Consumer Studies, 48*, e13057. https://doi.org/10.1111/ijcs.13057

Rotarou, E. S., Sakellariou, D., & Pizarro-Mena, R. (2025). Satisfaction with health facility personnel among older people with disabilities in Chile: An observational study based on the 2024 DISCA survey. *IJERPH, 22*, 1103. https://doi.org/10.3390/ijerph22071103

Santos, S. B. D. L., Kupczynski, L., & Mundy, M.-A. (2019). Determining academic success in students with disabilities in higher education. *IJHE, 8*, 16. https://doi.org/10.5430/ijhe.v8n2p16

Sedláčková, D., Kantor, J., Belkin, L., Marečková, J., Smrčková, A., Du, J., et al. (2025). The experiences of students with physical disabilities in inclusive education: A qualitative systematic review. *Educational Research Review, 49*, 100715. https://doi.org/10.1016/j.edurev.2025.100715

Shahraki, A. A. (2021). Urban planning for physically disabled people's needs with case studies. *Spatial Information Research, 29*, 173–184. https://doi.org/10.1007/s41324-020-00343-9

Shakespeare, T. (Ed.). (2015. [cited 2025 Sept 29]). *Disability research today [Internet]* (0th ed.). Routledge. https://doi.org/10.4324/9781315796574

Shater, A., AlMahdawi, A. J., & Khasawneh, M. A. S. (2023). The digital learning of disabled students: Perceptions of teachers in public schools. *Information Sciences Letters, 12*, 879–887. https://doi.org/10.18576/isl/120227

Soldatic, K., Lee, M., Tunggal, E., Liao, A., & Magee, L. (2025). Rethinking digital and AI inclusion: Participatory and intersectionality-informed methods for disability and migrant justice. *Frontiers in Sociology, 10*, 1593330. https://doi.org/10.3389/fsoc.2025.1593330

Stone, D. H. (2019). The least restrictive environment for providing education, treatment, and community services for persons with disabilities: Rethinking the concept. *Touro Law Review, 35*, 523.

Stumbo, N. J., Martin, J. K., & Hedrick, B. N. (2009). Assistive technology: Impact on education, employment, and independence of individuals with physical disabilities. *Journal of Vocational Rehabilitation, 30*, 99–110. https://doi.org/10.3233/JVR-2009-0456

Su, T.-T., & Mejía, S. T. (2024). The impact of disability and assistive technology use on well-being in later life: Findings from the National Health and Aging Trends Study. *The Gerontologist, 64*, gnae013. https://doi.org/10.1093/geront/gnae013

Sudharsanan, R., Mishra, A., Barua, B., Rane, P., & Pv, G. (2025). Windows sphere: Multimodal operating system control for disability support using artificial intelligence. *EPJ Web Conferences, 328*, 01039. https://doi.org/10.1051/epjconf/202532801039

Sutko, D. M. (2020). Theorizing femininity in artificial intelligence: A framework for undoing technology's gender troubles. *Cultural Studies, 34*, 567–592. https://doi.org/10.1080/09502386.2019.1671469

Tsamados, A., Aggarwal, N., Cowls, J., Morley, J., Roberts, H., Taddeo, M., et al. (2022). The ethics of algorithms: Key problems and solutions. *AI & Society, 37*, 215–230. https://doi.org/10.1007/s00146-021-01154-8

Watermeyer, B. (2012. [cited 2025 Sept 29]). *Towards a contextual psychology of disablism [Internet]* (0th ed.). Routledge. https://doi.org/10.4324/9780203112762

Xiang, X., Yang, Y., Cheng, J., & An, R. (2021). The impact of late-life disability Spectrum on depressive symptoms: A fixed-effects analysis of panel data. *The Journals of Gerontology, Series B: Psychological Sciences and Social Sciences, 76*, 810–819. https://doi.org/10.1093/geronb/gbaa060

Yahya, R., Jailani, R., Hanapiah, F. A., & Zakaria, N. K. (2024). A scoping review of artificial intelligence-based robot therapy for children with disabilities. *IJEECS, 33*, 1855. https://doi.org/10.11591/ijeecs.v33.i3.pp1855-1865

MIX
Papier aus verantwortungsvollen Quellen
Paper from responsible sources
FSC® C105338

If you have any concerns about our products,
you can contact us on
ProductSafety@springernature.com

In case Publisher is established outside the EU,
the EU authorized representative is:
Springer Nature Customer Service Center GmbH
Europaplatz 3, 69115 Heidelberg, Germany

Printed by Libri Plureos GmbH
in Hamburg, Germany

Time – Space – Places

Dietrich Henckel
Elke Pahl-Weber
Benjamin Herkommer
(eds.)

TIME
SPACE
PLACES

PETER LANG
Frankfurt am Main · Berlin · Bern · Bruxelles · New York · Oxford · Wien

Bibliografische Information der Deutschen Nationalbibliothek
Die Deutsche Nationalbibliothek verzeichnet diese Publikation in der Deutschen Nationalbibliografie; detaillierte bibliografische Daten sind im Internet über <http://www.d-nb.de> abrufbar.

Cover illustration by
courtesy of the editors.

ISBN-10: 3-631-54800-1
ISBN-13: 978-3-631-54800-4
US-ISBN 0-8204-9837-8

Printed in Germany 1 2 3 4 5 7

www.peterlang.de

TABLE OF CONTENT

PREFACE

The world is becoming more and more urbanised. In other words, an increasingly high proportion of the world population is living in cities, and people's life spaces are changing. New technologies, particularly in transport and telecommunications, enable greater freedom of choice between locations, which has induced some authors to question the importance of the city. On the other hand, there are signs that cities that had declined in importance over past decades in favour of surrounding regions are regaining status. There are many indications that the population of cities in the industrial countries, too, is once more increasing, and that cities as loci of knowledge generation are again experiencing an upswing, particularly in high-quality, knowledge-intensive activities. The more the production of information and the development of knowledge become key motors for the economies of developed countries, the more intensive will be the debate on the renaissance of cities.

Such opposing development trends and interpretations of current phenomena were the subject matter of the international conference 'Time Space Places', where experts from different countries and disciplines discussed key aspects of the future development of cities. The concept was the subject of appointment negotiations for the new chairholders Elke Pahl-Weber (1st March 2004) and Dietrich Henckel (15th March 2004) and become part of the appointment agreements with the Technical University Berlin. The University funded the conference and provided the venue. The papers presented by the two chairholders newly appointed to the University were also their public inaugural lectures. We would like to thank the Executive Board of the University for the support they provided and for making the conference possible.

We would also like to extend our thanks to a number of people who contributed to the success of the conference. Grit Podstata bore much of the responsibility for preparation and organisation. Anja Besecke, Mandy Chang, Manuela Graetz, Galene Haun, Benjamin Rütenik, Grete Seels were also involved in implementing the project. Our heartfelt thanks are due to all. Ricarda Römer and Christian Meyer took care of guests from abroad on a tour of Berlin. Many thanks to them, too.

Translation of the German texts and revision of texts by authors whose mother tongues were other than English was entrusted to Rhodes Barrett. We thank him for his cooperation. Editorial work, revision of quotation procedures, and layout were the responsibility of Grit Podstata and Robert Hänsch. Our thanks are also due to them. Last but not least, we extend our thanks to the publishers for making the publication of this volume possible and for their uncomplicated cooperation.

The usual disclaimer: the editors are the due addressees of any criticism of the publication as a whole, its coordination and conception.

Dietrich Henckel, Elke Pahl-Weber and Benjamin Herkommer
Berlin, June 2006

TIME – SPACE – PLACES: INTRODUCTION

by Dietrich Henckel, Benjamin Herkommer and Elke Pahl-Weber,

In both fiction and scientific literature, the city is doubtless among the human inventions that has most frequently been declared obsolescent. Within only half a century, cities appeared to lose the spatial compactness they had maintained for thousands of years, dissolving into an endless sprawl of less and less dense development. The process was driven by steadily declining transport costs and by the steadily increasing speed of transport, by the replacement of rail-bound mass transport by private motorised traffic, and by the growing demand for space concomitant with rising affluence. Cities and their environs turned into agglomerations with urban cores, and some of these urban agglomerations have grown into semi-continuous corridors of cities.

Towards the end of the 20th century, technological revolutions in microelectronics and communications technology inspired some commentators to declare the fate of the city as a way of organising human social life as sealed. The spread of new communications technologies sparked speculation about the far-reaching virtualisation of urban functions: cyberspace instead of city. The anticipated 'death of distance' (Cairncross 1997) – the eclipse of distance as a key factor in the genesis of cities – was expected to lead inevitably to complete spatial ubiquity: work, home, consumption, and recreation would be divorced from any sort of urban context (Mitchell 1995). Moreover, the flexibilisation of time structures which set in with the arrival of flexible specialisation and horizontal integration in the economy began to add a temporal dimension to the fragmentation of urban regions. The city as a phenomenon of spatial and temporal compactness – a thing of the past?

Looking back on the apocalyptic prophecies of the 1990s, it is encouraging to discover that the city is still among the living. The disconsolate vision of its spatial and temporal disintegration has not become reality. However, the vision has not proved entirely misleading. There is indeed a simultaneity of dispersion and concentration, progressive decentralisation of certain urban functions and increasing centralisation of others. Contrary to the expectations of most urbanist literature in the early 1990s, spatial and temporal density as key determinants in urban development are not in the process of dissolving: they are being redefined. The importance of density, centrality, cohesion, and context is changing.

The international conference Time Space Places, which is at the origin of this volume, undertook to trace the course of this redefinition and the new constellations of our urban system.

The title of the volume paraphrases that of a publication by Don Parkes and Nigel Thrift (1980). But the thrust of the present book is quite different. Parkes and Thrift undertook the ambitious task of processing and expanding the entire time geography of the 1970s. The present volume is concerned not with reproducing and modernising the approach but with central categories of future urban development. Placing the concepts time, space, and place in one context signals the high ambitions of the conference in probing the future of the city. Two of these concepts play a key role in the much-discussed work of Manuel Castells (1997) on the network society: the transition from the 'space of places' to the 'space of flows' which he posits announces the declining importance of 'place'. However, the choice of concepts – time, space, places – also indicates an intention to investigate fundamental aspects of future urban development.

Time has been a largely neglected category in space-oriented disciplines and sub-disciplines, even though it has been gaining in importance for some three decades past. As so often, changes in underlying conditions have dissolved constellations long taken for granted and therefore hardly investigated, hence engendering awareness of new scarcities. The dissolution of traditional rhythms and temporal arrangements is attracting increasing attention in modern social research. Similarly, spatial studies have been investigating the time dependence of spatial configurations and the impact of time on spatial structures.

Like time, space, as an abstract category of area availability, is subject to far-reaching changes. Depending on the specific urban situation, there is an extreme shortage of land or a loss of functions producing vacated areas that await reoccupation and offer new potential.

The place as appropriated space filled with identity seems to be losing in importance in the space of flows that knows only ubiquities. But the technologies that provide seeming ubiquity also impose a redefinition of space. Work is changing, spatial and temporal proximity are being reappraised, and competition between locations is being intensified in symbolic form by producing 'brands'.

Setting out from the three concepts in the title: 'time, space, places', the book covers a broad and heterogeneous spectrum, dealing with the general development of the city and its future role and importance. As indicated, the city is exposed to far-reaching changes, varying from region to region in the world and according to the specific conditions prevailing. There are particularly big differences in the extent, course, and conditions of urbanisation between developed and developing countries, between the so-called First and Third Worlds. A detailed treatment of these differences is beyond the scope of this volume, which must restrict itself to analysing cities in the developed world, principally in Western countries. For, although all cities are in principle subject to the same conditions for structural change, varying general economic, social, and institutional settings produce vastly different impacts. Given the considerable differences that exist between Western cities, too, concentrating on this category much facilitates a (comparative) examination.

Discussing structural change in our cities demands not only looking at the past and ascertaining what has changed up to the present day. Future developments must also be addressed. Unceasing societal change requires the continual re-examination of the future of cities, even though it is by no means a new undertaking.

The one-sided view of the future of the city taken in the 1990s, almost complete spatial and temporal dissolution, has given way to a recognition of simultaneous, opposing developments: disintegration and (re-)concentration. Edge cities are developing at exurban transport nodes and former key economic functions are retreating from the city core. Major losses of population in certain cities or urban areas contrast with the reurbanisation of other areas, sometimes the rediscovery of entire inner cities. In many places major urban infrastructures like port facilities, shipyards, railway stations, or even airports have been decommissioned, leaving urban wasteland for years to come. Elsewhere, the same facilities have become agents of urban renaissance, be it through successful conversion or because the infrastructures themselves become new focal points of urbanisation. At the same time, the acceleration of processes and the extension of activity times make the new, urbanised railway stations and airports into places of greater temporal density, of more intensive time use. They contrast with the many neighbourhoods where temporal de-concentration prevails, reflecting both the functional obsolescence of their residents and the superfluity of their time.

This urban change manifested in individual phenomena is caused by a whole range of different conditions and processes:

- the introduction of new technologies, especially 'time-saving' and 'space-shrinking' technologies,
- structural change in industry towards greater knowledge-intensity and a relative decline in the importance of material production,

- changes in societal time structures,
- demographic change due to declining birth rates, ageing of the population, and the heterogenization of the population composition,
- changes in the supply of public goods, especially infrastructure, with an impact on accessibility and its spatial and social distribution,
- increasing spatial and social polarisation,
- changes in the extent and structure of the demand for land,
- changes in locational requirements for business and industry,
- growing internationalisation and globalisation.

To restrict and bundle the vast range of issues, we have categorised contributions under four main headings. Despite varying emphasis, the three concepts time, space, and place run like a thread through all four thematic areas:

- *Temporal Topography of the City.* There are at least three levels of change in urban time structures: broad acceleration processes; the extension of working, operating, and activity times; and the flexibilisation of working and service times. The privatisation and disintegration of urban infrastructures are also generating new forms of urban time landscape. This thematic area addresses the role of the city as a 'time-saving machine', the influence of deregulated infrastructural services on the temporal accessibility of various urban spaces, and differing speeds in the city.
- *Network Cities and New Urban Fringes.* Density is a decisive factor in understanding cities and how they come into being. Meanwhile, density is progressively declining in many core cities while growing on the periphery. Key aspects of this section are the role of density in various parts of the urban region and the implications of the network city concept for our understanding of urban density.
- *Urban Places.* Whereas the loss of identity in inner cities is widely deplored, urbanisation is producing new identities in areas previously considered 'non-places' like transit corridors, transport nodes, and other major infrastructures. On the other hand, many inner cities are staging major improvement processes often charged with more or less authentic identity. This section of the book is accordingly concerned with examining where and how new places are produced with new forms of urbanity and new identities.
- *The Future of the Urban Core.* Finally, attention focuses on trends susceptible to strengthening the cores of urban regions. For a considerable period, core cities were judged to be the obvious losers in urban structural change. But there are signs that economic change, new forms of work, new life styles, and demographic change may mean a come back for cities in the medium term.

This volume addresses key aspects of the future development of urban regions. The contributing authors come from various countries and adopt a variety of perspectives. This inevitably places the stress on issues of development rather than control. If we had wanted to produce a comprehensive treatment of the future of the city, such control issues as government and governance, the financing of cities, or the provision of infrastructure would have had to be dealt with in depth. This would have been beyond the scope of the project, and especially of the conference on which this publication is based.

References

CAIRNCROSS, F. (1997), *The Death of Distance. How the Communications Revolution will Change Our Lives*, Boston

CASTELLS, M. (1997), *The Information Age: Economy, Society and Culture. Volume 1, The Rise of the Network Society*, Oxford, Malden

MITCHELL, W. (1995), *City of bits. Space, Place, and the Infobahn*, Cambridge/Mass.

PARKES, D., THRIFT, N. (1980), *Times, Spaces, Places. A Chronogeographic Perspective*, Chichester

CHAPTER I

THE TEMPORAL TOPOGRAPHY OF THE CITY – URBAN TIMESCAPES

THE TEMPORAL TOPOGRAPHY OF THE CITY – URBAN TIMESCAPES: INTRODUCTION

by Dietrich Henckel, Benjamin Herkommer and Elke Pahl-Weber

The discussion on the relationship between space and time in the city is not altogether new, there is at least some – if little – tradition in the literature. Approaches and perspectives have differed greatly. To name just a few:

- Futurists and early modernists praised the all-embracing acceleration and proclaimed that buildings would not last long, that every generation would build its own new city (Sant' Elia 1914).
- In his seminal work 'Space, Time and Architecture', first published in 1941, Sigfried Giedion celebrated the acceleration of individual movement through urban space that was made possible by modernist urbanism and the proliferation of the automobile. Behind a steering wheel, moving fast through the urban landscape, Giedion discovered a new space-time perception characterised by simultaneity and an unprecedented, intense awareness of space and time.
- In 'What time is this place?' published in 1976, Kevin Lynch was the first to take a temporal approach to questions of urban design. On the one hand, he demonstrated how urban places have different characteristics at different times of day. On the other, Lynch dealt with issues such as how to manage change in the shape of cities and how to connect the traces and images of different historical eras within the physical and aesthetic landscape of the city.

A first wave of intensive investigation into spatio-temporal issues came with the appearance of 'time geography' in the 1970s. Prompted by first indications that Fordism's rigid time patterns were being superseded by new, more flexible work schedules, the spatial consequences of temporal changes became the focus of examination. Attention also began to turn to the implications of steadily growing leisure time and of – paradoxically – increasing concern about tightening time resources caused by the surge of commercial leisure options (Hägerstrand 1970; Linder 1970; Chalendar 1972; Parkes/Thrift 1975; Parkes/Thrift 1980).

The late 1980s and 1990s witnessed increasing interest in time issues, particularly among social scientists. Focus now shifted towards the social conflicts that accompany major changes in societal time patterns. In 'Time Wars' (1987), Jeremy Rifkin analysed how social conflicts over time appear as expressions of temporal changes that go hand in hand historically with periods of major technical, economic and social change.

During the 1990s, the spatio-temporal effects of radical changes in communication and transportation technologies were a predominant issue for studies with a space-time approach. But the temporal perspective remained a scientific niche in urbanist research while in social sciences its importance continued to grow. Time conflicts as analysed by Rifkin received particular attention, but there was a shift in interest from mere analysis to questions of governance and time policy. Italian approaches to urban temporal policy played a very important role. Induced by the women's movement, a regulatory body for time issues was established on the local level, obliging all Italian local authorities to integrate the temporal perspective in public policy (Mareggi 2000).

But despite this development, research on the interaction of space and time in the city is still not very well established. Research on the urban and regional implications of temporal changes has remained a niche pursuit despite the important ramifications of major temporal changes such as acceleration, extension, flexibilisation, and differentiation for the work of urban planners and urban researchers alike. These changes in time structures and time conflicts have a profound impact on the role of the city.

This first section of the volume examines three aspects of spatial and temporal change in cities and city-regions:

- Time and infrastructure networks. Internationalisation and new technical options in operating infrastructures have diminished the importance of natural monopolies and led to the deregulation of infrastructure. Stephen Graham examines the effects on urban time structures of increasing privatisation and the disintegration of infrastructure networks and their spatially selective restructuring and thinning out.
- City and speed. One characteristic of urbanised space has always been a variety of speeds and rhythms differing from one specific area to another. In his contribution, Benjamin Herkommer looks into the meaning of different urban speeds and analyses aspects of fast and slow in the urban context. He concludes with a brief consideration of urban policy issues in the light of increasing polarisation and time conflicts in the city.

- The city as a time and space-saving machine. One purpose of the city has always been to organise the division of labour efficiently. It can therefore be defined as a time and space-saving machine. But how it operates has changed dramatically. In his paper, Dietrich Henckel looks at the function of spatial concentration (building high) and speed and temporal aspects (running fast) for the development of the city. A look into the present and future of this time-space saving function is the focus of the contribution.

All three papers in this section argue that post-Fordist society and the post-Fordist city have seen a fundamental shift in spatio-temporal patterns. In adopting a time-space perspective, the authors thereby contribute to completing the complex analysis of the post-Fordist configuration and condition of urban space. To fully comprehend the scope of change that cities undergo in the evolution of postmodernism, an integrated look at spatial and temporal developments is required in addition to the more conventional approaches of urban sociology, urban economics and urban political science.

References

CHALENDAR, J. de (1972), *Die Neuordnung der Zeit*, Aldingen, Hengstler Fachverlag

GIEDION, S. (1941), *Space, Time and Architecture, The Growth of a New Tradition*, Harvard, Harvard University Press

HÄGERSTRAND, T. (1970): "What about people in regional science?", *Papers of the Regional Science Association*, Vol. 24, p. 7-21

LINDER, S. B. (1970), *The Hurried Leisure Class*, New York, Columbia University Press

LYNCH, K. (1976), *What Time is This Place*, Cambridge/Mass., MIT Press

MAREGGI, M., (2000), *Le politiche temporali urbane in Italia*, Florence, Alinea Editrice

PARKES, D. N., THRIFT, N. (1975), "Timing space and spacing time", *Environment and Planning A*, Vol. 7, p. 651-670

PARKES, D., THRIFT, N. (1980), *Times, Spaces and Places. A Chronogeographic Perspective*, Chichester, New York, John Wiley & Sons

RIFKIN, J., (1987), *Time Wars. The Primary Conflict in Human History*, New York, Simon & Schuster

SANT' ELIA, A. (1914), *L' architettura futurista.* Manifesto, Milan

TEMPORAL ASPECTS OF SPLINTERING URBANISM

by Stephen Graham

Introduction: Cities, Infrastructure, Time-Space

My perspective on urban time and space is very much derived from a fascination with the material infrastructures of the city. The communications, transport, energy, the water systems are at the very heart of what allows modern cities to function. And yet, paradoxically, they are often neglected or ignored by social science as a taken for granted urban background – the 'technical' domain of engineers. My intention of this chapter is to examine how time and space in the networked, globalising cities are actually being socially reco nfigured. I do this by looking at the ways in which the material infrastructures through which the times and spaces of urban life are continually reworked are themselves being reconfigured, as we shift away from the emphasis on monopolistic provision and Keynesian modes of management of public infrastructure, towards a much more fractured and splintered world – to adopt the language of the book I wrote with Simon Marvin (2001). This chapter will spotlight how the temporal aspects of what we have called splintering urbanism might be understood. It will also raise some questions about how the politics of infrastructure might map onto the politics of time-space in the city. I use this word 'time-space' because it is very difficult to talk about space and time separately when you are looking at the ways in which network systems reconfigure both simultaneously, in mutually constitutive ways.

Traditionally, cities developed to help overcome time constraints by minimising space constraints. By concentrating multiple activities within a spatially confined area, interactions of various sorts become possible which would be much more problematic if that area was stretched across a much larger geographical zone. In a way, however, network technologies have the opposite function. They overcome space constraints by minimising time constraints. With the advent of near real-time electronic communications, for example, one can Email someone in Australia as instantly as one can someone in the next room. It follows that it is necessary to adopt a parallel perspective of the mutual constitution of urban spaces and networked technologies, to start to grapple with how times and spaces are being remade within globalizing, networked cities. It is necessary to stress this point because, very often, urban social science has treated urban infrastructure separately from reconfigurations of the city.

1. Beyond Totalizing Discourses

Once you start with such a perspective it becomes apparent that many of the debates, particularly in the last thirty years, about how new technologies might 'impact' upon cities have actually been very unhelpful. Very often, globalization discourses, especially in the media and business press, have rested on some a priori assumption that 'globalization' entails a generalised shift towards some sort of compressed, speeded-up, accelerated world. There has also been far too much reliance on big, meta-level metaphors like the 'networked society' and a widespread recourse to the idea that new networked technologies like the Internet somehow remake the fabric of cities through generalised technological 'impacts' which somehow derive from the intrinsic logics of the technology for transcending spatial barriers through speeding up flow. However, this concept of 'impact' is highly problematic because it suggests that cities and the social agents that shape urban spatiality are somehow passive and that technologies come into the social domain from some outside space, as if from outer space in fact, to smash into cities, as meteors might do with a planet.

Such deterministic, generalistic and totalizing readings of the relations between cities and flow provide a very unhelpful conceptual framework for understanding how technologies are actually socially configured and shaped in places within very particular social conditions. So, whilst such perspectives may help illuminate some parts of the debate, I would argue that ideas about 'time-space compression' (Harvey 1989), for example, need to be treated with care because they by no means describe all of the aspects of new technology used in cities. Similarly, Castells' (1996) ideas of the 'space of flow' as almost overpowering the 'space of places' can be criticized because it separates the two realms so absolutely. Arguably, cities have always been about flow and connection. It is not particularly new that we all have multiple net-work connections reaching out to many geographical scales in our daily lives and economic lives. Admittedly, these configurations are deepening and accelerating. But to separate some local realm of authentic places from some externalised domain of accelerating technological flow is, I would argue, an unhelpful theoretical starting point which misses the ways in which transnational economic, social and cultural systems are enacted through myriads of practices, flows and connectivities which simultaneously involve shifts in the practices and places of everyday urban life.

Similarly, the French urban philosopher Paul Virilio repeatedly stresses what he sees as the generalised collapse of the meaning of urban place and space, and the general-ised destruction of a traditional idea of the city, through what he calls the 'generalized arrival' caused by the almost infinite transnational speeds and connectivities sustained by electronic technologies. To Virilio (1993), "the city of the past slowly becomes a paradoxical agglomeration in which relations of immediate proximity give way to relationships over distance".

However, by overemphasising the deterministic power of external technological networks impacting on, and remaking, 'local' urban places, Virilio abandons any notion of the richness of urban place or of the ways in which the 'local' and everyday prac-tices of urban life are heavily involved in remaking the rhythms, landscapes and what Doreen Massey has called 'power geometries' of transnational capitalism, as new networked technologies are socially enrolled in a myriad of ways to connect urban places and sites with more of less distant elsewheres. Moreover, Virilio's totalising reading of the relations between networked technologies and urban life are one dimensional. They give no space for social constructions of flow and infrastructure which might add meaning to local interactions and local places. Such readings thus give very little space for the contingent social shaping of technologies. If you think about it, an Internet computer can be used for hundreds or thousands of different applications, all of which might have different implications for time space mobility, flows, materiality, local places, and so on. By maintaining top-down perspectives of the links between globalisation and urban change, within which the 'global' is seen as some techno-economic steamroller riding over 'local' places, the contingent enaction of new urban timespaces which simultaneously involve many scales of interaction – from the body to the globe – are overlooked. This is an inevitable problem when one adopts a binary and static binary perspective of geographical scale. The 'virtual' domains of electronic interaction are always seen 'out there,' separate from the body, the book, the city, the materiality of the city, whereas actually that perspective misses a lot of the subtle interdependence between new communications technologies and urban practices. And arguably, one of the biggest problems here is that these perspectives miss the crucial role of cities in shaping technologies. In overwhelmingly stressing how technologies might reshape cities, we forget that it is in cities that these innovations are actually shaped to have meaning, in very dif ferent ways, in very different places.

2. Remediating Urban Time-Space

I would argue that one really useful perspective which allows us to sidestep all of those problems derives from the work of Bolter and Grusin in their media theory book Remediation (1999). Their concept of remediation usefully destroys all of those over-familiar binary dichotomies like virtual and real, material and online, online and offline, and so on, which, it is increasingly clear, so inhibited an understanding of contemporary urban change. Instead, Bolter and Grusin suggest that 'cyberspace', rather than being some virtual world existing separately from the 'real' world, is actually very much part of our contemporary world. And they argue that it is constituted through what they call a series of 'remediations'. New technologies, for example, subtly shift the way in which telephones work, which have been going on for over 150 years. As virtual reality, they shift how newspapers, television and film work. Film and television, newspapers, telephones, streets, and constructed urban spaces have not gone away with the growth of computer networks, virtual reality and so on. Rather, they are being remediated. They have altered their time-space-arrangements as new electronic connectivities are subtly combined with, and superimposed upon, the older forms and practices. The UK Guardian is now perhaps the most widely read left-leaning newspaper in North America. This does not mean that newspapers die, or that hard copy necessarily

Figure 1. Electrification in Pennsylvania and Maryland, 1900-1930.

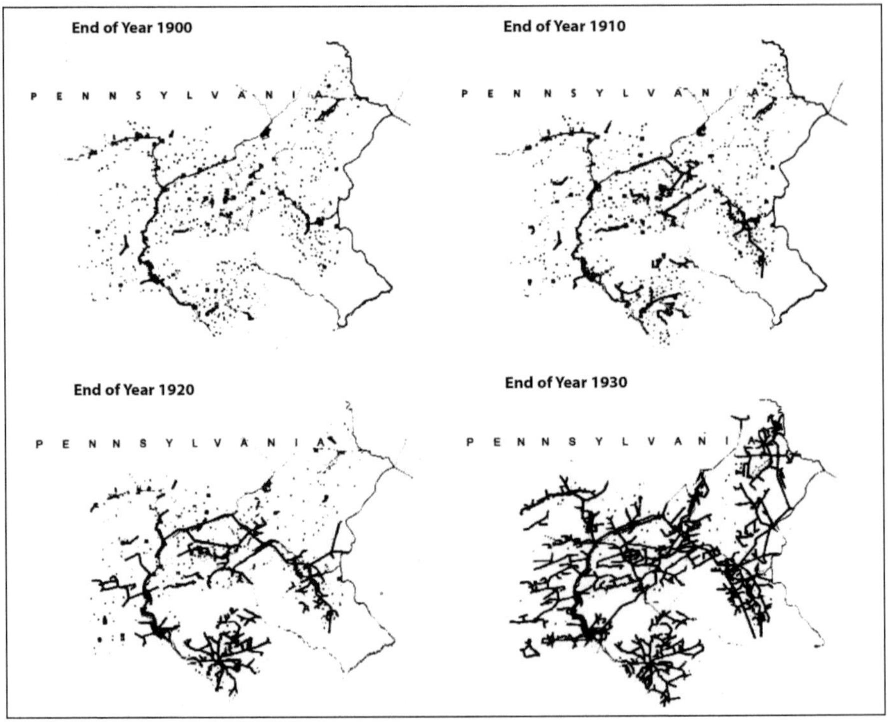

Source: Hughes 1983:10-13

disappears. Rather, newspapers become remediated; they become enacted locally and globally, and electronically and materially, at the same time.

Urban streets, meanwhile, are now being remediated and re-enacted through all sorts of electronic communication; countless more or less distant elsewheres continually erupt within urban public space and urban public transport spaces. This does not mean that such domains cease to have meaning, importance or power as central domains of urban life. Far from it: most people do not stay at home, online, bunkering themselves in the virtual reality caves and fortressed pods of countless urban dystopias or futurist imaginations. Rather, their physical tracings and nomadic patterns of movement within and between cities become animated, facilitated, and sometimes enriched and extended, by a bewildering array of continuous and flexible electronic devices and connectivities. This means that people, social groups, social movements and so on use mobile phones and PDA's to actually reshape streets, to reshape how they use streets, and to remediate the meanings and functions of urban space and place.

This perspective really helps because it shows how the urban aspects of technologies are very fine-grained and they are very much shaped in partnership with new uses of technology. Rather than being separated in a binary way, urban practices and techno-logical practices increasingly merge into a seamless and inseparable whole. Under-standing the social construction of new urban practices, and space times, without ad-dressing the simultaneous enaction of new networked flows and connectivities becomes impossible, and vice versa. In a way, as McKenzie Wark (1998) suggests then, the city is not totally overwhelmed by a speeding-up process; rather, it becomes what he calls a 'gearbox, full of speeds', juxtaposing multiple velocities and connectivities to more or less distant elsewheres within the fine-grained and banal practices of everyday urban life. Such multiple speeds and connectivities, which are always politically contested, clash together in the reformation of urban processes, imaginaries, and landscapes.

3. Urban Remediation and Splintering Urbanism

My work with Simon Marvin suggests that many contemporary urban remediations are pushing us towards what we have called 'splintering urbanism'.

We argue in the book 'Splintering Urbanism' that the relationship between infrastructures and cities is going through a fundamental shift at the moment. We argue that, in general late 19th and most of the 20th century, especially within western cities, urban-infrastructural relations were dominated by efforts to build monopolistic infrastructures to systematically integrate cities, city regions, and nations as unitary spaces. Think of the classic gas, electricity, telephone monopolies, the street monopolies and the transport monopolies of cities during this period. Hand in hand with this process, cities and national states developed what we have called the modern infrastructural ideal. This was very much embedded in the elaboration of Fordist societies, of Keynesian modes of governance and in the efforts to try and nurture developmental states in the Global South. Melvin Webber captures how this idea was constructed within the urban discipline with this concept of the 'unitary city'.

And the ideology of modern urban planning during this period was dominated by this idea of shaping the city as a unitary object through monopolistic orchestrations of infrastructure. This was based on using monopolies, cross-subsidies, and regulatory devices like universal service obligations, to try and constitute coherently integrated and unitary cities. There was often a very strong sense of social welfare and justice underpinning the ideology of infrastructure development, planning and urban politics. It has to be said that in reality this notion of an egalitarian network city was very rarely, if ever, actually achieved.

What we suggest in 'Splintering Urbanism' is that whilst this mode of development is not being abandoned completely, it is under very severe pressure. We witness very common processes of privatisation and liberalisation and the application of new technologies to turn public infrastructural goods into private infrastructural commodities through new electronically organised access control and surveillance systems. In many cities, especially those where neoliberal modes of governance have been embraced most fully (as in the UK, for example), there are often now multiple, privatised, and competitive commercial plazas, malls, and Business Improvement District street systems, or multiple governance and provision systems for energy, telecommunications, transportation and urban spaces. There is a pervasive sense of sprawl, peripheralisation, fracturing and fragmentation, which is partly due to the proliferation of different infrastructure systems in different parts of cities. Crucially, these systems selectively connect only valued nodes and spaces bypassing intervening territories. Very commonly we have efforts to build high-quality infrastructures or street systems or energy systems for premium and highly valued users and spaces which make the old monopolies increasingly problematic and even untenable as they are starved of new investment, or are left with rump of less profitable users or territories as those who can migrate to the new, splintered spaces and systems. Through their complex and uneven geographies of urban remediation, these complex patchworks of local, interurban and global infrastructure also bring into being new time-space configurations in cities.

4. Multiplex Urbanism

I think, broadly speaking, what we are seeing is that, whilst mobilities might accelerate for certain groups in the city, who have access to high-quality communications, transport or urban street systems, it is by no means a universal experience. And this is why many of the generalised accounts have failed. Often, valued and affluent spaces and users of the city do have very intense access to communications. Think of the WiFi bubbles and optic-fibre grids in the city; university broadband systems as well are an excellent example here. However, that by no means implies that these experiences of time-space compression and acceleration are generalised. Often, people in more marginal positions may actually have worsening connectivities, at least in relative terms, as general universal service obligations and modern infrastructural monopolies are withdrawn or undermined, service qualities deteriorate, cross-subsidies are withdrawn or charges rise to 'market' levels. One of the French geographer, François Ascher's, important arguments is that we witness what he calls 'tunnel effects' for premium users by new infrastructures bypassing time and space to link together across global areas. The result is a sort of archipelago economy of cities where high quality infrastructure is configured only to connect valued economic and social enclaves within and between urban areas. This is why discussions of urban splintering must adopt a flexible approach to the telescoping of spatial scale as new connectivities emerge at the interurban or transnational scale which simultaneously involve shifts in the fabric and geography of 'local' urban life (Figure 2).

Of course these enclaves and these premium infrastructures are actually configured within rapidly sprawling urban environments that constitute patchwork urban landscapes, and urbanised rural spaces, where the breakdown of urban-rural binaries becomes a dominant feature. The above part of the diagram below shows a model of the traditional European city with a rather simple, diurnal, commuting pattern and a dominant, central, core. In the second part of the diagram this traditional European City has

Figure 2. Schematic representation of 'hub and spoke' infrastructure networks which use 'tunnel effects' to traverse non-valued territory.

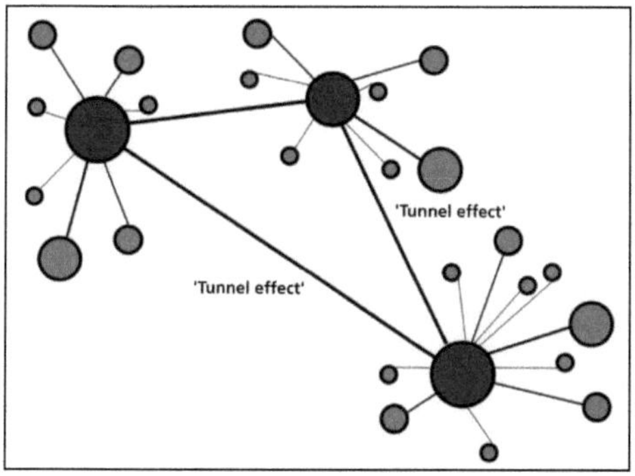

Source: Graham/Marvin 1996:59

Figure 3. Transoceanic fibre-optic networks connecting the 'global archipelago economy'.

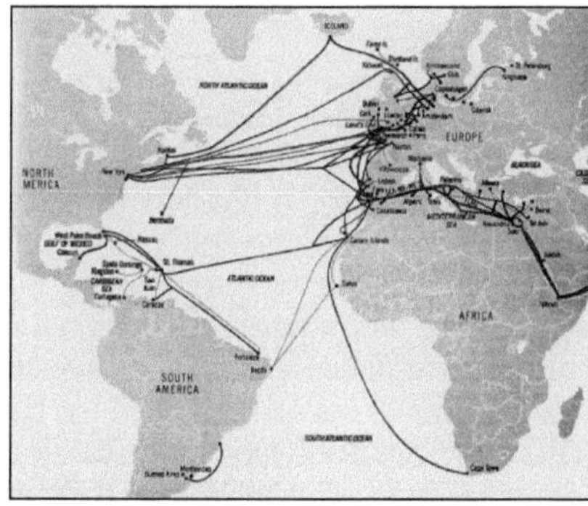

Source: Vedel 1997:34

Figure 4. Model development of city regions from a uniplex metropolis (left) to a multiplex urban region (right).

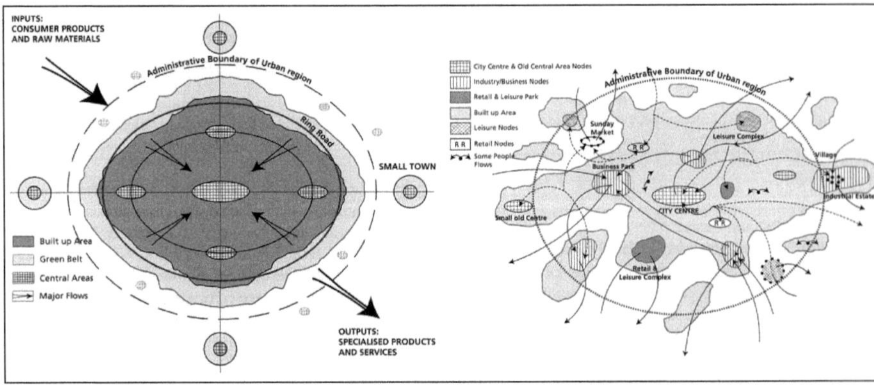

Source: Author's diagrams (after Patsy Healy)

sprawled into an urban region with multiple centres, multiple fractured infrastructures in many cases, multiple growth poles and leisure and consumption spaces, and corridors sustaining transnational connectivities and flows etc. And each of those has different configurations of infrastructure and different experiences of time.

5. Bypass as Remediation

Broadly speaking there are three types of splintering urbanism which are particularly relevant to discussions about time.

5.1 Glocal Bypass

First, there are logics of infrastructural bypasses that we called 'glocal bypass'. These are systems which link local sites across global space and thus do much to help constitute the transnational urban architectures of neoliberal capitalism.

As an example one may look at the many private optic-fibre grids which cross the oceans of the world to sustain informational capitalism. During the age of national telecommunications monopolies, transoceanic phone cables would have stopped at the edge of national borders and then the traffic would have gone through national monopoly systems to reach key local businesses in cities. But today the fibre infrastructures go directly from the desk of a stock market trader in the city of London to the desk of a stock market trader in New York. They bypass national space and the respective borders almost completely and are configured with classic 'glocal' logics which simultaneously remake both local and global geographies of connection and disconnection.

On the urban scale there are at the same time a whole load of new private optic-fibre grids which are only being built in the cores of key 'global' cities like London. Figure 5 shows London City's autonomous optic-fibre network built by a company called COLT. It is basically confined to the very core of London's key producer service and global finance and corporate head office areas – the most profitable parts of the market of central London with a little string down to Docklands. At the same time, however, the COLT network, and many others like it which concentrate in similar ways, connect directly to transnational networks which in turn lead to 'fibre to the desk' connections in similar global city cores around the world. Thus the archipelago geographies of neoliberal capitalism are directly reflected in archipelago materialities of premium connectivity and flow, which bypass urban, national, and transnational intervening spaces. This illustrates how very local the new 'global' networks are and how very powerful remediations often have startlingly 'local' urban geographies. This is not a process of urban evisceration: London is growing faster than at any time in the last 50 years. Rather, it is a process through which the necessary urban centrality of global cities is enhanced at the same time as very partial remediations of global connectivity are configured very specifically for the most valued and profitable core markets, whilst excluding even urban districts a few hundred metres outside, which suffer the indignities of not being nodal points on premium electronic circuits.

Figure 5. The COLT fibre-optic network in the City of London, 1998.

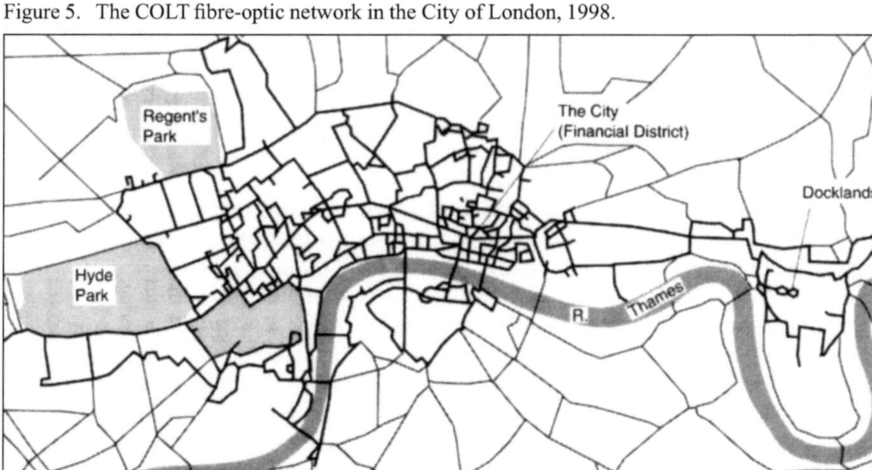

Source: Colt Telecom 1998

Interestingly, then, as global cities like the City of London 'reach out' across transnational corridors and connections, there is also a palpable sense of local fragmentation within the fine-grain geographies of urban life. This applies to other infrastructural domains to communications technology well.

Figure 6. Surveillance Cameras in Central London.

Source: Author's Photograph

For example, the street systems into the City of London have automatic CCTV cam-eras, anti-terror surveillance systems, road closures and more and more walls or bar-ricades (figure 6). Paradoxically, then, processes of global connection and local disconnection are being combined in London's financial core.

The articulation of air travel networks and urban centres is another very interesting example of this sort of 'glocal' bypass. Aircraft systems, in effect, are exemplar time-space tunnels. In addition, new, high-quality rail systems are increasingly being constructed as glocal bypass networks which link airport complexes directly to highly valued parts of city cores, whilst bypassing intervening territories (or, at least, not allowing network access through them). The tunnel effect of air travel is thus prolonged into the very hearts of the cities connected, to selectively minimise time space distances, and distribute the global accessibilities and connectivities of airports through premium rail to city cores. A good example of this is the Heathrow Express system. One of a very small number of new rail infrastructures in the UK, this links, built by the private British Airports Authority, connects Heathrow direct to central London (and, in the future, possibly to the financial core, too). But it offers no network access to intervening parts of west London.

Such bypass architectures increasingly involve remediations of human bodies in their reconfigurations of glocal time space. Many emerging immigration control systems, for example, are organized using biometric scanning and tracking systems. The 'Privium' system at Amsterdam's Schipol airport is a good example. These allow valued, premium, business travellers to bypass the often-intensifying scrutiny of national borders by having their irises, faces or palms scanned at special access points adjacent to normal passport control. Valued users are allowed to bypass immigration while at the same time, people under scrutiny, the immigrants and the mobile people who's mobility is deemed illegitimate or malign (asylum seekers, 'illegal' migrants), become more and more held back at borders. So again, such logics are determinedly not about time space compression for everybody; they are about certain bypass configurations that privilege and enhance mobilities and connectivities deemed legitimate whilst undermining those labelled malign, threatening, or simply unprofitable.

5.2 Local Bypass

Secondly, we look at what we call 'local bypass'. Here, parts of cities are actually bypassed by new infrastructures as in the case of the private, tolled highway, Highway 407 ETR (Express Toll Route), that goes around the northern edge of Toronto. One of many emerging private and fully commodified electronically organised highway corridors emerging across the world, 407 is a new highway that parallels the old fairly congested public highway. Access restriction is organised through new technology obliging users of the highway to pay for it each time they use it. For surveillance purposes, each car has to have a small radio transponder. The road, in effect, provides guarantees of free traffic flow for paying customers, and ultimately buys them time. Users literally buy time by using such local bypass networks.

Similar local bypass highways exist in Melbourne/LA, San Diego and Manila. All are developed through private capital. They become a sort of de facto highway sys-tem for the city. Often, as in Melbourne, they generate new rounds of urban sprawl because subscribers are suddenly able to cover bigger spatial distances in the same amounts of time. Some of these systems are experimenting with realtime pricing. In-stead of just paying, say, five dollars to use the system, the price of accessing the system will actually vary in real time depending on how busy the traffic is. This will enable developers to literally guarantee for free traffic flow, no matter how bad sur-rounding congestion is on public road systems. In case there is a vague hint of congestion, prices simply go up, discouraging some drivers to decide not to access the system.

Figure 7. From open gridded street systems (left) to laddered street systems (right) where every destination has an exclusive highway entrance/exit.

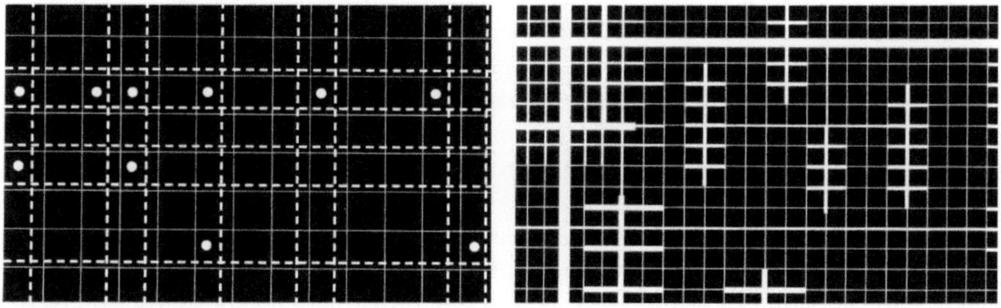

Source: Pope 1996:60,94

Figure 8. The Fashion Island mall developed by the Jerde Partnership in Newport Beach, California.

Source: Jerde Partnership International 1999:82

Car culture in general is an important area to look at in terms of the remediation of urban time and space. On a larger scale we have urban sprawl bringing about road networks which increasingly form what Albert Pope has called 'ladders' and thus change away from the old grid systems of central cities to roads that actually end, capillary-like, at a single, suburban point (figure 7). On a smaller scale, the increasing capsulelike nature of cars furthers the alteration of the whole fabric of cities. With more and more services on the inside of cars, automobility itself is being remediated. Car capsules are not just dead spaces anymore. If you are in a traffic queue, increasingly the car is full of things to do. Nor is such time 'dead' time anymore. Most cars provide equipment for mobile phones; some of them have Email, DVD players and other entertainment and communication devices.

Other examples of local bypass are more urban. The shift towards skywalk cities, where privatised streets and tunnel systems erupt within, through and above traditional city cores (as in Houston) is being paralleled by the growth of master planned malls and city-scale leisure resorts (figure 8). Gated communities, whilst not completely new, are a dominant mode of housing development in many parts of the world these days. In all of these cases, one of the main commodities in the trade is the separation between the more public environment outside and the usually privileged gated space inside, accessible only via controlled entry points.

5.3 Virtual Network Competition

A third type of bypass involves what we term 'virtual network competition'. Moderated by state legislation and monitored by the respective regulating institutions, previously monopolistic systems are now again a source of competition. In the case of electricity supply in the UK, the average customer has to think: How on earth can I have electricity from forty different companies when I have only got one wire coming to my house? There is only really one trunk system. But new technology allows a single system to offer many competing services. More than that, it allows people to actually understand the market much more and to tailor what they do based on surveillance of the market.

A more worrying example is the case of call centres. All over Europe call centres deliver a growing universe of services with many of the service providers actually located in Africa and India these days. Call centres are a major part of the global outsourcing movement. On the one hand, this implies new time configurations for employees who are increasingly staying up in the middle of the night to phone and deal with Western consumers. Some call centres, however, can actually detect the phone number that customers are calling with. They can detect who is calling and then queue people differently based on judgments about how profitable they are. A person living in a wealthy part of a city in Europe might actually be answered quickly whilst a person living in a less wealthy part of a city might be queued. This sort of splintering logic is a much more subtle process than watching people with transponders on their cars driving on a new private highway. In this example, the real and relative accelerations and decelerations are fairly visible and corporeal. But the crucial fact about these new techniques of call centres is that they remain totally invisible to the people who's mobilities, connectivities and temporal lives are shaped by them. If a user is being answered straight away, they are not going to know that there are other people being queued for longer, and vice versa.

Such a logic, which I term the software-sorting of urban time-space, is thus rendered almost completely opaque, stretched out as it is within and through the logics of transnational flow. Similarly, there is evidence that the flows of data packets on the Internet are themsleves being prioritised by algorithms designed by private network operators to allow more profitable services and users to maintain high service standards whilst actively decelerating or even stopping those packets and users deemed to be unprofitable or somehow parasitic on the increasingly market and e-commerce driven infrastructure networks that sustain Internet traffic. Importantly, such soft-ware-sorting of mobility and service rights in call centres and electronic service systems are being superimposed on the more familiar processes through which certain parts of cities are electronically 'red-lined' by insurance companies, mail order and e-commerce companies, and financial and retail service providers, so that they are unable to access services.

6. Conclusions: Opening Black Boxes

This chapter has argued that critical analyses of the changing time-spaces of urban life must move beyond generalised discussions suggesting that urban life is being revolutionised en masse through some all-encompassing new round of time-space compression, based on the infrastructural architectures of globalisation 'impacting' urban life. Instead, such research needs to get into the minute configurations and infrastructural architectures of emerging mobility, communications and surveillance systems. This is necessary to expose how these systems are socially produced and configured to produce the diverse urban time-spaces which characterise splintering urbanism. It is those systems that increasingly structure how people experience time and space, as they act as such electronically-mediated infrastructure, logistics, service and media systems act as what sociologists of technology call 'obligatory passage points' mediating and managing access to essential private, public and mobility systems. As part of their remediating effects on the politics of urban space and place, the configurations of the smart highways, of the call centre systems, of the increasingly market-driven Internet, and of a wider universe of electronic service systems, actually do prioritise certain flows, certain people's access whilst actively inhibiting all others.

The language of a general impact of technology on the city within an overall logic of globalisation and society is therefore profoundly unhelpful. One's position in relation to the new mobility systems depends on how one is ranked within the software code that acts as the access control to the right to the city with increasing degrees of auto-mation. Therefore, a person's experience of time and space might be very much con-tingent, based on these sorts of systems and their specific forms of judgments.

All this raises major questions about the changing politics of urban life. Relatively or absolutely, who's speeded up and who isn't? Who shapes the code that mediates and prioritises traffic and flow and what is the geography of such a code? Are such prioritisations visible or are they opaque – the result of the operation of a hidden background of geographically-stretched technological assemblages themselves operating at increasingly transnational scales? And what points of resistance exist through which social activism or social movements might change bring their influence to bear is changing the politics of remediating cities?

Clearly, the pervasive ideology implying that everybody might enjoy liberating ex-periences of new technology is undermined by the proliferation of the various reme-diated infrastructure, mobility and service systems discussed in this chapter. We thus need much more sophisticated research approaches to look at how the social produc-tion of diverse, contingent, times and spaces are locked into what Doreen Massey has called the 'power geometry' through which certain people's activities and spaces and interests become the dominant priority, within the overall network architectures of neoliberal architectures.

Importantly, however, resistance to the logics of splintering and remediating urban-ism is not just emerging from social movements and people and places experiencing new forms of networked marginalisation. Many capitalist firms themselves are increasingly worried about these new modes of infrastructure development. There are many classic market failures. In Queensland, Australia for example, chambers of commerce have asked the government to go back to a tax-and-spend approach to the generalised provision of Keynesian-style infrastructure. This is because the prevalent landscapes of splintered infrastructure in Queensland means that these firms are struggling to get their goods to market efficiently and speedily; they cannot get their workers to the actual workplace; and they are being hampered in their efforts to compete through the just-in-time orchestration of their supply chains. Perhaps the market failures and contradictions of splintering infrastructures – one of the main contradictions of transnational neoliberal capitalism – will, ultimately, lead to a resurgence of monopolistic, egalitarian and universalist infrastructure regimes?

References

BOLTER, J., GRUSIN, R. (1999), *Remediation: Understanding New Media*, Cambridge/Ma., MIT Press

CASTELLS, M. (1996), *The Rise of the Network Society*, Oxford, Blackwell

COLT TELECOM (1998), *The colt fibre-optic network in the City of London*, www.colt-telecom.com/english/countries/uk/mn_technology.html

GRAHAM, S., MARVIN, S. (1996), *Telecommunications an the City: electronic Spaces, Urban Places*, London, Routledge

GRAHAM, S., MARVIN, S. (2000), *Splintering Urbanism: Networked Infrastructures, Technological Mobilities and the Urban Condition*, London, Routledge

HARVEY, D. (1989), *The Condition of Postmodernity*, Oxfrod, Blackwell

HEATHROW EXPRESS (2005), *Porduct Brochure*

HUGHES, T. (1983), *Networks of Power: Electrification of Western Society 1880-1930*, London, Baltimore/MD, John Hopkins University Press

JERDE PARTNERSHIP INTERNATIONAL (1999), *You are Here*, London, Phaidon, p.82

POPE, A. (1996), *Ladders*, New York, Princeton Architectural Press

VEDEL, T. (1997), "The ecology of games", *Trends in Communication*, no. 3, p. 34-45

VIRILIO, P. (1993), "The third interval: a critical transition", in: Andermatt-Conley, V. (ed.), *Rethinking Technologies*, London, University of Minnesota Press, p. 3-10

WARK, M. (1998), "On technological time, Virilio's overexposed city", *Arena*, Vol. 83, p. 1-21

SLOW CITY – FAST CITY
AN EXPLORATION INTO URBAN SPEED

by Benjamin Herkommer

Introduction: What is Urban Speed Made of?

Urban speed as such is an almost unexplored subject, yet – some, albeit little research has been done on the question of 'time and the city'. This paper reviews some of the initial moves towards investigating urban speed and takes a look at some of the research investigating 'time and the city'. Some sections of the paper are more in the way of a preview of research I would like to conduct rather than a presentation of results already achieved.

In physics, speed is defined as the rate of change of position, the distance travelled per unit of time. Speed is how we measure movement and movement is what makes us feel the interrelation of time and space. Talking about speed and the city thus primarily evokes associations of movement in space, of traffic, transportation and infrastructure.

Research has also been done on the pace of life, which has been defined as the "relative rapidity or density of experiences, meanings, perceptions and activities" (Werner/Altman/Oxley 1985:14). To explore what could be understood as urban speed we must investigate the interrelation of movement in space with the pace of life and the factors that determine it. We must ask "what drives a city to make it move fast or slow"? This also means entering the complexity of cities' 'personalities' and how we experience them. If we ask "What speed is this place?" we need to look at a number of factors influencing how we experience the speed of a city:

- The speed of pedestrians, people hurrying and people strolling;
- People resting in parks or cafés and other images of calm and relaxation;
- Incessancy: persistence of activity in the streets, opening hours, people working late or on weekends, round-the-clock public transport;

- Access to high speed transport infrastructure, frequency and speed of public transport connections;
- The intensity and constancy of the urban white noise, largely resulting from traffic;
- Frequent changes in the physical city-structure, new buildings and new attractions;
- Visibility of the rhythms of nature.

In the following section, these components of urban speed are considered in the light of recent empirical evidence suggesting that there are differences in the speed of cities. Which city is the fastest might seem a rather trivial subject for research, since some people prefer to live at a fast pace while others like to take their time and prefer slow places. But there is more to it than that. I will be returning to this point in the conclusions of this paper.

1. Differences in Urban Speed

1.1 Empirical Research

In his 1997 book 'A Geography of Time', Robert Levine presents a study of the pace of life in big cities in 31 different countries. From the literature he reviewed, Levine drew up general assumptions about the factors influencing urban speed and proposed the following set of rules:

- Economic performance: the economy of a city has the strongest influence on its speed. The better the economic performance of a city the faster its pace of life will be. Where people earn high wages, time is precious.
- Degree of industrialisation: the more a country and its city regions are industrialised the less free time their citizens have.
- Size: bigger cities have a higher tempo than smaller ones.
- Climate: places with a hot climate tend to have a slower pace of life.
- Cultural values: individualised cultures move faster than cultures with collectivist values.

To measure urban speed – this experimental procedure then produced the ranking, which is shown in Table 1 –, Levine used three main indicators to show where time is particularly precious and thus most accurately measured and most efficiently used: walking speed, speed at work and accuracy of public clocks.

- Levine and his assistants recorded the time it took randomly chosen pedestrians to walk 20 meters in a bigger inner city street.
- As an example for speed at work he recorded the time it took clerks at a post office to hand out a standard stamp and to return the change.

- To measure the accuracy of public clocks, 15 randomly selected clocks attached to the buildings of banks were compared with the official time.

I will not discuss these results in detail, although they are debatable to say the least. It is questionable whether the speed of post clerks in Paris and New York can be representative of what constitutes the speed of these two centres of the global financial market.

Table 1. Speed Indices of Big Cities in 31 Countries.

City, Country	Overall rank	Walking speed	Speed at work	Accuracy of clocks
Bern, Zurich; Switzerland	1	3	2	1
Dublin, Ireland	2	1	3	11
Frankfurt, Germany	3	5	1	8
Tokyo, Japan	4	7	4	6
Rome, Italy	5	10	12	2
London, England	6	4	9	13
Stockholm, Sweden	7	13	5	7
Vienna, Austria	8	23	8	3
Amsterdam, Netherlands	9	2	14	25
Hong Kong	10	14	6	14
Paris, France	11	8	18	10
Warsaw, Lodz, Poznan; Poland	12	12	15	8
San José, Costa Rica	13	16	10	15
Taipei, Taiwan	14	18	7	21
Singapore	15	25	11	4
New York, USA	16	6	23	20
Toronto, Canada	17	11	21	22
Seoul, South Korea	18	20	20	16
Budapest, Hungary	19	19	19	18
Prague, Czech Republic	20	21	17	23
Athens, Greece	21	14	13	29
Nairobi, Kenya	22	9	30	24
Guanzhou, China	23	24	25	12
Sofia, Bulgaria	24	27	22	17
Bucharest, Romania	25	30	29	5
Amman, Jordan	26	28	27	19
Damascus, Syria	27	29	28	27
San Salvador, El Salvador	28	22	16	31
Rio de Janeiro, Brazil	29	31	24	28
Djakarta, Indonesia	30	26	26	30
Mexico City, Mexico	31	17	31	26

Source: Levine 1997:180

The merit of Levine's work may lie not so much in the concrete results of his experiments, but we can learn a lot from his general assumptions and his comments on the time-space-arrangements of certain cities. For instance, he admits the limitations of his experiments when commenting on a similar study he conducted on 36 American cities. The big cities in the northeast like Boston, Buffalo and New York ranked first while those in Southern California like San Jose, Sacramento and Los Angeles ranked last. Referring to his experiments in Los Angeles Levine commented that they hardly found any pedestrians at all to measure walking speed. Since Los Angeles is the number one example for car dependency among urban planners around the globe, his results on walking speed are more or less systematically invalid. Levine found people walking only in pedestrianised shopping centres where people arrive by car and then stroll from store to store. Levine quotes Joan Didion, who once concluded that the only form of secular community in Los Angeles was to drive down the highway (Levine 1997:203).

Figure 1. High Occupancy Vehicle Lane.

Source: Honda 2006

Unfortunately, Levine does not further investigate the consequences this has for the question of speed in Los Angeles. Time is perhaps more precious there than Levine's results would suggest. An indication is given by California's efforts to manage traffic on the innumerable highways in the Greater Los Angeles Region. During the 1990s, additional lanes where added but reserved for vehicles with more than one person riding. By the end of 2004, these so called 'high occupancy vehicle lanes' (HOV-lanes) or 'carpool lanes' covered 1,236 lane miles in California, 832 of which are situated in the metropolitan area of Los Angeles (Los Angeles and four neighbouring counties). They save commuters an average one minute per mile, amounting to 40 commute minutes per day. Yet no more than about 53 % of all commuters within the region have access to carpool lanes as they have been added only to certain sections of highways. This is altering the geography of slow and fast cities in the region. In terms of infrastructure access, Los Angeles neighbourhoods unable to access carpool lanes will have to be considered slow, as commuters are more likely to experience traffic congestion (Caltrans 2004; SCAG, 2001; Metro 2006).

Opinions on the success of carpool lanes being divided, the State of California recently implemented a new program, the so called HOT lanes (High Occupancy Toll Lanes)

(Jaskevich 2001). Buses and vehicles with occupancy higher than one have free access or receive price reductions of about 50 %. Solo drivers are charged a varying fee depending on traffic levels. On an eight-mile long test section near San Diego, prices range from 50 cents to $ 4.

Urban highways that feature access-restricted fast lanes are an example of how closely 'fast city' and 'slow city' can coexist.

1.2 A Theoretical Framework: Space-Time Zones

Urban speed not only differs from city to city but also within different areas of a single city. In his research, Robert Levine implicitly acknowledges this when he explains that he was conducting his experiments in central business districts only because of the supposedly comparable temporal characteristics of these areas. Inner city business areas all over the world function in more or less the same ways. While there are differences, some basic factors remain constant. In the search for comparable – if different – time structures, spatially and functionally comparable types of areas are chosen instead of a random selection of urban neighbourhoods. We are accustomed to studying the spatial, social and economic fragmentation of cities. But there is a temporal dimension to this fragmentation, as well. Spatial, social and economic differences between urban neighbourhoods produce differences in time structures. The concept of space-time zones can serve as an analytic tool for capturing this spatial-temporal fragmentation (Henckel/Eberling 2002).

Rather than a complete and detailed account on the concept of space-time-zones, this paper can only give a brief illustration of the idea behind it. If we talk about New York as 'the city that never sleeps', we are not speaking of the city as a whole but of certain areas with a tendency towards incessancy. Where there is urban activity at any hour of day and night, with people consuming, producing, communicating and strolling. We can define urban areas of this sort as 24/7 districts. They seem to be on the move 24 hours a day, seven days a week. Naturally, we experience places that never sleep as very fast. Empirically there may be very few places in the world that literally never stop.

Las Vegas, for instance, is certainly one. But a number of cities have areas displaying at least a tendency towards continuous activity. This can be said for many gentrified central areas like the Marais in Paris, Soho in London, Harajuku and Shibuya in Tokyo or the Spandauer Vorstadt in Berlin. Time works different there than in mono-functional, residential areas of the Fordist type, where activity is very low and time moves slowly outside the morning and evening commuter peak hours. Figure 2 shows four examples of space-time zones and some of their key temporal and socio-spatial characteristics.

Figure 2. Preliminary Characterisation of Space-Time Zones.

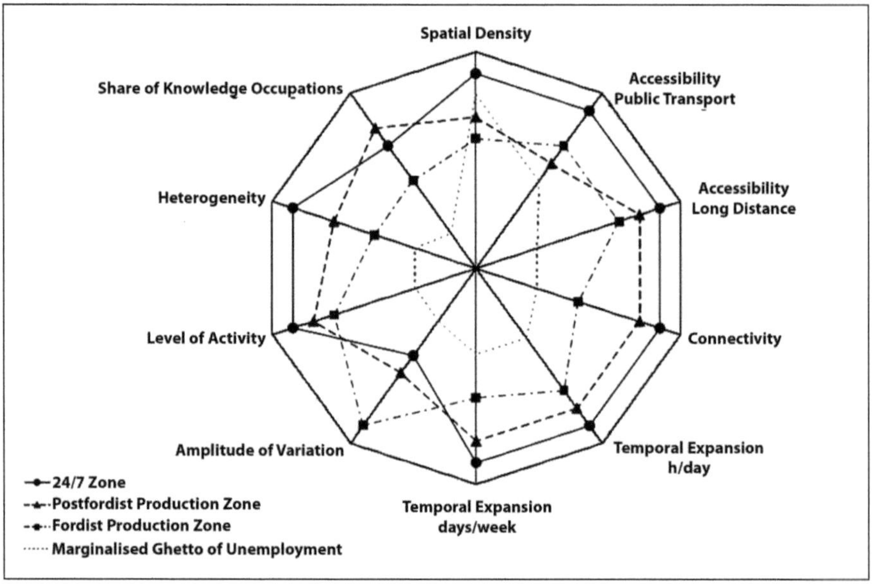

Source: Author's diagram

Space-time zones describe differences in time patterns and differences in urban speed at the city level. However, the example of Californian highways shows how closely 'fast' and 'slow' can coexist, how thin the dividing line can be. Sometimes the very same spot changes speed from fast to slow for a certain period of time, witness the example of 'Paris Plage'. This is a part of an urban freeway skirting one bank of the Seine, which is converted into a kilometre-long beach during the summer season. Paris generally is completely deserted at this time of the year and loses much its hectic pace, thus allowing a major traffic artery to be shut down and turned into an oasis of slowness (Figure 3).

Finally, another type of spatial cohabitation between different speed zones fully integrates a fast and a slow place into one system. Airports and railway stations, for example, can be seen as a kind of temporal hybrid because of the mixture of transitory population (passengers) and permanent population (employees) they host. Many airports today offer places of worship: A service for religious travellers to give them a spiritual rest before entering a machine that flies at 900 km/h.

Along German autobahns, too, there are signs directing drivers to an adjacent 'autobahn church'. Travellers are invited to renounce speed for a while and immerse themselves in peace and spirituality. These churches have minimum opening hours from 8 am to 8 pm

Figure 3. Paris Plage.

Source: Author's Photograph

Figure 4. Autobahn Churches in Germany.

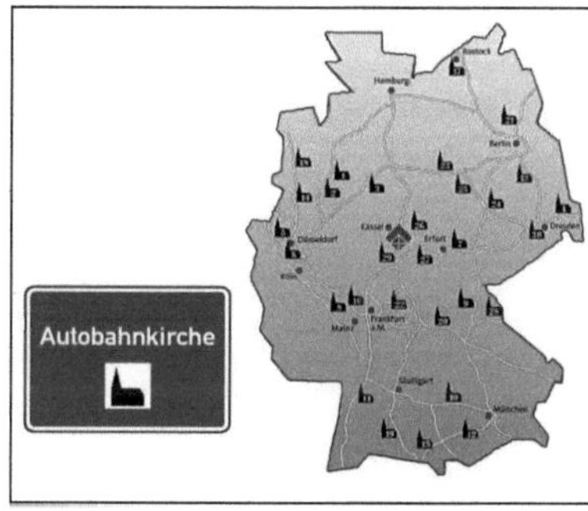

Source: Akademie Bruderhilfe 2005

seven days a week and are thus adapted to the incessancy of the traffic flow before their doors. This is an interesting paradox: if you want to provide rest for an incessant world you must be willing to offer it around the clock.

In comparing the speeds of different cities we must take account of the temporal heterogeneity of different areas within a city. The dividing line between slow and fast can be very thin, different speeds even overlap. Using the concept of the space-time zone can help avoid such methodological difficulties. It helps in the selection of comparable space-time zones, for instance only 24/7 districts. When comparing entire cities, it is useful to take the full variety of a city's space-time zones into account. A 'temporal variety index' can show how great the difference is between the slowest and fastest parts of a given city.

2. Urban Speed – Identifying Driving Factors

A systematic comparison of space-time zones on an international level has not yet been undertaken. But this alone will establish where life is fast and how fast, and, most importantly, why this is so, and what the costs and benefits are of a city's speed. We have some ideas about some of the factors involved, but many questions remain to be answered.

2.1 Economy

In the temporal landscape of a city, the spatial distribution of spaces of production and spaces of consumption plays a decisive role. Working and opening hours direct the movements of people at different times of the day. Industrial and service sector firms have different work schedules, the centres of commerce have varying opening hours and thus have a varying impact on activity levels and our experience of speed in a place.

On a more general scale, a city's economic performance obviously has a very strong impact on the city's speed (Levine 1997:38-45). In a place where the economy is doing well, time is an important and scarce resource. Where time is scarce, it is precious and not to be 'wasted'.

2.1.1 Acceleration in the Globalised Information Economy

The general trend of acceleration is most pronounced in information economies. The time in which information is modified by knowledge and subsequently exchanged and codified into information again is crucial. Highly skilled employees in tertiary economies will earn high wages and be short on time. This makes the places where these people work especially fast. Vice versa, this creates demand for the city to provide the spatial and infrastructural means this fast crowd needs. Clusters of firms and the supplemental infrastructure of communication spaces such as cafés, restaurants and public spaces work as 'creative milieus' (Camagni 2000) that have the important capacity of quickly mobilising the exchange of information, ideas and knowledge (Herkommer 2005:358-359). The working environment of the so called 'creative class' (Florida 2002) is a special breed of fast city.

Links within and between the companies this 'creative class' works for constitute what Manuel Castells called the 'space of flows' (Castells 1996). The global network of cities within the space of flows has been characterised as a multiple-level hierarchy (Taylor 2004). This hierarchy is comprehensible if we compare the numbers of affiliates of global companies and organisations and assess the intensity of flows – the amounts of data and the number of people – that are moved between the different nodes of the network. Figure 5 shows the intensity of global data transfers in 1993; the economic triad of North America, Europe and South and East Asia is clearly visible.

Since 1997, the Globalization and World City Study Group & Network (GAWC) has been publishing research bulletins on the hierarchical system of cities integrated in the global economy. Table 2 lists the cities the GAWC sees at the centre of the global economic system, i.e., cities with a large number of global companies with strong inter- and intra-firm linkages throughout the world and extraordinarily high connectivity (measured in relation to all other cities in the matrix). At the top of the hierarchy are London and New York that form a distinctive dyad, while cities within arenas B to D feature decreasing integration in global economic circuits as well as decreasing numbers of global service firms whose activities form a substantial part of the global economic network. Cities in Arena D are regional centres spearheading their respective

Figure 5. Intensity of data flows within countries, 1993.

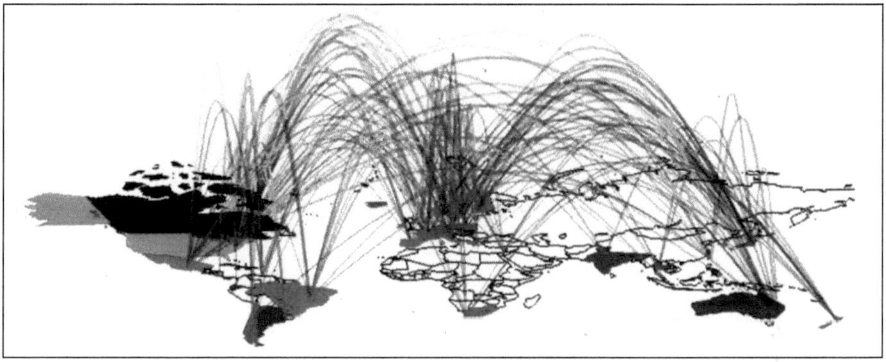

Source: Dodge/Kitchin 2001:117C

national economy and linking global and regional flows with one another. It is not the aim of this paper to discuss whether the cities listed here have been adequately ranked or not. The illustration should simply give an idea of ways to explore and describe hierarchical tendencies within the global city network.

It is important to point out that what constitutes the 'global city' applies to only part of each of the cities listed here as members of the higher strata within the so-called space of flows. The areas concerned are usually central business districts and related sites of informational production in other urban areas.

It is in these nodes of the global urban network that we witness the effects of one important means of acceleration: incessancy. In the core areas of the global economy, in the nodes of the global city network, people work longer hours than on the periphery. A high degree of integration into a network of cities spread over different time zones prompts firms to operate not only during the regular working hours of their specific time zone but to extend their operating hours so that they can monitor foreign markets

Table 2. Centre and Band I Arenas of Globalisation.

A	B	C	D
London New York	Frankfurt Hong Kong Paris Singapore Tokyo	Chicago Los Angeles	Amsterdam Zurich Madrid Milan Sao Paulo Mexico City

Source: Taylor 2004:169

and communicate with their affiliates, partners and clients. Goods, information, ideas, work in progress are all increasingly traded around the globe, 'following the sun'. Some part of the network is always in operation. Information and communication are immediate and instantaneous: the network never sleeps. The incessancy of the global economy translates firstly and most powerfully to the nodes of the urban network. But there are cascade effects that influence the operating hours of less globalized branches of the economy and the activity hours of less networked urban areas, too. The more highly globalized firms expand their operating hours, the more the demand for business as well as consumer oriented services will expand temporally. The tendency towards incessancy thus originates from the nodes of the global business and transport networks

Figure 6. Arenas of Globalization.

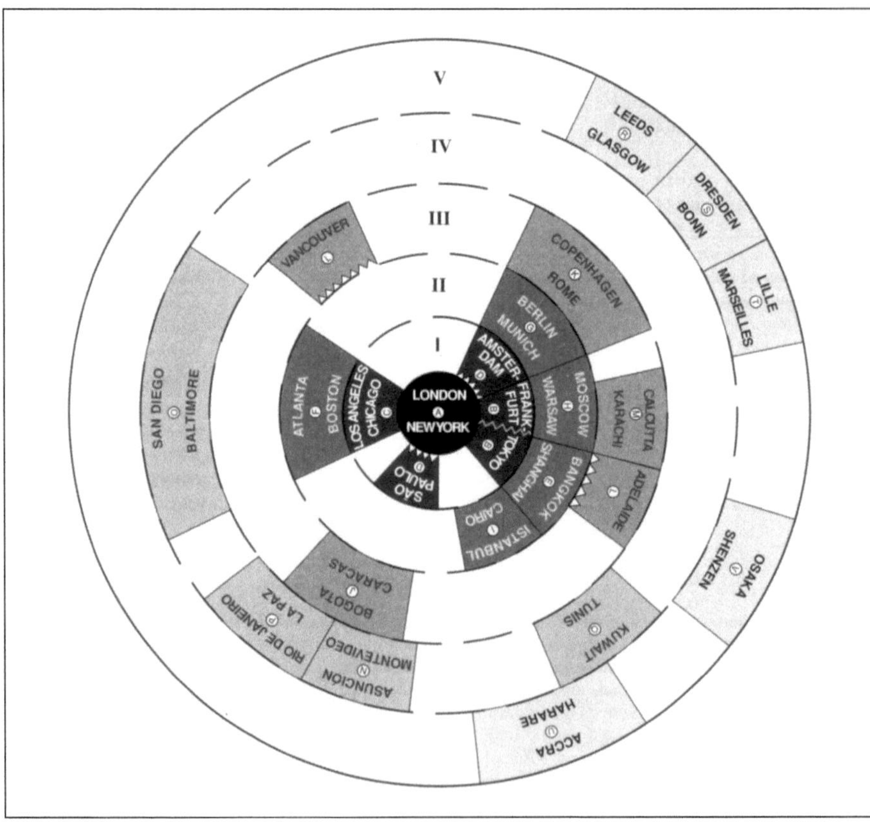

Source: Derudder et al. 2003:881

and is increasingly infiltrating related economic sectors, as well as adjacent urban areas. Arguably, we experience incessant cities as very fast (Herkommer 2002).

If the French researcher Luc Gwiadzinski is right in arguing that the continuous time of the network is increasingly imposing itself over natural and societal rhythms, (Gwiadzinski 2003:12-14) this process is likely to be apparent first of all in the centres of the globalized economy. It would therefore be important for further research to test the hypothesis that a 'world time' is overlaying and influencing local time patterns within the urban areas that constitute the global city network and the space of flows. This would imply the existence of a specific type of space-time zone that could be called the 'global flow area'.

This raises many questions; I will just name a few:

- Do the business districts of cities that are highly integrated into global economic circuits have converging temporal patterns?
- Does the City of London have a systematically higher pace than CBDs in cities on lower strata of the space of flows?
- Can incessancy create jobs or do the same employees work longer hours? Will night work necessarily remain precarious, undesirable, and stigmatized?
- Could incessant urban activity provide for more socio-temporal and socio-spatial liberty?

2.1.2 Economic Cycles and Urban Speed

If cities integrated into the global economy and the space of flows are accelerating, places whose economic performance is poor, where factories, offices and infrastructures have become obsolete, should be slowing down. A lack of economic importance tends to impose a slow pace on the areas concerned. Where there is little integration in economic circuits and a shattered labour market, there is no great need to hurry. We experience declining areas as slow, however rapid the process of devalorization might be. Simply the amount of superfluous time of the remaining inhabitants and the amount of superfluous space of defunct buildings and streets that carry a fraction of the traffic they were designed for give us an impression of standstill.

In 2004, the 'shrinking cities' project presented vivid images of abandoned, decaying urban areas around the world. They are involuntarily slow cities, disconnected from global economic development and increasingly spatially and mentally disconnected. In spatially and temporally fragmented cities, slow 'ghettos of unemployment' can be situated in close juxtaposition to fast, gentrified areas with incessant activity.,

Figure 7/8. Shrinking Cities: aerial view of the city centre of Halle, East-Germany, 2004 (left) and an impression of brownfield sites and left-over housing in Everton, England, 1993 (right).

Source: Oswalt 2005:649

Source: Wood 2005:142

But of course 'slow' cities have positive connotations, too. Some of the wealthiest urban areas might be just as slow as decaying areas. It is simply that slow pace has not been imposed involuntarily on these areas. Here, slow time is quality time because it gives balance to an otherwise active life. This distinction points to how strongly the spatial distribution of different social groups and temporal lifestyles influences the temporal map of a city.

The images of decay forebode another dimension of urban speed. They are images of neighbourhoods with a perhaps fast and vibrant past. For cities are subject to the cyclicity of urban structural change. The London Docklands are a good example. Ticking along at a very high pace from 1800 until the 1940s, they came to standstill in the 1970s. 25 years later they were turned into a centre of the information economy and began to run at a considerable pace again. There are places where these cycles are far shorter and others where they are much longer. Different cities have different turnover rates for areas subject to structural change. This of course also depends on the size of the area and the general economic condition of the city concerned.

Again, many questions remain open:

- Are there methods for predicting such cyclicities?
- How can cities become aware of these cycles and develop methods of countercyclical intervention?
- How could easy-to-construct throw-away architecture be used to intervene in decaying areas and provide for intermediate usage and activity?
- What consequences arise from the economic space-time fragmentation of cities? Do the trans-national managerial elites increasingly live in their own space and time, staying relatively disconnected from the local population (Castells 1996)?

2.2 Infrastructure

Closely related to what has been said about the influence of economic factors on urban speed is the question of integration in infrastructural networks (Henckel/Herkommer 2004:62).

Parallel to the hierarchical integration of cities in the global economic framework, there is a hierarchy of infrastructural connectivity. Connectivity is defined as the quality of access to and the bandwidth of the accessible infrastructure. In the space of flows, cities need to be closely connected since it is crucial to quickly transfer data and information as well as knowledge[1]. In other words, in both, the material and immaterial dimensions of transport, cities like New York, London, Paris, Hong Kong and Tokyo have a particularly broad-ranging infrastructure for conveying large numbers of people and large amounts of data at maximum speed. Connection intensity – the amount of flows – is highest in the two cities heading the hierarchy, London and New York. Berlin, in contrast, had no direct intercontinental flights apart from Ulan Bator, Mongolia, for many years. This is a feature typical of nodes in networks: high bandwidth nodes tend to connect with other high bandwidth nodes while medium bandwidth nodes tend to connect with other medium bandwidth nodes and so on.

This means that urban speed in terms of infrastructure is highly selective. The faster you want your connection to be, the more money needs to be invested in infrastructure. High connectivity costs a lot of money. And there is spatial selectivity as well: first, because infrastructures tend to need more space the faster they are. Second, because access to high speed infrastructures is highly selective. With each step of infrastructural acceleration, access becomes spatially more and more uneven.

One example is how the development of high-speed trains in Europe alters temporal distances between regions. As indicated by the maps below, geographical and temporal distances between different European regions are hardly equivalent. High-speed train connections shrink distances between certain parts of Europe, while distances grow in parts where travel times are slow.

By high-speed train, Paris is now only three hours away from Marseille. But there are regions between the two metropolises which, although geographically very close take a long time to reach. This is because the TGV does not stop in these areas, which are accessible only by very slow trains.

1 Knowledge transfer – as opposed to the transfer of information – necessarily implies the transport of people because knowledge is modified information that can only be carried personally.

Figure 9. Space-Time Distortion Induced by European High-Speed Trains. Left: Assumed train speeds of 60 km per hour on all tracks; Right: prognosis of temporal distances for 2010 with all proposed projects for high speed train connections realised.

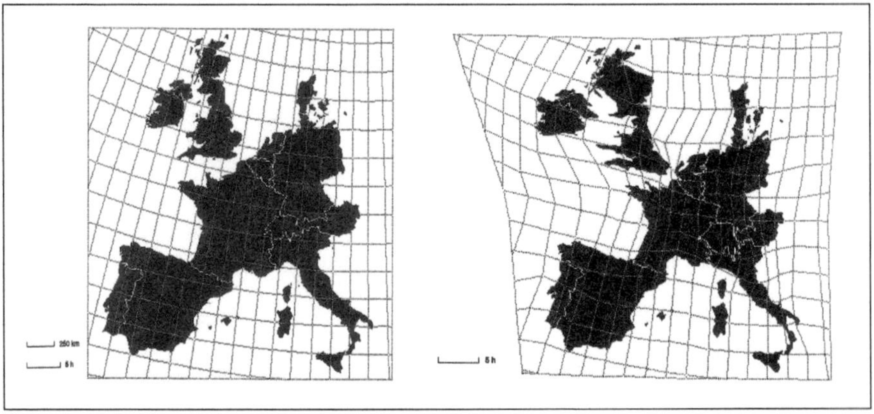

Source: Wegener/Spiekermann 1993:476-478

Gerhard Stiens recently outlined a scenario for the spaces in between the nodes of the network (Stiens 2002). In this scenario, the future of these spaces is one of agricultural production and craftsmanship, of a slow but comfortable life. These regions predominantly attract people that can no longer take the high pace of incessant urbanised areas, preferring the sense of (temporal) community and full integration in natural rhythms. The differences are not yet that great, but disparities, especially between connected and disconnected regions, are growing. So far, convergence within the European Union has primarily meant that regions of the same type have become more similar while the disparities between regions of different types have grown.

On the local level too, access to infrastructure and its bandwidth influence the speed of urban areas. And there is similar spatial and financial selectivity, as well. An inner-city metro line, for instance, typically carries by far more people per hour than a small bus circulating in the outskirts. In terms of cost-effectiveness, public transport networks generally tend to privilege city centres, which reduces the speed of the outskirts. Night services, in particular, are spatially selective, and tend to be very limited service outside the inner city. A different form of spatial selectivity is apparent in attempts to restrict the use of space by defining minimum speeds. In 2000 there was a debate on the introduction of a 'pedestrian fast lane' in London's Oxford Street, one of the city's busiest shopping areas. Here, shoppers and non-shoppers have widely differing walking speeds and, because pavement space is very scarce, slow people prevent others from moving faster. This increases the theoretical walking time of 19 to 20 minutes for Oxford Street to 38 minutes at lunchtime on a usual day and to a maximum of almost an hour during the weeks before Christmas. After numerous incidents of so-called 'pavement rage' – verbal or physical aggression among frustrated pedestrians – local businessmen launched a campaign calling for the installation of a fast lane, in which people would be obliged to walk at a speed of at least 3 mph or face a £ 10 fine (Baumgardner 2005). The project has not been realized, having been put on hold by the Westminster Council.

The access-restricted fast lanes on highways in dense urban and suburban areas discussed above are an example of financial selectivity in local infrastructure. People with limited time budgets have to pay more to move faster within their region whereas people with limited monetary budgets are more likely to lose time in congested traffic corridors. A striking example for this trade-off between time and money spent on journeys through urban agglomerations is provided by taxi services that use motorbikes. These can be found in London and Paris, perhaps Europe's most time sensitive cities, where businessmen, politicians, celebrities and other time-pressed people pay relatively high fares to bypass congested roads or service interruptions in public transport. In London there are two bike-taxi companies, one of which was founded as early as 1995 (Virgin Limobikes 2006a) . In Paris, the concept was introduced several years later but was all the more successful. A first company offering transits on motorcycles throughout the French capital and its surroundings started in 2003 with only a handful of vehicles. Today there are more than eleven such companies, many among them with ten vehicles or more. Their big advantage is to offer journey times that cars can only achieve at around five o'clock in the morning when traffic-flow is completely fluid. When absolutely necessary, employees can stay in their office half an hour longer and still catch their flight or train respectively, because in heavy traffic, motorcycles take up to 70 % less time than a car for a given distance (Scootexpress 2006a) . Fares range from 15 to 30 Euros within Paris and 45 to 95 Euros for journeys from the city-centre to one of the airports (Amoto 2006, Citybird 2006, Scootexpress 2006b) . In London, fares for inner-city journeys (inside the M25) range from £ 25 to £ 45 and from £ 60 to £ 150 for direct transfers to one of London's airports (Passenger Bikes 2006; Virgin Limobikes 2006b)

The use of differing speed regimes as a regulatory and/or commercial strategy in traffic is not limited to individual transport only. One example is differences in price for the journey from Heathrow Airport to the City by non-stop express line, which takes approximately 15 minutes, and by standard metro or bus lines, which take 45 minutes and more. Calculability risks also play a role. The 'Stansted Express' train linking Stansted Airport with Liverpool Street Station in the City, is currently running a massive advertising campaign emphasizing the risk of delays on London's streets and motorways. The argument is that while customers pay about five times less on the bus they can never be sure to be on time for their flight in Stansted or their appointment in the City.

The increasing replacement of old infrastructural monopolies by fractured and fragmented commercial solutions – a phenomenon that Stephen Graham and Simon Marvin so appealingly term 'splintering urbanism' – has its temporal dimension in the differential speed of the infrastructures (Graham/Marvin 2001).

The questions this raises include:

- How can spaces in between the nodal points of high speed infrastructure retain a minimum of connectivity?
- Could planning benefit from the explicit designation of certain disconnected regions as reproductive resources for high connectivity areas with a high pace of life?
- Will the advantage of infrastructural connectivity and the higher speed it generates for denser areas contribute to the future attractiveness of inner cities?
- How do 24-hour infrastructures influence their immediate surroundings?

Table 3. Connectivity characteristics of different areas in city regions.

	high accessibility	**low accessibility**
high bandwidth	FAST: city centres, areas around infrastructure nodes	INTERMEDIATE A: suburban areas between the access points of high speed infrastructure
low bandwidth	INTERMEDIATE B: low density areas within the urban core reached by infrastructure networks but with low speeds, low service frequencies and reduced night or holiday services	SLOW: areas without direct access to transport infrastructure / closer to an access point with low bandwidth than to high-speed networks

Source: Author's complilation

2.3 Culture and Tradition

What strongly impressed Robert Levine in his research was the differences existing between time cultures. For example he talks about 'amanha' – 'gum-time' that prevails in Latin American countries, where peoples' attitude towards punctuality tends to be incompatible with the European and North American version of the concept (Levine 1997:185).

Even within Europe there are differences in time structures depending on climate and culture. In many Mediterranean cities the midday 'siesta' has survived industrialisation and the invention of air conditioning. Public life stops completely for an hour or two, and such places become incredibly slow. In the evenings people work longer hours and shops stay open late. In many regions where the siesta is still practiced, religion and religious rituals continue to play a dominant role. This also affects local speed, since urban activity is rare on a Sunday. In all, these elements of Mediterranean time culture generate urban rhythms completely alien to Northern Europeans, and even northerners in the same countries. These cultural particularities are under pressure to adapt to standardisation. The continuous time of the network has a tendency to impose itself over local traditions (Gwyadzinski 2003:12). While we must be careful not to overemphasize the notion of the 'imposition' of globalization[2], there is certainly pressure to standardize, and cultural adaptation to national and international standards has an impact. These processes primarily affect parts of cities integrated into national and global economic circuits. Outside these areas, local traditions and rituals have a moderating and balancing function in between global and local time patterns. For instance, Madrid's 'global flow area' does not take a siesta while some adjacent neighbourhoods may still do so.

There is not much empirical evidence. A proper analysis of cultural differences is very difficult. Moreover, it is not even clear how to draw the line between areas within the space of flows and those outside it. There are many interdependencies and links even among very different urban areas. Another interesting question in the context of cultural influence is about the specific time patterns of tourists. It is conceivable that the geography of sights and tourist attractions tends to impose tourist rhythms on local ones.

In its cultural dimension, the urban temporal landscape is shaped by the allocation of cultural offers and leisure activities and the distribution of places of temporal rituals. Places for traditional rituals can be used to integrate islands of slow city into otherwise fast moving areas. Vice versa, cultural facilities and spaces of leisure consumption can help to activate otherwise slow neighbourhoods. The conversion of London's Bankside Power Station into the Tate Modern gallery, which has affected the destinies of almost an entire borough, is one example. Another example is the conversion of the old slaughterhouses in La Villette, Paris into a giant park, whose cultural institutions and activities such as the Cité de la Musique or the large open-air cinema helped to open up a door between ethnically and socially highly isolated neighbouring suburbs and the rest of the French capital.

Yet another very important cultural aspect of urban speed is a city's relation to its architectural past, the manner in which its built heritage is treated. This is closely related to the questions of economic cyclicities and the turnover rates of buildings, neighbourhoods and entire socio-economic regimes. Modern urbanism strongly accelerated the demolition of historic buildings – now its own products are being replaced all over the world, sometimes by urban design schemes that replicate exactly those structures that had been targeted by modernism. For issues of local identity and socio-historic struc-

2 The power of globalization to level cultural differences is often overemphasized. There is a tendency to overlook the extent to which globalization and cities' adaptation to it are not imposed by an external, natural process but constitute a political project often pursued by cities themselves.

tures it is absolutely crucial to keep up the debate on how quickly we actually write off entire architectural strata.

2.4 Natural Rhythms

Modern civilization has always struggled to gain independence from nature's rhythms. And the city has always been the place where this process has made the greatest advances. Yet most cities have left at least parts of their areas to nature. In these spaces, time seems to move at a significantly lower speed than within the urbanised parts of a city. Natural processes take a lot of time and it takes patience to observe them. Once we enter a park or take a rest beside a lake we automatically adopt a slower speed. Even more, to slow down, to relax we explicitly head out of the city and into nature – to profit form the absence of hurry and speed.

The more visible natural rhythms become – be it in parks, forests or lakes – the stronger is our impression of being exposed to slow rhythms. Sound and vision play a major role, too. Paris, for example, is a city that remains completely illuminated over night. It is much harder to see the difference between day and night in Paris than in Berlin, where one has the impression in winter that it is bedtime at three o'clock in the afternoon. Moreover, Paris emits constant urban white noise throughout night. Taken together, these effects give people unused to such conditions a sense of unease.

3. Conclusions – Relevance of Urban Speed for Urban Policy and Planning

3.1 Economic Performance

Urban speed plays an important role in a city's economic fate. Grasping the significance of speed in information-producing economies gives cities a key perspective on how to maintain or even improve their economic position. It means examining what speed parameters influence a place's position within the space of flows. This could imply cities pursuing the paradoxical goal of becoming 'sticky places' (Markusen 1996) in fluid processes. Global economic circuits show a preference for cities that are able to mobilise information and knowledge and to process the flows of goods, people and information as quickly as possible. It is these abilities that induce global corporations to stick to cities. For planning this implies providing the conditions a specific breed of fast space – the 'creative milieu' – needs to unfold its productive potential. Integration into high-speed infrastructure networks is therefore crucial. Yet having access to infrastructures of global high speed transport does not automatically place a city in the higher strata of the global economy. But cities aspiring to play in this league are strongly recommended to ensure they are served by high-speed trains and intercontinental air connections.

3.2 Design for Time

Taking account in urban design and architecture of the notion that places have a specific speed allows attention to be paid to the speed preferences of local users. Some railway stations and airports, for example, are increasingly becoming multi-functional urban nodes where people do a great deal more than take a train or plane. Some do their shopping, some wait, some have lunch or a coffee, and others work there. A good 60,000 people work at Frankfurt Airport. The demands these groups make on the speed of their environment differ, but this is scarcely reflected by the environment.

Especially for places that are 'temporal hybrids', where slow and fast overlap or coexist side by side, the urban speed perspective permits deliberate design to alleviate time or speed conflicts. This does not to repeat the demand for functions and traffic modes to be separated. On the contrary, the mix of spaces or spatial objects with differing temporalities and speeds is a key to the success of many places. Visual communication between spaces with different speeds becomes an aesthetic and sensual quality of cities. Nevertheless, any attempt to achieve communication, exchanges and mutual influence between different time zones without fostering conflict requires temporal and speed aspects to be taken into account in urban design.

3.3 Social Balance – Temporal Needs

Different people have different temporal lifestyles. The choice between fast or slow may merely be a matter of taste. Problems arise, however, when constraints come into play, where life in a slow place equals boredom, exclusion and the involuntary possession of time. This is also true where life in a fast place means foregoing peace and quiet, relaxation and any possibility of forgetting about time. The crux of the matter is temporal sovereignty. There is accordingly a temporal dimension to the 'quartered city' that Peter Marcuse posits in socio-spatial terms (Marcuse 1996). Cities are socially, spatially and temporally fragmented.

For urban policy this means finding how to compensate for this temporal fragmentation. The concept of urban speed could play an important role in a city's struggle for more social equity – or more generally for the contentment of its citizens. The speed perspective draws attention to the need for measures to tie islands of slowness into areas of high speed and to speed up the lives of people leading involuntarily slow lives. Obviously, most cities do not have the means to stage urban life where there is none. But allowing or still better encouraging the intermediate use of defunct buildings is important to inject temporary life into areas otherwise off the temporal map of a city. It could already be important to prevent neighbourhoods with high rates of unemployment from losing track of society's time structures.

Much of the future temporal work of urban planners will be about keeping a balance: between slow and fast micro-places within a district and between slow and fast areas within a city region. A city where people with accelerated lives and people no longer find times and places where their paths cross, where their activities take place on the same spot, at the same time and at the same pace is unlikely to maintain social cohesion for long. In addressing the needs of a population faced with splintering multiplicities of time, a new development goal for time-sensitive cities could emerge.

'The variable speed city' would be a place where differences between space-time-zones are not neglected, where fast and incessant areas are not re-regulated to the point where they lose their character but where an effort is made to maintain a temporal and spatial balance and where the times and places of individual lifestyles cohabit with times and places for cohesion and shared activity.

References

ALTMAN, I., OXLEY, D., WERNER, C.M. (1985), "Temporal Aspects of Homes: A Transactional Perspective", in: Altman, I., Werner, C. M. (eds.), *Home Environments: Human Behavior and Environment, Vol. 8*, New York, Plenum Press, p. 1-32

AMOTO (2006), *Tarifs*, in: www.amoto-express.com/lire/index.php?rubid=30, accessed June 5th, 2006

BUMGARDNER, W. (2005), *Fine The Slow or Cool Your Heels?*, in: http://walking.about.com/od/holiday/a/pavementrage.htm, accessed May 10, 2005

CALTRANS (California Department of Transportation), District 7, (2004), *HOV Annual Report*, in: www.dot.ca.gov/dist07/aboutdist7/hov/annual/2004%20HOV%20Annual%20Report%20rev%2011_14_05.pdf, accessed August 8, 2005

CAMAGNI, R. (2000), "Das urbane Milieu: Voraussetzung für Innovation und wirtschaftlichen Erfolg", in: Matejowski, D. (ed.), *Metropolen. Laboratorien der Moderne*, Frankfurt, New York, Campus, p. 292-307

CASTELLS, M. (1996), *The Information Age. Economy, Society and Culture, Vol. 1: The Rise of the Network-Society*, Oxford, Blackwell

CITYBIRD (2006), *Tarifs*, in: www.city-bird.com/tarifs.php, accessed June 5th, 2006

DERUDDER, B., TAYLOR, P. J., WITLOX, F., CATALANO, G. (2003): "Hierarchical Tendencies and Regional Patterns in the World City Network: A Global Urban Analysis of 234 Cities", *Regional Studies*, Vol. 37, No. 9, London, p. 875-886

DIE AKADEMIE BRUDERHILFE, Familienfürsorge (2005), Autobahnkirche, in: www.autobahnkirche.info/, accessed May 10, 2005

DODGE, M., KITCHIN, R. (2001), *Mapping Cyberspace*, London, New York, Routledge

EBERLING, M., HENCKEL, D. (eds.) (2002), *Alles zu jeder Zeit? Die Städte auf dem Weg zur kontinuierlichen Aktivität*, Difu-Beiträge zur Stadtforschung 36, Berlin

FLORIDA, R. (2002), "The Economic Geography of Talent", *Annals of the Association of American Geographers*, Vol. 92, No. 4, p. 743-755

GRAHAM, S., MARVIN, S. (2001), *Splintering Urbanism. Network Infrastructures, Technological Mobilities and the Urban Condition*, London, New York, Routledge

GWIAZDZINSKI, L. (2002), *La ville 24heures sur 24? Regards croisés sur la société en continu*, Paris, Editions de l'aube

HENCKEL, D., HERKOMMER, B. (2004), "Gemeinsamkeiten räumlicher und zeitlicher Strukturen und Veränderungen", in: Siebel, W. (ed.), *Die europäische Stadt*, Frankfurt/M, Suhrkamp, p. 52-66

HERKOMMER, B. (2002), "Hoch vernetzte Städte", in: Eberling, M., Henckel, D. (eds.), *Alles zu jeder Zeit? Die Städte auf dem Weg zur kontinuierlichen Aktivität*, Difu-Beiträge zur Stadtforschung 36, Berlin

HERKOMMER, B. (2005), "Nachmoderne Formen der Nutzungsmischung", in: Bodenschatz, H. (ed.), *Renaissance der Mitte. Zentrumsumbau in London und Berlin*, Berlin, Braun, p. 357-365

HONDA Motor (2006), *Press Release April 21, 2005*, http://world.honda.com/news, accessed May 25, 2006

JASKEVICH, M. (2001), "Mixed reviews for HOV lanes", *American City & County*, www.americancityandcounty.com/mag/government_mixed_reviews_hov/, accessed May 10, 2005

LEVINE, R. (1997), *Eine Landkarte der Zeit*, München, Zürich, Piper

MARCUSE, P. (1996), "Space and Race in the Post-Fordist City: The Outcast Ghetto and Advanced Homelessness in the United States Today", in: Mingione, E. (ed.), *Urban Poverty and the Underclass*, Oxford, Cambridge, Mass., Blackwell, p. 176-216

MARKUSEN, A. (1996), "Sticky Places in Slippery Space: A Typology of Industrial Districts", *Economic Geography*, Vol. 72, No. 3, p. 293-313.

METRO (Los Angeles County Metropolitan Transport Association) (2006), *Carpool FAQ*, in: www.mta.net/riding_metro/commute_services/carpool_faqs2.htm, accessed March 11, 2006

OSWALT, P. (ed.) (2005), *Shrinking Cities, Volume 1: International Investigation*, Ostfildern-Ruit, Hatje Cantz

PASSENGER BIKES Ltd (2006), *Cost*, in: www.passengerbikes.com/cost.html, accessed June 5, 2006

SCAG (Southern California Association of Governments)(2001), *The Book on Ridesharing*, in: www.scag.ca.gov/publications/pdf/1078bkonridesharing.pdf, accessed May 10, 2005

SCOOTEXPRESS (2006a), *Sérénité*, in: www.scootexpress.com/index.htm, accessed June 5, 2006

SCOOTEXPRESS (2006b), *Tarifs*, in: www.scootexpress.com/tarifs.htm, accessed June 5th, 2006

SPIEKERMANN, K. WEGENER, M. (1993), "Zeitkarten für die Raumplanung", *Informationen zur Raumentwicklung*, No. 7/1993, Bonn, p. 459-487

STIENS, G. (2002), "Wie unterschiedliche 'Timescapes' Staatsraum und Landschaften verändern können", in: Henckel, D., Eberling, M. (eds.), *Raumzeitpolitik*, Opladen, Leske + Budrich, p. 163-188

TAYLOR, P. J. (2004), *World City Network. A Global Urban Analysis*, London, New York, Routledge

VIRGIN LIMOBIKES (2006a), FAQ's, in: www.virgin.com/subsites/virginlimobike/link.html, accessed June 5th, 2006

VIRGIN LIMOBIKES (2006b), *Payment*, in: www.virgin.com/subsites/virginlimobike/link.html, accessed June 5th, 2006

WOOD, T. (2005), "Bus Odyssey", in: Oswalt, P. (ed.): *Shrinking Cities, Volume 1: International Investigation*, Ostfildern-Ruit, Hatje Cantz

BUILDING HIGH AND RUNNING FAST – CITIES AS SPACES AND TIME SAVING ENTITIES

by Dietrich Henckel

Introduction

The novel 'Einstein's Dreams', which portrays different concepts of time and their social and spatial aspects, gives a description – dated on 26 of april in 1905 – of a spatial order engendered by the knowledge that the farther one is from the centre of the Earth the more slowly time passes. There is hence no building development on the plain. The demand for housing is greatest in the mountains, and even there buildings are raised on stilts. People with business in the valley deal with it in great haste so they can return to the mountain as quickly as possible. Only an intrepid few unperturbed by the slight time differences stroll leisurely through the valleys enjoying life. This story stresses two aspects relevant to our purposes: time and how it is assessed provokes social and spatial differentiation reflected in the speed of human activities and where and how building development takes place. This complex is wonderfully captured in the tale.

The title of this paper plays with these elements, which are also embodied in the traditional image of the city: the (big) city as a place where activities take place at a greater pace, much faster than in small towns and the countryside; the city as an aggregation of tall buildings, if not skyscrapers. The city is demonstrably not only a place of spatial concentration but also of temporal agglomeration and acceleration (Levine 1997). The city, this concentration of many people and many functions in a small area, has always served to save space and time. The greater the density of the city, the more people and functions it has to accommodate in a small space and the less time is needed for widespread contacts or for using services. Hence, real estate that offers the best conditions, that is best serviced and allows the greatest utilisation, is also the most expensive (Franck 2002). Among the factors that have always limited the size of the 'city machine' are the degree of density considered reasonable and the time and costs for overcoming distances regarded as acceptable. However, ideas about what is reasonable and acceptable change over time, depending particularly on the technology available and on material prosperity.

Referring to the city as a 'space-time saving machine'[1] may at first sound somewhat too technical and banal. Banal because the definition of city, at least the economic definition, actually states this: the function of the city is to contribute to the efficient socio-spatial organisation of society (Hirsch 1975; Jacobs 1970), to help distribute work effectively – in other words, to use the resources space and time economically and efficiently. In a nutshell: 'economics is urban' (Coyle 1997:192). Agglomeration (= saving space) and the spatial proximity of similar and different functions with concomitant potential for contact between actors (= saving time) are the essential elements in the economic definition of the city.

Even if we accept this basic notion of the city's space-time saving function, it should not be forgotten that the conditions under which it operates are continually changing. These non-constant conditions include:

- the time structures of a society and how it handles time;
- the production conditions of a society;
- reachability, transport and traffic conditions;
- communication conditions and requirements;
- the (relative) availability (scarcity) of space;
- the (relative) availability (scarcity) of time.

Keeping to the image of a 'machine' for saving space and time, the function and significance of the machine will obviously change radically in response to changes in technological and production conditions, capital intensity, operative skills, and affluence, i.e., the pressure to use resources economically. Examining these changes, their extent and importance, also means investigating what the city – in the more or less traditional sense – still means or can mean in the future. Temporal changes and the connection between temporal and spatial changes that raise the issue of the future role of the city are the main focus of this article. Four principal aspects of temporal change can be identified, which, although not discrete, can usefully be dealt with separately for analytical purposes (Eberling/Henckel 2002; Geißler 2004):

- *Acceleration*. Many authors have regarded the modern age as a time of general mobilisation. Many areas of the economy and society are showing signs of acceleration. They range from shorter product life cycles and faster transport to accelerated telecommunications networking. This affects the spatial differentiation of the division of

1 The title of an Italian publication on local time policy also refers to the city as a time machine: La città macchina del tempo (Paolucci 1998).

labour, the size of catchment areas, the useful life of locations, and the need for lifelong learning. The effects are apparent in almost all facets of economic life, in the city, in (local) policy reactions, and in private, everyday life.

- *Flexibilisation*. Flexibilisation includes the dissolution of the rigid, 'mass' rhythms characteristic of industrialisation and the full-employment era. Not only are jobs being flexibilised. Working times are also being differentiated in terms of duration and scheduling. A key goal of flexibilisation is to adapt labour input to the demand for products. The logical consequence is the 'breathing factory', which breathes in or out in response to the state of the market. The extreme case is work on call. Temporal rhythms become individualised, dissociated from collective rhythms, and temporal coordination is left up to the individual. People have to 'put together' their own working times as best they can.
- *Expansion*. The expansion of working hours refers to the use of times previously largely excluded from economic activity, the advance of activities into previously protected times, especially in the evening, at night, during the weekend, and on public holidays. However plausibly it may be argued that there have always been cycles of expansion and shrinkage in this domain, it must nevertheless be assumed that times once 'conquered' will not be surrendered for good. In other words, there is a trend towards 24/7 continuousness even if our society is still far from fully implementing it. One important outcome is the linearization of rhythms, at least a levelling off and smoothing of transitions and an increase in working times and employment beyond the normal working day. Here, too, there is a wide spectrum of effects, including expanded demand for public transport services, function compatibility problems in the city when economic activities, especially traffic, continue far into the night, and growing risks arising from night work and overtiredness.
- *Temporal agglomeration, simultaneity*. Temporal agglomeration or intensification refers to carrying out several activities at the same time. New information processing and telecommunications technologies have made this considerably easier. The general reachability afforded by the cell phone has integrated occupational activities more strongly into other spheres of life (leisure time, household chores, etc.); the possibilities offered by laptops and networking are making travel time more and more into working time in the narrower sense of the word. Simultaneity is firstly a consequence of the differentiated division of labour, which now makes it necessary for actors from different and perhaps distant companies to be present at the same time in the same place, and secondly a result of time saving strategies which require activities traditionally carried out in sequence (e.g., development and marketing) to be performed simultaneously (simultaneous engineering), with corresponding consequences for factory organisation (Wendt 1995).

With these temporal changes in mind, space-time issues and their implications for the future role of the city can be identified. This brings us to the focal proposition of my article, that space and time, and therefore proximity in space and time, are generally directly related in the city. Spatial proximity has always been a key topic in the debate on the city about such issues as density, agglomeration effects, neighbourhood. Since the time dimension has tended to play a minor role, we are concerned primarily to examine the implications of an explicitly more time-oriented analysis.

The emphasis is on the following questions:[2]

- How does the role of the city as a time saving machine change in response to temporal changes?
- How do temporal changes affect the 'demand' for spatio-temporal proximity?
- What role does acceleration play?
- How are spatial and temporal proximity conceptualized? How close is close?
- What future trends can be identified, and what do they mean for the role of the city?

1. Theories of Agglomeration and the Functioning of the Machine

As we have seen, the city is considered to be the wellspring of agglomeration effects, of positive externalities, and that these are a constitutive element in the economic definition of city.[3] The role of these externalities has mostly been described in the spatial dimension, in spatial proximity. To the best of my knowledge, time aspects that can be important for agglomeration, for the development of spatial concentrations of firms from related or complementary sectors, have been almost ignored. The role of the city and hence the importance of positive external effects has repeatedly been called into question. Almost every new technological wave (in transport and communications) has provoked new doubts about the economic importance of the city as a site for business. Official statements by the German Federal Ministry of Building and Housing provide evidence of this in relation to IC technologies and the accelerated technologies of material transport, and the EU, too, has considered ICTs to be a source of rural prosperity. Authors like Mitchell (1995) have claimed that "the very idea of the city is challenged" and Cairncross (1997) declared the death of distance and the completely arbitrariness of site selection. Questioning the future of the city means assuming that externalities are becoming less important. The attack on a key symbol of the urban economy, the Twin Towers in New York, considerably reinforced uncertainty about the sustainability of big, dense cities.

2 A comprehensive analysis of the city as a space-time saving machine would have to deal with a much broader spectrum than that covered by these questions, which address only an excerpt from the catalogue of issues.

3 Roberto Camagni (2000) has discussed the parallels between milieu and city.

Although there have always been counterarguments rejecting doubts about the future of the city, the fog of fears and hopes about the impact of ICTs has meanwhile lifted a little to reveal that forecasts about the death of the city are premature, that, especially in an economy driven by information and knowledge, the positive external effects of spatial agglomeration are becoming greater (Glaeser 1996; Läpple 2003; Gornig/Geppert 2003). As Coyle puts it (1997:197): "The forces for geographical concentration are becoming stronger as the economy becomes increasingly weightless", leading him to conclude "that the weightless economy, the product of the latest technological wave, will renew concentration in great cities" (1997:201). One explanation offered by McCann (2004) is the relative increase in transaction costs when communication becomes more complex, more intense, and more frequent. There are many explanations for the spatial concentration of economic activities, all of which essentially go back to positive external effects. More recent theories of regional development, in particular, propose various explanatory patterns or priorities for interpreting spatial agglomeration (McCann 2004). It is striking, however, that all theories or explanatory concepts treat space very abstractly, making practically no empirically concrete statements about spatio-temporal distances and extents. Even considering that 'region' and regional boundaries are variable, issue-dependent concepts, it is astonishing how little concepts stressing the importance of spillovers, of the need for personal exchanges, for embeddedness in milieus and institutional framework conditions concern themselves with distance sensitivity.

Even when discussion focuses on physical proximity, space remains a strangely dimensionless concept, as though it had no boundaries, despite the stress many authors place on its importance for the exchange of knowledge, especially implicit knowedge, and for positive externalities.[4] This is particularly noticeable in cluster theories. Depending on the study, the spatial extent of clusters ranges from a neighbourhood to an entire country. But this makes statements on space, on proximity, on spatio-temporal proximity almost arbitrary. It is accepted that proximity can contribute to economic interaction and to economic success, but it is not clear what is meant by the term, since proximity can have different dimensions – cognitive, physical, organisational (Boschma 2005). This indicates that proximity and common location are not the same thing (Rallet/Torre 2005). Boschma, for example, shows that geographical proximity is neither necessary nor sufficient for innovative learning processes, but that it facilitates these processes, especially by strengthening other dimensions of proximity (Boschma 2005). Geographical proximity is a matter of physical distance, and empirical studies show that knowledge externalities are geographically limited (Audretsch/Feldman 1996). But statements about geographical boundaries remain vague (Feldmann 2003).

4 One example: "Though the milieu has a spatial dimension, it does not correspond to a well defined geographical area; the milieu is an organic framework including market and non-market links" (Maillat/Lecoq 1992 quoted in Capello/Faggin 2005:78).

Central to the issue of spatio-temporal proximity is not only co-presence, the face-to-face contacts assumed to be indispensable for the exchange of implicit knowledge, but also the speed with which contacts can be established and knowledge transferred. Moreover, the 'half-life' of any edge in knowledge plays a role, that is to say, the rate at which a lead is lost if too much time passes between gaining a knowledge advantage and being in a position to use and exploit it.

We will now look at two aspects in greater depth:

- The discussion on the temporal aspects of the question 'How close is close?' and the relationship between absolute and relative spatio-temporal proximity,
- The importance of acceleration for space-time proximity (acceleration of knowledge production, rate of knowledge obsolescence, loss of information edge).

2. How Close is Close? Spatio-Temporal Proximity Factors

Financial services can be a useful point of departure in answering the question How close is close? No industry is so globalised and so permeated by information and communication technology as the financial sector, and therefore – measured against the technical possibilities – it offers the best chance for demonstrating the death of distance (Cairncross 1997). And we discover that it demonstrates nothing of the sort: hardly any other industry is as heavily concentrated: in only a few cities of the world and, within these cities, in small, inner-city areas. The key factor for the spatial concentration of financial services is claimed to be "the tremendous importance of access to sensitive knowledge through face-to-face interaction and a tightly woven network of personal relationships between industry-professionals, clients, suppliers, and other decision makers" (Fürst quoted in Russel 2004). Many studies have shown that the extreme expression of spatio-temporal density, highrise development, is thriving and has a great future ahead of it: "Tall buildings, ..., seem bigger news than ever" (Russel 2004). "Skyscrapers make sense where density and the urban infrastructure make it the logical way to occupy land" (Willis quoted in Russel 2004). A cursory assessment of tower occupancy shows that hotels and financial services are the most frequent users of tall buildings, but that mixed uses are making progress[5]. After these preliminaries, we must consider the different types of space-time proximity, the various spatial and especially temporal dimensions and trends towards change. The city offers particularly advantageous conditions for spatio-temporal proximity compared with other spatial units and despite the changes that are occurring.

5 For instance see www.emporis.com

- A *density* that is generally higher than in all other spatial units makes the relative proximity of functions to one another greater than elsewhere.
- The *size* of cities means they assemble a disproportionately high number of functions.
- The city displays great functional *heterogeneity*.
- The *speed* of access to the city by public transport and long-distance traffic systems, to some extent also by road, makes functional catchment areas particularly large.
- Even if telecommunications are now almost omnipresent, systems generally offer much faster access and higher capacities in cities.

Size, density, heterogeneity are the three factors that Simmel had cited as conditions for urbanity and which can be described as the probabilistic aspect of exchange (Capello/Faggin 2005:79), i.e., the greater likelihood of meeting other actors, of gaining new information. The two other factors are the ones most affected by technical change. If we consider the historical development of spatio-temporal proximity in the city, the specific scarcities that led to agglomeration, and the trends that contributed to dispersion, i.e., to relativising specific scarcities, it emerges that in many traditional areas, specific scarcities that had made agglomeration necessary no longer exist, but that new scarcities occur that (can) require renewed concentration (Table1).

Table 1. Specific scarcities in history contributing to density and concentration of city-functions.

Historical phase	Specific scarcity	Density due to	Dissolution due to
Middle ages	Transport costs, external security	Walled towns	New transport technology, new military technology
Industrialisation	Transport costs, space	Close spatial relationship of primary resources and production, demand for labour, railway stations, harbours	Railway, decreasing transport costs
Fordism	Space, options for expansion	Growth, demand for labour, economies of scale, mass production	Automobile, acceleration of transport, decreasing transport costs, substitution of proximity by telecommunication
Postfordism	Knowledge and its modes of production, milieu, attractiveness	Role of face-to-face contacts, reurbanisation of certain functions, importance of knowledge spillovers	Extension of substitionability

Source: Author's compilation

Table 2. Change of conditions for space time proximity.

	Change	Causes
Size	Expansion of conurbation	Acceleration, ICTs, Suburbanisation
Density	Contradictory developments	Functional specialisation, skyscrapers, housing preferences
Heterogeneity	Inhabitants vs. economy; large scale vs. small scale	Individualisation, international migration
Accessibility	Acceleration	Technology, new infrastructures
Connectivity	New possibilities, capacities, spatially selective	Technology, density, types of de-mand and supply strategies

Source: Author's compilation

Analysis of specific scarcities and changes in the conditions for spatio-temporal proximity suggest that, after a marked phase of dispersion we might well be on an historic threshold to urban reconcentration. A preliminary systematisation of changes and their causes (Table 2) indicates that the effects on (inner) cities are not unambiguous, that some developments have occurred that reinforce the potentials of space-time proximity in the city while others have a relativising impact.

Contradictory developments are particularly apparent with regard to density. In some places density is increasing strongly and is being reinforced by multi-function centres (cf. Christiaanse in this volume) and by concentrations of high-rise buildings, whereas in other locations it is decreasing owing to dispersion and demographic developments.

Contradictory trends are also apparent as regards heterogeneity. Heterogeneity is increasing at the macro-level but is tending to be overlaid by homogenization trends at the more local level. Nonetheless, it can be shown that heterogeneity is of considerable importance for the economic growth of cities and crucial for innovation (Feldman 2003). Reachability is increasing strongly owing to the acceleration of transport and the growth of often highly specialised infrastructures. However, infrastructural specialisation leads to strong spatial and social selectivity (cf. Graham in this volume). The same is true of connectivity, which may also have a very strong spatially and socially selective impact.

3. Proximity and Speed

The pivotal question for the future of the city is what activities still require any spatio-temporal proximity. A temporal dimension, speed, and its importance for certain economic activities, play a key role in this context. Different aspects of speed can be distinguished (cf. Grabher 1998:9).

- A *high frequency* of personal exchanges between actors can generally be (cost-effectively) ensured only through spatio-temporal proximity.
- The need for *short notice* contact between actors also makes demands on spatio-temporal proximity.
- *Simultaneity* between actors, especially if it occurs in conjunction with the factors already mentioned, can also be achieved cost-effectively only in spatio-temporal proximity (Grabher 1998:9ff).
- The *rate of knowledge obsolescence*, the loss of a knowledge lead can be interpreted as a further dimension of short-termedness. Where knowledge and an edge in knowledge are crucial competitive parameters, such leads need to be secured and premature diffusion prevented.[6] This can best be achieved through proximity, social control, and avoiding the integration of knowledge into the network. In this context the cost of transforming implicit knowledge into explicit knowledge can under certain circumstances be too high.
- The brevity of product life cycles (time to market) and transport time can also contribute to making spatio-temporal proximity a necessity.
- *Sensitivity* to disturbance and *calculability* require space-time proximity.

This suggests that temporal factors (frequency, simultaneity, and speed) are of prime importance in sustaining the need for spatio-temporal proximity. Taking due account of the relations between space and time, it can be said that saving time is becoming relatively more urgent than saving space, that temporal proximity is becoming relatively more important.

4. The Relationship between Absolute and Relative Space-Time Proximity

It has been implicitly assumed that spatio-temporal proximity implies physical vicinity. However, under the conditions created by new transport and telecommunications technologies, this is not necessarily the case. In fact, a distinction needs to be drawn between absolute and relative spatio-temporal proximity or between material and virtual spatio-temporal proximity. This distinction is necessary because of the ambivalent effects of technical development on space-time proximity. A range of technological developments make it possible to substitute both spatial and temporal proximity in varying degrees. These technologies include: The telephone, the first device to permit direct personal contact without physical co-presence. Studies on the impact of the telephone describe not only what far-reaching hopes were raised by the introduction of the tech-

6 "In market environments characterised by rapidly changing information, such clustering affords the clustered co-located firms an information advantage relative to all other firms." (McCann 2005:34) or "Industries with high average annual rates of knowledge obsolescence, we may hypothesize, would face the greatest pressure to locate near the source of new knowledge" (Feldman 2003:386).

nology (including lasting world peace), which were revived with the expanded possibilities introduced by informatics. They also show its spatially ambivalent effects: spatial dispersion was facilitated (in conjunction with mass transport) and concentration in the form of skyscrapers was enabled (Sola Pool 1981).

The advanced telecommunications options offered by new ICTs show, as many studies have emphasised, similarly two-edged effects. Contrary to the hopes that telecommunication would replace traffic, there has been a net increase in material traffic. In other words, information precedes material and personal exchanges. As the level of information rises, contact potential and actual contacts increase, as well. Catchment areas are expanding. At the same time, co-presence is promoted.

One key condition for these effects of telecommunication is the parallel upgrading of transport modes, the acceleration of transport at various levels. The expansion of catchment areas this permitted is well mirrored by the European railway network. It also shrinks space (space time compression) (Harvey 1990). However, spatial compression involves the torsion of space because 'shrinkage' does not occur proportionately and homogeneously (cf. figure 9 in Herkommer in this volume). The relationship between spatial and temporal proximity shifts disproportionately, so that spatially close places (in terms of kms) move to a great temporal distance while spatially distant places come closer in time.

As telecommunication facilities change, so does the relationship between material and virtual proximity. The theoretical possibilities are summarised in Table 3. As we see, the two top quadrants are the most important for the present issue. The top right-hand quadrant shows the possibilities of personal co-presence with the (limited) means of telecommunication and thus the potential for substituting proximity by telecommunication – or, to put it more precisely, for renouncing spatial proximity while maintaining temporal proximity – and thus for the dissolution of the city.

Table 3. Relationship between material and virtual space-time proximity.

	Proximity in space materially	**Proximity in space virtually**
Proximity in time materially	Same location, walking distance, 'appropriate' (?) transport distance, (transport mode specific isochrones)	Coordination of telecommunication in time (e.g. telephone call over time zones, telephone conference, videoconference)
Proximity in time virtually	Inaccessible location in close vicinity (e.g. social barriers, no go areas, divided cities)	Disjointed telecommunication in time (e.g. answering machine, email, letter)

Source: Author's compilation

The top left-hand quadrant is of particular interest because it deals with the urban – or at least locally bound – variant of spatio-temporal proximity. However, this variant is also not clearly defined, because temporal distance is variable and spatio-temporal boundaries are generally indefinite. We are therefore dealing with a variable calculation of spatio-temporal distance in conjunction with other variables such as costs. Spatio-temporal distance could be measured in transport mode-specific isochrones whose overlap identifies the places with greatest space-time proximity. Crucially important is how 'demand' develops according to this variant.tab3

The relationship between absolute and relative spatio-temporal proximity cannot be determined theoretically. The necessary empirical studies on the role of temporal parameters of proximity are lacking. Furthermore, the problem of (relative) spatio-temporal proximity is specific to each spatial reference level – local, regional, supraregional, international – and depends on the given functions. There is much to suggest that actual space-time proximity is particularly necessary for innovative and information and knowledge-intensive sectors of the economy (as we have seen with financial services) that depend on complex and frequent communication in which implicit knowledge plays a major role. Depending on the quantitative development of these functions this means:

- greater differentiation/polarisation of small-scale and large-scale spaces, or at least the redistribution of functions within spaces;
- changes in demand for infrastructural facilities for securing material and virtual space-time proximity, resulting in preferences for certain areas (Graham/Marvin 2001).

Satisfying this demand engenders spatially selective changes in space-saving possibilities, thus magnifying spatial torsion. Shrinkage and torsion take place at the same time in both material and virtual space. The resulting differences in accessibility amplify spatio-temporal differentiation. This differentiation proceeds both on a small scale within the city between different districts and on a large scale as a speed advantage of the big city at various levels over network gaps (material, virtual, absolute, and relative).

5. Changes in Spatio-Temporal Proximity – Future Development Trends

We have seen how important spatio-temporal proximity is, and especially what role temporal aspects play. The future role of the city – or rather of agglomerations with functions of an urban character – will depend on function-specific demands on spatio-temporal proximity and how they change. These dimensions are decisively influenced by a number of parameters:

Foreseeable trends in the future organisation of work suggest that the structure and organisation of work will increase the 'demand' for spatio-temporal proximity.

- High growth potential is attributed to knowledge production activities with a strong need for face-to-face contact.
- The parallel increases in material traffic and informational networking shows that contact optionality has increased and is also taken advantage of. A decisive empirical issue, however, is development of the 'communicative modal split', the relationship between technically mediated and direct communication and types of indirect communication, because it will determine spatial allocation. The greater the role played by simultaneity, time sensitivity, and speed considerations, the greater will be the demand for highly central locations.
- In proportion to how knowledge-based activities (creative industries) flourish in the mix of firm, scene, cultural life, and housing in which employees move, the stronger will be the demand for inner-city locations.
- The organisation of work in the narrower sense of the term also determines the need for spatio-temporal proximity. Widely differing aspects are involved, such as the ratio of fixed to free-lance employment, the role of short-term project work in cooperation between many participants, the level of precarious employment, where those affected are obliged to take on more than one job, and the influence of urban lifestyles.
- The demand for urban locations is also increased by new lifestyle groups – which are becoming more important owing to changes in the organisation of work and because of an 'option demand' for the wide-ranging possibilities the city offers. Certain return migration trends towards cities are already apparent. Läpple/Thiel (2005) have shown the extent to which new everyday time structures contribute to making urban life, if not more attractive, at least more advantageous. The underlying assumption is that the time sensitivity of activities in various groups and livelihood ties and relations are tending to increase (many find their time budgets becoming finer-grained) (Sieverts 2002), so that spatio-temporal proximity again becomes more important than it long appeared to have been owing to shorter working hours and the flexibilisation of working time.
- The demographic developments (the ageing of society and the shrinking of the population) that are emerging in many European countries and to some extent in Japan, once again raise the question of the role of the city and agglomeration, i.e. space-time proximity. As the population shrinks and ages, reduced structures, especially in social and technical infrastructure, become extremely prone to undersupply (e.g. retailing, old-age care). The question of space and time distances must be put anew for a smaller and older society, because such societies probably can no longer easily afford spatial and temporal dispersion.

Even leaving aside such short-term factors, there are arguments that will come to bear in the longer term and which suggest that the space and time-saving function of urban structures will again play a growing role. One important aspect is the economies of energy offered by spatial structures in the light of rising energy costs and dwindling reserves. It is therefore questionable whether relative transport costs will remain as low as they are at present (Krugman 1999). In particular, measures favouring distance-intensive lifestyles (home ownership allowance, flat-rate commuter allowance as in Germany) are likely to disappear, thus changing incentive structures in the long term.

6. Conclusion

This article has sought to show that spatio-temporal proximity in the city not only continues to be very important but also that the role of speed is tending to increase. This and other temporal aspects have been neglected by theory and empirical research, although they are crucial for vital functions of the city. This is the context in which continued high-rise development must be considered. It is not by chance that running fast and building high coincide in places that act as the control centres of national and global economic flows.

With the growing importance of temporal aspects, speed is becoming more vital, especially in the core city. Nevertheless, there is no disputing that the core city is no longer the sole locus of spatio-temporal proximity and the corresponding advantages, because new crystallisation points for urbanisation have developed. However, time aspects play a salient role with regard to these locations, too.

We have outlined the necessary supplementation of traditional approaches, which have hitherto concentrated almost exclusively on space, by temporal perspectives. This neglect of time considerations has left many questions unanswered and a great deal of theoretical and empirical work to be done. Empirical research will need to address:

- the analysis of contact networks and their spatio-temporal distance dependence;
- the modal split of communication and the consequences for the demand for spatio-temporal proximity;
- sector-structural conditionalities of demand for spatio-temporal proximity;
- the question of what the city can do that other spaces cannot;
- the analysis of control approaches in the spatio-temporal context.

In concluding, I allow myself a normative remark. For a wide range of reasons, the city has often been pronounced at death's door – whether in a spirit of wishful thinking or prophecy. Similarly, the prospects of rural areas have repeatedly been evoked, most recently in connection with the development of telecommunications systems. But telematics favours urban centres in many ways. Cities change, the 'construction of the space-time saving machine' modifies as a result of technological and other developments. In essence, cities remain space-time saving machines. The extent to which they can remain so – for whom and through whom – can be influenced, and hence depends on policy decisions, on, for instance, the development of infrastructure, on the financial framework conditions set by the tax system, and on development promotion. Everyone who has a vision of liveable cities is therefore called up to play his part.

References

AUDRETSCH, D., FELDMAN, B., MARYANN, P. (1996), "R&D Spillovers and the Geography of Innovation and Production", *American Economic Review*, Vol. 86, No. 3, p. 630-640

BIRKEFELD, R., JUNG, M. (1994), *Die Stadt, der Lärm und das Licht – die Veränderung des öffentlichen Raumes durch Motorisierung und Elektrifizierung*, Seelze, Kallmeyer

BOSCHMA, R. A. (ed.) (2005), "Role of Proximity in Interaction and Performance: Conceptual and Empirical Challenges", *Regional Studies*, Vol. 39, p. 41-45

BOSCHMA, R. A. (2005), "Proximity and Innovation: A Critical Assessment", *Regional Studies*, Vol. 39, p. 61-74

BRIOSCHI, L. (1997), "Le cittadelle a tempo continuo", in: Bonfiglioli, S., Mareggi, M. (eds.), *Il tempo e la città fra natura e storia. Atlante di progetti sui tempi della città*, Urbanistica Quaderni, No. 12, Rome, p. 214-218

CAIRNCROSS, F. (1997), *The Death of Distance. How the Communications Revolution will Change Our Lives*, Boston, Harvard Business School Press

CAPELLO, R., FAGGIAN, A. (2005), "Collecitve Learning and Relational Capital in Local Innovation Processes", *Regional Studies*, Vol. 39, p. 75-87

CAMAGNI, R. (2000), "Das urbane Milieu: Voraussetzung für Innovation und wirtschaftlichen Erfolg", in: Matejowski, D. (ed.), *Metropolen. Laboratorien der Modern*, Frankfurt, p. 292-307

CASTELLS, M. (2003), "European Cities, the Informational Society, and the Global Economy", in: LeGates, R. T., Stout, F. (eds.), *The City Reader*, Third Edition, London, New York, Routhledge, p. 474-485

COYLE, D. (1997), *The Weightless World. Strategies for Managing the Digital Economy*, Oxford

EBERLING, M., HENCKEL, D. (2002), *Alles zu jeder Zeit? Die Städte auf dem Weg zur kontinuierlichen Aktivität*, Difu-Beiträge zur Stadtforschung Vol. 36, Berlin

FELDMAN, M. P. (2003), "Location and Innovation: New Economic Geography of Innovation, Spillovers, and Agglomeration", in: Clark, G., Feldman, L., Gertler, M. P., Meric, S. (eds.), *The Oxford Handbook of Economic Geography*, Oxford, Oxford University Press, p. 373-394

FLORIDA, R. (2002), "The Economic Geography of Talent", *Annals of the Association of American Geographers*, Vol. 92, No. 4, p. 743-755

FRANCK, G. (2002), "Soziale Raumzeit. Räumliche und zeitliche Knappheit und zeitliche Diskontierung, reale und temporale Veränderung", in: Henckel, D., Eberling, M. (eds.), *Raumzeitpolitik*, Opladen, Leske-Budrich, p. 61-80

GEISSLER, K. A. (2004), *Alles. Gleichzeitig. Und zwar sofort. Auf der Suche nach dem pausenlosen Glück*, Freiburg/Breisgau, Herder

GLAESER, E. L. (1994), "Cities, Information and Economic Growth", *Cityscape* Vol. 1, No. 1, p. 9-47

GLAESER, E. L. (1996), "Why Economists still like cities", *City-Journal*, Vol. 6, No. 2, p. 70-89

GLAESER, E. L. (2003), *The Rise of the Skilled City*, Harvard Institute of Economic Research Discussion Paper 2025, Cambridge/Mass

GORNIG, M., GEPPERT, K. (2003), "Die Renaissance der großen Städte – und die Chancen Berlins", *DIW-Wochenbericht* 26/2003.

GRABHER, G. (1998), "Urbi et Orbi. Lokale Ökonomien in Global Cities", *Der Öffentliche Sektor*, Vol. 24, No. 2/3, p. 1-18

GRAHAM, S., MARVIN, S. (2001), *Splintering Urbanism. Network Infrastructures, Technological Mobilities and the Urban Condition*, London, New York, Routledge

HÄUSSERMANN, H. (2004), *Phänomenologie und Struktur städtischer Dichte*, Zürich

HALL, P. (2003), "The end of the city? The report of my death was an exaggeration", *City*, Vol. 7, No. 2, p. 141-152

HARVEY, D. (1990), *The Condition of Postmodernity. An Enquiry into the Origins of Cultural Change*, Cambridge/Mass., Oxford, Blackwell

HELBRECHT, I. (2004), "Denkraum Stadt", in: Siebel, W. (ed.), *Die europäische Stadt*, Frankfurt/M. Suhrkamp, p. 422-432

HENCKEL, D. (2003), "Die Stadt als Raumzeitsparmaschine", in: AG Stadtleben Hannover (ed.), *Lücken und Tücken. Die Europäische Stadt zu Beginn des 21. Jahrhunderts*, Hannover, p. 44-46

HENCKEL, D., EBERLING, M. (eds.) (2002), *Raumzeitpolitik*, Opladen, Leske+Budrich

HIRSCH, W. Z. (1975), *Urban Economic Analysis*, New Delhi, Tata McGraw-Hill

JACOBS, J. (1970), *Stadt im Untergang. Thesen über den Verfall von Wirtschaft und Gesellschaft in Amerika*, Frankfurt/M, Ullstein

JAHODA, M., LAZARSFELD, P. F., Zeisel, H. (1975), *Die Arbeitslosen von Marienthal. Ein soziographischer Versuch über die Wirkungen langdauernder Arbeitslosigkeit*, Frankfurt/M, Suhrkamp

KRUGMAN, P. (1999), *"Looking Backward"*, in: Krugmann, P. (ed.), *The Accidental Theorist and Other Dispatches from a Dismal Science*, London, Penguin, p. 196-204

LÄPPLE, D. (2003), "Thesen zu einer Renaissance der Stadt in der Wissensgesellschaft", in: Gestring, N., Glasauer, H., Hannemann, Ch., Petrowsky, W., Pohlan, J. (eds.), *Jahrbuch StadtRegion*, Opladen, Leske+Budrich

LÄPPLE, D., THIEL, J. (2005), *Synthesebericht Sozioökonomischer Strukturwandel, Raum-Zeitkonfiguration und Alltag in Metropolregionen. Eine konzeptuelle Skizze mit empirischer Illustration*, VERA-Working-Paper No. 3, www.forschungsstelle-zeitpolitik.de/pdf-files/SyntheseTUfinal.pdf, accessed February 10, 2006

LEVINE, R. (1997), *Eine Landkarte der Zeit. Wie Kulturen mit Zeit umgehen*, München, Zürich, Piper

LIGHTMAN, A. (1994), *Und immer wieder die Zeit. Einstein's Dreams*, Hamburg, Heyne

MARKUSEN, A. (2003), "Fuzzy concepts, scanty evidence and policy distance: the case for rigour and policy relevance in critical regional studies", *Regional Studies*, Vol. 33, p. 869-84

MATTHIESEN, U. (ed.) (2004), *Stadtregion und Wissen. Analysen und Plädoyers für eine wissensbasierte Stadtpolitik*, Wiesbaden

McCANN, P. (2004), "Urban Scale Economies: Statics and Dynamics", in Capello, R., Nijkamp, P. (eds.), *Urban Dynamics and Growth. Advances in Urban Economics*, Amsterdam, Elsevier Science and Technology , p. 31-56

MITCHELL, W. (1995), *City of bits. Space, Place, and the Infobahn*, Cambridge/Mass., MIT Press

PAOLUCCI, P. (ed.) (1998), *La città macchine del tempo. Politiche del tempo in Italia*, Milano, Franco Angeli

PAWLEY, M. (2004), *A Disurbanist Manifesto*, shrinking cities, standpoint 06, www.shrinkingcities.com/fileadmin/shrink/downloads/pdfs/Pawley.pdf, accessed February 10, 2005

RIFKIN, J. (1988), *Uhrwerk Universum. Die Zeit als Grundkonflikt des Menschen*, München, Kindler

ROSENTHAL, S., STRANGE, S., WILLIAM, C. (2001), "The Determinants of Agglomeration", *Journal of Urban Economics*, Vol. 50, p. 191-229

RUSSELL, J. S. (2004), "Do skyscrapers still make sense?", *Archtitectural Record*, No. 11/2004, http://archrecord.construction.com/innovation/2_Features/0411SkyscraperSense.asp accessed May 26, 2005

SCHMITZ, S. (2001), *Revolutionen der Erreichbarkeit. Gesellschaft, Raum und Verkehr im Wandel*, Opladen, Leske+Budrich

SIEBEL, W. (2002), "Urbanität ohne Raum. Der Möglichkeitsraum", in: Kornhardt, D. (ed.), *Mögliche Räume. Stadt schafft Landschaft*, Hamburg, Junius, p. 32-40

SIEVERTS, T. (2002), "Zeitverwendungsmuster und Raumordnung", in: Henckel, D., Eberling, M. (eds.), *Raumzeitpolitik*, Opladen, Leske+Budrich, p. 251-264

SINGER, W. (2002), "Die Architektur des Gehirns als Modell für komplexe Stadtstrukturen", in: Singer, W. (ed.), *Der Beobachter im Gehirn, Essays zur Hirnforschung*, Frankfurt/M, Suhrkamp, p. 200-210

SORKIN, M. (2003), "The Center Cannot Hold", in: LeGates, R. T., Stout, F. (eds.), *The City Reader*, Third Edition, London, Routhledge, p. 290-295

SOLA POOL, I. de, DECKER, C., DIZARD, S., ISRAEL, K., RUBIN, P., WEINSTEIN, B. (1981), "Foresight and Hindsight. The Case of the Telephone", in: Sola Pool, I. de, (ed.), The Social Impact of the Telephone, Cambridge/Mass, MIT Press

STIENS, G. (2002), "Wie unterschiedliche 'Timesscapes' Staatsraum und Landschaften verändern können", in: Henckel, D., Eberling, M. (eds.), *Raumzeitpolitik*, Opladen, Leske+Budrich, p. 163-186

TORRE, A., RALLET, A. (2005), "Proximity and Localization", *Regional Studies*, Vol. 39, p. 47-59

WENDT, R. (1995), "Drehscheiben des Wissens", in: Sommer, D. (ed.), *Industriebau. Radikale Umstrukturierung. Praxisreport*, Basel, Birkhäuser

ZEDDA, R. (1999), "La carta di cronontopi urbani", in: Bonfiglioli, S., Zedda, R. (eds.), *Comune di Pesaro. Il piano dei tempi e degli orari della città di Pesaro*, Urbanistica Quaderni, No. 18, Rome, p. 32-36

CHAPTER II

NETWORK CITIES AND NEW URBAN FRINGES

NETWORK CITIES AND NEW URBAN FRINGES: INTRODUCTION

by Dietrich Henckel, Benjamin Herkommer and Elke Pahl-Weber

The heading points to a new phase in urban structures and developments, the blending of cities with regions, the region as a new city, and a new division of labour between cities in the region. The shift of functions from the city to the urban fringe is a process that began long ago and which has advanced in repeated waves of functional relocation. The exodus from the city was led by large manufacturing facilities, followed mainly by transport-intensive activities. Commerce was next to depart, and with mass motorisation and the development of public transport networks, it was joined by housing and finally by services. The relocation to the periphery of functions constitutive of the urban core is a well-documented phenomenon. On the one hand, this development is considered an opportunity for more evenly distributing economic activities in space and for integrating rural areas into the economic and cultural development of society. Those adopting an anti-city stance have to some extent welcomed this dissolution of the city. On the other hand, the decline of traditional cities is lamented, and not only for cultural reasons. Attention is drawn to the ecological and economic impacts of heavier traffic, growing infrastructural costs, and various forms of negative externalities.

At any rate, new spatial structures have developed involving new ways of dividing labour, new forms of work and production, and the spatial re-allocation of functions. These developments, to which authors have given various names such as 'edge city' (Garreau 1992), 'in-between city' ('Zwischenstadt') (Sieverts 1999, Bölling/Sieverts 2004), or 'network city' long found little favour among planners. Only gradually was it acknowledged that there was 'life beyond the city bounds' (Müller/Rohr-Zänker 1995), and that a highly dynamic and efficacious process was underway, which was permanently modifying spatial structures and exerting considerable influence on the economic competitiveness of regions. Only if these processes, what underlies them and where they are heading are subjected to scrutiny can issues of influence and control be realistically addressed.

In adopting such a regional view of the city, this second section of the book takes a more intensive look at three complexes:

- Elke Pahl-Weber focuses on density in its spatial, physical, and social dimensions as a key category of city formation. The city is always characterised by high densities. Nevertheless, densities have declined in very many cities of the developed world as cities have spread out and regions have been restructured. This raises the question of what factors and agents produce or promote density. Crucial is also the question of the spatial contexts in which density increases and decreases. For it is evident that density is growing precisely on the fringes of urban regions. This also raises questions about types of density, their granularity, about functional mix and mix intensity in different spatial units.
- Roberta Capello concentrates first on the issue of urban growth and optimum size for cities. This issue has repeatedly been a matter of intense concern for the urban economy. It shows that traditional concepts for explaining urban growth are unable to explicate growth beyond certain sizes because many factors like location and specialisation play an important role. Only the additional advantages offered by the networking of cities can explain further growth. In the second part of her article, she demonstrates empirically that cities integrated into networks enhance their growth, thus overcoming limits to growth.
- Finally, from the perspective of a globally operating firm in the automobile sector, Stephan Carsten examines how the product, the car, shapes the organisation of space and how the organisation of production in the international context determines the spatial requirements of firms. Taking as his point of departure the role of automobility and the motor industry and the organisation of production in the sector, he describes the path-dependency, cultural specificities, and role of world-wide competition. He comes to the conclusion that the city is becoming less and less important, that with growing competition between locations and diminishing scope for action, the once close links between city or urban region and car production are weakening. In this connection not only economic conditions but also the cultural setting are extremely important.

The three articles shed light on the emergence of 'new' dimensions of development on the urban fringe as a new crystallisation of density and show the role of strategic network formation for enhancing growth and thus for the spatial extension of urban dynamics.

Both Capello and Carsten show clearly that traditional territorial ties with the city are loosening and that larger-scale links are becoming more important, links vital for both the development of individual enterprises and the development of the city and city region. However, even on a more extensive level, a range of dimensions clearly play a role. Both regional networks and international networks of cities are involved; Capello cites the Healthy Cities Network. Density plays a particularly important role in connection with regional issues.

The importance for cities and firms of soft factors like the general cultural setting and cooperative capacity is also evident. This raises issues of institution formation, leadership, and organising capacity (van den Berg 2001).

References

BERG, L. van den, BRAUN, E., WINDEN, W. van (2001), *Growth Clusters in European Metropolitan Cities*, Aldershot, Ashgate

BÖLLING, L., SIEVERTS, T. (eds.) (2004), *Mitten am Rand. Auf dem Weg von der Vorstadt über die Zwischenstadt zur regionalen Stadtlandschaft*, Wuppertal, Müller+Busmannn

GARREAU, J. (1992), *Edge City. Life on the New Frontier*, New York, Anchor

HÄUSSERMANN, H. (2004), *Phänomenologie und Struktur städtischer Dichte*, Zurich.

MÜLLER, W., ROHR-ZÄNKER, R. (1995), "Neue Zentren in den Verdichtungsräumen der USA", *Raumforschung und Raumordnung*, No. 6/1995, p. 436-443

SIEVERTS, T. (1999), *Zwischenstadt. Zwischen Ort und Welt, Raum und Zeit, Stadt und Land*, Braunschweig, Wiesbaden, Birkhäuser

PRODUCTION OF URBAN DENSITIES – QUO VADIS DENSITY?

by Elke Pahl-Weber

Introduction: Urban density – Really a Topic for Urban Planning and Development?[1]

"The city is more than a contemporary and passing phenomenon" (Giedion 1941:821) wrote Siegried Giedion in his 'Time, Space and Architecture', published 65 years ago, in which he examines the emergence of a new tradition in architecture to verify the thesis that the methods of developing the city, of working with architecture, urban planning, science and building display a high degree of similarity over the years. He ascribed a paradigmatic shift in urban planning methods to the Amsterdam planner and architect of the 1920s C. van Eesteren: "He thinks no longer in linear terms of street and axis, but in terms of population densities. His approach to the town is conditioned by this population ratio, which in the Amsterdam extension plan, for example, was allowed to range between 110 and 550 inhabitants per hectare." (Giedion 1941:817). He described urban density, or at least the population density aspect, as the crux of city planning.

Whether or not cities are a passing phenomenon is still open to question, and implicitly involves postulates about urban density. There is intense debate on how urban structures develop in post-Fordist societies. Three years ago, John Friedmann argued that "the city is dead" (Friedmann quoted in Läpple 2003:61). In August 2005 the German weekly 'Die Zeit' published an article on 'Neue Heimat Stadt' (City – The New Home). In its series 'Principal Voices', Time Magazine published Zaha Hadid's view that "those cities which can shake off their inherited aesthetic regimes and dare to adopt a contemporary urbanism and architecture within their very centres will be the vital places where the next, most advanced sectors of the economy will flourish" (Hadid 2005).

---

1 I would like to thank Nikolai Roskamm for his intensive support in producing the conference presentation and this article.

'Urban density' is a term often used in this context, both in explaining and planning the city. It is used explicitly ("density generally equals City and City equals density" [Lampugnani 2004:2]) or implicitly as a categorical imperative, and hence with both positive and negative connotations. Planners and users associate urban life with urban density, with diversity, the spatial proximity of cultural services, housing, and places of work. The 'New Urbanism' movement pleads for greater density in the city and the rediscovery of urban attractiveness (Bodenschatz 2001:7). On the other hand, professionals, residents and policy makers alike understand density to mean physical density, which they reject, associating it with high-rise canyons and excessive traffic. In the sustainability debate, 'density' is the superlative concept for land conservation and the compact city, best able to meet ecological, social, and economic demands. Density is also a vehicle for transporting the city as space, but it is a very broad concept, so broad that, although it can and has been theoretically defined, its practical implications have still largely to be apprehended and its significance for urban development subjected to thoroughgoing scholarly investigation. What is well established is spatial monitoring at the level of population densities in urbanised areas.[2] Innumerable research projects, dissertations, conferences, and publications have been devoted to specific aspects of urban density, such as the relationship between urban density and green and open spaces.[3] There is broad debate on density in suburbia and the city, especially with regard to mobility. Topics range from deteriorating environmental conditions and road traffic nuisance attributable to high densities because of public transport's inability to satisfy the growing demand for mobility (Cox 2000:1) to cost effectiveness aspects under the motto: "urban density is more cost-effective than urban sprawl" (Scheidegger 2001; Gutsche 2004).

However, we lack the empirical and theoretical basis for any comprehensive treatment of relations between the individual components of urban density and urban structures, of their strategic importance for urban development, and of the role played by different components of urban density in planning and developing cities – for any investigation

2 Spatial monitoring is carried out at the national, state, and local levels in Germany; but interest in the subject now goes beyond government agencies. For example, Wendell, Cox Consultancy has published density profiles for Los Angeles in comparison with European, American, and Japanese cities, a comparison on population densities in the high income new world urbanised areas in Canada, the United States, and Australia, and on the comparative development of population densities in core cities and suburbs in all major American cities between 1950 and 1990; source: Cox Consultancy 2006

3 Some examples: Urban Density and Green Structure, European Research Network on Urban Density and Green Structure; Secretariat 2000-2002: Prof. Kimmo Lapintie, Laboratory of Urban Planning and Design, Department of Architecture, Helsinki University of Technology; source: European Research Network on Urban Density and Green Structure 2000; information Olli Maijala, Centre for Urban and Regional Studies, Helsinki University of Technology, May 2006; French publications on density and urban expansion (Fouchier/Merlin 1994, 1997); Switzerland: Avenir Suisse, March 2004 with articles by Lampugnani, Häußermann, Frey; Germany: Ingrid Krau 2000:79-84

that can relate these components to economic ratios, demographic developments, and cultural and civilizational achievements. Given the popularity of the concept in urban planning and development, this is astonishing.

Defining 'urban density' is prerequisite to any scholarly exploration of the concept. This brings a first dilemma, for "the concept 'density' as such is intension-free" (Spiegel 2000:39). It is used in physics[4], in optics[5], in electronics, in mathematics, and in statistics[6], in sociology[7], as well as in psychology and in urban planning.

In the urban planning context, three dimensions of the density concept come most frequently to bear: spatial, physical/building, and social density. In the urban context, density is ambivalent. Although the three dimensions are interlinked, they are not mutually contingent. They may correspond but they can also be in absolute contrast to one another. Even in abstract definition it is clear that urban density may involve simultaneous but dissimilar developments. Population density is not only a measure of spatial density, it is also an indicator of the structure of residential areas, and possibly has something to say about the concentration of employment. A low population density may point to a thinly settled neighbourhood with low building density, or to a central, inner-city neighbourhood with high building density, numerous jobs, but only little residential development. Building or physical density describes the ratio of developed land to surface area and, where appropriate, the height of buildings and the ratio of developed land to open space. But high physical density does not automatically mean high population density or high social density. The mistaken idea that high physical density promotes 'urbanity' has necessitated a great deal of urban repair from the 1990s to the present day. As a dimension of urban density, social density refers to the degree of division of labour as defined by Durkheim (Spiegel 2000:43) and associated contact possibilities in the working world. It also refers to gender roles and the resulting contact patterns, to social differentiation and the permeability of contact and communication structures within and between social groups. It relates to access to mobility and mobility technology and to the possibilities offered by communication technologies.

4 In physics it denotes the ratio of a physical quantity to volume, area or length, e.g., current density (current strength/cross-sectional area); (Die Zeit 2005:444).
5 Optical density is a property of an optical medium, expressed as refractive index, in producing refraction; the medium with the higher refractive index is described as optically more dense (Brockhaus 1988:458).
6 In statistics, density describes the function ascribed to continuously distributed random variables (Die-Zeit 2005:444).
7 According to Emile Durkheim, density in sociology describes the differention of the population into dynamic and moral density, the number of inhabitants per area unit and the number of interrelating individuals. 'Real' distances do not correspond to spatial distances, and not spatial proximity but accessibility is the precondition for social relations (Spiegel 2000:43).

The relationship between density and urban planning is one of tension. Statements and forecasts on spatial density provide our discipline with framework inputs for the planning of neighbourhoods; they supply guidelines and recommendations for designing social infrastructure facilities and green and open spaces, which are calculated in terms of residents per unit area. High population density has made its way into urban planning guidelines and recommendations at the local level in large-scale concepts like preparatory land-use plans and urban development concepts. Building density has been a subject of debate at all levels of the discipline, in design, in the distribution of building volume, in the utilisation of existing plots. Physical density is tied to urban planning tools and is thus a subject and result of binding urban land-use planning. Since the beginnings of urban planning as a discipline, development trends in spatial density and population projections have been an important basis for a wide variety of planning tasks and decisions, as the quote from Giedion shows. This is true not only for planning to deal with growth but also for the Europe of today with its ageing populations and shrinking societies. The challenges this situation poses for urban planning in Germany currently dominate many aspects of the expert discourse.

This paper is concerned with the future role of urban density in the development of cities. No global answer is sought, although the emergence of megacities in the South calls for urgent action with respect to the development of urban density in existing cities and raises questions about the sense of developing new towns. I begin with a brief review of the historical development of the symbiotic, paired concept 'density and urban planning', going on to consider the three dimensions of density in the German context. Since the production of density is not restricted to urban planning alone, the plural 'urban densities' is appropriate. Finally, the prospects for urban density are considered in thesis form, reuniting the different aspects of density in the urban development context.

1. 'Density' in the History of Urban Development

There are two quite distinct lines of development in the history of urban planning as a discipline. The first concerns the regulatory regime and policing and hygienic requirements in the prodigiously growing cities of the industrial revolution. The second pursued ventures of the imagination, the utopias and ideal cities of the utopian humanists and socialists (Roskamm 1997:58). Beginning with Renaissance humanism, the first urban utopias were designs for ideal cities and social systems. In this 'no place', as the Greek term 'utopia' can be translated, the humanist imaginings were still very utopian and far removed from any concrete realisation. Humanist utopias (Thomas More and the 'Island Utopia', Tomaso Campanella and his 'Cittá del Sole') were followed by the utopias of the socialists (Etienne Cabet's 'Voyage en Icarie', Charles Fourier and the 'Phalanstère'), who first undertook to put their ideas into effect in practical experiments. The socialist utopias are regarded as predecessors of scientific socialism. This brought a radical break with the ideal city designs and their illustrative quality, and put an end to the utopian line of development (de Bruyn 1996:151ff). This coincided with the first major phase of growth in European cities, generated by industrialisation. The emergence of the capitalist or post-liberal (Benevolo 1991:813) city with its planning requirements also signalled the birth of governmental urban planning and of the scholarly discipline bearing the same name (Albers 1995:250).

By the end of the 19th and the beginning of the 20th century, the capitalist city had produced enormous physical density. The resulting traffic and housing conditions were, however, soon felt to be extremely burdensome, and from the turn of the century one of the chief aims of the new profession of urban planning was to reduce building density by deconcentrating and extending built-up areas into the urbanised region. In 1960 the economist and sociologist Edgar Salin coined the term 'urbanity through density', giving a new direction to urban planning thinking. The formal schematism of spatio-functional separation and simple housing sociology concepts were to be replaced by mixed uses and greater physical densities. By 'urbanity' Salin meant the manifestation of a specific urban quality in political participation and cultural openness and tolerance, and believed he had found the missing link between architecture and urban society. The 'urbanity through density' model prompted an understanding of lifestyles and mentalities as the products of certain physical configurations in the built environment. This misunderstanding produced the next radical about-turn in the debate on urban planning models in the 1980s. Any monocausal relationship between the built environment and the living beings that inhabit it was denied, urbanity was no longer simply equated with a certain density of urban interactions. Building density or high population density without cultural and social diversity, it was recognised, only intensify the monotony characteristic of homogeneous places. In the present urban-development discussion, density is treated as a component in the model of the compact, mixed-use, short-distance city. Physical density is considered a tool and supposed guarantee for sustainable urban development and accordingly as a safeguard against undue land take, wastage of energy, and unnecessary traffic. In many cases, the generation of social density can be assumed to the be underlying aim of this model. However, probably because it is not amenable to planning, such a goal is not explicitly formulated. But the 'human scale' has been an enduring theme of planning, suggesting that a demand for the production of spatial facilities for social interaction may be implied. One objection to the model is that physical concentration is worthwhile only to a limited degree beyond which, while exacerbating housing conditions, it contributes little towards conserving land (Sieverts 1997:41).[8] The concept of density has thus repeatedly aroused fears, wishes, and hopes.

8 A study by the German Institute of Urban Affairs also comes to the conclusion that, under prevailing conditions, residential development up to three storeys high is the physical density that 'saves' most land (Difu 1995:83).

2. Spatial Density

Data and forecasts on demographic developments provide the basis for urban planning and the planning of spatial densities. At present we know that there are fewer births in Germany than deaths and that the population of the country is declining in absolute terms. Immigration can cushion this development but not compensate for it.[9] Population projections range from 67 to 81 million by 2050. More seriously, the population is also ageing. Two falls in the birth rate – in about 1900 and 1965 – resulted in so low a level of births that the child generations are always smaller in numbers than their parent generations. The long-term, continuous rise in life expectancy has meant that earlier large birth cohorts reach a great age. Since the two causes coincide, ageing is accelerated.

An ageing population and falling population figures are crucial factors in producing spatial densities in the city. A brief analysis of the development of spatial densities and economic development over the past decade shows that the expansion of urban regions has not occurred in parallel to economic growth. The trend is apparent in both economically prosperous regions and in economically weaker regions (BBR 2005a:85). Following the economic growth of the 1970s, spatial development is now being disrupted by current trends, bringing simultaneous but dissimilar developments in the various regions and cities of Germany, some with growing populations, some with fewer people living in existing structures. A look at the current Spatial Planning Report (BBR 2005a) and Regional Planning Forecast (BBR 2006) shows that almost everywhere outside the Berlin region the population is falling in East Germany, whereas the population is growing in the West and South, especially in border areas. Population in the cores of agglomerations is declining. It remains to be seen whether this will affect the production of spatial densities in different ways. The forecast shows that population developments could produce new edges, borders between growing and shrinking regions, which can be fixed or fuzzy. If these borders coincide with differing spatial densities, they pre-

9 In 2000 the UN Population Division investigated how many people would have to immigrate if the population were no longer to age (so-called replacement migration). It asked how many people would have to come to Germany to ensure three things: constancy of the population, constancy of the population of working age, and constancy in the ratio of population of working age to that of retirement age. It would be relatively easy to maintain the level of population. Some 320,000 more people would have to come to Germany each year than leave the country. Over the entire projection period, this would amount to 17.8 million immigrants. To keep the population of working age constant until 2050, an annual migration gain of 458,000 would be needed. This would give a total of 25.2 million, so that the population would rise to 92 million. But the ageing of the population could not be halted by such a development. The third scenario calculates a constant ratio of population of retirement age to population of working age. To achieve this, an annual migration gain of 3.4 million would be required. Over the years until 2050, this would add up to 188.5 million; the population would increase to 300 million with immigrants constituting 80 % of the total. The outcome of this scenario would thus be the complete urbanisation of the country (cf. Bundesinstitut 2004:14ff).

sumably also draw lines between areas with differing infrastructure endowment. In its present extension and according to the current development concept, technical infrastructure requires minimum spatial densities, minimum numbers of customers and users – whether for water or energy supply, sewage or waste disposal.

In an expert report on the framework conditions for downsizing infrastructure in communities and neighbourhoods with falling population figures (BBR 2005b), we ascertained that the technical efficiency of the technical network infrastructure and the cost of operating it depend absolutely on population density. The social infrastructure, on the other hand, can react very flexibly, and in the urban context (but not in rural areas) it is therefore less dependent on population densities as far as cost trends are concerned. This raises the question whether the new edges indicated by the Spatial Planning Report 2005 will in future constitute new borders for infrastructure endowment, and hence in the long term further reduce spatial densities – whether they will mark a transition from decentralised to centralised systems of infrastructure provision. This is indicated by the drastic falls in population forecast from 2012 onwards. In the past, by contrast, population densities have tended to decline moderately without any obvious implications for infrastructure endowment. A brief analysis of data (BPW Hamburg 2003) on the BBR (Federal Office for Building and Regional Planning) field of research 'Cities of the Future' (BBR 2004) shows that population density in the fifty cities under study with seven different types of spatial and settlement structure has fallen everywhere over the past ten years – least of all in urban cores and most of all in rural areas. Absolute population figures have also fallen in all types except suburbanised areas of polycentric agglomerations and agglomerations with outstanding centres. Settlement areas are growing in all types, and population densities relate to these settlement areas and not to the administrative borders of municipalities .[10]

Figure 1. Basis data on 50 cities from the BBR field of research 'Cities of the Future'.

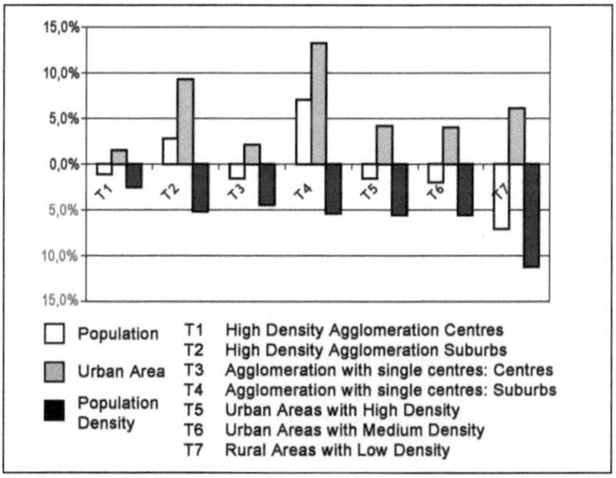

Source: Authors' diagram based on data from BBR 2004

10 This is to avoid misinterpretations when comparing cities with much or little green and open space, with woodland or agricultural land within the bounds of the municipality.

The conclusion is that spatial density declines independently of spatial and settlement structure type. What is more, spatial density in the cases under study decreases quite independently of population growth and population decline, at least on the scale experienced to date.

In a study of five global metropolises entitled 'Phenomenology and Structure of Urban Density', Häußermann (2004:14) shows that spatial density displays no homogeneous structures in relation to population or to employment in the various areas of a city. Paris, Tokyo, London, and New York have the highest employment density in the inner urban core. In the urban core as a whole, population density is higher than employment density. The only exception among these metropolises in Tokyo, where population density in the inner urban core and in the urban core as a whole is very much lower than in the entire remaining city. Berlin is the only city where population density and employment density in the inner core and the whole urban core is equally high. It is also the only city where employment density in the remaining urban area is extremely low.

These big differences in the population and employment density landscape – even in relation to very general and average spatial densities for the total urban area – reflect the differing physical structures and living conditions that have developed in the course of history, as well as differential property prices across the city. In the global context

Figure 2. Changes in population density (number of inhabitans) in four selected cities.

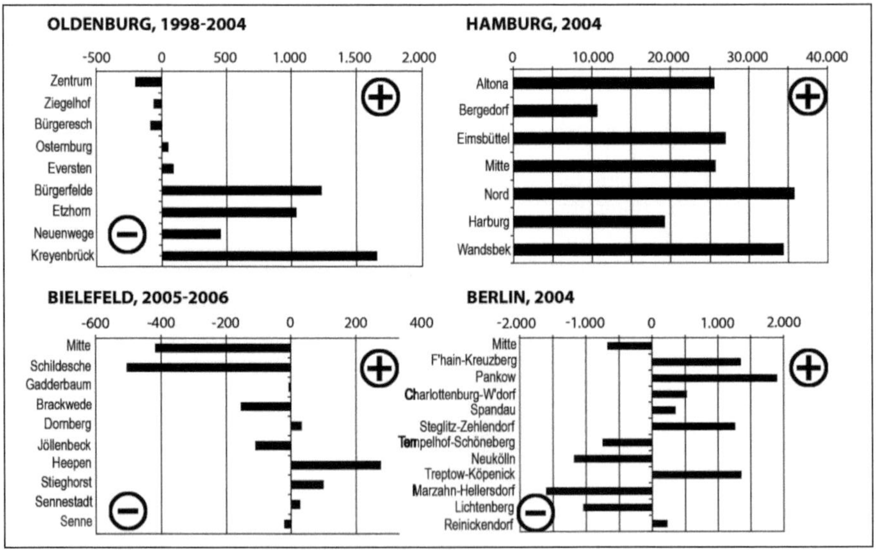

Source: Author's diagram

and in metropolises, urban density clearly obeys no generalizable patterns in relation to population and employment densities: it is inhomogeneous in structure.

This is presumably also the case for smaller cities that cannot claim to be metropolises. A brief analysis of changes in population figures and population densities in urban neighbourhoods shows a strong trend towards centrifugal migration. Suburbanisation takes place not only in relation to city bounds and beyond. Within cities, too, spatial density changes in the city centre, in inner-city areas, and in edge-city neighbourhoods and urban expansion areas.

No homogeneous development is apparent. Light could be thrown on the subject by a systematic study of changes in spatial density that develops typologies of density structures showing the relationship between spatial structure, spatial density, and quality of life. The on-going trend in spatial density, population density, and dwelling occupancy density ranges from decline to strong decline. Whether this entails losses in spatial quality and quality of life need not be discussed at this point, but the planning dichotomy of evoking and rejecting high spatial density can be demythologised.

This can point the way for adjusting or completely restructuring requirement values for planning. For, in view of continuously declining spatial densities, requirement values stated in terms of catchment areas and distances no longer reflect actual needs.

3. Building Density

Building or physical density refers to the ratio of the floor area of buildings to total area. It is an indicator for the structure of cities and regions, but is informative in other connections, too. The paired concept 'low rise – high density', for example, shows that high physical density can be achieved in other ways than with high buildings (Schramm 2004:11ff). The urban context is not a homogeneous container but a complex system of different structures, which grows logically out of historical structures and "is organised in a field of density and space" (Humpert 1997:42). Humpert shows the relations between cultural context and urban structure. European cities are clustered and produce numerous edges, American cities are extremely spread out, whereas in Africa and Asia cities are very compact. Physical densities relate closely to these structures, and the edges and boundaries between the various, differently structured areas mark their identity. Population density is less visible. We have noted that population density does not relate to economic development: it cannot be said that greater economic growth brings higher or lower population density.

There is no empirical basis for any generalised description of how economic development relates to building density. In analysing these relations we turn first to residential development. We looked at the number of dwellings built in West Germany between 1960 and 2002. Over the years, completion figures follow the ups and downs of economic development. The share of single-family homes remains relatively constant, and the proportion of new dwellings completed in existing building stock is almost marginal. The difference in the curves, and especially major swings reflect multi-storey housing development. As a rule, higher physical densities are expected in multi-storey buildings than in single-family housing. And indeed, the rate of multi-family housing development has been high when economic output has been high, for example in the early 1970s and in the mid-1990s. During these periods greater building densities were accordingly reached in residential development than in times of economic depression. This gives us a starting point for determining the relationship between physical density and density of development, namely that they do indeed correlate: building density increases in step with economic growth. This has yet to be tested for specific sectors and markets – office space, industrial premises.

Development of the older building stock is also significant in the context described. Considering that, of every 100 Euros spent for building purposes, 65 Euros are invested in existing buildings, it would appear that the money is spent chiefly on maintaining the building stock and not on producing new dwellings. If, however, a significant number of dwellings are not produced in the existing housing stock, it suggests that physical densities remain approximately constant. This would mean that most investment in residential development goes into constant building density. And if a distinction is also made between publicly subsidised and private investment in housing development, it could be hypothesized that most private investment in housing (namely in existing buildings) does little to change physical density.

Figure 3. Number of dwellings completed in West Germany and East Germany.

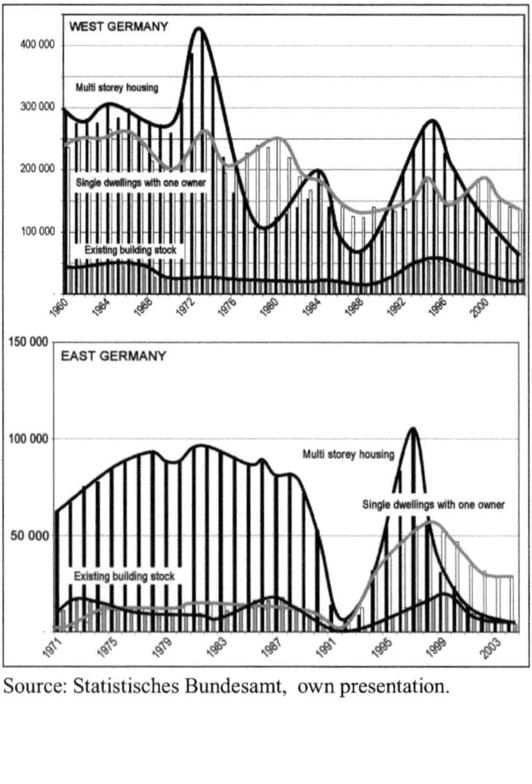

Source: Statistisches Bundesamt, own presentation.

The housing construction sector in West and East Germany differs strongly in the development of building densities. Until the beginning of the 1990s, the completion rate for multi-storey buildings was approximately six times higher than that for single-family homes. After unification, the share of single-family houses in East Germany reached a level comparable to West Germany. Since the end of the 1990s, single-family housing has been the dominant line (see figure 3). In both East and West Germany, physical density has fallen over the past seven years.

In the early 1990s, tremendous efforts were made in Berlin to create a new urban context with new suburbs of relatively high building density. The aim was to build between 80,000 and 100,000 new dwellings within four years. Some 80 % were to be built with public subsidies, and 57,000 were to be located in the new suburbs (Stimmann 1995:9). The present senate building director of Berlin Hans Stimman envisaged a floor-space index of 1.2 (Stimmann 1995:15). But once public grants for this project had been stopped, the physical density for the projects fell and the full number of buildings planned was not constructed. The following example shows the decrease in building densities in Karow Nord, where planning was revised to give a much lower FSI and a new building structure.

Figure 4. Karow Nord, former (left) and revised (right) planning.

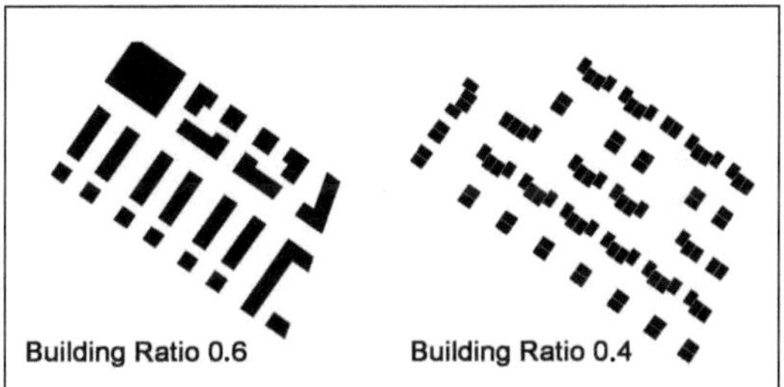

Source: Diagram by Nikolai Roskamm (Freie Planungsgruppe Berlin)

There are, of course, quite contrary examples, like Munich-Riem, a project where the former airport was redeveloped into a new district. High building densities were concentrated in the northern section, and housing areas were linked with large, undivided open spaces. But in the residential areas the average floor-space index was 1.2, and in industrial areas an FSI of 1.3 to 2.0 was planned and partly realised. The urban development concept also allowed relatively dense building structures to be combined with extensive open space structures including a large landscape park, and direct allocation and accessibility of social infrastructural facilities. Moreover, the latter are 'marginal phenomena' between the landscape park and building structure, lending this edge its own urban planning significance in the context of all three forms of urban density. This is a holistic concept for the production of urban density. The ecological footprint is better than for the overall city of Munich. Some 50 % of the entire area is devoted to green and open spaces as compared to the mean 40 % for the whole of Munich (BPW Hamburg 2005).

Over the past five years in Germany, both building density, especially in residential development, and population densities have declined. But the Munich example demonstrates simultaneous but contrary currents, which will strongly affect spatial development in Germany over the coming years, depending on how population figures develop. Munich Riem points the way for all areas where higher building densities can be realised.

4. Social Density

Social density refers primarily to interactions between people, whether deliberate or chance, multi-dimensional and manifold, and which are relatively easy to establish in the spatial proximity offered by the urban context (Spiegel 2000:43). Proximity and density are not necessarily identical, but they are directly related. This is one of the findings of Emile Durkheim in his work on the social division of labour and the organisation of civil society in the late 20th century (Spiegel 2000:43).

Proximity and accessibility are the key components of social density in urban space. And they depend not least of all on the development of communications technologies and mobility. Communication density and the city are mutually sustaining. High communication density in the city developed with the rising complexity of the urban space – and the urban space gained in complexity through communication density. Social density, the expression of the division of labour and heterogeneity in society, is decisive in producing innovative milieus.

Communications technologies have made major advances over the past five to ten years. Cities have become the central places of communication, but the Internet offers innumerable opportunities for obtaining information, and, increasingly, for communication and even participation for all spaces regardless of physical or population density. For instance, there is intensive communication via the Internet between Europe and the United States. It is striking that building and population density in Germany declined particularly during the years following the establishment of these technical communication services. But technical possibilities are no real substitute for direct contact. Social density can certainly be supplemented by electronic communication, but it is doubtful whether it can replace it, at least in Durkeim's understanding of the concept.

Social infrastructure has a decisive function in social density. Schools, for example, are one of the crucial places where children not only gain knowledge but also learn to establish personal relationships and to develop social contacts. As the population and the number of children falls, more and more schools are being closed.

In an expert report for the Federal Office for Building and Regional Planning (BBR) on the development of infrastructure in shrinking regions (BBR 2005b), we worked on thresholds for the cost-related viability of these institutions. The assumption was that declining utilization in shrinking regions causes high costs, especially high per capita costs for social infrastructure facilities.

Figure 5 shows the example of Frankfurt/Oder, where the school population has fallen by 45 % over the past decade. In accordance with Brandenburg state regulations, almost half of all schools in Frankfurt had to close their doors. Nevertheless, accessibility has not essentially suffered in the urban context. Even in the absence of direct ties with the district, accessibility has been ensured and a range of schools with differing profiles has also been maintained. This shows that social infrastructure, in this case the school system, relates not only to a particular neighbourhood but is important for the city as a whole. In the overall context, social infrastructure facilities can assume the role of urban nuclei, which perform a vital function for social density in the different areas of the city. Hence, they contrast strongly with the technical infrastructure.

Figure 5. Case Study Frankfurt (Oder).

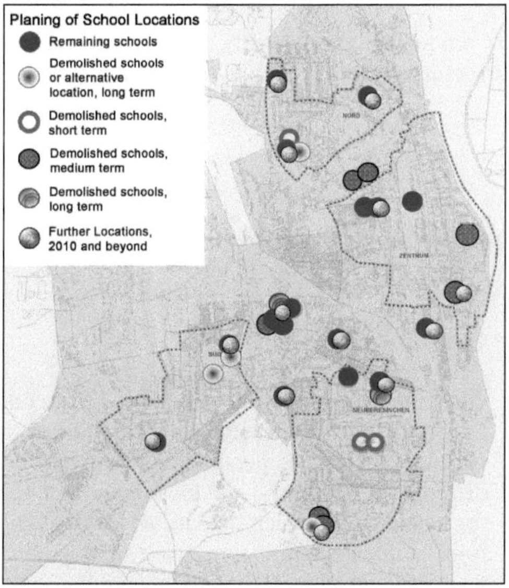

Source: BBR 2005b:50

5. Quo Vadis Density?

On the assumption that the construction of cities in Germany has now largely been completed, that the major phase of urban expansion has come to an end, future planning will be concerned with developing the existing building stock.

Disregarding all local differences, population and building densities in Germany are generally falling. But this applies primarily to the new urban structures of recent years. In existing building stock, population densities have been redistributed, and a shift has taken place between centre and periphery, but density in the building stock has largely remained constant. The social infrastructure has a linking function, which can suffer if population density falls too strongly in single neighbourhoods.

Development of the building stock is therefore the major challenge in shaping the urban density of the future. Urban renewal, urban regeneration in the classical sense is not meant. What is needed is new, vital layers of urban complexity. This will not succeed if major conversion areas in inner cities form the edges of the inner core because a lack of demand or excessive land prices prevent their adequate development.

In producing urban density, such new edges must be avoided and new complexities and structures created – also in cities that are shrinking.

Case Study Münster

Generally, population density varies from one neighbourhood to another. Average figures of a city's density can hardly reflect the very different developments in the various districts. As population density is a crucial factor for the stabilisation of the different neighbourhoods' local identities, urban development must try to provide for a balance between the city as a whole and its single parts. The following four brief examples, taken from a case study on the city of **Münster**, indicate that there is no simple correlation between a neighbourhood's density and characteristics such as its location and its housing stock.

The relationship between the three elements of infrastructure depends on the particular location and site. This is one result of the work we have been doing in Münster over the past year. The city's districts show a broad range of constellations of spatial density, building density and social density. In a concerted action, politicians, administrators, investors, banks, stakeholders and external consultants have been developing strategies of communication and discussion to stabilise the identity of the areas involved with respect to the different elements of density. The following pictures may illustrate that the spatial structure and spatial density, the growth and ageing of the population differ from one neighbourhood to another. The equipment with and the quality of technical infrastructure is similar in all neighbourhoods but social infrastructure shows a broad range of variation. Major societal trends such as demographic change will affect the single areas in very different ways. Instead of "one-size-fits-all" solutions, area specific approaches will be needed.

Hansaviertel: The Hansaviertel is located in the inner city, the buildings date from the beginning of the 20th century. Spatial density changed in the last 12 years due to a decrease in the number of inhabitants of about 14 %. Over 40 % of this figure were represented by children. The provision of social infrastructure is very good with approximately 170 % of the demand.

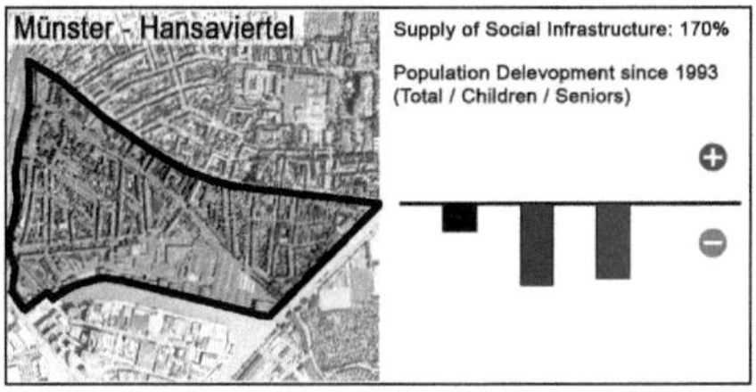

Uppenberg-East: This neighbourhood is also part of the urban core, the building structure shows the typical form of single houses built in the 1950s and 1960s. Here, the decrease in spatial density over the last 12 years was mostly represented by elderly people. The supply of social infrastructure is only at about 65 % of the demand.

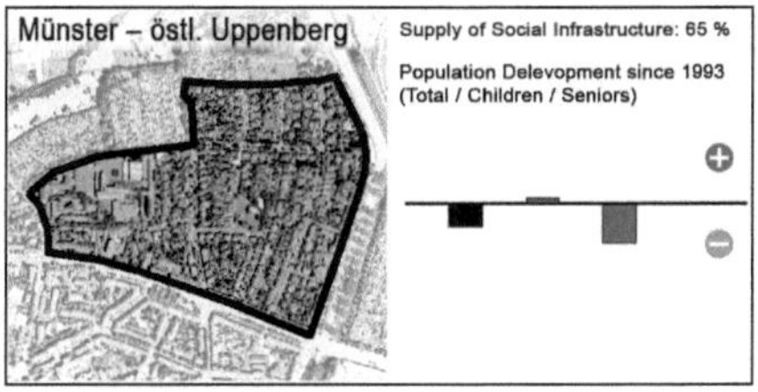

Mauritz-East: This neighbourhood on the outskirts of Münster is a well established area with villas on large tracts of land. The spatial density slightly decreased by 6 % over the last 12 years, again with a large share of older people leaving the quarter. The supply of social infrastructure almost meets the demand at approximately 100 %.

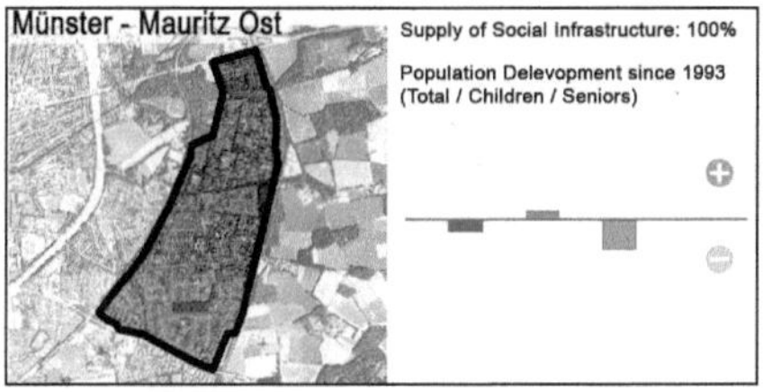

Hiltrup-East: The second area located at the periphery of Münster features small single family houses. Spatial density remained constant, however, during the last 12 years the rate of older people in this area grew by more than 50 %. The supply with social infrastructure fits the demand at approximately 100 %.

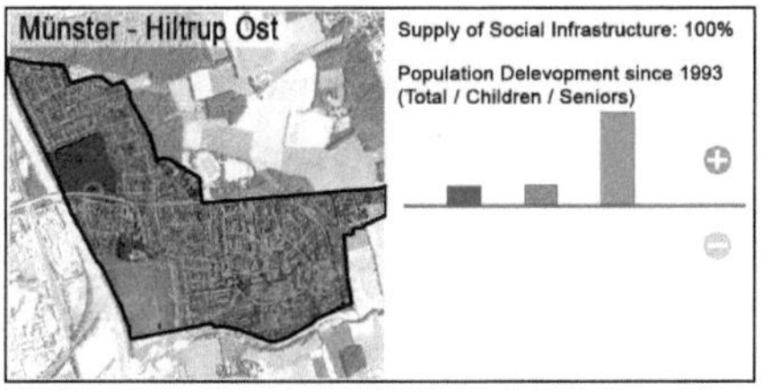

References

ALBERS, G. (1995), *Zur Entwicklung der Stadtplanung in Europa*, Braunschweig, Vieweg

BENEVOLO, L. (1991), *Die Geschichte der Stadt*, Frankfurt/M, Campus

BUNDESINSTITUTS für Bevölkerungsforschung (2004), Bevölkerung: Fakten –Trends – Ursachen – Erwartungen. Die wichtigsten Fragen, Sonderheft der Schriftenreihe des Bundesinstituts für Bevölkerungsforschung, Wiesbaden

BODENSCHATZ, H. (2000), "Suche nach einem besseren Leben. Die Amerikaner wollen wieder Stadtluft atmen: Die Reformbewegung des 'New Urbanism' hat bereits 200 Neustädte hervorgebracht", *Berliner Zeitung*, Issue January 15/16, 2000, Magazin

BPW HAMBURG (2003), *Datensammlung im Rahmen der Testphase 'Städte der Zukunft' im Auftrag des BBR*,unpublished

BROCKHAUS (1988), Enzyklopädie in 24 Bänden, Vol. 5, Mannheim, Bibliographisches Institut & F. A. Brockhaus A.G.

BBR (Bundesamt für Bauwesen und Raumordnung) (2004), *Städte der Zukunft, Kompass für den Weg zur Stadt der Zukunft*, Bonn

BBR (Bundesamt für Bauwesen und Raumordnung) (2005a), *Raumordnungsbericht 2005*, Berichte 21, Bonn

BBR (Bundesamt für Bauwesen und Raumordnung) (ed.) (2005b), *Rahmenbedingungen für die Rücknahme von Infrastruktur* , BBR-Online-Publikation, September 2005, www.bbr.bund.de/exwost/pdf-files/SQU-gutachten_zusammenfassung.pdf, accessed May 12, 2006

BBR (Bundesamt für Bauwesen und Raumordnung) (2006), *Raumordnungsprognose 2020/2050*, Berichte 23, Bonn

BRUYN, G. de (1996), *Die Diktatur der Philanthropen: Entwicklung der Stadtplanung aus dem utopischen Denken*, Braunschweig, Wiesbaden, Vieweg

COX, W. (2000), *How urban density intensifies traffic congestion and air pollution*, Arizona Issue Analysis 162, Phoenix, Goldwater Institute

COX CONSULTANCY (2006): *Demographia*, www.demographia.com, accessed Januaryy 21, 2006

DIFU (Deutsches Instituts für Urbanistik) (1995), *Möglichkeiten zur Steuerung des Flächenverbrauchs und der Verkehrsentwicklung*, Berlin

DIE ZEIT (ed.) (2005), *Zeit-Lexikon*, Vol. 3, Mannheim, Bibliographisches Institut

EUROPEAN RESEARCH NETWORK ON URBAN DENSITY AND GREEN STRUCTURE (2000): *Urban Density and Green Structure*, www.arbeer.demon.co.uk, accessed January 21, 2006

GIEDION, S. (1941), *Space, Time and Architecture, The Growth of a New Tradition*, 5th ed. 1982, 14th impression, 2002, Harvard, Harvard College

GUTSCHE, J. M. (2004), *Verkehrserzeugende Wirkungen des kommunalen Finanzsystems*, Hamburg, Analytica

HADID, Z. (2005): *The role of urbanism and architecture in economic development*, www.principal-voices.com/voices/zaha-hadid-white-paper.html, accessed September 20, 2005

HÄUSSERMANN, H. (2004), *Phänomenologie und Struktur städtischer Dichte*, Zürich

HUMPERT, K. (1997), *Einführung in den Städtebau*, Stuttgart, Kohlhammer

KRAU, I. (2000), "Urbane und bauliche Dichte im Kontext der Stadtregion", in: Institut für Städtebau und Wohnungswesen (ed.), *Aktuelle Fragen zur Stadt*, Veröffentlichungsreihe Planung, Vol. 3, München, p. 79-84

LAMPUGNANI, V. M. (2004), *Die Ästhetik der Dichte*, Zürich

LÄPPLE, D. (2003), "Thesen zu einer Renaissance der Stadt in der Wissensgesellschaft", in: Gestring, N., Glasauer, H., Hannemann, Ch., Petrowsky, W., Pohlan, J. (eds.), Jahrbuch StadtRegion, Opladen, Leske+Budrich, p. 61-77

Landeshauptstadt MÜNCHEN (ed.) (2005), *Evaluierung Messestadt Riem – Nachhaltige Stadtentwicklung in München*, Ergebnisband, München

PAHL-WEBER, E., REHSÖFT, N. (2005): Arbeitskreis 'Wohnen in Münster', Dokumentation der 3. Sitzung am 6. April 2005, Münster

RAUTERBERG, H. (2005), "Neue Heimat Stadt", *Die Zeit*, No. 34, August 18, 2005

ROSKAMM, N. (1997), *Von den Schwierigkeiten, eine Stadt zu planen*, Institut für Stadt- und Regionalplanung Berlin (Thesis)

SCHEIDEGGER, P., MERCHAND, L., DELVA G., QUIDORT, M., VIVIER, J., ALLEN, H. (2001): Urban Density is More Cost-effective than Urban Sprawl, www.uitp.com/publications/ brochures/better.cfm, accessed August 5, 2004

SCHRAMM, H. (2004), *Low Rise – High Density*, Wien, Springer

SIEVERTS, T. (1997), *Zwischenstadt: zwischen Ort und Welt, Raum und Zeit, Stadt und Land*, Braunschweig, Wiesbaden, Vieweg

SPIEGEL, E. (2000), "Dichte", in: Häußermann, H. (ed.): *Großstadt*, Opladen, Leske+Budrich, p.39-47

STIMMANN H. (1995), "Wohnungsbau für die Großstadt", in: Senatsverwaltung für Bau- und Wohnungswesen (ed.): *Stadt Haus Wohnung*, Berlin, Ernst&Sohn, p. 9-27

URBAN GROWTH AND CITY NETWORKS EMPIRICAL EVIDENCE FROM ITALY AND EUROPE

by Roberta Capello

Introduction

In the real world, the number of people living in cities is growing in all countries and continents. The urbanisation process is a phenomenon which, in the last decade, has been increasingly intense in the developing countries. The share of urban population in the more developed continents, such as Europe and North America, is extremely high, and is nearly 50 % at the world scale. This share, according to the forecasts of the World Resources Institute (World Resources 2003), is expected to rise yet further in future decades. As a consequence of increasing population, cities physically expand through processes which have been defined as 'ville éclatée', 'ville éparpillée', 'ubiquitous city'. The population of large cities continues to grow, though sometimes more slowly than previously (Camagni 1996). The constantly increasing size of cities encountered in the real world is in contrast with the famous 'optimal city size' theory, which envisages a size above which an increase in physical dimension decreases the advantages of agglomeration. The declining rate of urban population growth recorded in the last decade in most developing countries appears to be common to all cities, independently of physical size, and represents a general slowing down, rather than a specific crisis in the larger cities. Indeed, during the seventies, there were negative population growth rates in the urban system of the Po Valley in Northern Italy not only in the major cities, but also a number of secondary centres of 75,000 to 150,000 inhabitants (8 out of 19) and even some smaller towns of 20,000 to 75,000 inhabitants (27 out of 113) (Camagni et al. 1985; Camagni et al. 1986). According to the theory, however, medium-sized towns are expected to increase their size, since the advantages associated with the physical dimension are still higher than location costs. This seemingly mistaken interpretation of the real world by the 'optimal city size theory' has already been pointed out by various authors. Richardson (1972) was the first to present a 'sceptic's view', by underlining that an apparent paradox existed between the theoretical acceptance of an 'optimal city size' and the contradictory development patterns of urban systems in the real world. According to Richardson, this paradox could be explained by the existence of other determinants influencing urban agglomeration economies, not merely physical size. Since Richardson's paper, other interpretations have been given to this apparent paradox, through the 'urban life cycle' theory (cf. van den Berg et al. 1982; Camagni et al. 1985), and through the integration of dynamic elements, such as innovation, continuous information and knowledge acquisition, into the static framework of 'optimal city size theory'.

After the sixties, with the neoclassical approach to urban size, other studies have been carried out with the aim to understand urban dynamics. One theory is the so-called 'urban life cycle theory' which was launched by the Vienna group within the CURB project (costs of urban growth) (cf. Klassen/Molle/Paelink 1981; van den Berg et al. 1982; van den Berg 1987). The main elements of this theory, as well as its limits, are already well known. It provides an elegant way of describing urban trends and dynamics by interpreting them as the result of a natural process of physical diffusion of urban population from core areas to the periphery. The opposite movement, from periphery to core, is explained on the other hand by the existence of scale diseconomies. However, some aspects remain unresolved: for example, is there a city size threshold at which the process of decentralisation starts? At what city size do scale economies become scale diseconomies? At what point in time does this happen? Should we expect cities like Milan and Rome to grow to the size of London and Paris before they start to decline[1]?

Many empirical analyses have proved the existence of an optimal city size through the measurement of economies or diseconomies of scale, generally applied either to the costs of urban services or to elegant econometric estimates of urban and sectoral production functions. But, unfortunately these studies have never produced a common result, and have often been subject to criticism for their restrictive hypotheses[2]. The aims of the present paper are threefold. The first aim is to describe urban dynamics in Italy, through a descriptive analysis of the population changes in core and ring areas in the 95 provincial capital, and some data on land use presented in order to describe the urbanisation process (Section 2). The second aim of the paper is to understand how cities are able to face the expected decreasing returns to scale that they reach up to a certain critical size. As we will see, urban size is only one of the elements explaining urban advantages and costs. Other elements are important in this respect, in particular the functional specialisation of the city and its networking capacity (Section 3).

1 These are the well-known criticisms of the urban life cycle theory and the theory of optimal city size. See, among others, Camagni 1994 and Capello 2004.

2 See, among others, Henderson 1974, 1985, 1996; Kamashima 1975; Shefer 1973; Sveikauskas 1975; Sveikauskas et al. 1988; Segal 1976; Marelli 1981; Ladd 1992; Catin 1991; Rousseaux/Proud'homme 1992; Rousseaux 1995; Capello 2004, Capello/Camagni 2000.

It is on this latter element that the paper will put its attention on in its remaining part. In fact, the third aim of the paper is to analyse more in depth goals and advantages cities may have in developing a network approach and in particular:

- whether it is true that network behaviour provides advantages to cities, i.e. has network cooperation an impact on the performance of cities? (Section 6);
- whether some structural features of cities (size, location, specialisation) explain the capacity of a city to derive advantage from city networks, i.e. who gains the most in a city network? (Section 7);
- whether there are common behavioural patterns in the use and exploitation of a network, in terms of the aims and goals partner cities have, i.e. which kinds of behaviour exist in a network of cities? (Section 8).

Some concluding remarks are presented in Section 9.

1. Urban Dynamics in Italy

This section provides a description of urban dynamics in Italy over the last thirty years through an empirical analysis of demographic changes in the inner core and suburban ring areas of the 95 provincial capitals (ISTAT 2005). For the core, data refer to the municipality and for the ring to the difference between the province and the municipality. The analysis is based on simple regressions between population in core areas and changes in population in core areas, for different periods of time, starting from the end of the sixties. Table 1 contains the results of the regressions for the 95 Italian provincial capitals and for the North, Centre and South of Italy, which look rather interesting.

A first result is that some correlations are more significant than others: especially in the case of the Centre of Italy, in each time period analysed changes in population in core areas are not affected by the size of the core areas, being T-students and R-squares statistically insignificant. This result witnesses that there is a lot of pure random (or idiosyncratic) elements in the change processes which are not captured in the analysis (R-square insignificant and high T-student values for the constant term), and therefore that urban size is not relevant to explain population changes.

However, some results are significant, and stress that a tendency exists in core areas to lose population. It can be seen that trend affects cities in the North as well as the South of Italy. This trend first appears in the North, where by the early seventies on an average towns are already registering a negative population growth rate (Table 1, second column). In the South of Italy the phenomenon is less evident during the seventies, when most southern cities still has a positive population growth rate, probably due not so much to the attractiveness of the core areas, but to the inefficiency of peripheral areas, which probably pushes population towards the centre (Table 1, fourth column).

Table 1. Changes in core population on population size in core areas: regression analyses in five different time periods (T-student in brackets).

	% Change in Population in the core 1969-1975			
	Italy	North	Centre	South
Constant	5.86 (8.62)	4.65 (6.21)	6.27 (3.85)	8.18 (5.76)
Population in the core 1969	-0.0030 (-1.88)	-0.0038 (-1.91)	-0.00044 (-0.16)	0.0010 (-2.13)
R-square	0.037	0.085	0.001	0.13
	% Change in Population in the core 1975-1980			
	Italy	**North**	**Centre**	**South**
Constant	1.30 (3.53)	-0.83 (-2.22)	1.50 (2.43)	4.15 (8.08)
Population in the core 1975	-0.0017 (-1.98)	-0.0027 (-2.78)	-0.00016 (-0.17)	-0.0038 (-2.10)
R-square	0.04	0.16	0.001	0.12
	% Change in Population in the core 1980-1985			
	Italy	**North**	**Centre**	**South**
Constant	-1.07 (-2.62)	-2.59 (-6.33)	-1.05 (-1.74)	1.24 (1.44)
Population in the core 1980	-0.0025 (-2.16)	-0.0044 (-3.97)	-0.0009 (-0.98)	-0.0042 (-1.38)
R-square	0.06	0.28	0.05	0.05
	% Change in Population in the core 1985-1991			
	Italy	**North**	**Centre**	**South**
Constant	-2.54 (-5.11)	-2.99 (-6.45)	-1.46 (-1.76)	-1.27 (-1.03)
Population in the core 1985	-0.0032 (-2.69)	-0.0052 (-3.52)	-0.0009 (-0.70)	-0.0106 (-2.57)
R-square	0.07	0.24	0.02	0.17
	% Change in Population in the core 1991-1996			
	Italy	**North**	**Centre**	**South**
Constant	-2.70 (-0.72)	-1.24 (-3.18)	0.13 (0.16)	0.94 (1.08)
Population in the core 1991	-0.002 (-2.1)	-0.0028 (-2.27)	-0.0014 (-1.09)	-0.0035 (-1.02)
R-square	0.04	0.11	0.06	0.03

Source: Capello 2002

Table 2. Changes in ring population on population size in core areas: regression analyses in five different time periods (T-student in brackets, values of the slope parameters multiplied by 1 million).

	% Change in Population in the ring 1969-1975			
	Italy	North	Centre	South
Constant	2.42 (3.72)	3.58 (3.01)	2.34 (2.86)	0.30 (0.27)
Population in the core 1969	0.0077 (4.96)	0.0087 (2.77)	0.0057 (4.33)	0.012 (3.20)
R-square	0.21	0.16	0.51	0.25
	% Change in Population in the ring 1975-1980			
	Italy	**North**	**Centre**	**South**
Constant	1.65 (6.67)	1.06 (3.01)	1.55 (3.53)	2.14 (4.47)
Population in the core 1975	0.0028 (4.84)	0.0023 (2.57)	0.0026 (3.99)	0.005 (3.18)
R-square	0.20	0.14	0.46	0.24
	% Change in Population in the ring 1980-1985			
	Italy	**North**	**Centre**	**South**
Constant	-0.094 (-0.22)	-1.19 (-1.42)	0.49 (1.37)	5.20 (0.95)
Population in the core 1980	0.0031 (3.24)	0.0028 (1.26)	0.0026 (4.95)	0.0061 (3.17)
R-square	0.10	0.03	0.57	0.23
	% Change in Population in the ring 1985-1991			
	Italy	**North**	**Centre**	**South**
Constant	-0.086 (-0.15)	0.88 (0.66)	-0.36 (-0.89)	-0.96 (-1.60)
Population in the core 1985	0.00373 (2.63)	0.0011 (0.29)	0.0042 (6.77)	0.0061 (2.83)
R-square	0.07	0.002	0.71	0.20
	% Change in Population in the ring 1991-1996			
	Italy	**North**	**Centre**	**South**
Constant	(6.87)	1.71 (5.19)	1.61 (4.42)	0.85 (2.28)
Population in the core 1991	0.0031 (5.63)	0.00072 (0.68)	0.0031 (5.36)	-0.0065 (4.45)
R-square	0.25	0.01	0.61	0.38

Source: Capello 2002

During the nineties, the situation appears to change in favour of large urban areas, where a slowing of the population loss in the core is registered: during the first part of the nineties (1991-96) cities with more than 1 million inhabitants register an average annual growth rate of -4 % in comparison with the -8 % of the 1985-91 period. These results suggest that large cities seem to attract population again, thanks to the increase in their net locational advantages. This positive (or better less negative) trend in population growth of the cores of large cities has characterised the North since the mid eighties. A plausible assumption for this reversal is that these cities are no longer primarily dependent on manufacturing activities, but that a new economic cycle had begun, based on managerial and tertiary economic functions, which find their natural location in large cities.

Table 2 shows the results of regression analyses between population growth rates in the outer 'ring' around the city and population in the core. It is clearly evident that the demographic decline of the city core has always been accompanied by an increase in the population of ring areas (positive values of parameters). During the seventies, there are positive growth rates in these peripheral areas, indicating that processes of peri-urbanisation are occurring especially in the large cities. Demographic increases in ring areas are in fact typical of large cities, (significant values of T-student for the slope parameters). Lastly, Table 2 shows that the strong peri-urbanisation process which previously characterised the North of Italy has declined in strength over the last ten years. In the nineties, lower rates of increase in ring areas have been associated with lower loss of population in the core areas. The analysis presented provides prima facie evidence that the concept of 'optimal city size' is difficult to be applied to the real world. The reason of the continuous increase in city size, despite the size cities have already reached, is that urban costs and advantages do not depend merely on urban size, but also on the functions firms perform and the degree of network participation they have. This is the subject matter of the next section.

2. Urban Advantages and Costs: Size, Functional Specialisation and Network Organisation

Despite the size cities have already reached, the rapid and constant increase of urban size finds a plausible explanation in the fact that other elements beyond physical size influence advantages and costs of cities. Two elements have been highlighted, namely the functional specialisation and the city network participation. The aim of this part of the work is to analyse the relationship between advantages and costs of urban size and the size of cities, the functional specialisation and the degree of participation to a city network.

The analysis we present is based on two indicators: the 'city effect' indicator, which contains all positive externalities associated with an urban location, and the 'urban overload indicator', measuring on its turn the disadvantages associated with an urban location. Table 3 presents the data used to built the two indicators[3]. The database on which these indicators have been built regards 58 Italian cities and refers to the year 1991. The geographical area analysed is the NUTS 3 administrative level. Figure 1 (graphs a and b) shows the estimated city effect and urban overload functions for different levels of urban size. In economic terms, the calculated parameters reflect the elasticity of the city effect with respect to size, i.e. how the city effect and urban overload change with an increase in size of 1 %, for different urban sizes. The results obtained are in line with the abstract interpretation of the optimal urban size theory.

In fact, the curves are 'well-behaved', showing a city-effect which increases with urban size up to a certain point (approximately 361,000 inhabitants) and then decreases

Table 3. Statistical Definition of City Effect and Urban Overload Indicators.

	Interaction between economic and physical environment	Interaction between economic and social environment	Interaction between social and physical environment
City effect indicator (ALB)	• Per capita energy use • Per capita petrol use • Per capita water use	• Number of graduates/ population • Number of schools/ population • Number of banks/ population • Supply of public services/population • Urban rent per m^2	• Square meters of green areas in city per capita
Urban overload indicator (ALC)	• Per capita NO_x emissions • Per capita kg of urban waste • Number of vehicles per m^2	• Unemployment/ population	• Number of murders/ population

Source: Author's compilation

3 Each data has been divided by its maximum value, in order to standardise the different values and thus sum the different indices. The general 'city effect' indicator is in fact calculated as the unweighted sum of the different indices obtained; the indices refer to cross-effects between the different environments, and therefore the choice of a weighted sum would imply an arbitrary choice of weighs. The first group of indices, relating to the interaction between the economic and the natural environment enter the sum with their 'complement to one' value, reflecting their negative correlation with city size.

(Table 4). As far as the city effect is concerned, the results in fact show the possibility for a city to exploit:

- *economies of scale.* Our analysis shows that economies of scale exist for public services (like schools, public transport and banks), but also environmental resources, like water, petrol and energy use;
- *indivisibities* of public services in general, since the larger the city, the greater the possibility of exploiting a critical mass of users.

The city effect, however, is exploited up to a certain urban size, after which its slope becomes negative. The expected congestion effects and diseconomies of scale prevail in large cities. As far as the urban overload effect is concerned, our results show a decreasing trend up to a certain urban size (approximately 55,500 inhabitants) and an increasing trend afterwards, once again in line with the traditional expectations.

Two elements seem to generate this trend:

- *in small cities, an economic and territorial effect.* For very small cities, the results show that an increase in the physical dimension decreases urban overload, in terms of unemployment rates and all the social diseases associated with a peripheral local economy, dependent upon larger surrounding centres;
- *in large cities, a negative environmental effect.* For larger urban areas the results are the opposite: the increase in urban size increases the level of overload. The explanation is related to the natural environment indices contained in the general overload indicator. Large cities pollute more and generate more environmental damage than medium ones; higher levels of production, linked to increasing physical urban size, is likely to mean a higher pollution density.

The picture changes (Figure 1) when the analysis is made on the basis of the different types of economic functions which can characterise a city. The results are quite interesting. As far as the city effect is concerned, these results show that higher order functions guarantee a greater city effect, due to the positive returns generated (Figures 1c). Only if the city achieves a substantial share of tertiary activities (49 % of its total activities), it can exploit the advantages of urban size.

The urban overload effects increase at a decreasing rate when there is a strong presence of high level functions[4]. This means that the increase in tertiary activities tends to entail congestion and location costs, but that this negative aspect does not occur in a

4 High order economic functions developed in the city are estimated as the share of private tertiary value-added produced by the city is used.

Figure 1. City advantages and disadvantages according to urban size, urban specialisation and network integration.

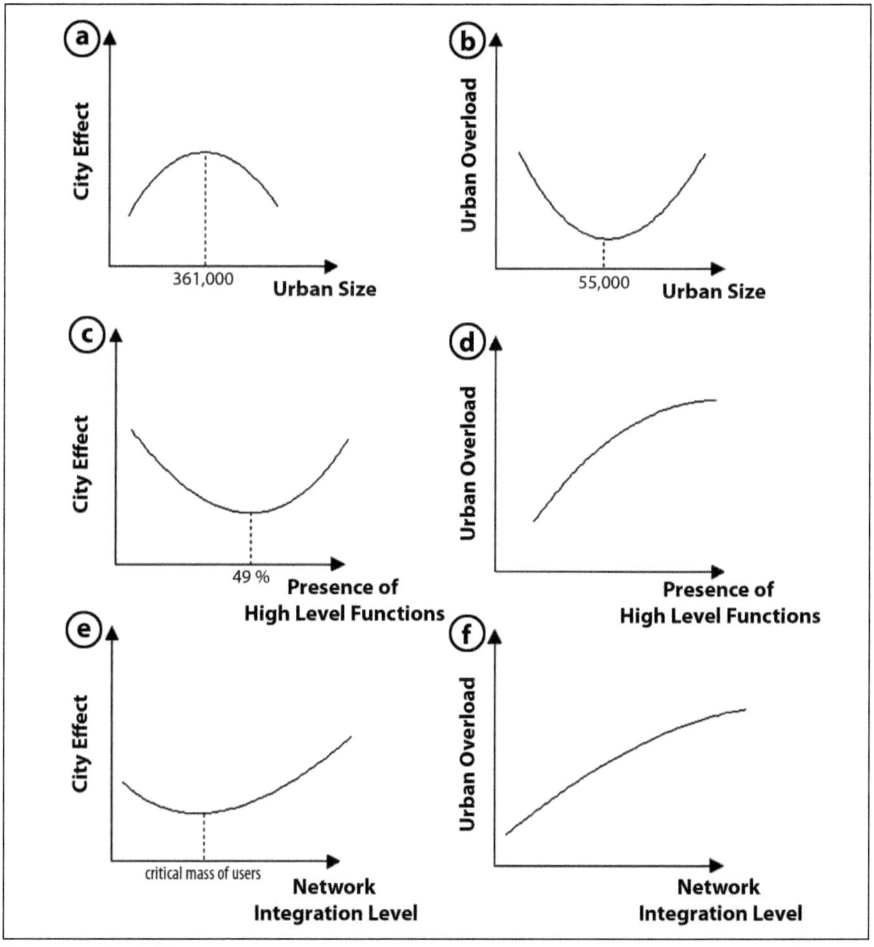

Source: Author's diagram

disruptive and uncontrollable way, as in the case of increasing urban size (Figure 1d). The urban overload effect increases at a decreasing rate, which indicates that higher order functions produce economic development and also local congestion costs, but with a decreasing marginal productivity, and thus in a more controlled way. The decreasing order of magnitude with which overload is generated in the presence of higher order functions may be explained by the following reasons:

- from the point of view of environmental indices involved in the overload indicator: a) tertiary activities are by definition less polluting activities than industrial ones, b) higher income level communities (stemming from economies based on higher order functions and higher profit levels) treat the environment as a luxury good, due to the emergence of new social values with respect to the environment (Camagni 1996). These results are in line with the apparent paradox described by Baldwin (1995) in his provocative and very important statement: 'sustainability requires growth';
- from the point of view of the economic and social costs involved in the overload indicator, tertiary activities have in the last decade been characterised by high employment rates, and thus a higher percentage of these activities in a city guarantees a lower level of social disease resulting from the lack of jobs;
- from the economic point of view, the increasing overload is the consequence of the broad economic development that higher order functions generate. Higher order functions stimulate strong economic development because of their capacity to generate greater multiplicative effects than more traditional functions. This is a mechanism which has been widely overestimated in the empirical analysis.

The results of the size elasticity of the city effect and urban overload for different levels of network integration[5] produce an interesting picture (Figure 1e and f). As far as the city effect is concerned, the effect decreases up to a certain level of network integration, when it starts to increase. These results are stimulating, since they suggest that:

- for low levels of network integration, advantages of autarchy and independence take place, although these results seem to be statistically weak;
- when the network integration process starts, cities are vulnerable and are weak partners, risking in general being exploited by the network, rather than exploiting the advantages of a network. This result is in line with the general idea that being part of a network does not necessary mean obtaining advantages from it (Camagni 1994; Capello 1994). As expected, this is true up to a certain level of network integration;
- after a certain threshold level, the city is able to exploit the advantages associated with the interconnected economy and network externality advantages are in full operation[6]. Through the network, the city is able to exploit more dispersed information collection, the acquisition of more know-how and more qualified input factors, as well as a wider market for final goods.

5 The level of network integration of the city with the rest of the world is calculated, because of the lack of statistical information on the flows of interaction between our sample cities (duration of phones calls or number of phone calls) for these groups of cities, as the stock of per capita telephone subscribers. However, the share of flows of international phone calls (both duration and number of phone calls) and the per capita telephone subscribers available for a different group of cities (municipalities) in the metropolitan areas of Milan have shown a correlation equal to 0.80.

6 See the vast literature existing on network externalities (i. e., Hayashi 1992 and Rohlfs 1974).

For the urban overload effect, the picture which emerges is similar to that for different levels of high order functions (Figure 1f). When the level of network integration increases, urban overload increases, too. This is what would be expected: higher levels of network integration stimulate more economic activities and generate higher city effects, but with the negative counterpart of an increasing overload. What is rather interesting is that urban overload has decreasing growth rates. Again, this result is different from the exploding situation which occurs when the city size is taken into consideration.

As the level of network integration increases, positive mechanisms come into effect, decreasing the size elasticity of the overload:

- from the *economic point of view*, as the city increases its ability to exploit network externality advantages, unemployment and social diseases related to a stagnating economy decrease;
- from an *environmental point of view*, the city economy increases via the network, by keeping under control the local pressure in terms of environmental costs. The networked city can reorganise its production system by decentralising the most polluting and less attractive functions, while specialising in higher order functions, like control and decision-making processes. In this way, it benefits from the advantages of an expanding economy, while keeping environmental costs and local pressures under control.

The results are quite interesting. Through the investigation of a number of hypotheses, it is revealed that an optimal city size *does* exist, but that it differs from one city to another, depending on the structural characteristics. Functional structure and the spatial organisation of activities appear to be the main reasons for the differences. For the latter, a more in-depth analysis of the advantages which stem from it is presented in the rest of the paper.

3. City Networks: a Definition

A way of facing the challenges imposed to cities is a growth through cooperation; this new rationale of economic behaviour has come to the fore in the last decade, and may be described as 'network behaviour'. By this term, a metaphor for cooperative behaviour among individuals, corporate or territorial partners is intended – which is increasingly becoming the reference paradigm when innovation processes are involved[7]. This new economic behaviour allows cities to respond to the challenge imposed by the globalisation process in two ways. Cooperation, or 'networking', provides a less costly and more

7 The concept of network externalities is at the basis of this network behaviour. See, among others, Capello 1994; Capello/Rietveld 1998; Hayhashi 1992; Katz/Shapiro 1985, 1986 and 1992.

profitable way of achieving new and strategic resources to control multiple technological paths, otherwise impossible to be achieved through traditional economic behaviour; internal competence can expand only at a limited rate; resorting to the market faces limitations – in the form of transaction costs, risks and timing – that often make it non-viable, especially in businesses characterized by a high speed of technological evolution[8]. Moreover, cooperation allows for the achievement of a critical mass of markets for both goods/services and skilled factors, without imposing a physical growth to cities.

Therefore, cooperation seems to be an interesting way of facing competition, and on this idea a new concept has been elaborated, that of 'city network'; it refers to mainly horizontal linkages among centres of similar size, of a cooperative nature, addressed to the achievement of a critical mass in terms of markets for both outputs and skilled factors[9]. Still keeping a limited size, and thus benefiting from a series of environmental advantages, urban centres may develop higher order functions (thus benefiting from higher per capita incomes) either:

- through the so-called *complementarity networks* which basically consist of specialized cities that generate a territorial division of labour by avoiding duplication; the network of relations between the cities of the Randstad in Holland and between the medium-sized cities of the Veneto and Emilia in Italy fall into this category;
- through the so-called *synergy networks*, developed by cities that are basically similar in their specialization and therefore form a single integrated market and present a common image to the outside; among great cities, this is the case of the financial 'world cities', which all act in an integrated market; among the small and medium-sized cities, on the other hand, we have the example of tourist cities organized either into regional 'itineraries' or coastal belts (Romagna being a case in point) or of the port cities of one and the same region who cooperate in allocating demand rather than engaging in competition with each other (the cooperation project of the Ligurian ports, for example); or
- through the so-called *innovation networks*, built by cities which cooperate in the provision of a common territorial innovation (infrastructure, airports etc.).

The city-network model not only allows the functions established in the individual centres to be upgraded without their individual size necessarily being increased, but it also brings in its wake some advantages of considerable potential as far as mobility management is concerned. In fact, whenever activities that constitute the productive 'vocation' are integrated into such a pattern, one can readily imagine that most transport interac-

8 Similar reflections have been made for what concerns firms networks. For a review on firms' cooperation agreement, see Camagni 1993a and Teece 1989.

9 For a theoretical and empirical reflections on city networks, see Camagni 1993b, 1994; Camagni et al. 1998; Dematteis 1985; Emanuel 1988; Emanuel/Dematteis 1990; Diappi/Pompili 1989.

tions will occur within the city itself (or within its productive district). The cooperative element is essential in these cases, because it allows joint development of some ambitious projects that would be uneconomic if undertaken by a single city. This is the direction in which the European Commission is moving – and very rightly so – in the case of historically-penalized border cities, since these cities can achieve yet another integration goal by means of trans-frontier collaboration.

4. Goals and Advantages in City Networks

In general, the literature on city networks is mainly concerned with the general economic rationale explaining network behaviour. There is however still some space for further reflections on the different goals that may characterise cities' decisions to work with other cities. These may be defined, in increasing order of importance, as (cf. Capello 2000):

a *Efficiency goals.* As in the case of private firms, public administrations may increase their efficiency in the sphere of decision-making processes through network behaviour. Additional information and know-how acquired from the network provide a basis for reducing uncertainty, risks and information asymmetries. They may inspire operational solutions to urban problems, improving the efficiency of each city's urban policy, but leaving them to be run and managed in a traditional way, without requiring the implementation of joint local policy actions among partner cities and local institutions.

b *Synergy goals.* Synergy goals are associated to what have been termed 'synergy networks', made up of similar cooperative centres. In this case, the necessary economies of scale are provided by the network itself, which integrates the market of each single centre, breaking the value additivity principle of utility (i.e. $1 + 1 > 2$). Examples of synergy networks are the financial cities, whose markets are virtually integrated through advanced telecommunications infrastructures, or tourist cities connected via cultural or historical itineraries. As previously mentioned, this may be the case of cities which cooperate in allocating demand rather than engaging in competition with each other (the cooperative project of the Ligurian ports). Synergy goals allow the achievement of a sufficient critical mass for the implementation of specific projects, both with respect to demand (market) and to supply (production) conditions.

c *Competence goals.* City networks allow partners to obtain locally unavailable know-how for efficient and advanced urban policies, managed in a cooperative way with other partner cities. Technical innovation (e.g. new techniques for a more efficient management of urban traffic), and/or new organisational solutions for urban policy management (concertative and participative processes for common projects among institutions, and with citizens, as well as intersectoral approaches to the solution of urban issues) embodied in success stories previously experienced by partners, easily become a strategic starting point for locally successful urban policies.

These advantages reflect the rationale for network behaviour: they are all achieved via a network behaviour, but the advantages achieved are expected to be rather different in the three cases. The achievement of new information in specific urban projects may easily represent a solution to a contingent urban problem (e.g. management of new policies, like waste management disposal); the achievement of a wider market through synergy networks is a more strategic medium-term goal, strengthening the position of the city in international urban competition.

However, long-term sustainable urban growth calls for an integrated approach to different urban negative externalities (in social, economic and environmental spheres), and requires innovative technical and organisational solutions. In this perspective, competence goals represent the most useful strategic aims for a city's participation in a network, achieved through a joint cooperative effort of similar cities with similar problems. However, achieving the most strategic advantages of network participation requires specific preconditions to be met:

- *commitment of the city to participation in the network.* Competence goals require serious investment and participation in the network, e.g. attendance at business meetings by qualified representative administrators and interest in organising meetings of the network itself;
- *flexibility regarding organisational changes.* A long-term sustainable urban programme requires organisational changes to the public administration's traditional procedures. The transition towards intersectoral approaches to urban problems (among different responsible bodies) and concertative procedures between institutions and citizens, are difficult changes for administrations to make. Concertative procedures and intersectoral approaches require functional integration, the elimination of previous management positions, and the creation of new professional activities;
- *open attitudes to network behaviour.* Active participation in the network presupposes city managers have attitudes towards organisational change that are required to achieve network externalities: these attitudes are frequently the result of previous experiences of network participation.

As Figure 2 shows, a strong interrelation is envisaged between the following elements and the achievement of the most strategic advantages of being part of a network of cities: greater commitment to participation, more open attitudes to network behaviours and greater organisational changes all lead to greater network advantages. Network behaviour seems rational. However, empirical evidence proving its validity would strengthen the strategic importance of this economic behaviour in a situation of rapid and turbulent dynamic environments. The existence of a network of European cities, labelled Healthy City Network, managed by the World Health Organisation, Regional Office of Europe, located in Copenhagen, provides a good empirical case on which to measure the advantages of cooperation. This network links together cities of different sizes and countries in a joint programme dealing with quality of life and health in urban areas: common projects are developed in the field of health and related sectors (e.g. tobacco use, urban traffic control, AIDS, social equity) under the management of the World Health Organisation (WHO 1994, 1995).

Figure 2. Preconditions and goals in city networks.

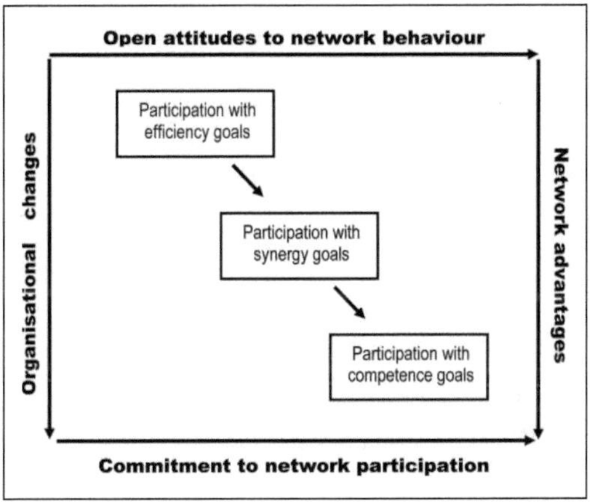

Source: Author's diagram

The existence of this network provides a interesting opportunity to develop an empirical analysis on the city network theory since it provides a concrete case of an institutional network of different cities with the aim a) at widening the information exchange among public managers on policy strategies in specific health related areas; b) at providing the opportunity to cities to launch and run joint policies in specific health related areas.

In particular, the existence of this network allows to test[10]:

- whether it is true that network behaviour provides advantages to cities, i.e. is network cooperation worth the effort? (section 6);
- whether some structural features of cities (size, location, specialisation) explain the capacity of a city to derive advantage from city networks, i.e. who gains the most in a city network? (section 7);
- whether there are common behavioural patterns in the use and exploitation of the HCP network, in terms of the aims and goals partner cities have, i.e. which kinds of behaviour exist in a network of cities? (section 8).

10 The empirical results presented here are drawn from the research project 'Evaluation of integrated health promotion and innovation in a network of European cities', run by Roberto Camagni and Roberta Capello as subcontractors of the London School of Economics, for the European Union.

5. Is Networking Worth the Effort?

The empirical analyses are run on primary data collected via a questionnaire filled out by all cities taking part in the HCP network, run by WHO (1994, 1995). The questionnaire addresses different issues, with the aim of obtaining information on:

- structural features of cities;
- aims of cities in joining the network;
- investment in terms of finance and time involved in network participation;
- degree of involvement in the network (number of projects and number of cities involved in the networks);
- degree of involvement in national networks;
- degree of satisfaction in international and national networks;
- policy outcomes from participation in the network;
- advantages obtained via the network;
- willingness to enlarge network behaviours in the future.

Looking at the results obtained from this information, partner cities are positive regarding their participation in the network: one third of the cities involved recognise their network involvement has strategic importance for local policy actions, and 60 % of cities participating in the HCP network declare that local projects were successful thanks to their network participation (Figure 3).

Figure 3. Success stories of local projects developed in cooperation with the HC network.

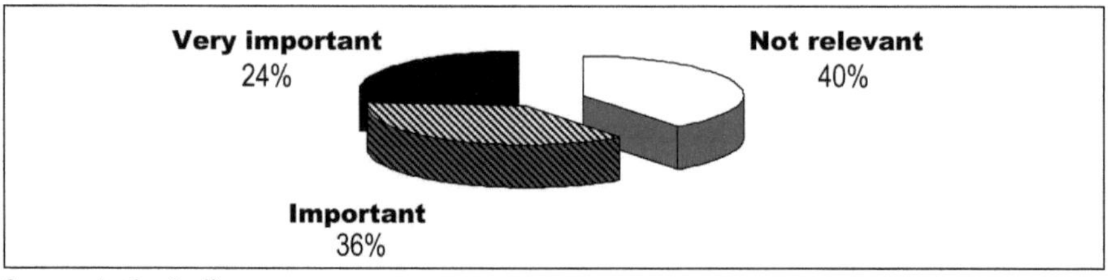

Source: Author's diagram

The reasons for cooperation mentioned by cities vary: a) opportunistic reasons, such as getting funds from the EU, or attracting new organisational and technological competences; b) solidarity reasons, i.e. provide new organisational and technological competences; c) cooperative reasons, i.e. cooperating in order to achieve new organisational and technological competences. The replies obtained show an average degree of importance for each reason mentioned: as Figure 4 shows, there is a general tendency to reply 'important', rather than 'not relevant' or 'very important'. Opportunistic behaviours seem to predominate as very important reasons for joining the network, while altruistic reasons seem to be the lowest in terms of the share of 'very important' replies.

Table 4. Estimates of Urban Network Externality Measurement.

	First regression**	Second regression**
Constant	0.08 (-1.09)	-0.05 (-0.55)
Network connectivity	0.005 (2.21)	0.006 (2.51)
Intensity of use of the network*		0.47 (2.23)
R-square	**0.12**	**0.25**

* weighted sum of the number of Multi City Action Plans (MCAPs) in which cities participate multiplied by the number of cities-partners involved in each MCAPs and the number of HC network business meetings

** measured as the number of success stories replicated by each city on the weighted sum of the number of MCAPs in which each city participates and the number of HC network business meetings cities have participated to

Source: Capello 2000

Another important feature which emerges from the analysis is given by the cities themselves, through their declared interest and willingness to develop network projects in the future. As Figure 5 shows, this is true for nearly 90 % of network cities. A more statistical analysis shows that a strong positive correlation exists between the degree of participation in networks (measured in terms of numbers of national and international networks cities take part in within the HCP organisation) and the number of successful local policies achieved thanks to participation in the HCP: the higher the degree of participation in a network, the higher the outcome in terms of successful local policies. This also means that cities achieve an advantage through the network, despite the inten-

Figure 4. Reasons for cooperation.

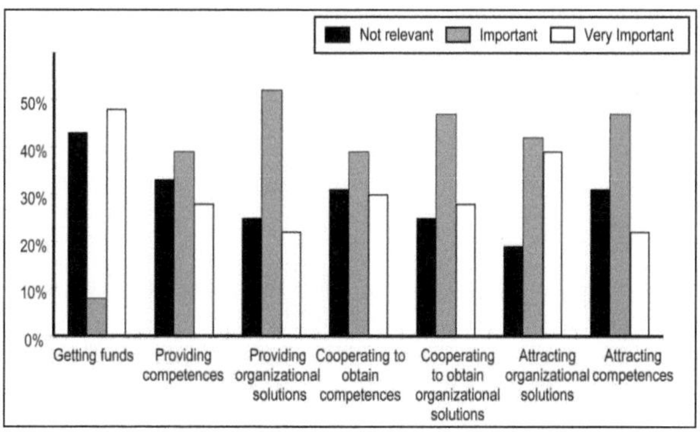

Source: Author's diagram

Figure 5. Willingness to develop other projects in cooperation.

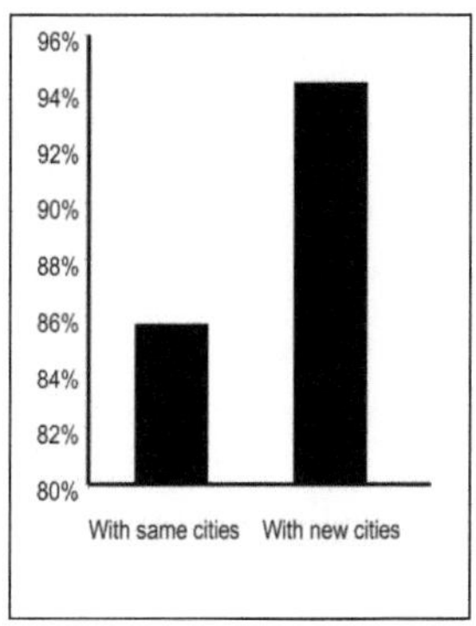

Source: Author's diagram

sity of use of the network itself. The correlation becomes statistically more robust if an index of connectivity is built which also takes into consideration the intensity of participation in a network; this indicates that active participation in the network increases the advantages achieved through the network (Table 4).

6. Who Gains the Most?

A legitimate question at this stage is to ask whether the positive conclusions achieved before are true for specific cities, characterised by specific structural features, like Western vs. Eastern European cities (i.e. richer vs. poorer cities), Northern vs. Southern European cities, large vs. small cities, cities joining the HCP network in the first or in the second phase, capital vs. non-capital cities, EU vs. non-EU cities. In other words, we are interested in showing whether the advantages, use and exploitation of the HCP network are concentrated in specific categories of cities. Generally speaking, the capacity to exploit network cooperation is not related to specific categories of cities. For example, the outcome, in terms of local successful policy actions, is not related to the richest categories, like Northern or Western cities. This result seems to contradict the idea that the richest cities are those able to achieve the highest and most strategic advantages from the network, by exploiting weaker partners. If we look at the degree of satisfaction demonstrated by cities, this seems to be even higher for the poorest and weakest cities. The smallest Eastern and Southern cities find their participation in the network is a useful instrument on which to build efficient policy actions. Paradoxically, this indicates that the network is more appreciated by weaker and less economically developed cities than by richer ones. The above interesting result may be explained by another important finding stemming from our empirical results: each category of cities uses the network for its specific requirements and, from this perspective, finds a way of exploiting it. For example, in the case of Eastern cities, network cooperation is regarded as a vehicle for sharing costs of large urban projects when local funding is insufficient. From their perspective, the network is an extremely strategic instrument to cope with the scarcity of financial resources which characterises their countries. A similar case exists for small cities, which stress the importance for cities to achieve economies of scale in urban projects: for these cities, a critical mass to achieve efficient urban size and thus a minimum average cost for the project is again an extremely important use of the network.

An important element that emerges in our analysis is the learning process in cooperation. Cities which entered the network in the first phase show a greater capacity for exploiting the network and for adopting more strategic aims. They show a change in their stated most important goals for joining the network. While these cities were initially more oriented towards less strategic advantages, they are now emphasising more strategic goals to justify their participation in the network. This is confirmed in the results describing the approach cities adopt to their network participation: cities of the first phase are also those adopting a more strategic approach to the network, probably due to the experience developed during the longer initial period when they were active in the network. While no specific categories of cities show a greater capacity to gain from network participation in general, the analysis quite clearly indicates that the cities gaining the most in a network are those which seriously participate in the network, by investing in human capital and by devoting resources to introduce the necessary organisational changes in the institutional structure governing the network locally. The presence of these preconditions, rather than being part of a particular group of cities, allows them to exploit the network and achieve the most strategic advantages, such as acquiring know-how and developing innovative projects.

7. Which Kinds of Behaviours Exist in a City Network?

The analysis run on the behaviours developed by cities in the network demonstrates that a range of completely different behaviours exist in the HCP network, namely:

- *a* *Opportunistic behaviour*. The first group of cities shows opportunistic behaviour in the network: the main advantage they achieve through the network is political legitimisation for local policies, and their reasons for joining the network are not for the wider public benefits. These are in general the largest cities, characterised by a low unemployment rate. These cities are aware of the advantages achieved, but seem to play a 'hit and run' strategy, in the sense that they seem to maximise their advantages when they join the network, without manifesting a willingness to develop this behaviour further. Another advantage obtained from the network is their choice of partners, which is not incompatible with an opportunistic behaviour: if the partner is chosen for self-serving purposes only, it may turn out to reflect an opportunistic behaviour too. Opportunistic behaviour, using the name of the network for political legitimisation, seems to be accompanied by a very low commitment to participating in the network, as would be expected.
- *b* *Exploring behaviour*. A second, rather different, profile in network behaviour is what can be termed an exploring behaviour. These cities show a great commitment to participating in the network, investing in the experience and putting into place a learning process to make use of the network. These cities have so far registered a limited degree of satisfaction in participating in the network, and also in success policies resulting from the existence of the network. This cluster mainly seems to contain small cities from Western countries.
- *c* *Economic efficiency behaviour*. Another kind of common network behaviour is the pure economic efficiency behaviour. Cities belonging to this group enter the network with simple information gathering goals, and achieve typical advantages which

increase economic efficiency, like increasing information and economies of scale. Eastern and non-European cities belong to this cluster, once again proving that for Eastern cities the achievement of economic efficiency may turn out to be extremely strategic for them. These are also cities with a limited capacity, compared to all other clusters of cities, for successfully developing local policy actions. So the profile of this cluster is of a group of cities whose primary goal in joining the network is very simple, that of information gathering. This increases their economic efficiency and they are relatively satisfied. These are also cities with no tradition of success in local projects, belonging primarily to Eastern Countries.

d *Strategic behaviour.* A last cluster of cities is labelled cities with a 'strategic behaviour'. In these clusters, cities obtain the greatest and most strategic advantages from the network, that of acquiring know-how, and are the ones achieving more local success stories from the network. This result underlines once again the relationship between network participation and a high proportion of successful local policies achieved through the network. Furthermore, these cities are also those characterised by an open attitude to network behaviour and are cities that do not join the network for simple reasons, like information gathering. Interestingly enough, these cities are also those having a high rate of unemployment, indicating once again the idea that the network does not provide the greatest advantages to the strongest (richest and most developed) cities. These cities are mostly Western European cities.

The empirical analysis provides initial evidence that different behavioural patterns exist in the network. The most cooperative behaviour leads to the greatest proportion of successful local policies deriving from network participation. However, it also requires commitment to participation and an open attitude to network behaviour.

8. Concluding Remarks

The aim of the present paper was to study urban dynamics in Italy and to identify the role of city networks in urban growth. In the first part of the study, the empirical evidence on urban growth with respect to Italy showed that the tendencies of urban areas to grow is typical of all cities, despite their size. From the theoretical point of view this means that the concept of an optimal city size, for which the net urban advantages are maximum, does not exist in reality. From the practical point of view, this means that other elements, despite size, influence urban advantages and costs, which have been identified as the functional specialisation of an area and its participation to city networks. The paper finds validity of this assumption in an empirical evidence which shows the role of networking and of functional specialisation in determining the degree of urban advantages and disadvantages.

Thanks to the existence of a city network created by the World Health Organisation, we were also able to prove empirically the reasons and advantages achieved by cities joining the network; in particular, our assessment of the Healthy City network was not focused on identifying *what* cities have developed in the sphere of health planning, or *why* they chose this or that strategy, but on *how* (fully or partially) they achieved network advantages, both in the phase of policy conception and policy implementation. Three main conclusions have been reached.

Participation in a city network is worth the effort. Cities express positive judgements on their participation in the network, indicating a strategic role played by the network for the implementation of their local policy actions. This result has gone far beyond expectations, since even mere passive participation in a network provides advantages to cities.

Moreover, *no particular category of cities gains more than others from being part of a network.* The outcome, in terms of successful local policy actions achieved via the network, is not in fact a characteristic of the richest and economically strongest partners in the network. Each city exploits the network for its specific purposes and needs, finding a way of obtaining from cooperative behaviour the specific support they need.

Different kinds of behaviours exist in a network, from opportunistic to exploring behaviours, and to more strategic ones. Behaviours generally change over time while cities are part of the network: cities generally enter a network with an exploring behaviour and gradually move to more strategic behaviours, thanks to learning processes in cooperation. Commitment to network participation and an open attitude to cooperation are the main conditions for achieving the greatest advantages from city behaviour.

Interestingly enough, from the analysis of the HCP network some important lessons can be learnt which can be useful for every organisations managing and running a city network. A first aspect is that the participation to a network risks a saturation level, in terms of interest and advantages that partners may obtain from the network. In the case of the HCP network, this is witnessed by the fact that more satisfied partner cities are also those having a lower willingness to develop other cooperative projects in the future. A second aspect is that large cities, and especially capital cities, are the ones showing a lower degree of satisfaction in the participation to the network. If one thinks that these cities guarantee ideas, success stories and 'examples' of policy actions and solutions to local problems to replicate in other cities, this may turn out to be another weak element for the future of the network.

A primary role of an organisation running a network should be to keep the network alive by taking these weak elements as the starting point for future activities, through some specific actions having the aims:

1) to maintain the interest of cooperation for important partners like large cities alive. Activities more oriented to large urban metropolies should be strengthened, like the launch of large projects on urban mobility, both within the area (solving traffic congestion) and within the whole metropolitan area (solving connectivity problems between the city centres and the most important nodes of international infrastructures – airports, international train stations), largely linked to health problems and quality of life in large cities;
2) to underline the importance of the network itself among partner cities. In this respect, it would be very helpful to demonstrate the existence of successful policy actions launched by partner cities thanks to the existence of the network.
3) to disincentivate opportunistic and 'hit and run' behaviours, by demonstrating the role that a cooperative behaviour can play to achieve strategic advantages through the network. Opportunistic behaviour seems to characterise large cities: once again, an activity programme more oriented towards cooperative and innovative urban projects for large cities could highlight a feeling of cooperation rather than of opportunism.

In general terms, the HC network assessment has highlighted the importance that a city network can play in terms of local policy outcome, and the general degree of satisfaction that partner cities demonstrate. If the weak elements which have been highlighted, are kept under control with specific policy actions, the importance of a city network among partners is destined to increase in the future.

References

BALDWIN, R. (1995), "Does sustainability require growth?", in: Goldin, I., Winters, A. L. (eds.), *The economics of sustainable development*, Cambridge, Cambridge University Press, p. 51-82

BERG, L. van den (1987), *Urban Systems in a Dynamic Society*, Aldershot, Gower

BERG, L. van den, DRWETT, R., KLAASSEN, L. H., Rossi, A., Vijverbert, C. H. (1982), *Urban Europe: A Study of Growth and Decline*, Oxford, Pergamon Press

CAMAGNI, R. (1994), "From City Hierarchy to City Networks: Reflections about the an Emerging Paradigm", in: Lakshmanan, T. R., Nijkamp, P. (eds.), *Structure and Change in the Space Economy, Festschrift in honor of Martin Beckmann*, Berlin, Springer Verlag, p. 66-87

CAMAGNI, R. (1996), "Città in Europa: Globalizzazione, Coesione e Sviluppo Sostenibile", in: Presidenza del glio dei Ministri (ed.), *Sviluppo del Territorio Europeo*, Rome, Il Poligrafico dello Stato

CAMAGNI, R., CAPELLO, R., NIJKAMP, P. (1998), "Towards Sustainable City Policy: an Economy, Environmental, Technology Nexus", *Ecological Economics*, Vol. 24, No. 1, p. 103-118

CAMAGNI, R., CURTI, F., GIBELLI, M. C. (1985), "La città tra sviluppo e declino", in: Bianchi, G., Magnani, I. (eds.), *Sviluppo multiregionale: teorie, metodi, problemi*, Milan, Franco Angeli, p.197-234

CAMAGNI, R., DIAPPI, L., LEONARDI, G. (1986), "Urban Growth and Decline in a Hierarchical System: a Supply-oriented Dynamic Approach", *Regional Science and Urban Economics*, Vol. 16, p. 145-160

CAPELLO, R. (1994), *Spatial Economic Analysis of Telecommunications Network Externalities*, Avebury, Aldershot

CAPELLO, R. (2000), "The City-Network Paradigm: Measuring Urban Network Externalities", *Urban Studies*, Vol. 37, No. 11, p. 1925-1945

CAPELLO, R. (2002). "Urban Rent and Urban Dynamics: the Determinants of Urban Development in Italy", *The Annals of Regional Science*, Vol. 36, No. 4, p. 593-612

CAPELLO, R. (2004), "Beyond Optimal City Size: Theory and Evidence Reconsidered", in: Capello, R., Nijkamp, P. (eds.), *Urban Dynamics and Growth: Advances in Urban Economics*, Amsterdam, Elsevier, p. 57-86

CAPELLO, R., CAMAGNI, R. (2000), "Beyond Optimal City Size: an Evaluation of Alternative Urban Growth Patterns", *Urban Studies*, Vol. 37, No. 9, p. 1479-96

CAPELLO, R., RIETVELD, P. (1998), "The Concept of Network Synergy in Economic Theory: Policy Implications", in: Button, K., Nijkamp, P., Priemus, H., (eds.) *Transport Networks in Europe,* Cheltenham, Edward Elgar, p. 57-83

CATIN, M. (1991). "Economies d'agglomeration et gains de productivité", *Révue d'Economie Régionale et Urbaine*, No. 5/1991, p. 565-598

DEMATTEIS, G. (1985), "Verso strutture urbane reticolari", in: Bianchi, G., Magnani, L. (eds.), *Sviluppo multiregionale: teorie, metodi, problemi*, Milan, FrancoAngeli, p. 121-132

DIAPPI, L., POMPILI, T. (1989), "Sistemi di città come reti di interazione: un approccio dinamico di tipo Löschiano", in: Martellato, D., Sforzi, F. (eds.), *Studi sui sistemi urbani*, Milan, Franco Angeli, p. 265-291

EMANUEL, C. (1988), "Recenti trasformazioni nell'organizzazione urbana e regionale: il caso padano", IX. Conference of Italian Regional Science Association, Turin

EMANUEL, C., DEMATTEIS, G. (1990). "Reti urbane minori e deconcentrazione metropolitana nella Padania centro-occidentale", in: Martellato, D., Sforzi, F. (eds.), *Studi sui sistemi urbani*, Milan, FrancoAngeli, p. 233-261

HAYASHI, K. (1992), "From Network Externalities to Interconnection: the Changing Nature of Networks and Economy", in: Antonelli, C. (ed.), *The Economcs of Information Networks*, Amsterdam, North-Holland, p. 195-216

HENDERSON, J. (1974), "The Sizes and Types of Cities", *The American Economic Review*, Vol. 64, p. 640-656

HENDERSON, J. (1985), Economic Theory and the Cities, Orlando, Acadenmic Press

HENDERSON, J. (1996), "Ways to Think About Urban Concentration: Neoclassical Urban Systems vs. the New Economic Geography", *International Regional Science Review*, Vol. 19, No. 1/2, p. 31-36

ISTAT (Istituto Nazionale di Statistica Italia) (2005), *Italian Statistical Yearbook*, Rome

KAWASHIMA, T. (1975), "Urban Agglomeration Economies in Manufacturing Industries", *Papers of the Regional Science Association*, Vol. 34, p. 157-175

LADD, H. (1992), "Population Growth, Density and the Costs of Providing Public Services", *Urban Studies*, Vol. 29, No. 2, p. 237-295

MARELLI, E. (1981), "Optimal City Size, the Productivity of Cities and Urban Production Functions", *Sistemi Urbani*, Vol. 1/2, p. 149-163

ROHLFS, J. (1974), "A Theory of Interdependent Demand for a Communication Service", *The Bell Journal of Economics and Management Science*, No. 5/1974, p. 16-37

ROUSSEAUX, M. P., Proud'homme, R. (1992), *Les Bénéfices de la Concentration Parisienne,* Paris, l'Oeil-Iaurif

ROUSSEAUX, M. P. (1995), "Y a-t-il une surproductivité de l'Ile-de-France?", in: Savy, M., Veltz, P. (eds.), *Economie Locale et Réinvention du Local*, DATAR-Editions de l'Aube, Paris, p. 157-167

SEGAL, D. (1976), "Are There Returns to Scale in City Size?", *Review of Economics and Statistics*, Vol. 58, p. 250-339

SHEFER, D. (1973), "Localisation Economies: in SMSA's: a Production Function Analysis", *Journal of Regional Studies*, Vol. 13, p. 55-64

SVEIKAUSKAS, L. (1975), "The Productivity of City Size", *Quarterly Journal of Economics*, Vol. 89, p. 393-413

SVEIKAUSKAS, L., GOWDY, J., FUNK, M. (1988), "Urban Productivity: City Size or Industry Size", *Journal of Regional Science*, Vol. 28, No. 2, p. 185-202

WHO, Regional Office for Europe (World Health Organisation) (1994), *Action for Health in Cities*, Copenhagen

WHO, Regional Office for Europe (World Health Organisation) (1995). *Twenty Steps for developing a Healthy Cities Project*, Copenhagen

WORLD RESOURCE INSTITUTE (2003), *Resources 2002-2004: Decisions for the Earth*, Washington D. C., World Bank

CITY REGIONS: PERSPECTIVE OF A GLOBAL PLAYER

by Stefan Carsten

Introduction

For more than a hundred years, urban development and all aspects of manufacturing have been interlinked in the narrowest sense of the term. This can also be said of the integrative aspect of urban design and the automotive industry. Not only has the urban environment been the locus of industrial production, a function which it continues to perform to a considerable degree, but the car, with a global fleet of over 700 million units, is now undisputedly the key article in mass production (Fordism) and mass consumption. Both affect spatial organization through road planning, city layout, suburban housing and shopping malls, etc. In the past, urbanization and industrial mass production formed an inseparable and unique symbiosis. Present and future conditions require new standards. The way business is conducted has changed dramatically in recent years. The debates on shareholder value, return on investment (ROI), unique selling propositions (USP), and, most importantly, corporate reputation have generated significant new perspectives in evaluating companies and business activities. It is also crucial to assess how, when and – in the face of increasing internationalisation – where investment is made, especially large-scale, long-term investment. Merely extrapolating from past conclusions would not only be too simple but would not do justice to the complexity of economic, socio-cultural, and technological developments. Understandably, this situation demands particular skill on the part of urban protagonists. Urban policy makers realise that, in competition with other cities, stable capital commitments are essential. The globally operating enterprise needs to weigh up economic interests, historical and cultural conditions, and political requirements. Under these circumstances, it is not surprising that future developments prove difficult to predict, all the more so because the prerequisites for sustainable urban development and durable corporate development are far from congruent. The paper looks at the pertinent environment and influences from the perspective of a globally operating enterprise. It concentrates on causal effects with regard to city regions, production and space. Continuity in change has always characterised relations between the automotive industry and regional development. This is also the case for the sub-categories this study examines, passenger vehicle production and the development prospects of city regions. The focus is on assessing whether independent development will be possible or if the century-old links between functional and spatial units will persist. This assessment requires an analysis of the nucleus of production – the automobile – and economic and customer demands on the automobility of the future.

1. The System of Producing Automobility in Germany

Every society produces spatial specificities. Every (industrial) enterprise is a substantial part of a society and thus produces space with either positive or negative effects on that society. This interrelation becomes conspicuous when, owing to economic uncertainty and social fragility, negative entrepreneurial investment has a far stronger impact on city regions than usual. It is hence far more important to analyse what local factors provoke negative investment or (capital) withdrawal than vice versa. The conjunction of spatial practices, representations of space and representational spaces (Lefebvre 1991:33-39) is more important than ever. Like any other firm, a multinational automotive company will take these factors into consideration when deciding about a new production site. Any choice of location has to take account of economic, regulatory, and socio-cultural aspects. Attracting a business to a given city now requires company-specific aspects to be stressed – often historical values. Mostly this is done under the heading of economic patriotism (e.g. Leipzig for BMW, Kolleda for DaimlerChrysler, Dresden for VW). Unfortunately, not all the actors involved share the same spatial notions. Not surprisingly, sustainable urban development and corporate development are not identical processes even if local decision makers often try to construct an artificial congruence.

A look at history suggests an obvious historical extrapolation of urban development from industrial production. "During the Industrial Age, urbanization and the rise of manufacturing were so closely linked as to be almost one and the same thing" (Glaeser 1996). For industrial production, the presence of a big city meant that the existing market could be served without incurring transport costs. Economies of scale could be exploited by spreading fixed costs through mass production. In recent years, local authority scope for organizing the city region has steadily declined. In Germany, federal legislation has weakened the income position of local government while increasing its mandatory expenditures. As a result, municipalities are now almost unable to pursue an active industrial location policy. This also makes it difficult (if not impossible) to guarantee sustainable urban development (Carsten 2005). This is particularly true for the social component of sustainability, making it more and more difficult to ensure equivalent living conditions for all. All too often, urban and public space is abandoned in obedience to some economic rationale. In the German debate on neo-liberal economics, it should not be forgotten that some local government policy makers can be obliged to adopt a neo-liberal course against their will in global competition for capital investment.

Local policy makers thus face the challenge of tying up capital as long as possible to maximize wealth and achieve ecological sustainability. Industrial production plays an important role because only high capital investment and spatial embeddedness can guarantee durability and stability in planning. This is not the case with soft economies that normally tie up less capital and offer no exclusivity in spatial organisation. Tying up capital clearly needs certain basic local conditions to be met, conditions often (but not necessarily) reflected in potential investors' requirements. For instance, demands on the educational landscape are similar in the national and regional/local contexts. The urban region needs abundant and high-quality human resources to attract organisations away from other localities. For organisations, the availability of ample, skilled human resources is an essential condition for permanently improving the value creation process (Glaeser 1996).

In Germany, the automotive industry is one of the sectors most courted by local authorities, and not without reason. It distinguishes itself by enormous investment and a consistent research and development strategy. In 2003, the German automotive industry invested 13 billion Euros – more than a quarter of all German industrial investment. In research and development, too, it takes first place, having spent 14.5 billion Euros in 2003 or a third of total R&D spending in Germany. Over the last ten years the sector has invested 110 billion Euros in research and development. With more than 3,300 patent applications – a third of worldwide patent applications in the industry – the German automotive industry leads the world. Japanese and US firms lag far behind. The German automotive industry plays a decisive role in guaranteeing growth and wealth and in safeguarding jobs in this country. In addition to the core workforce of over 770,000, 1.45 million people are employed in the supplier sector. Adding some three million people in the sales, repair and service sectors to give a total of 5.3 million, more than one out of seven jobs depend directly or indirectly on the automobile. This is 600,000 jobs more than ten years ago. Over the same period, other sectors of German industry lost 1.5 million jobs (VDA 2005).

In 2004, 5.6 million vehicles were produced in Germany (Table 1). An additional 4.8 million were produced abroad. Within the last ten years, the export rate has increased from 55 % to 70 %. It is an extraordinarily powerful complex constituted by technical and social interlinkages with other industries, including components, refining, and road building (Urry 2000). "Cars signify national identity as familiar, iconic manufactured objects emerging out of historic systems of production and expertise" (Edensor 2004:103). In

Table 1. Fleet of Passenger Vehicles in Germany.

Year	Passenger Vehicle Park (in 1,000)
1946	192
1953	1,057
1960	4,489
1970	13,941
1980	23,192
1990	30,685
2005 (August)	47,300

Source: Kraftfahrt-Bundesamt 2005

Germany this identity is particularly powerful and symbolic, all the more so because the automobile was an essential success factor for the German economy after World War II. It should not be forgotten that post-1945 industrialization went hand in hand with an impressive rate of automobilization (Krämer-Badoni et al. 1971).

To date, this history has been symbolised by the 'steel-and-petroleum' car. "Automobility is the quintessential manufactured object produced by the leading industrial sectors and the iconic firms within 20th-century capitalism (Ford, GM, Rolls-Royce, Mercedes, Toyota, VW and so on), and the industry from which the definitive social science concepts of Fordism and post-Fordism have emerged" (Urry 2004:25-26, cf. also Sheller/Urry 2000). The nucleus of the production regime is hence the automobile. For Urry (2004:28-29), however, path-dependence goes beyond merely economic coupling, being mainly expressed in social constraints: "Automobility is a source of freedom, the 'freedom of the road'. Its flexibility enables the car-driver to travel at any time in any direction along the complex of road systems [...] But this flexibility is necessitated by automobility. The 'structure of auto space' (Freund 1993; Kunstler 1994) forces people to orchestrate in complex and heterogeneous ways their mobilities and socialities across very significant distances. The urban environment has 'unbundled' territorialities of home, work, business and leisure [...] Automobility is thus a system that coerces people into an intense flexibility [...] Automobility thus produces desires for flexibility that so far only the car is able to satisfy."

This has understandably established a more than century-old path-dependence involving large sections of German industry, local and national politics and society. This interrelationship explains the demise of the myth of public transport superseding the car. However, the car system is non-linear, and Urry (2004:36) emphasizes that "small changes, if they occur in a certain order, tip it into a post-car mobility system", beyond the steel-and-petroleum car towards a new system of mobility. For him the 'post-car' is constituted by technological innovations, sometimes in the form of real technological and organisational breakthroughs, sometimes through wild cards, such as de-privatisation through car-sharing, car clubs and car-hire schemes. However, I doubt whether such developments will transform the system. Changing the 'steel-and-petroleum-car' system into another will require not a single, isolated development but an entire complex of long-term developments and effects. I suggest that the steel-and-petroleum car is likely to retain its dominant position for at least 10 to 15 years, because viable alternatives have only just begun to conquer niche markets (e.g. the hybrid technology, the fuel cell, etc.). Now and in the future, the shift from the steel-and-petroleum car to the intermediate metal-based hydrogen car and the convergent mobility concept will generate evolutionary change in the automotive production landscape in Germany, as well. However, the third stage in any kind of a convergent mobility concept will need more than 20 to 30 years to gain any kind of urban significance.

Figure 1. The intersecting set of surrounding fields that influence current and future production regimes.

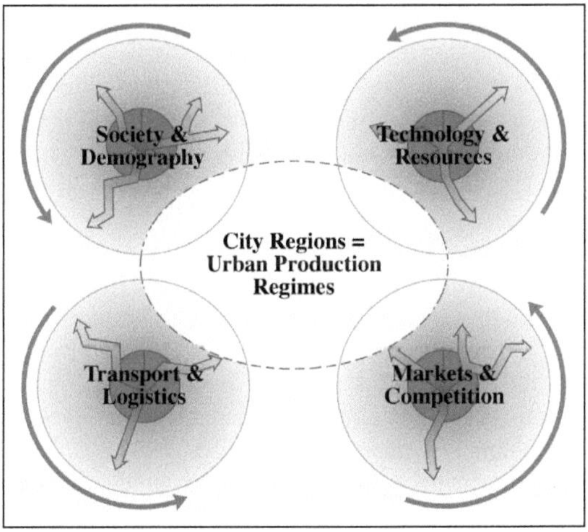

Source: Author's diagram

2. Areas of System Change or Preservation

As we have seen, changes in the production system occur first of all in the automotive industry. Thrift (1996:282) stresses that the automobile and the driver are part of a larger context: "the 'car-driver' is a hybrid assemblage of specific human activities, machines, roads, buildings, signs and cultures of mobility". The automobile has to be seen as an intersecting set of societal, technological, market and transport circumstances (Figure 1). This set has to be implemented in a long-term environment, because decisions on the production regime need several years of planning. Consequently, three potential spirals of system change emerge: social unrest, transport inefficiency, and rising costs.

2.1 Spiral of Social Unrest

Sheller and Urry (2000) address the link between automobility and consumers in relation to the social order and value systems and the automotive production system. They regard the 'car-driver' as a hybrid entity fusing vehicle and person. If this thesis is tenable, as I consider it to be, current social changes obviously play an important role. Although slow, as usual with social developments, their impact is profound, involving the interplay of socio-cultural developments and socio-spatial reactions.

German political, economic and social players are well on the way to eliminating one of the country's most valuable assets: a highly educated young population. The skills level of the workforce is an important factor in assessing the quality of a location (90 % of all companies relocating facilities to Eastern Europe and China stress the high qualifications of local labour) and in appraising the immediate environment of mobile interaction. Industry needs not only employees with good schooling but also sufficient and adequately qualified university graduates. In Germany today, some disciplines (notably engineering) are unable to produce sufficient graduates to replace retiring cohorts. This dangerous trend is aggravated by growing polarization in the educational landscape, where reforms are needed to enable general educational institutions to cope with this development. In winter semester 2003/04, there were 62 private universities in Germany with 33,000 students compared to 19 in 1992/93 with an intake of 11,700. To judge by all current developments and political affirmations, this trend is likely to continue. On the other hand, more and more German states are introducing tuition fees for state institutions. Two thirds of today's students are obliged to work to finance their studies because support and incentive systems (scholarships, grants, donations) are unable to meet the new financial challenges. As a consequence of this development, an educational elite is emerging which is contributing to the so-called information and knowledge society. Only the most popular enterprises with the best employment image are able to attract these people, while the companies have to provide an appealing work environment to serve the needs of this elite.

The labour market is also experiencing far-reaching structural change. The number of employees under the lower earnings limit (who are not liable for social security contributions) is rising while the number of people in contributory employment is falling. This suggests that the first category of employment is massively superseding the second type. This is not a problem in Germany alone, it is one of the biggest challenges the world faces today. The global labour market is having to cope with double the workforce potential and an enormous wage gap between the 'old world' (about 1.5 billion employees in North America, Western Europe and Japan) and the 'new world' (about 1.3 billion in China and India earning significantly lower wages). Not only in Germany is the gap widening. Economic growth is slowing down while productivity is rising exponentially, increasingly reducing the need for labour. The logical consequence is growing unemployment. Even if this process fluctuates in keeping with the business cycle, the basic unemployment rate is gradually rising. The base unemployment rate (lowest level in a booming economy) prevailing in 1960-70 put 200,000 people out of work. The current figure is now almost four million (Konrad-Adenauer-Stiftung 2002). This development is excluding a growing number of people from the labour market permanently or for a long period. At the same time, undeclared employment is on the rise. In 2004 the shadow economy accounted for more than 16 % of German GDP. Structural change is also evident in the relationship between transforming industries and services. In 1990 in Cologne, for example, there were 290,000 jobs in services and 145,000 in manufacturing. By 2003 there were some 360,000 jobs in the service sector but only 91,000 in manufacturing. Manufacturing will continue to lose jobs, with repeated reports on plant closures (Linde) and job cuts (Bauer, Leybold). Dependence on a small number of big employers is an early warning sign. Today 20,000 people work for Ford AG and some 4,000 for Deutz. For Cologne, the loss of these jobs would be a societal, political and economic catastrophe.

Another serious problem, not only in Germany, is the age structure of the population. In the medium and long term, significant changes can be expected owing to declining birth rates and rising life expectancy. The average age of Europeans is now 37.5; this is much lower than the German average of 42. By 2050 it will reach 49.5 and Spain will then have the oldest population in Europe (cf. Statistisches Bundesamt 2002). Apart from the aging of the population, quantitative changes will be rather insignificant. Recent forecasts for Germany predict a population of 83.6 million in 2030. This is a million more than now. The population has grown almost continuously over the past ten years, by between 0 and 700,000 per year (depending on the migration rate, cf. DIW, 2004). A decrease in population is thus not imminent in Germany, rendering obsolete a number of urban worst-case scenarios. Generally speaking, city regions in Europe are less affected by basic demographic trends because they experience a much higher influx of young people. At the same time, a number of peripheral regions with poor infrastructure will register losses among this age-group, so that regions with widely diverging age structures will develop on the national and international levels.

In the public discussion in Germany, societal internationalisation has predominantly negative connotations. Since the proportion of immigrants and their descendants is increasing, particularly in younger age groups, and, for instance, will reach more than 40 % in North-Rhine Westphalian cities by 2040, a fundamental change of attitude is essential before certain ethnic groups and urban areas become irreversibly stigmatized. If marginalized population groups are concentrated in certain neighbourhoods, they inevitably withdraw into their own culture and ethnic networks or families. When social segregation is accompanied by ethnic segregation, those affected risk developing their own culture of poverty, or value systems incompatible with those of the majority of society. Stigmatizing these areas will further devalue them. Growing social segregation is evident throughout Germany. The poverty and wealth report of the Federal Government reveals the intensifying polarization between very poor and very rich population groups. The low-income population is growing in both absolute and relative terms. Spatial polarization translates this development into the spatial dimension, demonstrating society's incapacity for integration. Recent studies of segregation note an increase in the poor population of neighbourhoods already inhabited by many poorer households. This suggests that ethnic and social polarization will continue to increase in this society, also in the form of spatial segregation.

2.2 Spiral of Transport Inefficiency

The information society is in every respect creating greater market transparency. And this enhanced transparency is not only influencing transport efficiency, it is a crucial prerequisite for overcoming urban problems. Overwhelmingly, manufacturers report that the two central difficulties they will be facing over the next three to five years are coping with intensive cost pressure and the pitfalls of global supply chain management. The latter ranges from optimization of local transport organization – a more and more difficult task as traffic increases – to handling global production networks with simultaneously adjusted development and production processes.

The connection between shortening development and production periods in the sector and the urban environment are obvious when it comes to current and future traffic conditions. The functionality of traffic and measures for maintaining or optimizing flows are decisive for a city region's image and development potential. The heavier the burden on the traffic capacity of a city region due to the longer journeys necessitated by decentralization and the functional specialization of space, the higher will be emissions of every kind (traffic noise, for example, threatens the health of 40 % of the German population) and the stress and physical strain to which the road user is subjected. Transport efficiency thus includes optimizing traffic flows in and around city regions. Many local authorities and infrastructure operators consider road pricing a key policy tool. The idea is to limit motorized individual traffic in heavily burdened inner city areas by imposing a fee, transferring traffic flows to public transport. The London road-pricing model is often cited. Since February 2003 every driver who wants to enter a 21 km^2 zone in the inner city has to pay a congestion charge of £ 5 per day, now raised to £ 8. Almost 700 CCTV cameras monitor the system. Mayor Ken Livingstone hoped this measure would remedy a situation where inner city traffic had become more sluggish than in Victorian times. More than two years after its introduction, there is still controversy about the system's efficacy. While car traffic in the charging area has declined and bus service capacity is better used, with bus traffic moving faster, 75 % of businesses in the area complain about losses in turnover, suggesting that Londoners do not find the inner city more accessible than before. Small businesses are particularly hard hit. 25 % are even considering moving out of the charging zone. Besides, a high proportion of traffic has merely shifted outside the charging zone and hours.

Better technical solutions for mobility services are available, for example wayflow (Frankfurt), mobinet (Munich), intermobil (Dresden) and mobilist (Stuttgart). These situational information systems are superior to inflexible regulations like access restrictions or road pricing because they are able to organize city traffic flexibly. Since mobile systems like the Internet, PDA (personal digital assistant), or mobile telephony are now widespread, more and more information services can be integrated into the car. Because these services no longer rely on collective equipment such as indicator boards but use individual facilities, they can be adapted to the driver's individual needs (route, time, maximum parking fee, shops or restaurants at destination, etc.).

The feverish search for intelligent traffic solutions is not limited to the immediate urban context but extends to the entire urban field, particularly major nodes in the highway and motorway systems. A quarter of the German highway network can still be considered bottlenecked (VDA 2005). A study by Cologne University shows that less than 80 % of German highways are fully usable. That means 20 % have extremely uneven surfaces, are badly rutted, are aquaplaning-prone or offer insufficient tyre grip. This percentage will double or even triple by 2015 (in function of the forecast growth in traffic).

The trend towards IT-based logistics systems will also continue in road goods transport. About 1.3 million new commercial vehicles will be equipped with telematics systems every year throughout Europe. By 2009 5.4 million will be thus equipped. The advantages of telematics for the freight forwarder are security, routing, and higher productivity. The improved logistical planning and organization possibilities offered by information and communication technologies (ICTs) give new impetus to intermodal transport. Because ICT service providers can coordinate traffic information from intermodal forwarders it is now possible to locate fleets and goods throughout all transport modes (cf. OECD 2002).

Another new development enabled by ICTs is the electronic market place, which flexibilizes supplier-customer contacts and business transactions. They offer an electronic platform for large numbers of customers and suppliers to interchange information and do business. Specialised electronic market places have already developed separately for goods and logistics, the latter focussing on the planning and management of logistical process chains. There are now more than 200 electronic logistics market places worldwide, about 80 in Europe and 120 in the USA (in 2002).

Informatization is another factor in shortening automobile development and production time. The average life cycle of a model is consequently also becoming shorter and shorter. In 1990 a model was replaced after nine years, in 1999 after seven years. In

2004 the average life cycle was less than six years. Development times have been reduced even more drastically, in certain sectors from three years to one. Global and in-time sourcing increases the complexity of supply chain management and can disrupt high-level company objectives.

2.3 Spiral of Rising Costs

From the perspective of original equipment manufacturers (OEMs) in the automobile sector, the spiral of rising costs is a major aspect of system change. OEMs are under pressure to rethink their current production regime to cope with rising transport and energy costs, growing emerging markets, and accelerating production costs. Until recently, transport costs were a negligible factor, since neither energy costs nor road pricing was an issue. For political reasons this is now changing. Political intervention cannot stop the rise in energy prices and road pricing is politically motivated.

For the time being, the crude oil price has levelled off at about $ 60 a barrel owing to growing demand from emerging markets like China and India (in 2004 the economic boom in China alone contributed 40 % to the record price of crude oil), extraction problems in the USA following Mexican Gulf hurricanes, and unresolved conflicts in the Middle East which has some 60 % of global crude oil reserves and 20 % of petrol resources. Furthermore, uncertain global exploration prospects provide little reassurance about the future development of transport and energy costs. Although known energy deposits should suffice for several decades or more, future exploration costs are quite another matter.

Price developments depend on the so-called depletion mid-point, the point in time when half the known reserves of crude oil will have been extracted. When demand becomes higher than the quantity extracted, prices will explode, provoking economic disorder. When the depletion mid-point will be reached has, however, been a subject of debate for many years. But there is broad agreement that non-OPEC countries are supplying a declining proportion of oil. The USA reached their extraction maximum in 1971, the Soviet Union in 1979/80. Most European crude oil is extracted by Norway and the United Kingdom, both of which reached maximum production in 2000/01. In this situation, a crude oil price of over $ 100 per barrel can no longer be considered an unrealistic scenario. Emerging markets are now an increasingly crucial factor in the development of crude oil prices and the global production landscape. These markets, namely China, India and ASEAN (Association of Southeast Asian Nations), now report the highest growth rates for gross domestic product and per capita income (Table 2).

Future automotive demand thus also depends on these markets. China has doubtless attracted most attention over the last five years. Thanks to extremely high foreign di-

Table 2. Comparison of China, India and ASEAN.

	China	India	ASEAN
Population (in mio.)	1,300	1,100	500
Per Capita Income (in $)	970	580	1,400
GDP growth 2015 (p.a. in %)	7.5	6.8	4.9

Source: Author's compilation

rect investment (FDI), in 2004/05 to the tune of $ 60 billion (compared to $ 6 billion in India), the government was able to realize its plans for infrastructure investment and the networking of logistics infrastructures (waterways, road, rail). China has hence created excellent conditions for attracting more FDI. Furthermore, the mobility market has reached impressive dimensions with about 5.1 million vehicles. Nevertheless, China remains a very contradictory country. It is still a dictatorship with one of the highest capital punishment rates in the world and an economic success story based on a copy-and-paste logic hardly compatible with Western economic ethics. While about 120 million jobseekers are in daily migration (often without ever being paid), architectonic visions and utopias are being constructed in the metropolises (mostly with Western aid) to project the image of a modern and urbane country. It will take some years to discover what lies behind this façade.

Only in the early 1990s did India start opening its economy, far later than China, which had taken initial measures as long ago as the late 1970s; nor are the dynamics of reform the same in the two countries. But development in India is on a broad front and mainly based on democratic principles, so that a number of institutions now consider India the most sustained growth market worldwide. The young population structure and the high fertility rate (3.1 in India, compared to 1.7 in China and 1.3 in Germany) guarantees that the section of the population able to contribute to economic development will remain stable. Moreover, the highly skilled Indian labour force is a major growth factor. India has over 1,000 institutes for computer applications, more than 900 schools of management, and more than 250 universities. Every year more than 50,000 computer specialists and more than 360,000 engineers graduate from these institutions. Not only the high number but also the quality of graduates ensures a high international ranking for India year after year, far ahead of China, South Korea or Taiwan. Only the deficient transport infrastructure will hamper substantial growth for the coming years. Corruption in public administration is one reason why infrastructure measures are poorly sustained, causing persistent problems for investors dependent on reliable systems.

ASEAN member countries are making every effort to resist the influence of their powerful neighbours. Their primary tools are the ASEAN Free Trade Area (AFTA) and political and economic relations with China and India. The establishment of an ASEAN-China free trade area by 2010, an ASEAN-India free trade area by 2015, as well as an

ASEAN-China-South Korea-Japan free trade area are under discussion. The diversity of ASEAN members nevertheless poses problems. It is practically impossible to reconcile their multifarious economic, social and political interests. Moreover, none of these countries is economically and politically in a position to take an active lead. They are either too small (Thailand), politically isolated (Singapore), or plagued by internal conflict (Philippines, Indonesia).

Globalization is not only introducing new, dynamic economies into international markets. It also exerts massive influence through global purchasing policies and the worldwide exploitation of labour cost advantages. In recent years, the discussion on labour costs as a location factor has become more animated. Although labour costs are doubtless only one of many aspects, Germany with its high wage costs has recently been losing (automotive) production capacity to low wage countries. The German share of value added per vehicle has steadily fallen. Labour costs are clearly an important factor in automotive development and production. The German automotive industry has the highest labour costs in the world. At 33 Euros per hour in 2003 they were 20 % higher than in the USA and Japan, and 50 % higher than in the average for western European competitors (Dudenhöffer 2004). The gap between Germany and the new eastern European members of the EU, not to mention Asian countries like South Korea, China or India, is even much greater.

Both automotive OEMs and their suppliers are following the trend to outsource production to eastern Europe. Over the past decade, component suppliers have created about 100,000 jobs in accession countries. The greater the role the supplier plays in production, the more important this is for the German production site. By 2015, suppliers will be expected to shoulder almost 80 % of automotive development and production

Table 3. Labour costs in the automobile industry.

Country	Labour costs in the automobile industry (Euro per hour)
Germany	33.0
Japan	28.6
USA	27.4
France	22.7
England	22.3
Italy	16.8
Poland	6.5
Czech Republic	5.1
Slovakia	4.3
Romania	1.8

Source: Author's compilation based on Duddenhöffer 2004

(IML/IPA/MMC 2004), reducing the OEM workforce and increasing supplier employment. At the same time, the number of suppliers is predicted to fall from 5,000 today to between 2,500 and 3,000 in 2015. The same trend is apparent with automotive OEMs (2005: 13, 2015: 6-8). The market will hence be equilibrated between OEMs and system integrators (OESs). For volume producers (VW, Opel, Ford, etc.) this means reducing self-production and transferring their share of value creation in all main modules to suppliers (IML et al. 2004). Premium manufacturers (Mercedes-Benz, BMW, Audi, etc.) will concentrate even more strongly on brand issues, redefining self-production and outside service.

The growing pressure for integration between actors is also affecting spatial distribution. At the micro-level, automotive research and development and production centres will benefit from spatial synergies. At the macro-level, suppliers must decide the extent to which they participate in OEM engagement abroad in order to furnish the required quality. The surge of quality problems and product recalls in the automotive industry (there were 137 recalls in 2004, 41 % more than the year before) illustrates the dilemma (VDA 2005). Since all modules and systems are becoming increasingly complex and have to be adapted to local market conditions, there is growing pressure at all levels for efficient cooperation. Thailand, the 'Asian Detroit', is a good example for the regional concentration of OEMs and OESs. German and other European suppliers have followed the OEMs to ensure joint compliance with local content and quality requirements and in pursuit of labour cost advantages.

2.4 System Preservation: The Historical Lock-in

The German automotive industry is facing complex challenges with enormous impact on urban production regimes. They include a rising number of models superseding one another at ever shorter intervals, falling prices, and greater price-performance awareness and declining brand loyalty among customers, and, last but not least, the progressive liberalization of the motor vehicle trade in the EU. These market-related challenges are compounded by developments in the product, the car itself, most importantly in electric and electronic elements. It is estimated that by 2010 no less than 90 % of innovations will be in electronics, 80 % of which in software. Even conservative forecasts put the share of software innovations at between 60 % and 70 %. Electronics and software are expected to increase their share of vehicle value from the current 25 % to between 35 % and 40 % by 2010. However, the numerous quality problems and product recalls indicate that the high penetration rate of electrics and electronics has had unwanted side effects.

These developments point to the weaknesses of traditional orientation on the German location as opposed to a flexible, global production landscape integrating many actors. Nevertheless there are also factors emphasizing that Germany should remain an important automotive production location. The notion of the historical lock-in, constituted by brand embeddedness, political embeddedness and socio-cultural embeddedness characterizes this preservative force. "Automeanings shifted from car parts to wholes and back again, and from individual cars to national and transnational levels" (Koshar 2004:139). In the pursuit of greater scale and broader product ranges, OEMs are facing increased challenges in brand management. The local presence of an OEM is an important part of its brand image. In other words, a premium brand image based on trust and future stability must be rooted in the history of the brand. "The identity between space and national identity produces a variegated and multi-scaled geography constituted by borders, symbolic areas and sites, constellations, pathways, dwelling places and everyday realms" (Edensor 2004:108). The national identity of brands will blur with increasing cross-border mergers in the OEM and supplier systems. OEMs seem to be aware of this and react with similar strategies (e.g., Volkswagen, Porsche and Mercedes-Benz).

Volkswagen has launched two important projects enhancing the link between production and brand value: the Autostadt in Wolfsburg and the 'Gläserne Manufaktur' (the Transparent Factory) in Dresden. The central message of the Autostadt is: "There is future in experience. Innovation cannot prosper without experience. Nevertheless, experience seems to have lost ground in recent times against the new, the latest. The new, whether acclaimed or mistrusted, is the focus of public interest. But what would mankind make of it without the backing of experience?" (Autostadt 2005). The Autostadt has meanwhile welcomed over ten million visitors, and VW stresses that it is an important communication platform where the values and visions of the company and its brands can be experienced. The location of the Autostadt next door to company headquarters symbolises this link. The mission of the Gläserne Manufaktur in Dresden is somewhat different: "New Paths: Only those who take new paths can create new values. Volkswagen's Gläserne Manufaktur in Dresden reflects our thoughts and actions on automobiles." (Die Gläserne Manufaktur 2005). VW puts the stress on the combination of production and event world, choosing a site in the very centre of a city famous for its wealth of art and lively culture, as well as industrial tradition.

Although the new Porsche factory in Leipzig does not directly visualise the relationship between brand and production, "'Made in Germany' was considered a competitive advantage on the broad world market" (Porsche Leipzig 2005). A total of 17 potential locations in former GDR (East Germany) were assessed in a multilevel selection process. It was clear from the start that the brand message could be transported only by a factory in Germany. And from the very outset, the factory's communication strategy has sought a very special design stressing experience value for both workers and visitors. One of the assembly lines, for example, traverses the transparent roof of a canteen so that the workers are always close to the vehicles they are assembling.

Mercedes-Benz puts the accent less on production-specific issues than on brand and product history, which it has been presenting for many years in the Mercedes-Benz Museum in Stuttgart. The museum, with about 480,000 visitors per year, is one of the most successful in southwestern Germany. Its first task has been to establish the historical links between the innovative brand symbolized primarily by the engineering genius of Karl Benz und Gottlieb Daimler and a "fascinating mobility" (Mercedes-Benz International 2005). It culminates in the statement: "We do not need to invent a good story – we have been writing history since 1886", and it is this Mercedes-Benz tradition that "builds a bridge from the tentative beginnings of motorization in the last century via the current high technology standards into the future."

Overall, the German automotive industry ideally represents the link between national identity formation by engineers such as Benz, Daimler, Maybach, Porsche plus an unequalled post-war success story and the associated industrial, social and technological developments and interrelations that have led to an automobile culture unique in the world. Many see this culture threatened by the perennial debate about speed limits on German motorways, and by the introduction of electronic toll collecting schemes for commercial vehicles, not to mention issues such as road pricing in cities and tolls for passenger vehicles on German motorways, which might soon be on the agenda. A national automobile culture evolves from the regulatory environment and technical, social and mobility aspects. The brand culture of all automotive OEMs, as an element of Germany's national (automobile) identity, is an important contributory factor in the international production landscape. It is the old question of origin. 'Made in Germany' has always been offset against, for example, 'Made by Mercedes-Benz' and vice versa. A premium carmaker like Mercedes-Benz is also obliged to localize brand management, vehicle technology, and pricing in keeping with customer needs and requirements.

There is growing awareness that urban actors and urban policy makers need to rethink the value of the socio-historical lock-in. This means that societal and historical developments should not be taken for granted: they must inspire an overall goal or vision to guide all action. But what does this mean for the urban environment? The European city should not restrict development to preserving its compactness and beauty but seek to extend compactness and beauty to all areas of the city: to the urban periphery, the individual neighbourhood, even to industrial areas.

3. The Future Urban Production Regime

All organisations, whether in the public or private sector, operate in environments that are continuously changing. Although changes are sometimes minor in nature (or hidden to the observer), more often than not they are significant and can even pose a threat to the future existence of an organisation. How decision makers interact with their changing environment is therefore crucial to the success or failure of their organisations and, obviously, to that of the associated environment. The urban image and performance thus need to be integrated with organisational structures in a long-term approach.

The most important changes reflect a shift from an 'either-or' view towards an 'as-well-as' mindset, with the increasingly powerful consumer unwilling to accept the car as an interruptive element in daily activity. The driver-car assemblage as an integrated entity will come to the fore in satisfying individual mobility needs, meeting a wide range of demands and requirements (e.g., online *and* offline capacity, emotional *and* functional design, business *and* private use). Urban mobility and hardware routines in urban and transportation planning could generate a shift in system from the existing urban world to a new urban environment, for emerging developments are not as strongly limited to the existing infrastructure nor so constrained by traditional values. This means that consolidation of the global automotive industry will continue. Consolidation has been driven by OEM needs to create global economies of scale in procurement and manufacturing, to maximize returns on investment for product and technology development, to access emerging high-growth markets, and to broaden product and brand portfolios as well as the customer base. The industry's over-capacity of more than 30 %, the increasing burden of research and development for new technologies (alternative drivetrain technologies, recycling, etc.) and power shifts in the value chain – retailers and mega-suppliers will continue to gain power – will generate further consolidation, even greater scale and gains in efficiency.

In evaluating locations, OEMs will bring their capital power to bear, playing sites off against one another in the pursuit of increasingly capital-related strategies. This means intense competition between the urban core and fringe, urban region and regional, national periphery, between urban regions, and, of course, between locations in the developed world and in emerging markets. Modes of production are changing not only through technological innovation and interrelations but in response to social aspirations and requirements.

The driver-car assemblage can be varyingly and continuously restructured. It is a complex of societal transformation, technological developments, market dynamic changes and the emerging transport framework that reshapes spatio-temporal production regimes. Thrift shows how the dividing line between human (driver) and machine (mobile technological environment) becomes blurred (Thrift 2004). The cultural manifestations of how we produce automobility are thus crucial to the future of production and urban development. Only if the meaning and symbolism of the automobile as such are attenuating, can we seriously posit the reversibility of urban production regimes in countries such as Germany. However, the forces capable of shifting the national car system into a new mode are growing in strength: "The car cum driving of the 21st century is no longer the same knot of steely practices that it was in the 20th" (Thrift 2004:48).

And it is these underlying forces that will reconfigure the spatio-temporal production practices of the future.

Table 4. The emerging production regime.

Past/Present	Future
Production (= core competence)	Brand-specific integration (= core competence)
Export-oriented (serving the world from Germany)	Market-oriented
Long-term investment (historically locked-in)	Long-term but flexible
Technology push (high investment in plant)	Market pull
High local content (beneficial for national supplier)	High regional content
'Made in ...'	'Made by ...'
Functional (focus on production)	Emotional (Porsche Leipzig; VW Dresden, Wolfsburg)
Focus on Cities	Focus on Regions

Source: Author's compilation

References

AUTOSTADT (2005), www.autostadt.de, accessed May 10, 2005

CARSTEN, S. (2005), *Zukunftsfähiges Handeln in Stadtregionen*, Norderstedt

DIE GLÄSERNE MANUFAKTUR (2005), *Philosophy*, in: www.glaesernemanufaktur.de/gmd.jsp?dok=, accessed May 10, 2005

DIW (Deutsches Institut für Wirtschaftsforschung) (2004), *Potential Migration from Central and Eastern Europe into the EU-15: An Update*, Berlin

DUDENHÖFFER, F. (2004), "Zwischenschritte auf dem Weg zur Wettbewerbsfähigkeit", *ifo-Schnelldienst*, Vol. 17, p. 9-12

EDENSOR, T. (2004), "Automobility and National Identity: Representation, Geography and Driving Practice", *Theory, Culture & Society*, Vol. 21, No. 4/5, p. 101-120

FREUND, P. (1993), *The Ecology of the Automobile*, Montreal, New York

GLAESER, E. L. (1996), "Why Economists still like Cities", *City Journal*, Vol. 6, No. 2, p. 70-89

IML (Fraunhofer-Institut für Materialfluss und Logistik), IPA (Fraunhofer-Institut für Produktionstechnik und Automatisierung), MMC (Mercer Management Consulting) (eds.) (2004), *Future Automotive Industry Structure (FAST) 2015*, Dortmund

KONRAD-ADENAUER-STIFTUNG (ed.) (2002), *Die Entwicklung des Arbeitsmarktes 1962-2001*, Sankt Augustin

KOSHAR, R. (2004), "Cars and Nations: Anglo-German Perspectives on Automobility between the World Wars", *Theory, Culture & Society*, Vol. 21, No. 4/5, p. 121-144

KRÄMER-BADONI, T., GRYMER, H., RODENSTEIN, M. (1971), *Zur sozio-ökonomischen Bedeutung des Automobils*, Frankfurt/M

KUNSTLER, J. (1994), *The Geography of Nowhere: The Rise and Decline of America's Man-Made Landscape*, New York.

LEFEBVRE, H. (1991), *The Production of Space*, Oxford

MERCEDES-BENZ INTERNATIONAL (2005), www.mercedes-benz.com, accessed May 10, 2005

MEYER,C.,ZIMMER-HEGMANN,R.(2004)."Wohnungsmärkte und Segregation. Rahmenbedingungen für ein Belegungsmanagement", in: ILS (Institut für Landes- und Stadtentwicklungsforsc hung NRW) (ed.), *Belegungsmanagement in der integrierten Stadt(teil)entwicklung*, Dortmund

OECD (Organisation for Economic Co-operation and Development) (2002), *Benchmarking Intermodal Freight Transport*, Paris

PORSCHE LEIPZIG (2005), *Porsche & Leipzig: Wie alles begann. Warum Leipzig?*, in: www.porsche-leipzig.com/de/porscheleipzig/howitbegun/warumleipzig.aspx, accessed May 10, 2005

SHELLER, M., URRY, J. (2000), "The City and the Car", *International Journal of Urban and Regional Research*, Vol. 24, p. 737-757

STATISTISCHES BUNDESAMT (2002), *Datenreport 2002*, Bonn

THRIFT, N. (2004), "Driving in the City", *Theory, Culture & Society*, Vol. 21, No. 4/5, p. 41-59

URRY, J. (2000), *Sociology Beyond Societies*, London

URRY, J. (2004), "The 'System' of Automobility", *Theory, Culture & Society*, Vol. 21, No. 4/5, p. 25-39

VDA (Verband der Automobilindustrie) (2005), *Autojahresbericht 2005*, Frankfurt/M

CHAPTER III

PLACES OF URBAN CHARACTER

PLACES OF URBAN CHARACTER: INTRODUCTION

by Dietrich Henckel, Benjamin Herkommer and Elke Pahl-Weber

Among most planners and architects, mega-infrastructures such as motorways, airports, train stations etc. never enjoyed the reputation of being very urban types of spaces. They were regarded as key components of modernity's agenda to separate and decentralize urban functions.

Together with innumerable low-density residential areas, shopping malls, business and technology parks, modern transport infrastructures form the fragmented conglomerate of sprawling city regions, also referred to as 'Zwischenstadt' (Sieverts 1999) or 'metapolis' (Ascher 2004). The peripheral 'Zwischenstadt' is conventionally regarded as a sort of antipode to traditional forms of urbanity and placeness. And wherever we find large-scale infrastructures cutting through (more or less) historic core cities, they seem to produce a sort of 'inner periphery', promoting 'Zwischenstadt' inside the traditional compact city. Especially transport infrastructures have been attributed with Marc Augé's (1994) term 'non-lieu' – a place without identity, deprived of the socio-historical relatedness that constitutes the identity of a place. Urbanity however, is thought to be a feature of only the traditional forms of placeness, of historical, relational places with a unique identity.

But new developments point in the opposite direction: increasingly, the 'non-places' like mega-infrastructures and transit corridors become hatcheries of urbanity. They become multi-functional and more and more often they are appropriated by people in a way that they develop new forms of identity. At the same time, urbanists bemoan the loss of identity in many historic city centres. The globalisation of consumption and image production has reduced the degree to which places are unique and authentic. Spatial identity as an individual quality has often been replaced by franchised brandscapes. To make a stand against the increasing conformity, many cities have reinvented themselves, trying to reconstruct a conceived authentic identity or creating new identities.

Spatial identity thus becomes footloose and detached from its social and historical context and serves as a 'hyperreal' (Baudrillard 1983) setting and cultural role model within the framework of mass consumption. Where modernism wanted one international style, postmodernism seeks the global propagation of various local styles.

Probably, identity and authenticity have never been valid categories in urban placemaking. In any case, the polarity between place and non-place is collapsing and urban planning needs to shift its attention towards the new urbanities, towards all places of urban character whether they possess a traditional form of identity and placeness or not.

- In their contribution, Michael Koch and Henrik Sander shed light on new urban developments along transport corridors. The authors not only explore the many ways in which traffic infrastructures have recently become urbanised, they also present design principles for the 'Corridor City' and the integration of traffic spaces into the regional cityscape.
- Architect Kees Christiaanse presents how megainfrastructures such as airports, industrial harbours and train stations become more and more densified and urbanised. These newly evolving micro-cities serve increasingly diverse interests and demands which also means that a large proportion of them function 24 hours a day, seven days a week. Kees Christiaanse and Partners (KCAP) have been and continue to be participating in this process over the course of several projects for example in Schiphol Airport, Zurich Station and Oslo Björvika. The paper shows, how former agents of low density, functional separation and largeness develop into high density mixed-use developments and how these projects can be integrated into the surrounding urban fabric.

Unfortunately, the third contribution to Chapter Three is missing. In the course of the conference 'Time Space Places', Werner Sewing gave a very interesting presentation on 'The Production of Place in the Postmodern City' but for personal reasons he was not able to hand in his paper in time.

References:

ASCHER, F. (2004), "Métapolis: A third Modern Urban Revolution", in: Bölling, L., Sieverts, T. (eds.), *Mitten am Rand. Auf dem Weg von der Vorstadt über die Zwischenstadt zur regionalen Stadtlandschaft,* Wuppertal, Müller+Busmann, p. 24-37

AUGÉ, M. (1994), *Orte und Nicht-Orte,* Frankfurt/M, Fischer

BAUDRILLARD, J. (1983), *Simulations,* New York, Semiotext(e)

SIEVERTS, T. (1999), *Zwischenstadt. Zwischen Ort und Welt, Raum und Zeit, Stadt und Land,* Bauwelt Fundamente No. 118, Basel, Boston, Birkhäuser

WHERE THE HECK IS URBANITY?

by Michael Koch and Henrik Sander

Introduction

The dissolving of our cities into broad, regional urban landscapes makes us ask one central question: Where the heck is urbanity? To get an idea where the answer to this question is to be found, we need to take a look at what forces drive urban developments today and how people adapt their daily routines and daily lives to this new urban cosmos of traffic corridors, parking lots and gas stations (Garreau 1992). This paper is more a phenomenological picture story than an extensive analytic or scientific paper. However, it proceeds with the same degree of seriousness, based on observations that are easily repeatable (which is what science is about). Whoever wants to check on our research may do so by chatting with the attendant or whoever comes by while having a coffee at his local gas station.

The reality of the city today is the city region; it is the network city which by definition does not mean that only the nodes of the network are urban spaces. Instead, urbanity should also be found on and along connecting infrastructure lines (Figure 1). Transit corridors as new urban places do more than connect A with B. Our research interest lies in exploring more than the mere connection. What happens in between is what we are interested in: is there some kind of a new urbanity?

Urbanity has to do with attraction and exoticism, difference, neurosis, freedom, beauty, and community. The new urbanism of the transit corridor has to do with the real daily life of people, so called dirty realism. It is about daily urbanism, a little bit ugly and unwanted and somewhat against our discipline's terms of political correctness, which habitually associate private transport with 'bad' and public transport with 'good'. This way of thinking is less than helpful in discovering new ways of looking at places. With such blinkers you will not see the beauty of places like the combined commercial/rest

Figure1. Ruhrstadt, the aesthetic of a region.

Source: Willamowski 2002: Cover

Figure 2. 'Motopia' by G. Jellico.

Source: Neuer Berliner Kunstverein 1982:117

area/housing estate 'Dückerweg' on the A40 freeway in Bochum. In a way, our position is similar to that of the artist in the early 20th century, who discovered the beauty and urbanity of the big city, like Ernst Ludwig Kirchner in his 1914 picture capturing the atmosphere of Friedrichstraße, or August Endell who wrote in his article 'The Beauty of the Big City': "But it is amazing how the big city, despite all the ugly buildings, despite all the noise and everything it can be reproached with, is a miracle of beauty and poetry for anyone who has eyes to see. It is a fairytale – more colorful, many-hued and variform than any poet has ever told. It is a home, a mother prodigally lavishing happiness on her children over and over again. This may sound paradoxical and exaggerated. But whoever is not blinded by prejudice, whoever is capable of devotion, whoever intensively engages in the city will soon become aware of the thousand beauties, the countless wonders, the abundant riches its streets embrace – visible to all and seen by so few." (Endell/David 1995:163ff).

1. The History of a Relationship

Some historical remarks: city and traffic are an integrated whole, they are two sides of the same coin. Cities come into being where flows of traffic cross. It is not possible to think of a city without traffic; nevertheless the relationship is always problematic. Leonardo da Vinci's design for a separation of pedestrian and street traffic in two levels is not only a precursor of modern concepts, it also describes the immense traffic problems of historical cities. At the same time, mobility has always been used to escape traffic problems: the country estates of the Roman aristocracy and those of the British bourgeoisie in the 18th century were no more than early forms of suburbanization. Only the technical possibilities and price of mobility limited this movement to the fringes of urban settlements to a relatively small social group. The mass mobility offered by trains, and later by private cars made traffic the Trojan horse of the classical pedestrian city. The spatial needs of different means of transportation broke up confined urban structures and enabled the city to grow beyond all traditional limits.

Baron Hausmann was one of the first modern planners who adapted the historical city to the needs of modern traffic. Hausmann inserted 165 km of new streets into the city of Paris, 95 km within the center, mainly connecting the different train stations. He thus created a modern street system, which served as a basis for the further existence and future growth of Paris (Schüle 1997:22ff). The modernism movement was a reaction to the needs of growing traffic. Le Corbusicr with his 'plan Voisin' – named after the famous French car brand – and all his successors like Hans Reichow with his 'car-oriented city' or Geoffrey Jellico with his 'motopia' designed new cities for new traffic structures (Figure 2).

But all their designs were visions of almost baroque idealism – totally new urban structures that never really worked, given the complexity and dynamics of real life. In contrast, Archigram's 'walking cities' can be regarded as a first attempt to describe the anarchic and chaotic relationship between mobility and urban development (Figure 3). Walking cities is a metaphor for urbanity on the road and quite well describes present day reality. Traffic-based urban agglomerations developed around stations, airports and as a nearly ubiquitous phenomenon along highways. Their appearance disturbs us and after 100 years of 'automobile revolution' we are just starting to understand them.

Figure 3. Archigramm's 'Walking Cities'.

Source: Archplus 1997:35

2. The Perception of Space in Speed

These new environments of urban agglomerations are based on speed and lead to dramatic changes in the perception of urban spaces. Paul Klee's 1910 drawings of the city of Bern show a new, blurred view of the city. Zaha Hadid's sketch 'The peak' from 1983 for the Hong Kong competition recalls these drawings. In the 1930s, the first freeways and expressways were seen as monuments of speed. Due to the lack of traffic they were less of a subject of debate on efficiency and safety but became a land-art-like landscape element to open new views on home country. In Germany, so called 'landscapeadvocates' designed not only the highway as part of the landscape, but the surrounding landscape in relation to the highway. These highways are far from being a symbol of destruction and pollution. Still today there are many places where the infrastructure is like a sculpture in the landscape.

Many of today's photographers explore these new landscapes urbanized by traffic infrastructure: the Swiss Nicolas Faure, the Dutch Theo Baart and Cary Markering or the German Uschi Huber. Artists help us to realize special qualities of 'strange' urban surroundings and to explore new possibilities of using them. In 1999 Sigrid Lange transformed the top of a parking deck in Puhlheim near Cologne into a 'light and air spa' with artificial lawns, sun chairs and parasols. This new view of urban landscapes is nowadays often used for advertising. A campaign for the car brand Smart showed a couple hand in hand in a parking lot, picnicking with a view of a skyline under a romantic sunset. The infrastructure becomes the emotional background for a moment of individual happiness. A campaign for the furniture company de Sede called 'The Art of Seating' also used traffic spaces. It showed design chairs on bridges and in tunnels. The message was simple: feel comfortable and at home on the road; or feel connected with the world while sitting in your living room.

Figure 4. CD-Cover 'Neue Heimat 2'.

Source: Ministry of Sound Recordings 2002

Similarly, the music label 'Ministry of Sound' has a popular series of electronic music compilations from Germany, called 'Neue Heimat' (New Homeland). The CD covers show young people listening to music in front of highways, noise barriers and in trains (Figure 4). These and similar cover art works indicate a high level of acceptance and appreciation for mobility and transit corridors among the young generation (Figure 5). Photographers, artists and musicians are cultural pioneers, playing the role of the urban flaneurs of the 21st century. Their new way of looking at things is becoming more and more widely accepted. A Sunday walk on the verge of the highway no longer is considered a quirky oddity and a race with electric scooters for elderly people, which took place in Zandvoort, Netherlands in 2004 demonstrates how much speed and traffic are integral parts of the daily urban life of every generation.

Figure 5. Cruising culture of elderly people.

Source: Parr in BBC 1994

Apart from this phenomenological approach, architects and urban planners like Kevin Lynch and Allison Smithson have tried to develop a more systematic approach in describing the driver's perspective of space in motion as the way most citizens perceive their urban environment on a daily basis. In 'AS in DS' (2001) the British architect Allison Smithson describes the journey in her Citroen DS 19 from London to a Wiltshire cottage in the form of an illustrated story. The contrast between the technically advanced car and the pre-industrial landscape increases sensibility for mobile perception and makes the route a longitudinal section through contemporary civilization.

At the same time, Kevin Lynch, Donald Appleyard und John R. Myer examined the Boston ring road. They developed a system to map the spatial perception of the motorist. On the basis of their visual analysis, they tried to find optimized routing for the ring road. For their procedure, they renounced film and photographic techniques. Instead, they used drawings and mental mapping in order to give priority to individual perception. Owing to this approach, their design looks more like a screenplay then a traditional urban design scheme. This parallel certainly is not by pure chance, because Lynch experiences moving in much the same way as he experiences film and music: "The sensation of driving a car is primarily one of motion and space, felt in a continuous sequence. Vision, rather than sound or smell, is the principal sense… The continuity and insistent temporal flow are akin to music and the cinema…" (Appleyard/Lynch/Myer 1966).

Nearly 40 years after Kevin Lynch, Francine Houben, director of the first architecture biennale '1ab' 2003 in Rotterdam, restarted exploration of the perception of urban motorways. The exhibition 'World Avenue' compared ten global metropolises on the basis of their highway networks. Each region was represented by a typical car with

Figure 6. Six typologies for the aesthetices of mobility.

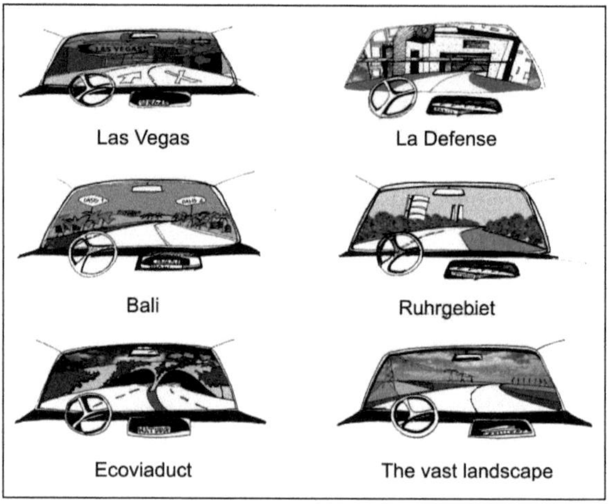

Source: Houben/Calabrese 2003:27

typical equipment and local radio shows, like Mexico City by a beetle, L.A. by a van or the Ruhr District by a BMW. The visitor could directly experience the different regional (car) cultures all over the world. On the basis of case studies, Francine Houben (2003) developed a kind of typology of metropolises in terms of the view through the windshield: "To give the aesthetics of mobility some form, I introduced six typologies that can deal with the alternation from the scale of the city to that of the country side" (Figure 6).

Christophe Girot, landscape architect at ETH Zurich, showed that the representation of our perception of new urban landscapes formed by mobility today can use moving images and film to explore the character of urban landscapes. He developed a method called Movism to use video as a tool of perception. The film 'Idylle' by Marco Sträuli and Sascha Mathis shows a day in the landscape around Zurich airport in time-lapse photography. It describes the overlapping of landscape and traffic infrastructure. And it raises questions like: What is this? Landscape, urban-scape, agglo-scape, rural-scape? In any case, this space aside some transit corridors is both: quite banal and simultaneously a place of Heimat as well as Sehnsucht.

3. The Vehicle as Living Space

A train station generally is regarded as a public space. Stations are more or less synonymous with urban atmosphere. Their beauty and the fascinating flows of crowds were described and celebrated by artists like the Italian futurists. Train stations as well as the trains themselves have more functions than facilitating travel from one place to another. There are sleeping cars, dining cars (which sometimes become a meeting place for entire commuting communities), conference compartments, experiments with onboard convenience shops, and you can even book 'flying teachers' who accompany you (Figure 7). Unfortunately, a process of privatization is becoming evident in these places: the conversation with fellow passengers is more and more often replaced by the conversation via mobile phone, or it is avoided by escaping to the computer – to work or just watch films.

Compared to the train, the car is generally regarded as the epitome of the private capsule. Isolated and thrown back on ourselves, we are lonely in the traffic jam. Seen from without, this description may be correct, the internal perception is often different. Many commuters describe the seemingly wasted time in the car as quality time, one of the rare moments of the day when they do not need to worry about anything: no boss, no kids, just time for themselves and their thoughts. The daily trip serves as relief from omnipresent stimulus satiation. And then there is the radio. From hit parade to high-class talk show, everything is present in the car. Interestingly, in radio shows a rather high proportion of listeners call in on their mobile phones while sitting in the car.

At the same time, the isolation of the car creates an atmosphere of seriousness. The automobile is often the place where people reveal their feelings. It is often the place where important questions are settled. In this respect, Abbas Kiarostami's film 'Ten' (Hesler 2006) is remarkable, as the film is based on these unique characteristics of the car. The whole film is set inside a car showing a woman having conversations with several passengers while driving through the streets of Teheran. The dialogues, spread over two days and a night, revolve around the role of women in Iranian society. In this way, the car, driving through the city of Teheran, is turned into a tool of subversion. The car (still) seems to be the only place in Iran where this topic can be discussed.

The automobile also is a hybrid space. You can find busses for conferences, the mobile phone makes a car into an office space, in vans you can change the ground plan, and, with office equipment like a notebook holder, there is no need to fear a traffic

Figure 7. The train as living space.

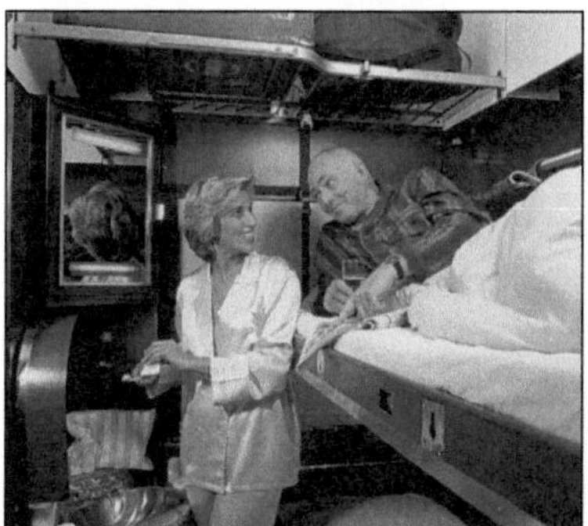

Source: SBB 2005

Figure 8. The automobile as a hybrid space.

Source: Parr in BBC 1994

jam anymore (Figure 8). In 1990, in an interview with Arch+ Cedric Price pointed out that "when you take into account what happens in a car, apart from pure movement – dreams, music, family reunions, business chats – then I regard the car as one of the most human spaces. Nowadays, the family only comes together and talks with each other in the car, while at home the family members withdraw to their bedrooms watching different television programs and do not have their meals together" (Price 1998:330). Cars are living spaces, the still growing mobility and our ability to adapt to new environments (with new technologies) steadily increases its public character. Urbanism is somewhere inside.

4. Transit Corridors as Living Space

'Transit corridor' is an abstract term, describing high speed connections between A and B. But corridors are not only a paved line in the landscape. As on every road, there are links with the surrounding space: exits, parking lots, gas stations and feeder roads. A closer look shows that the corridor is strongly interlinked with its environment. As paradoxical as it may sound, corridors should be regarded as linear cores of a network and, like every core, they have more than one function. They attract and develop 'parasites' that make a business out of them.

Apart from the dominating billboard advertising, there is an ever growing number of 'cultural signs' on highways. Standardized bay-colored signs, indicating historic monuments as well as tourist attractions somewhere in the region, like Hockenheim, the famous Formula One racetrack, or small historic towns with odd traditions like the 'Schäferlaufstadt Markgröningen' (Shepherd-run town Markgröningen) (Figure 9). Meanwhile there is a series of special guidebooks on these signs, helping to explore the hinterland of a corridor.

Parking and rest areas are a cosmos of their own, well described in their beauty by Julio Cortázar and Carol Dunlop. Their book 'Los autonautas de la cosmopista' describes a six week discovery tour of the Paris-Marseille freeway. Cortázar and Dunlop stopped at every rest area and stayed for the night at every second, 'no matter how ugly it might be'. The car park as a transition zone between the speed of the car and the speed of the pedestrian is a place without any fear of entering. As the car park is rarely totally blocked by cars, it is something like an ephemeral wasteland, open for temporary occupation. Not surprisingly, you can find a beach bar (resembling illegal bars on wasteland sites in the early 1990s in Berlin, which are now back in fashion), on top of the multi-storey car park of a downtown department store in Dortmund. Nor is it surprising to find a junkshop in an underground car park in Zurich. Not to mention the meeting places for swingers and temporary trucker villages, that emerge night by night in our freeway rest areas – to disappear again at sunrise.

Figure 9. Culture on the way along german 'autobahn'.

Source: Renner Verlag 2005

Figure 10. The gas station as a neighborhood meeting place.

Source: orange.edge

The gas station is the classical node in a car based infrastructure (Bremer 2001) and these places are being converted more and more into little urban centers for shopping, recreation, meeting points not only for transit passengers but also for local residents (Figure 10). Nowadays you can get much more than the classic deep frozen pizza for singles. In places like Sandau in the German state of Saxony-Anhalt, a 'Stammtisch' (regulars' table) for retirees was established at the gas station, the Putbus service station on the island of Rügen is a tourist attraction and won an architectural prize, and the gas stations along Berlin's East Side Gallery (a part of the former Berlin Wall) are heavily frequented by the party crowd on weekend nights. In Münster, North-Rhine Westphalia, a gas station and a Burger King outlet share a building, and you can see people getting their car washed while enjoying a burger.

Within the context of his work on the Broad Acre City, Frank Lloyd Wright quite early gave an indication about the meaning of gas stations in modern urban landscapes. He wrote: "Watch the little gas station. ... In our present gasoline service station you may see a crude beginning to such important advance decentralization; also see the beginning of the future humane establishment we are now calling the free city. Wherever service stations are located, naturally these so often ugly and seemingly insignificant features will survive and expand. [The new city] ... is all around us in the haphazard making, the apparent forces to the contrary notwithstanding. All about us and no plan. The old order is breaking up." (Frank Lloyd Wright Gas Station Page 2005). Wright pins his hopes on the gas station as a decentral-central place and he even built a prototype in Cloquet Minnesota. A building more lounge than gas station, more neighborhood place than filling. What Wright planned in his time as a prototype is nowadays emerging in every corner of our cities. At first glance the public occupation of gas stations and parking lots is surprising. Their design is monofunctional. The gas station is a marketing machine for selling fuel, the parking lot an inhospitable space for cars. Their attractiveness is based on their social openness and the unplanned interaction between different social groups.

Figure 11. 'Our Lady of the Angels' by Rafael Moneo.

Source: Polidori 2005:109

Figure 12. The traffic jam as a happening.

Source: unknown private photographer

Figure 13. Urbanity is somewhere in-between.

Source: orange.edge

The public character of these spaces remains limited, though, and the intensity of public life is temporary and variable. Nevertheless, service stations should not be underestimated for the daily urban experience and individual forms of spontaneous occupation of urban spaces they provide.

Corridors are not only places of daily urbanity. In economic terms, they are also important locations for urban development, for large scale architecture by famous architects who build landmarks along corridors like the 'Allianz Arena' in Munich by Herzog & de Meuron or the Cathedral of 'Our Lady of the Angels' by Rafael Moneo in L.A (Figure 11). The importance of locations along traffic corridors is reflected by prices. Data from Dresden show that real estate prices can be five times higher along highways than in other comparably suburban locations. Office rents in locations close to highways – especially in mid-sized cities – are often equal if not significantly higher than in the city center (Schulten 2005:9). The Dutch ex-post analysis 'Infrastructure and urban development: the case of the Amsterdam orbital motorway' by Bruinsma, Pepping and Rietveld indicates the role of high quality urban design schemes for the development of prices. The survey shows significant statistical relationships between location on the highway and the price levels of office space. According to Bruinsma the price for office space is essentially determined by the urban context and the quality of the urban design (Bruinsma 1996).

But even the collapse of a corridor has certain urban qualities. Traffic jams are mostly hated, yet they are an integral part of the daily routines of commuters. They develop a certain 'urban' knowledge about the likelihood of traffic jams, and use them for work, breakfast etc. (Figure 12). The weekly traffic jam on the way to soccer stadiums in the Ruhr District is nearly part of the game; the street becomes a catwalk, with cars decorated with all kind of fan merchandise. The annual summer vacation collapse often turns into a happening. People use it for actually playing soccer, picnicking, sightseeing, and so on. The real catastrophe is the end of the jam, when this get-together comes to an end without warning.

To summarize what has been said up to this point: urbanity is an ambiguous spatial quality and is not confined to what our discipline regards as 'good urban space'. New forms of urbanity lie in the 'somewhere-in-between-spaces' of our post-modern 'in-between city' and transit corridors are actually key examples of new urban spaces (Figure 13).

5. Strategies

For several years now, there has been renewed discussion about traffic corridors within urban regions. The transport infrastructure authority of Zurich canton in Switzerland was in search of innovative planning procedures for new highways. Transport and urban planners jointly developed integrated solutions right from the routing phase. In Austria the federal ministry for transport and the ASFINAG, in charge for planning freeways and expressways, are looking for integrated urban solutions using toll charges. This is necessary to make new radial highways within the Vienna region acceptable. The Dutch ministry of transport initiated the project 'Roads to the Future,'examining innovative solutions to traffic and urban planning problems in several pilot projects. In France, the 'Institut pour la ville en mouvement' organised an exhibition on 'Architecture on the Move – Cities and Mobilities', which presented international examples for the reintegration of traffic infrastructure in the urban fabric. Japanese building law was liberalized in the 1990s to make way for establishing a closer relationship between city highways and activating spatial potentials. The 'Foundation for Road Enhancement' is now developing this instrument in the light of international experience.

In Germany, too, first efforts are being undertaken to adapt traffic and urban planning procedures to the new conditions of urban development. For example Dortmund and Leipzig are pursuing the urban integration of highways at the master plan level. The ‚City of Speed' conference (Huber/Koch/Sander 2005) was a first attempt to open the design discussion to traffic planners and developers. Straßen.NRW, the state-owned road construction and maintenance company, played an important part in the interdisciplinary debate on how different disciplines – urban and traffic planning – understand the urban integration of traffic corridors. The perspective of the debate was broadened by an international exchange of experience with Austrian and Swiss experts.

The conference showed how new solutions for the urban integration of highways depend mainly on the planning cultures of the cities involved and individuals in charge. The scope available can be utilized only if planning is coordinated and pursued with strong professional and political commitment at a very early stage in the process. As the institutional framework of urban and traffic planning is not compatible in terms of terminology, scheduling and financing structures, co-ordination is rarely successful. Furthermore, what the urban integration of transport infrastructure actually means, what its consequences are, and how planning processes are affected are subjects of controversy.

6. The Corridor City

We started our research on urban development and urban design along traffic corridors with the autumn academy ‚City Scape B1‘ in 2001 (Koch/Sander/Wachten 2002). It was an experiment in search of answers to the provocative question Prof. Kunibert Wachten posed: "Can the B1 become something like the Champs Elysées of the Ruhr District?". The autumn academy came up with various urban design visions, which, although they offered little in common with the traditional appearance of the Champs Elysées, still answered the question in the affirmative (Figure 14).

The Corridor City is a field for different urban design strategies, depending on the location, the cityscape and the intended urban character of a development. A typology of urban design opportunities consists of four basic elements: hide, show, over/under and connect. The first three can be seen as 'classical' approaches: the noise barrier, the billboard, and the large-scale structure. Most interesting is the fourth element. The connection circumvents the idea of a corridor. It not only creates a facade, but a new form of street, directly linking the different speeds, the 5 km/h of pedestrians and the 160 km/h of the cars.

This allows a new form of Highway Boulevard to evolve that has nothing in common with the traditional appearance of highways or boulevards, thus combining the two concepts of speed and urban life.

Examples all around the world show the opportunities that a corridor city offers. Jean Nouvel's 'red kilometer', a noise barrier painted in flaming red separating a freeway and the car supplier Brembo's site in Stezzano, Italy, makes a symbol of an infrastructure element we are used to regarding in purely functional, never aesthetic terms. This gleaming line of fiery red aluminium becomes a landmark behind which all buildings, a business park and a hotel are part of the landscape (Figure 15). The parking facility between the wall and the freeway, also in red, symbolizes the activities behind the wall.

Figure 14. Autumn academy 'City Scape B1'.

Source: Julia Biallas

The Apollo Varieté in Düsseldorf by Niklaus Fritschi, Benedikt Stahl and Günter Baum, situated under the Rheinknie Bridge, exemplarily demonstrates that dark and dirty non-places under bridges can become cultural icons and tourist attractions in a city. The theatre is an urban stepping stone for the riverfront developments along the city center and the new media harbor (Figure 16). The two were separated by the bridge. The Apollo Varieté not only attracts visitors to performances, its café makes the place a destination in itself. The hidden qualities of the place lie in the particular scenery, revealed after performances, when a panorama window reveals the view of the old town center and riverfront.

Figure 15. The red kilometer by Jean Nouvel.

Source: Ateliers Jean Nouvel, Artfactory

The Mercedes Benz car dealership Prodon in Nieuwegein, Netherlands makes use of a typical urban wasteland along highways. It is situated between the elevated highway, a prison and an office building – not an ideal place to sell premium automobiles. A twelve architects unlocked this situation by creating a visual connection to the highway via an 'Auto-lift system', similar to the Smart towers. This high rack storage not only reduces the footprint of the building, it also functions as an oversized shop window (Figure 17). It generates enough attraction to make the car dealership profitable at this location, and it avoids typical bill boards.

A key issue in the corridor city is the relationship between transport corridors and city space, more precisely the connection of highways to the surrounding city. While the city needs as many exits as possible, traditional highway design aims at as few exits as possible to ensure optimal traffic flow and safety. This contradiction can rarely be resolved. On the A40, the central freeway in the Ruhr District, there is some degree of close connection between city and highway. Originally, the A40 was not planned as a freeway. It was upgraded step-by-step from the B1 national road, leaving some anomalies in the current layout. Some exits are only 100 meters apart and in Dortmund there are still connections from the freeway into residential streets with a speed limit of 30 km/h. These anomalies work because the highway has a speed limit of 70 km/h. Traffic flow becomes more important than high velocity. Situations like these are an important element in a new concept of 'urban highways'.

Urbanity is somewhere out there. There are new urban spaces along traffic infrastructures that are used in unexpected ways. However, they are not yet appropriately designed as a spatial and social unity. Innovative planning procedures and design schemes

Figure 16. Apollo Varieté under the Rheinknie-Bridge.

Source: Atelier Fritschi/Stahl/Baum, Düsseldorf

Figure 17. Window shopping by A12 architecten.

Source: orange.edge

need to be developed in order to consolidate these spaces into a new form of a network and corridor city. Considering the existing legal and administrative framework, the real work on procedures, content and instruments will have to be individual handwork, specially adapted to the specific situation. But this can only be successful if we accept reality, work together across disciplinary borders and rethink the role of traffic infrastructure in shaping urban form.

References

APPLEYARD, D., LYNCH, K., MYER, J. R. (1966), *The View from the Road*, Cambridge/Mass., MIT Press

ARCHPLUS, Zeitschrift für Architektur und Städtebau (1997), "'Walking Cities' Archigramm", *Archplus*, No. 139/140

BAART, T, MARKERINK, C., MERZ, T. (1996), *Snelweg. Highways in the Netherlands*, Den Haag, Lakerveld

BBC, books division (1994), *From A to B – tales of modern motoring*, Manchester

BREMER, S. (2001), "Jenseits von Benzin", in: Koch, M., Sander, H., Wachten, K. (eds.), *Stadtraum B1 – Visionen für eine Metropole*, Wuppertal, Bergische Universität Wuppertal

BRUINSMA, F. (1996), "Infrastructure and urban development: the case of the Amsterdam orbital motorway", in: Batten, D. (ed.), *Infrastructure and the complexity of economic development*, Berlin, Springer

CORTAZAR, J., DUNLOP, C. (1996), *Die Autonauten auf der Kosmobahn*, Frankfurt/M, Suhrkamp

ENDELL, A., DAVID, H. (eds.) (1995), *Vom Sehen, über Architektur, Formkunst und 'Die Schönheit der großen Stadt'*, Basel, Birkhäuser

FAURE, N. (1999), *Autoland*, Zürich, Scalo

FRANK LLOYD WRIGHT GAS STATION PAGE (2005), www.geocities.com/soho/1469/flwgas.html, accessed January 1, 2006

GARREAU, J. (1992), *Edge City. Life on a new frontier*, New York, Anchor Books

HESLER, J. (2006) "Filmkritik: Kein Kuss für Mutter", in: www.filmtext.com/start.jsp?mode=2&lett=T&archiv=484, accessed January 19, 2006

HOUBEN, F., CALABRESE, L. M. (eds.) (2003), *Mobility: a room with a view*, Rotterdam, NAI Publishers

HUBER, F., KOCH, M., SANDER, H. (eds.) (2005), *Stadt der Geschwindigkeit – Wege zur städtebaulichen Integration von Verkehrskorridoren*, Wuppertal, Bergische Universität Wuppertal

HUBER, U. (2000), *Autobahn*, Düsseldorf, Richter

KOCH, M., SANDER, H., WACHTEN, K. (2002), *Stadtraum B1 – Visionen für eine Metropole*, Wuppertal, Bergische Universität Wuppertal

MINISTRY OF SOUND RECORDINGS (2002), *CD-Cover 'Neue Heimat* 2', Berlin

NEUER BERLINER KUNSTVEREIN (ed.) (1982), *Stadt und Utopie. Modelle idealer Gemeinschaften*, Berlin

POLIDORI, R. (2005), *Robert Polidori's Metropolis*. Göttingen, Steidl

PRICE, C. (1998), "Freude am Unbekannten", in: Prigge, W. (ed.), *Peripherie ist überall*, Frankfurt/M, Campus

RENNER VERLAG (ed.) (2005), Entdeckungsreise Autobahn, Band 1, Horben, Renner Verlag

ROTERS, E. (ed.) (1987), *Ich und die Stadt*, Berlin, Nicolaische Verlagsbuchhandlung

SBB (Swiss Federal Railway) (2005), *Nighttrain-Leaflet*, Zurich

SCHÜLE, K. (1997), *Paris – Vordergründe / Hintergründe / Abgründe*, München, Aries

SCHULTEN, M. (2005), "Standort Autobahn", in: Huber, F., Koch, M., Sander, H. (eds.), *Stadt der Geschwindigkeit – Wege zur städtebaulichen Integration von Verkehrskorridoren*, Wuppertal, Bergische Universität Wuppertal

SMITHSON, A. (2001), *AS in DS*, Baden, Lars Müller Publisher

WILLAMOWSKI, G. (ed.) (2002), *Ruhrstadt – die andere Metropole*, Essen, Klartext

4 HD MUD
HIGH-DENISTY MIXED-USE DEVELOPMENT

by Kees Christiaanse

Introduction

Station areas, airports and other urban hubs are increasingly evolving into urban concentrations known as high-density Mixed-Use Developments (MUDs). High concentrations of people from a diversity of backgrounds converge here, not only to travel, but also in search of social contact, for entertainment, shopping or work. These former agents of largeness of scale and division of functions are evolving an urbanism that has a stimulating effect on the development of specific forms of urban activity.

In a world of increasing mobility, major junctions of public transportation demonstrate a potential for becoming 'urban hubs' for their surrounding environment. In the Netherlands, for instance, the architectural complex of Schiphol Airport evolved until, at a certain point, it changed as it were spontaneously into 'a city'. Nowadays, Schiphol Airport enjoys everything that goes to make a city except housing: hotels, an intercity station, every conceivable kind of shop, entertainment, an annex of the Rijksmuseum with paintings by Jan Steen, even stables and a mortuary. Schiphol Airport handles 40 million passengers a year and directly or indirectly employs enough people to populate a city. Anyone who doubts the existence of urbanity at Schiphol Airport should simply go and have a beer in one of the 'brown cafés' on the plaza, where people from all backgrounds sit drinking into the small hours. These cafés, replicas of 'Old Amsterdam', infiltrated the airport like an architectural Trojan Horse. Since their arrival, Schiphol has been transformed from a homogeneous 'total design' environment into a labyrinth of heterogeneous stage sets. In contrast to American urban entertainment centres, Schiphol even has homeless people, since the covered plaza is officially a public space that is accessible to everyone.

Figure 1. Map by architect Maarten Kloos presenting Amsterdam Airport Schiphol as the capital of the surrounding agglomeration.

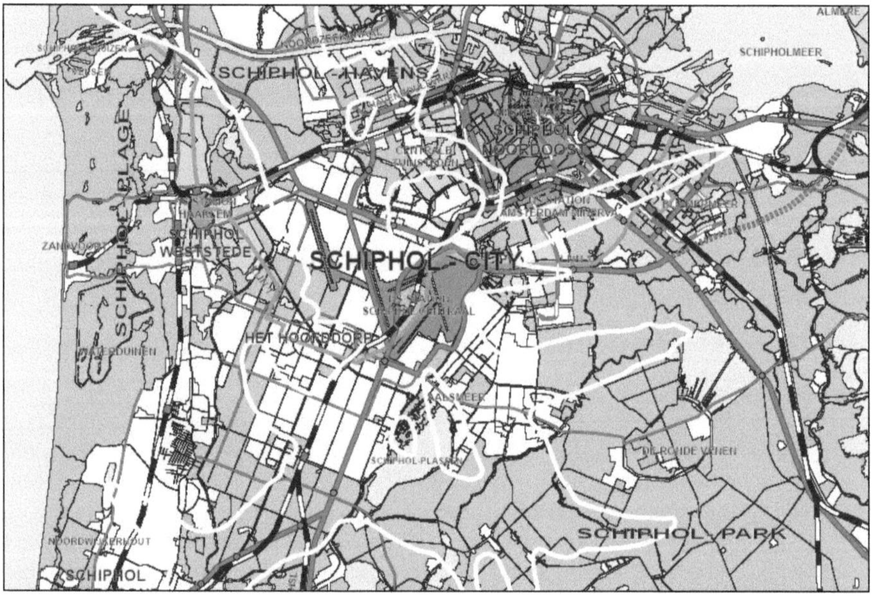

Source: Maarten Kloos

Due to the 24-hour flow of people at the airport and the steady expansion in size and programme, the laws of the architecture have turned into those of urban design. And the process may well continue. In a map by architect Maarten Kloos (figure 1), Schiphol even is presented as the capital of the surrounding agglomeration. On this map, the City of Amsterdam has been renamed Schiphol Noordoost (Schiphol North-East), Haarlem has become Schiphol-West and the seaside resort of Zandvoort is called Schiphol-Plage.

Although this is certainly taking it to the extreme, Schiphol Airport did prove to posses all the important features of a high-density MUD: a location next to a high-quality public transport hub and the proximity of a city centre or high-quality cluster with sufficient density to bring about an intensive mix of activities. In the case of Schiphol, which was originally just a small village in the polder, the high quality cluster was added on to the public transport hub by upgrading the airport building and inviting high-end boutiques to set up shop. Once the public caught on to the possibility of shopping at Schiphol, other than just tax-free on the way to the gate, the development acquired a momentum of its own.

1. Integrating Urban Hubs

High potential locations for high-density MUDs are also found where the 24-hour rhythm of high-density flows of people is combined with the proximity of a historical city centre. Zurich's station area, for instance, is the ultimate combination of public transport hub, shopping mall and urban entertainment centre. It also symbolizes a meeting place in the traditional sense of urbanity in terms of its interpenetration with the city (Figure 2).

Anyone entering Zurich's new station area designed by KCAP would be hard put to distinguish it from the surrounding city districts. It is only on penetrating deeply into the new area that anyone would be aware of being in a 'different' city, one that owes its naturalness to the continuation of the urban fabric. The structure of streets and squares is dominated by a diagonal pattern. It envelops a number of construction fields that range typologically from the perimeter block, with its secretive inner world, to more solitary, sculptural volumes. To avoid the risk of an isolated ensemble, such an urban district must not be subjected to any uniformity in architecture or programming. The quarter has therefore been designed 'without a programme' in order to allow the increasing dynamism of urban life to find its own way (Figure 3). However, minimum quotas have been established for vulnerable and sustainable functions, such as housing. Also, the street level and mezzanine are required to fulfil a highly public function.

Figure 2. The intersection of a new ‚diagonal' and the surrounding street layout creates differentiated building blocks.

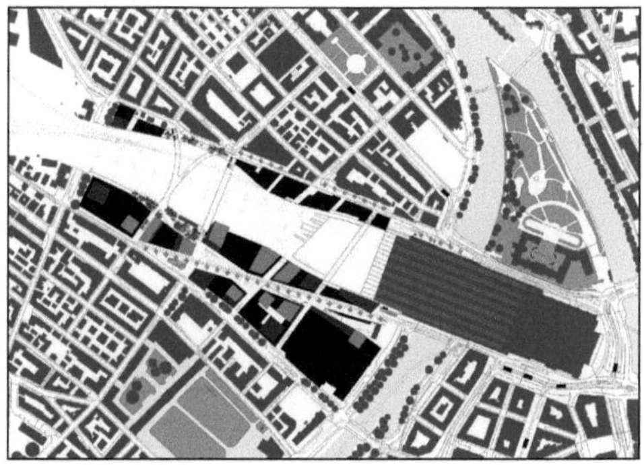

Source: KCAP

Figure 3. Zurich central station Nowadays, public space is one of many physical and virtual communication networks.

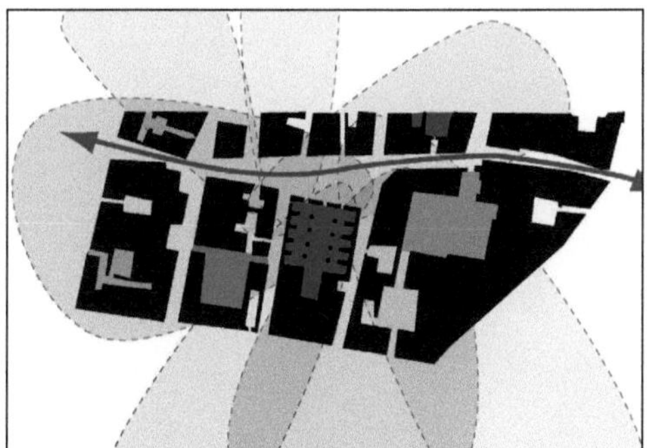

Source: Thomas Hildebrand

Big construction runs and mono-functional programmes notwithstanding, a fine-grained atmosphere becomes possible. As in Barcelona's Ensanche, building codes set a maximum construction height of about 22 metres. Taller buildings are permitted, providing they have a 'setback'. As in New York, the setback guarantees a stable 'streetscape', regardless of the number and position of the high-rise structures. This will, hopefully, lead to a 'gentrified' hybrid, something between the Paseo de Gracia and Greenwich Village.

The densification of station areas is not really altogether new. Development projects for large-scale shopping malls and office complexes close to big stations have been realised since the 1960s, like, for example, Hoog Catharijne in Utrecht and Euralille in Lille. Many of these projects consisted of covered shopping malls and self-contained office projects. In other cities, however, the development of the station area is held back by conventional city planning dogmas, which insist on forcibly reducing road traffic in order to stimulate use of public transport and on barring large-scale shops and distribution from the city centre in order to protect retailers. These dogmas certainly are no longer valid. We now know that, given a deliberately open structure that connects with the surroundings and a variegated mix of functions, station areas can reinvigorate the urbanity in city centre areas.

Figure 4. Groningen Station Area. Range of typologies within construction rules.

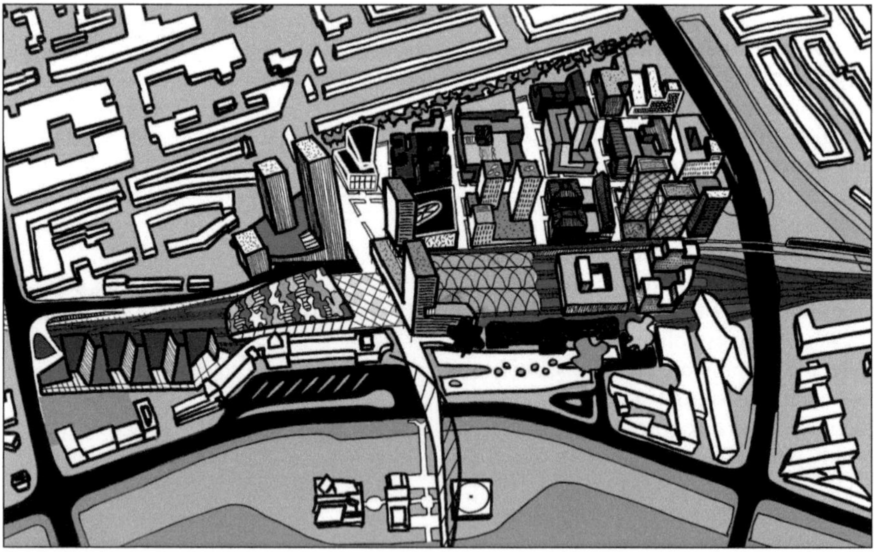

Source: KCAP

Figure 5. Amstel 3, Overview of the entrance area with the buildings and underneath parking.

Source: KCAP

Figure 6. Collage of the masterplan projected onto the aerial view of Oslo Bjorvika/ Bispevik.

Source: KCAP

The construction of highly accessible parking facilities close to Intercity stations demonstrably stimulates use of the train, just as the introduction of large-scale shopping centres close to the station stimulates the economy in the adjacent city-centre. For instance, the centre of Lille has experienced a tremendous revitalization thanks to the construction of the Euralille project with its TGV station, shopping mall, amenities and parking facilities.

2. Bridging the Barrier

In many cities, the density of a new development is decided by traffic volume or parking capacity. An absurd situation, for how can traffic possibly be considered the primary factor in a high-quality city? In a station area, where the permitted number of parking spots is negligible, density should not be a topic of discussion. As a 'social condensor', the station area can cope with any density. Physically, however, the development of urban hubs may well be hampered by the fact that in many major cities, the station area forms a formidable barrier dividing the centre into a prosperous central area and a poorer area 'behind the station'. A major construction effort is required to overcome the barrier of such a large-scale station precinct in the middle of the city. Except in centrally governed cities like Paris, where the city government could simply decide to cover over the railway at the Gare d'Austerlitz with an enormous concrete slab, such massive initial investment is politically and economically almost inconceivable. That is why such designs can only be realised by means of a 'growing' structure, allowing investments to keep pace with actual construction.

For the station precinct in Groningen (Figure 4), which forms a barrier between the medieval centre and Groningen-Zuid, KCAP designed a street layout that dovetails with the morphology of the surroundings. The resulting blocks will be filled with mixed development, ranging from townhouses with workspace to a hotel and conference centre, offices and cultural facilities. Thanks to an ingenious design, the street layout gradually ascends from south to north, reaching a height at which construction could, in the future, be extended above the railway, thus integrating the area with the city even more closely. Beneath this deck structure, distribution and transfer functions and major retail stores can be accommodated in close vicinity to a regional bus station and a Park&Ride transfer point that is directly accessible from the motorway. KCAP's 'growing roof' concept, as proposed for the Groningen Station Area, was first successfully implemented in the Amstel III project in Amsterdam (Figure 5). Here, an elevated road system on columns was constructed between nine blocks of 51 square metres each. The roads were set at a distance of two metres from the buildings, with little bridges connecting the buildings to the road.

The advantage of this structure is that it does not require any massive preliminary investment. The road system grows step by step according to the realization of the buildings. The buildings are not structurally dependent on each other or on the deck, which means that they can be realized to wholly autonomous specifications without any real coordination problems.

A similar construction was proposed for Björvika in Oslo (Figure 6). Here, a gigantic railway yard and the end of a motorway form a peripheral jungle right next to the station and the city centre. In order to overcome this barrier, the Amstel III principle was applied, domesticating the surrounding area to make it part of the city centre. The costs of building new structures above the existing infrastructure are partially covered by the realisation of a maximum built volume in the form of high-rise towers above the railway. As in Groningen, there are plans for a Park&Ride transfer point, big retail stores and mass entertainment beneath the superstructure next to the railway, functions which until recently were confined to the periphery.

3. Highest Density Development

All the conditions, factors and elements described so far are combined in an intensified form in the project for the Bishopsgate Goods Yard near Liverpool Street Station in London. Here, there are enormous pressures on development because of the proximity of the City of London's financial district. Commercial rents are the highest in Europe, and the Floor Area Ratio (FAR) in the office district around Liverpool Street is about 5, a density that is twice as high as the average in other densely built European cities. The problematic accessibility means that the car is no longer considered as the major determinant of scale in this area. The dimensions of pedestrian routes have become the norm because of the massive streams of pedestrians during rush hour.

Figure 7. Model of the ideal situation of the London Bishopsgate location.

Source: KCAP

In Bishopsgate there is a meeting of highly diverse lifestyles and cultures: the financial district, the burgeoning East End cultural scene and a diversity of communities, including the biggest Bangladeshi immigrant population in Europe. Part of the site is occupied by the vaulted brick viaducts of the former goods railway, which have been granted listed status and, in calling to mind the ruins of Ancient Rome, provide an 'atmospheric' basis for future development. This diversity of interests holds the promise of an exemplary 'high-density Mixed-Use Development'. High-performance offices, shopping, entertainment, cultural facilities, exclusive residential properties, social-sector housing, high-quality public spaces, an underground station and semi-permanent functions between the arches plus a new railway line are to be developed to an average Floor Space Index (FSI) of 5.

For the development of Bishopsgate (Figure 7), KCAP will have to mobilize the entire toolbox amassed in its previous experiences with complex developments. We expect to benefit considerably from our experience in the development of 'waiting lands' (former harbour and industrial areas), where we applied our so-called 'simultaneous chess' strategy to interact with a variety of actors and stakeholders. Also, with luck, pioneering forms of urbanity will evolve here, thriving on our experience in the development of waterfronts with their fertile symbiosis of high culture/low budget and high budget/low culture functions.

An example of such a successful waterfront development is the 'Pakhuizen' project on the Oostelijke Handelskade in Amsterdam. New buildings envelop old warehouses, creating a sequence of discrete spaces. While their form and texture refers to industrial architecture, their functions vary from social housing and living-working units for artists to luxury penthouses and offices. Investors and large companies have understood that these spatial, programmatic and historical mixed-use developments can produce a sustainable urbanity, a more inspiring working-environment and a good profit due to the increased value of the real estate.

4. Recreating Public Space

It is heartening to see that airports and station areas, once the motors of a large-scale division of functions, have now become the protagonists of an increasingly radical mix of functions that is redefining the concepts of public-ness and urbanity. Whereas public space used to be the interface for all forms of communication, it is now just one of many contexts in which human interaction takes place. In the words of A. Reijndorp "Real public space occurs when certain groups predominate without excluding others".

In 'Von Mob zur Mall', Werner Sewing argues that in Europe, unlike the USA, it is not so much the privatisation of public space and the exclusion of social fringe groups in urban entertainment centres that is the problem, but an increasing overabundance of public-ness for the masses, which results in the retreat of the elite. According to Sewing, it is this absence of the elite that poses a threat to urbanity, along with the homogenisation that goes hand in hand with the mass consumer behaviour fostered by big brands.

The big brands, influenced in turn by this homogenisation and saturation, are forced to evolve beyond mere shopping to encompass urban lifestyle and entertainment and hence, to present themselves as designers of the city. The question is whether these 'drivers' of urban activity can also establish structures that have an enduring impact on the city. The answer should be affirmative, if Alex Wall is right in claiming that 'Commerce is the engine of urbanity'.

CHAPTER IV

THE FUTURE OF THE URBAN CORE

THE FUTURE OF THE URBAN CORE: INTRODUCTION

by Dietrich Henckel, Benjamin Herkommer and Elke Pahl-Weber

The second section of this volume dealt with the changing structure of urban space, its expansion and regionalisation. The final section goes on to consider the future role of the traditional city, especially the urban core. As Edward Glaeser (1996) and Paul Krugman (1999) assure us, "economists still like cities". The death of the city has often been announced, always prematurely (Hall 2003), and now the debate on the renaissance of the city is gathering momentum. There is meanwhile sufficient, indeed abundant evidence that the urban core will (again) be playing an important role, that its importance is even likely to increase. This section examines some of the factors that stabilise or strengthen the traditional urban core.

- Taking the art community as an example of a population group with high personal potential for choosing where to live and work, Ann Markusen discusses the importance of the inner city for certain sections of the population if the urban core is attractive (or made attractive) for them. These groups have high prestige and enhance the image value of a city. From an economic point of view they offer high-quality services in the so-called cultural industries. A number of empirical studies on Germany show that this type of high-quality service activity has been increasing more strongly in inner cities than in other spatial units (Geppert/Gornig 2003, 2005).
- Another population group that could, and (as Taner Oc shows) is indeed likely to bolster the traditional city is the elderly, who constitute an ever growing proportion of the population in many developed countries. An ageing population exacerbates the problem of providing for the old. Decentralised support for old people in need of care is unlikely to be affordable in the long run. Services for the old are much easier to organise in urban contexts. The recentralisation of older people is therefore to be expected. This will perhaps not occur in the short run, but there is some evidence that many people now aged between 30 and 55 are becoming more cautious about mov-

ing to outlying areas in view of the risky services situation and considering a return to the city as a longer term precautionary measure.

- Although recreation requiring large-scale leisure amenities has to some extent relocated outside the city, integrated recreational concepts in mixed use projects can help strengthen the centres of metropolitan areas, as David Camp shows. However, this presupposes very careful and economically well-founded planning.

For a considerable period, core cities were judged to be the clear losers in urban structural change. But the articles in this section demonstrate that the traditional urban core is still alive and kicking and displays considerable potential for development. In the course of structural change there are a number of economic functions that still need the inner city or benefit from it (Markusen: art and culture; Camp: the role of recreational services), and the urban core offers advantages in meeting the needs of certain sections of the population like artists (Markusen) and the old (Oc). Recent empirical studies from Germany indicate that inner cities are experiencing a renaissance as a place to live (Brühl 2006) among a wide spectrum of the population. There is as yet little quantitative data on these core-oriented groups, for instance on their economic significance and the role of support and subsidies. The extent to which urban core-oriented groups and activities can enliven and sustain the inner city without support needs to be examined, as well as the extent to which inner-city vitality develops into a public good and image factor in inter-city competition that need to be supplied or at least stabilised through public sector intervention.

References

BRÜHL, H. (2006), "Neues Wohnen in der Innenstadt – wohin treibt die Stadtgesellschaft?", in: Spars, G. (ed.), *Wohnungsmarktentwicklung Deutschland: Trends, Segmente, Instrumente*, ISR-Diskussionsbeitrag 58, Berlin

GEPPERT, K., GORNIG, M. (2003), "Die Renaissance der großen Städte – und die Chancen Berlins", *DIW-Wochenbericht*, No. 26/2003, p. 411-417

GEPPERT, K., GORNIG, M. (2005), "Berlin: Potentiale einer neuen wirtschaftlichen Dynamik", *DIW-Wochenbericht*, No. 44/2005, p. 657-663

GLAESER, E. (1996), "Why Economists still like cities", *City-Journal*, Vol.6, No. 2, p. 70-89

HALL, P. (2003), "The end of the city? The report of my death was an exaggeration", *City*, Vol. 7, No. 2, p. 141-152

KRUGMAN, P. (1999), "Looking Backward", in: Krugman, P. (ed.), *The Accidental Theorist and Other Dispatches from a Dismal Science*, New York, London, Norton&Company, p. 196-204

VELTZ, P. (2004), *The Rationale for a Resurgence in the Major Cities of Advanced Economies*, Paper at the Leverhulme International Symposium 2004: The Resurgent City, London School of Economics, April 19-21, 2004

THE URBAN CORE AS A CULTURAL STICKY PLACE

by Ann Markusen

Introduction

Most analyses of the urban core stress the role of firms and entire industries in abandoning central locations for dispersed ones. Only those with strong ties to government or for whom face-to-face specialized interchanges matter remain tied to the core. This line of reasoning ignores the fact that workers are also urban actors and may make residential location decisions independent of firms. In this paper, I argue that one source of contemporary urban core stability and vitality is the commitments of certain groups of workers to work and live there. I explore this theme by looking at artists as a case study.

Most geographers and economists assume that it is firm location decisions that matter and that workers move to fill the jobs created by firms. I argue that many groups of workers are able to choose their locations independently of firms, who then must take differential labor quality and accessibility into account in making their location decisions. Workers' preferences can be inferred by studying them as members of occupational groups, just as we study firm behavior by grouping them as members of industries. In the first part of the paper, I present this occupational approach and introduce artists as a case study.

Artists exhibit very high levels of self-employment, giving them latitude to locate semi-independently of firms. In the US, artists gravitate strongly to larger metropolitan areas, and within them, to urban cores. Although some of this concentration can be explained by the presence of cultural industries, much of it cannot. Apart from the largest cities, artists congregate in some mid-sized urban cores and not others, drawn by a series of networking opportunities and amenities, including vacant historic and industrial buildings that offer ample artistic workspace in settings with cache. While gentrification processes may be a problematic counterpart of artistic enclaves, often this process is overstated, while the role of artists in stabilizing communities, diminishing crime rates and enlivening political discourse is understated.

1. The Urban Core as Sticky Place

Rapid transnational economic integration has undermined the traditional economic base of many cities. In the past twenty years, especially given devolution and the abandonment of central government regional policy in many countries, cities all over the globe have had to take on greater responsibility for strategizing and implementing economic development activities to provide jobs and incomes for their residents. Fashioning economic development policy is a difficult new project for cities emerging from centuries of growth, often rapid. Most traditional urban planning activities involve accommodating growth by building infrastructure, regulating land use and providing housing, and the tools cities had at their disposal were relatively powerful.

Economic development, especially in a deregulatory environment, is a much more daunting task. Not only are certain industries imploding and their redundant land, buildings and workers an adjustment problem, but economic developers have much weaker tools at their disposal. They have few regulatory powers and must rely on marketing and often costly incentives as ways of home-growing, attracting and retaining private sector establishments. They must also compete with cities within their nation and abroad that offer similar incentives and perhaps lower business costs or better access to markets. At the same time, the fringes of metropolitan areas are successfully competing for economic functions that previously took place in the core.

Recent strategies for cities experiencing structural change in their economies rely heavily on industrial targeting. Targeting requires that a city or region understand its competitive advantages and use incentives to play to these strengths, chiefly by targeting employers in these industries and related clusters. Targeting is quite controversial (Buss 1999; Finkle 1999; Wiewel 1999), but it is heavily used and is central to the recent spate of cluster strategies. Often, the distinction between what is good for the region and what works for the core is not clearly made – high tech activity, for instance, is remarkably suburban in its spatial orientation and may not contribute much at all to the core of a city promoting it.

In what follows, I explore the potential for core cities to use targeting as a means of reshaping its employment structure. I begin by asking what advantages the urban core still possesses as a center for economic activity – what makes it a sticky place in slippery space (Markusen 1996)? What activities seem to cleave to the urban core despite the accelerated obliteration of the friction of distance? I argue that especially for the urban core, industrial targeting is inadequate, because it is so expensive and because it focuses on firms as decision-makers, many of which are caught up in the dispersal process. Cities should also engage in occupational targeting, recognizing that many skilled workers have some discretion about where they will live and work and that some show strong preferences for the urban core. I then use a case study of artists in the US to show how this particular occupational group is strongly drawn to the urban core and why, and show how cities can use their influence over space to enhance the prospects for artistic enclaves in their urban core.

2. Core City Economic Potential

In an increasingly integrated world market, each locality must work harder to find and fashion its own niches – the activities in which it has a comparative advantage. It is in these sectors and occupations that civic and public sector leaders can anticipate a substantial economic development dividend if they invest their resources well. To do this in the longer run, such activities have to be 'sticky' – they have to be deeply anchored in particular places so that longer run returns are assured (Markusen 1996). Core cities – the inner areas of larger metropolitan areas that have lost many of their traditional industrial sectors to competition from suburbs, smaller cities or regions elsewhere in the world – face this need in a particularly pressing way. What economic activities can bring work and prosperity to the urban core?

I focus on seeing regional economies not just as assemblages of firms in particular industries (finance, business services, manufacturing…), but also as agglomerations of human capital and skill, captured in occupational profiles (Thompson/Thompson 1985; Markusen 2004; Markusen/Schrock 2005). I have used this framework to explore the existing distribution of occupational specializations across metropolitan areas in the US. I find that certain occupations are most apt to root in larger metropolitan areas, and within them, in the urban core, where they comprise a disproportional share of the area workforce. The occupations of computer expert, mathematician, lawyer, business and financial operations specialist, artist/designer/entertainer, media worker, architect, engineer, and life/physical/social scientist are over-represented in the US in metropolitan areas with labor forces of 1 million or more (Table 1). This table shows that smaller cities excel only in manufacturing operations – in the US, manufacturing work has become highly de-urbanized.

In similar industry-based studies, scholars find that government, education, finance, advertising, architecture/design, media, hospitals and cultural industries are highly urban core-centric.

How can urban core advocates and policymakers work from these general insights to a more precise understanding of their comparative advantages and how to nourish them?

Table 1. Occupational Specialization by Metro Size Class in the United States, 2000.

Occupational Group	Metro Size Class					
	All MSAs	4m+	1-4m	500k-1m	250-500k	<250k
Computer and Mathematical	1.17	1.05	**1.56**	1.06	0.84	0.75
Legal	1.15	**1.47**	**1.26**	1.06	1.02	0.84
Business and Financial Operations	1.12	**1.26**	**1.23**	1.10	0.98	0.85
Arts, Design, Entertainment, Sports and Media	1.09	**1.87**	1.05	0.97	0.95	0.83
Architecture and Engineering	1.09	0.79	**1.36**	0.96	0.98	0.96
Life, Physical, and Social Science	1.05	0.96	**1.26**	0.95	0.89	0.92
Office and Administrative Support	1.04	1.14	1.04	1.06	1.01	0.95
Management	1.04	1.09	1.11	0.97	0.97	0.95
Protective Service	1.02	**1.30**	0.97	1.06	0.93	0.91
Healthcare Practitioners and Technical	1.01	0.98	0.95	0.99	1.11	1.10
Sales and Related	1.00	0.92	1.01	1.03	1.01	1.02
Personal Care and Service	1.00	1.13	0.99	0.98	0.97	1.00
Building and Grounds Cleaning, Maintenance	0.99	0.98	0.99	0.97	1.03	0.98
Community and Social Services	0.98	**1.20**	0.87	0.94	1.05	1.06
Construction and Extraction	0.97	0.74	1.01	0.98	1.01	1.05
Food Preparation and Serving Related	0.96	0.75	0.94	1.00	1.03	1.11
Installation, Maintenance, and Repair	0.96	0.79	0.95	1.00	1.01	1.04
Education, Training, and Library	0.96	1.01	0.92	0.90	0.96	1.11
Healthcare Support	0.96	1.00	0.86	0.95	1.04	1.12
Transportation and Material Moving	0.95	0.95	0.90	1.01	0.97	0.96
Production	0.91	0.95	0.81	0.94	0.97	1.01
Farming, Fishing, and Forestry	0.68	0.17	0.31	0.32	**1.55**	**2.02**

Source: Own calculation, based of data from Bureau of Labor Statistics, Occupational Employment Statistics. Spezializations shown as location quotients. Those in excess of 1.20 in bold.

First, developing a view of within-metropolitan distribution of activity and dynamics is important. Studies in the US have found that some large metro-oriented jobs and industries, especially high technology, are chiefly suburban-oriented. They are largely new sectors and occupations in which employers prefer suburban campuses and employees prefer to live there as well. But others are quite core-centric, among them law, finance, media, marketing and cultural activities.

Second, an efficient and effective strategy can only be built on a substantive understanding of particular sectors and occupations. Why do firms and workers prefer to operate and live in the core versus other places? What costs and amenities and networking possibilities anchor them there? What are the challenges from other locations – either other core cities or other types of locales? What public sector interventions might help make them more sticky and provide something they cannot do for themselves?

I use the case of artists, a group with extraordinary location discretion, to probe to what extent they are core-oriented and sticky in their spatial orientation and why.

3. Artists as Case Study

The case of artists offers an exceptional opportunity to look at an occupational group that heavily favors core cities, semi-independently of job offers from core industries. Artists are much more apt to be self-employed than most other occupations in the economy – in the US, 45 % of artists are self-employed versus 8 % of the workforce as a whole (Table 2). Because they are self-employed, they are freer to choose a location to live and work that is detached from employers' location.

Why might artists favor core areas of large metropolitan regions (Markusen/Schrock 2006)? First, sheer size may matter. Residents who love big core cities may display a higher penchant for arts consumption, and producers may enjoy increasing returns to scale, especially in art forms such as the opera. Second, the demand for artistic activity from residents may be higher in the traditional elite cities like New York, Philadelphia, Boston, Chicago, San Francisco and Los Angeles where people with high, unearned (i.e. capital) income cluster and patronize the arts through philanthropy, attendance and collecting. Third, certain large city centric industries, such as advertising and media, may form a significant source of demand and income for artists. Fourth, artists and art spaces attract tourists, generating urban income flows that feed back into artists' livelihoods (Judd 1999). Fifth, synergies among different types of artistic activity may create agglomerative tendencies that enhance the draw of large, traditional city centers (Blau 1989). Such synergies can be informal as well as organizational; artists are highly networked with other artists and with workers in other sectors (Becker 1982). Sixth, artists may be drawn to the amenities offered by a plethora of cultural institutions

Table 2. Self employment trends, artistic occupations, 2002.

Occupational Title	Total Employed	Self-employed	% Self-employed	Primary job	Secondary job
Visual artists	**307,254**	**155,159**	**50 %**	**129,109**	**26,050**
Artists and related workers	148,682	80,022	54 %	70,731	9,291
Arts directors	*50,664*	*27,139*	*54 %*	*23,988*	*3,151*
Fine artists (painters, sculptors,...)	*23,192*	*12,866*	*55 %*	*11,372*	*1,494*
Multi-media artists & animators	*74,826*	*40,017*	*53 %*	*35,371*	*4,646*
Photographers	130,442	68,432	52 %	54,024	14,408
Camera operators, TV/Video/Motion picture	28,130	6,705	24 %	4,354	2,351
Performing artists	**176,463**	**42,724**	**24 %**	**38,174**	**4,550**
Actors	63,033	10,992	17 %	9,754	1,238
Producers and directors	76,125	24,995	33 %	21,683	3,312
Dancers & choreographers	37,305	6,737	18 %	6,737	0
Dancers	*19,992*	*3,854*	*19 %*	*3,854*	*0*
Choreographers	*17,313*	*2,883*	*17 %*	*2,883*	*0*
Musicians, singers and related	**215,425**	**83,121**	**39 %**	**56,770**	**26,351**
Music directors & composers	54,271	21,354	39 %	14,584	6,770
Musicians & singers	161,154	61,767	38 %	42,186	19,581
Writers & authors	**138,980**	**94,377**	**68 %**	**80,509**	**13,868**
TOTAL, ARTS OCCUPATIONS	**838,122**	**375,381**	**45 %**	**304,562**	**70,819**

Source: BLS 2002

in, and the diversity and innovativeness of, the largest cities (Florida 2002; Clark 2004.) Finally, the impact of these factors may be magnified by the behavior of artists themselves, who are more likely to patronize other artistic endeavors than any other group.

Do artists favor larger cities, and within them, core areas? In general, yes. In the US, artists comprise a much larger share of the labor force in the three arts super-cities – Los Angeles, New York, San Francisco – than in the nation as a whole (Table 3). However, the presence of artists is not fully explained by metro size or growth rates – other very large metro areas such as Chicago and Philadelphia have artistic concentration ratios at or near average, while in some of the fastest growth metros – Dallas, Phoenix, Denver – they are below average. Some 'second-tier' metros (Washington DC, Seattle, Boston, Minneapolis/St. Paul, San Diego and Miami) have relatively high concentrations, while other older industrial cities and newer sunbelt metros do not. Artists gravitate residentially towards core cities within metro areas. In the Twin Cities metro area, artists are heavily concentrated in the two core cities – Minneapolis and St. Paul, and within each, they are concentrated in inner city precincts (Figure 1).

Figure 1. Artists in the Twin Cities Metropolitan Region Labor Force.

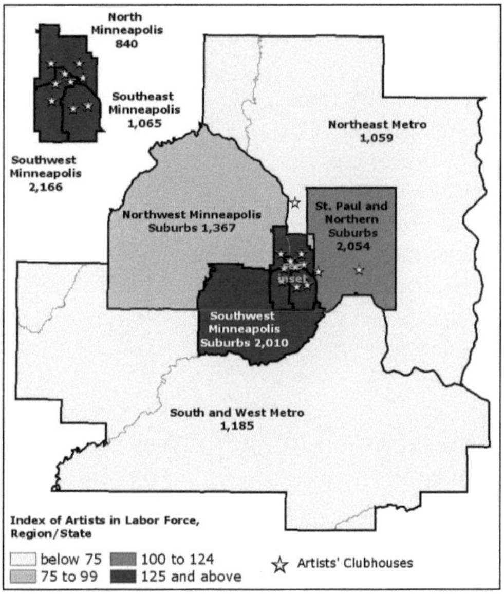

Source: Author's diagram

In extensive interviews with artists about why they chose to move to or stay in the region, we found that amenities (including the parks, alternative health care, a progressive political culture), strong regional foundation support for the arts, networking and marketing possibilities, the presence of artist-employing industries (e.g. publishing) and an unusual number of artists' centers and decentralized performing arts and artists studio and live-work spaces were most important (Markusen/King 2003; Markusen/Johnson 2006). There were several factors that countered this tendency. The higher cost of housing and workspace in cities and preferences for a slower pace of life and greater access to nature drove some artists to prefer smaller towns and rural locations. To some extent, the proliferation of digital technologies as ways of producing and distributing art work favored the latter.

4. Artist-centric Spaces for Cities

This characterization of artistic work and spatial preferences helps us think about what core city strategies might attract and hold this important occupational group. In our intensive examination of artists in the Twin Cities, involving more than 200 interviews, we have concluded that enhancing artistic space is a key way that urban core leaders can nurture a vibrant cultural economy (Markusen/Johnson 2006). Most cultural policymakers have little experience with urban planning and economic development strategies and tend to think organizationally, not in terms of space and place. It is difficult for them to see and appreciate the role of dedicated spaces for artists in urban economic revitalization.

Table 3. Artistic Concentrations for the Top 29 U.S. Metro Areas by Employment, 2000.

	Total	Performing Artists	Visual Artists	Authors	Musicians
Los Angeles, CA	2.99	5.44	2.34	2.71	1.95
New York, NY-NJ	2.52	3.71	2.01	2.99	1.85
San Francisco-Oakland, CA	1.82	1.85	1.83	2.51	1.12
ALL 29 METROS	**1.34**	**1.60**	**1.26**	**1.45**	**1.12**
Washington, DC-MD-VA-WV	1.36	1.51	1.01	2.27	1.08
Seattle, WA	1.33	1.15	1.48	1.48	1.06
Boston, MA-NH	1.27	1.24	1.02	2.00	1.15
Orange County, CA	1.18	1.21	1.36	0.92	0.98
Minneapolis-St. Paul, MN-WI	1.16	1.12	1.10	1.33	1.16
San Diego, CA	1.15	0.90	1.27	1.10	1.25
Miami, FL	1.15	1.48	1.05	0.82	1.28
Portland, OR-WA	1.09	1.12	0.99	1.50	0.87
Atlanta, GA	1.08	1.05	1.11	0.97	1.15
Baltimore, MD	1.08	0.96	1.10	0.92	1.30
Chicago, IL	1.04	0.83	1.14	1.27	0.84
Newark, NJ	1.02	1.07	0.97	1.24	0.83
US AVERAGE	1.00	1.00	1.00	1.00	1.00
Dallas, TX	0.99	1.08	1.11	0.73	0.87
Philadelphia, PA-NJ	0.96	0.90	1.04	0.94	0.88
Phoenix, AZ	0.96	0.70	1.13	0.88	0.94
Nassau-Suffolk, NY	0.93	0.83	1.10	0.84	0.76
Kansas City, MO-KS	0.90	0.59	1.16	0.82	0.76
Denver, CO	0.90	1.08	0.82	0.98	0.79
Tampa-St. Petersburg, FL	0.89	0.83	0.89	0.76	1.08
San Jose, CA	0.84	0.75	0.95	0.95	0.61
Cleveland, OH	0.79	0.61	0.79	0.74	1.05
Riverside-San Bernardino, CA	0.77	0.79	0.84	0.61	0.76
Pittsburgh, PA	0.76	0.63	0.74	0.79	0.91
Houston, TX	0.74	0.65	0.75	0.66	0.91
Detroit, MI	0.74	0.61	0.82	0.73	0.74
St. Louis, MO-IL	0.71	0.52	0.79	0.67	0.80

Sources: Minnesota Population Center 2002

Our prescriptions for artistic space enhancement are of two types. First, we advocate a decentralized, smaller scale mosaic of artistic space in contrast to the large, centralized arts district that has been favored by many cities in past eras (e.g. Lincoln Center in New York, the Civic Center in San Francisco). We believe that a multiplicity of galleries, museums, clubhouses, live/work and studio buildings and performing arts space brings healthy competition to the artistic economy in a city. It also embeds artistic space in neighborhoods, where artists and arts space managers interact with the larger community on issues of safety, community life and community development, often bringing artistic talent to revitalization campaigns and community-building efforts. In turn, communities hosting artistic space become advocates for artists and artistic programming. This vision of the cultural mosaic was first set out by Jane Jacobs (1961) in her depiction of New York as a series of ethnically differentiated live-and-work neighborhoods, each with its own distinctive culture – Little Italy, SoHo, Greenwich Village, Chinatown – where citizens felt invited to cross the porous borders between them and enjoy the amenities of the others.

Three types of artistic space are central to our vision of urban core artistic stickiness: artists' clubhouses or centers, artists' live/work and studio buildings, and performing arts centers. In what follows, I describe each of these and give a few examples.

4.1 Artists' Clubhouses

In some cities, non-profit or even for-profit entrepreneurs have created dedicated spaces that welcome artists at all levels of expertise and for nominal membership fees to participate in multiple types of activities, such as classes, access to equipment (photography labs, printing presses, kilns, rehearsal space), exhibitions and performances, mentoring, specialized libraries, websites and newsletters. Some were started by art who sought a way of continuing to share their work and get feedback beyond formal training; others by communities who believed that providing art ists studios and exhibition space in their neighborhoods would help counter crime and drugs, especially in their impact on youth. The Twin Cities hosts some eighteen of these clubhouses with $ 18 million in revenues and 8,500 members and which also serve the larger arts-loving community. They are mapped in Figure 1, spread out among a number of neighborhoods in a pattern reminiscent of the Jacobs vision.

An outstanding example of such a clubhouse is the Loft Literary Center, started in the 1970s by a group of politically active poets that survived six moves, several organizational overhauls and challenges to move to new literary forms, expand diversity and reach far out to the suburbs. Currently, the Loft occupies portions of 'The Open Book' (Figure 2), a series of three rehabbed industrial lofts that also houses the 'Minnesota Center for Book Arts' and a small non-profit press, Milkweed Editions. On the second floor, a large open space with moveable tables and chairs allows people to group themselves. Adjacent is an auditorium for readings and talks given throughout the year by master writers, spoken-word artists, award winners, and mentees. Along the back wall sit classrooms and a library of books by Minnesota authors and small presses, as well as regional and national literary magazines. To the west lies a series of writers' studios, each with a table and chair, an easy chair and an ample window with afternoon light. Writers may rent studios on a scheduled basis and keep their materials in a phalanx of lockers that line the corridor outside. More classrooms, a book-club room and a rooftop space are upstairs.

Figure 2. The Open Book, Minneapolis.

Source: Author's photograph

Today, the Loft has 2,700 members, mostly in the region, and a budget of $ 1.8 million. It offers classes on everything from beginning poetry and memoir to advanced novel-writing and business skills for writers. It runs prestigious competitions for fellowships and mentorships, some tailored to emerging writers and some for career writers to begin a new body of work. It raises about 55 % of its revenues from contributed funds, and 45 % from earned income – chiefly class fees. A survey of Loft participants found widespread agreement, among amateurs as well as accomplished writers, that the Loft's activities had substantially improved their writing skills and helped many to make careers of their writing (Markusen/Johnson 2006).

The Loft has also begun reaching out to its neighborhood and larger community. Although it originally chose the Open Book site because it was conveniently located near two freeways, it has come to understand that its original vision of itself as a destination site rather than a community-embedded center has hurt some of the other buildings' occupants, specifically the ground floor independent bookstore that was forced to close for lack of neighborhood traffic.

Central to the Loft's strategy, and that of the Minnesota Center for Book Arts, is to serve inner city schools as a place to visit and do hands-on work.

4.2 Live/Work Buildings

Artist live/work and studio buildings form another urban spatial element and constitute both an investment in the arts economy as well as a revitalization catalyst in neighborhoods. Generally developed out of used and discarded industrial space and involving extensive rehabbing, these buildings create residential communities that encourage artistic spillover among artists while enlivening the surrounding streets and bolstering local businesses. Artists tend to work odd hours, and their presence helps keep streets safer at all hours of the night and day. They patronize local merchants and often become active in community groups. They open up their space for periodic arts crawls, where the public is invited to view (and buy) their work in the very spaces where it was created, often in full view of kitchen sinks and clothes closets.

The Twin Cities hosts a large number of artist live/work buildings and is home to one of the pioneering American live/work space developers, Artspace Inc. Artspace is a nonprofit that was formed at the request of the Minneapolis City Council when sports bars (associated with a new entertainment arena) began forcing out galleries and restaurants that had thrived in the warehouse district. After developing a number of successful projects, Artspace found that if it did not continue to manage the buildings, artists were apt to move out or be bought out by higher bidders. Since 1991, they have continued to manage all of their live/work buildings for the long haul, preventing rents from rising to market rates.

Artspace has created large live/work buildings in the urban core. In the early 1990s, it developed two vacant former warehouses in downtown St. Paul – The Northern Warehouse and the Tilsner, both as artist coops (Figure 3). The two buildings house dozens of artists, and the former also provides rental space to cafes and arts-related non-profits on its first two floors. The buildings have brought stability and commercial revitalization to the surrounding neighborhood, inducing the start-up of the old outdoor farmer's market across the street and encouraging private developers to convert other empty buildings into housing.

Figure 3. Northern Warehouse and Tilsner Artist Coops, St. Paul.

Source: Author's photograph

As part of its complicated negotiations with the city to do these two buildings, Artspace agreed to do a project in a troubled low in-

Figure 4/5. Frogtown Family Lofts before (left) and after (right) regeneration.

Source: Author's photograph

Source: Author's photograph

come neighborhood in the inner city. It took an old printing building, a brownfield site (Figure 4) and converted it into Frogtown Family Lofts. Today, this complex houses dozens of artists with their children, including a number of Hmong artists from the surrounding immigrant community (Figure 5). It has brought activity and stability to its neighborhood, and some of the artists are using their work as a catalyst for community change.

4.3 Performing Arts Facilities

Smaller scale performing arts spaces, such as theaters and dance venues embedded in neighborhoods, stabilize and invigorate commercial areas and often relate to the unique character of the community. The Twin Cities hosts 55 theaters and a number of dedicated dance spaces, plus many music venues that serve similar purposes. While the largest of these are entertainment destinations surrounded by parking ramps and receiving disproportionate shares of public arts and economic development funding, many others have forged close ties to neighborhood residents.

An outstanding example of how artistic space has helped to revitalize and stabilize a low-income neighborhood is the In the Heart of the Beast Puppet and Mask Theater (Figure 6). Begun in the 1970s by counter-culture young people, Heart of the Beast Theatre (HOBT) works with larger-than-life puppets worn by the players, original scripts, and live music, much of it now international ethnic folk material. After working out of a series of churches and lofts, HOBT worked with the City of Minneapolis to lease and then buy a former porn theater (once a family theater) in the poorest neighborhood of town. After some dragging of its feet, the city gave the theater troupe a ten-year, interest-free loan of $ 325,000 to do the renovations, and HOBT also won a $ 150,000 loan from the Neighborhood Revitalization Program, to be repaid through service to the neighborhood. The neighborhood, increasingly Latino, rallied to help clean up the building – it needed a new roof, standing water pumped out, and every surface washed. Across the street, Latino merchants had redeveloped vacant space into a Mercado and new restaurants with rental housing upstairs, all with private money. Through a carefully built partnership of mutual respect, HOBT and the Latino Business Association are now taking over the huge, adjacent Minnesota Antiques building, vacant for more than a decade, to use as an incubator for Latino businesses, a Latino Community Network space, and for the theater, a place to rehearse, build puppets (previously done in the theater aisles) and run the office (previously in the old balcony).

Figure 6. Heart of the Beast Puppet Theater, Minneapolis.

Source: Author's photograph

Cities have been important investors in each of these forms of artist-centric space. In some cases, they have owned the buildings in question. In others, they have helped to finance the rehabbing of the space. Changes in land use regulations have enabled some projects, as has infrastructure provision. Some cities have designated cultural districts, while in others, opposition to such concentrations has ensured that projects are spread throughout the city.

5. Artists and Gentrification

The mushrooming of artistic activity in some inner city neighborhoods has prompted concerns about gentrification and community displacement. Planners and communities are also concerned that artists' space may reap subsidies – for low income housing, for instance – that may crowd out other poorer and worthy recipients. In some cities, like New York City, tensions between long-time working class and minority residents of a neighborhood and incoming young artists moving into apartments and industrial spaces has been high for decades, as described in Sharon Zukin's pioneering book, Loft Living (1982). Real estate developers often use artists as a vanguard for wholesale neighborhood turnover, even subsidizing galleries and performance spaces as a way of making the neighborhood more hip and benefiting from the sweat labor of artists. Yet in some cities, pioneering low-income artists have been displaced by wealthier galleries and more prosperous residents. This process is less problematic in de-industrializing and de-populating neighborhoods in older cities like Cleveland and St. Paul's Lowertown that have benefited from artists moving into vacant industrial space and increasing personal security and economic activity. Also, many artists occupying such space are of the neighborhood to begin with, so that the artistic use of such space constitutes a community retention success.

Many artists, along with other lower income residents, are displaced when property taxes and rents begin to rise with the incursion of higher income residents attracted to the buzz that artists create in neighborhoods they have helped to renovate. One way of preventing this dynamic, so powerful because of private land ownership rights, is to build and hold artistic space in common as cooperatives, in non-profit organizations, or in land banks as Artspace has done.

Beyond economic impacts, urban core artists make many contributions to community viability and life. Artists produce commissioned and informal public art that enlivens the community visually, and they often participate in planning parks and cultural facilities. Artists are often actively engaged in community events such as parades, festivals and fairs, and in neighborhood politics. The Heart of the Beast Theatre, for example, unfurls its puppets every year for a themed May Day parade down the south side, ending up in Powderhorn Park and drawing admirers from all over the city.

6. Conclusions

In general, contemporary discourse on cultural and economic development policy undervalues the significance of space and place. This is particularly true in the arts sector. Arts administrators and funders tend to think organizationally. But many artists and arts fans think instead of a place: a theater space, a gallery, a jazz club, an art crawl, or even an entire arts neighborhood that they love to visit and revisit. Ongoing access to spaces that offer novelty and serendipitous encounters with other artists and art lovers is a great gift for artists. It is not only the events and equipment that matter, but also the networks and friendships formed around them. 'More and better' artists, to use the rather crass terminology of economics, emerge in and are attracted to urban cores that offer a portfolio of dedicated spaces for living, working, learning, networking, exhibition, presentation and sharing tools and workspace. Once there, they contribute to the host economy by exporting their work, contracting with businesses to make them more productive and profitable, stimulating innovation on the part of supplies, and bringing income and energy to their neighborhoods.

Cities and towns can help generate, recruit and retain artists as a sticky occupational core that can in turn attract other firms and individuals. Providing artistic space that embeds artists in their communities is a fruitful way for cities to do so. In addition, cities nurturing their urban cores could apply the occupational approach illustrated here to identify and pursue other key urban occupations that are attracted to inner cities, amplify the cities' exports and generate multiplier effects via other business sectors and consumer spending.

References

BECKER, H. (1982), *Art Worlds*, Berkeley, Los Angeles, University of California Press

BLAU, J. (1989), *The Shape of Culture*. Cambridge/Mass., Cambridge University Press

BLS (US Department of Labor, Bureau of Labor Statistics) (2002), *National Employment Matrix*, www.bls.gov/emp/empoils.htm, accessed October 20, 2002

BUSS, T. (1999), "The Case Against Targeted Industry Strategies", *Economic Development Quarterly*, Vol. 13, p. 339-355

CLARK, T. N. (2004), The City as an Entertainment Machine, Research in Urban Policy, Vol. 9, Kiddlington/UK, Elsevier

FINKLE, J. A. (1999), "The Case Against Targeting Might have been More ...Targeted", *Economic Development Quarterly*, Vol. 13, p. 361-64

FLORIDA, R. (2002), *The Rise of the Creative Class*, New York, Basic Books

JACOBS, J. (1961), *The Death and Life of Great American Cities*, New York, Vintage

JUDD, D. (1999), "Constructing the Tourist Bubble", in: Judd, D., Fainstein, S. (eds), *The Tourist City*, New Haven/CT, Yale University Press, p. 35-53

MARKUSEN, A., KING, D. (2003), *The Artistic Dividend: The Hidden Contributions of the Arts to the Regional Economy*, Minneapolis/MN, University of Minnesota

MARKUSEN, A., SCHROCK, G. (2005), *Regional Job Growth through an Occupational Lens*, Working Paper 256, Minneapolis/MN, University of Minnesota

MARKUSEN, A., SCHROCK, G. (2006), "The Artistic Dividend: Urban Artistic Specialization and Economic Development Implications", *Urban Studies*, forthcoming

MARKUSEN, A. (1996), "Sticky Places in Slippery Space: a Typology of Industrial Districts", *Economic Geography*, Vol. 72, No. 3, p. 293-313

MARKUSEN, A. (2004), "Targeting Occupations in Regional and Community Economic Development?", *Journal of the American Planning Association*, Vol. 70, No. 3, p. 253-268

MINNESOTA POPULATION CENTER, University of Minnesota (2000), Census 2000, Minneapolis

THOMPSON, W., THOMPSON, P. (1985), "From Industries to Occupations: Rethinking Local Economic Development", *Economic Development Commentary*, Vol. 9, p. 12-18

WIEWEL, W. (1999), "Policy Research in an Imperfect World, Response to Terry F. Buss' 'The Case Against Targeted Industry Strategies'", *Economic Development Quarterly*. Vol. 13, p. 357-60

ZUKIN, S. (1982), *Loft Living: Culture and Capital in Urban Change*, Baltimore/MD, Johns Hopkins University Pres

THE AGEING SOCIETY – AN URBAN SOCIETY? THE BRITISH EXPERIENCE

by Taner Oc, Tzu-Yuan Chao and Nicholas Brown[1]

Introduction

The last census confirmed that Britain is an 'ageing society'. Life expectancy has been steadily increasing and the number of young people is in decline. (Centre for Future Studies 2002). Rather than heralding this increase in life expectancy as a positive effect of progress, there is a tendency to interpret the future outcomes in a rather pessimistic light. The media coverage of a so-called 'Global Ageing Crisis' has seen the process of ageing and the changes in the population profiles of western countries including Britain being identified as the population problem of our times (Centre for Future Studies 2002). Even demographers, social and political commentators are citing the growth in the aged population as a potential danger, particularly for the west.

The debate about pensions and potential changes to the age of retirement is on-going but this is only one aspect of the problem. Much of the discussion on older people restricts itself to the health and social care interface. The importance to older people of such issues as housing, transport, crime prevention, leisure activities, access and home

Figure 1. Under 16s and people aged 65+ in the UK.

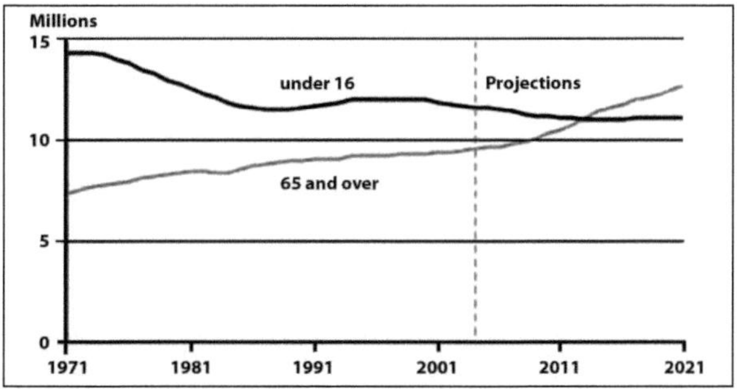

Source: Author's diagram based on National Statistics 2006

1 Part of this research was funded by the Ministere de l'équipement (Paris).

Table 1. Absolute numbers (in 1,000) and proportions of the oldest old in the UK 1901-2031.

		Population enumerated in Census			Estimated mid-year resident population	
		1901	1931	1951	1961	1971
All Persons	All	38,237	46,038	50,225	52,807	55,928
	65+	1,809	3,418	5,468	6,208	7,408
	85+	61	113	224	346	485
	Percentage 85+/Total	0.2	0.2	0.4	0.7	0.9
	Percentage 85+/65+	3.4	3.3	4.1	5.6	6.5
Males	All	18,492	22,060	24,118	25,528	27,167
	65+	784	1,470	2,247	2,385	2,841
	85+	23	36	70	105	126
	Percentage 85+/Total	0./	0.2	0.3	0.4	0.5
	Percentage 85+/65+	2.9	2.4	3.1	4.4	4.4
Females	All	19,745	23,978	26,107	27,279	28,761
	65+	1,025	1,947	3,218	3,823	4,567
	85+	38	77	154	241	359
	Percentage 85+/Total	0.2	0.3	0.6	0.9	1.2
	Percentage 85+/65+	3.7	4.0	4.8	6.3	7.9

Source: Author's compilation based on data from ONS 2004, ONS 2003, GAD 2003

maintenance is rarely acknowledged (Phillips 1999:69). The key concern is how to plan for the ageing population? Faced with the possibility that the elderly may become the majority of the population in the near future, policy makers, planners and housing officers are studying the emerging changes. The impact of new demands on the city is likely to have significant effects on all aspects of the urban environment.

1. Current Population Trends

A changing population structure is evident with people living longer and being active over longer periods. By 2010/11, life expectancy is set to increase from 74 years to 77.1 years for men, and 79.5 years to 81.6 years for women. This rate is increasing by approximately two years every ten years (HEA 1997). The gendered profile of the ageing population is well established (Bernard/Phillips 2000), with women progressively outnumbering men at later ages due to their greater longevity (Department for Work and Pensions 2004). Population predictions and projections for the next 20 years can be made with some certainty as the majority of the people that will be in the workforce in 2020 are already alive (Tables 1). However, Frank Shaw warns that,

Estimated mid-year resident population (continue)			Projected mid-year resident population			
1981	1991	2003	2021	2031		
56,357	57,439	59,553	63,835	65,700	**All**	**All Persons**
8,475	9,059	9,510	12,703	15,271	**65+**	
603	873	1,104	1,802	2,479	**85+**	
1.1	1.5	1.9	2.8	3.8	**Percentage 85+/Total**	
7.1	9.6	11.6	14.2	16.2	**Percentage 85+/65+**	
27,412	27,909	29,108	31,432	32,337	**All**	**Males**
3,327	3,630	4,038	5,777	6,976	**65+**	
141	212	313.1	680	978	**85+**	
0.5	0.8	1.1	2.2	3.0	**Percentage 85+/Total**	
4.2	5.8	7.8	11.8	14.0	**Percentage 85+/65+**	
28,946	29,530	30,446	32,4032	33,362	**All**	**Females**
5,149	5,428	5,472	6,926	8,296	**65+**	
462	661	791	1,122	1,501	**85+**	
1.6	2.2	2.6	3.5	4.5	**Percentage 85+/Total**	
9.0	12.2	14.5	16.2	18.1	**Percentage 85+/65+**	

as America has experienced over the last few decades, such demographic trends can change quite suddenly and unpredictably, with relatively immediate effects (Centre for Future Studies 2002).

Findings from the 'English House Condition Survey 1996' show that one third of households in England (6.8 million) are headed by someone over 60 and there are 3.1 million older people over 60 living alone, making up half of all single person households (Table 2). In comparison to 1996, there will be an estimated 300,000 additional homeowners aged 80 or over in England by 2011. Given this, services such as 'Staying Put' will need to increase and local authorities will need to plan for the resulting increased demand for grant aid (Forrest et al. 1997:6).

The survey's result suggest that regardless of ownership trends in the housing market as a whole, increases in the absolute numbers of older homeowners in England through the next two decades are inevitable (Appleton 2002:7).

Table 2. Proportions of people aged 65+ and 85+ by living arrangements in the UK, 2001.

	65+		85+	
	Men	**Women**	**Men**	**Women**
Living alone	22.5	46.4	42.1	70.5
In couple	71.2	41.5	46.4	10.6
Other	6.3	12.1	11.5	18.9

Source: National Statistics 2006

2. The Issues

The majority of older people live in general housing. Therefore, in the planning of neighbourhoods and the design of dwellings, the impacts of the ageing population need to be considered. Design features at all scales of the outdoor environment, including street layouts, building form, even signage detail, can all have an effect on the orientation and way-finding abilities of older people. Mitchell et al. speak of the need to design 'neighbourhoods for life', defined as a "neighbourhood that provides intelligible, high quality environment for the whole of the local inhabitants' life" (Mitchell et al. 2004:99). Similarly, architects are exploring 'Universal Design' so that buildings, including housing, respond to the needs of all able bodied and disabled equally. This approach would enable the ageing population to be accommodated without requiring special arrangements for them (Figure 2).

A recent survey by Halifax Estate Agents claims that respondents aged 65 and older are most concerned with being close to shops (NOP World Research 2005). A survey carried out by MORI reveals that key priorities for older people to live independent lives are bus services, shopping facilities, road and pavement maintenance and, interestingly, among those aged 55-64, better leisure and sports facilities (DETR 2001). There is a body of research that suggests city living should be explored as a sustainable alternative for this population. City living could effectively reduce their travel needs and if the mixed-use areas contained appropriate facilities and services, their quality of life would be improved with a wider range of choices within easy reach (Oc/Chao 2004) (Figure 3).

The actual location of the accommodation is an important consideration. Harding states that, "A 'sense of home' comes from the area people live in, their sense of familiarity and of belonging. Access to local shops, post offices, and places of entertainment and of community activity all contribute to well-being and staying in touch and in control of one's life. The availability of public transport, the location of bus stops and zebra crossings, the siting of street lamps can all make a difference in how mobile older people are

Figure 2. Primrose Hill, London, is an exemplary environment for all ages, including the very old. The vivid colours of the building make this highly navigable for the ageing.

Source: Author's Photograph

Figure 3. The café, the doctors' surgery and the pharmacy. On the same high street in Primrose Hill there are several grocery shops, a library, a dental surgery, dry cleaners and other amenities, enabling the residents to cater for their daily needs within walking distance.

Source: Author's Photograph

able to be and how safe they feel. Environmental planners need to take account of these human needs of an ageing population, and to ensure that both practical considerations and human interaction are core objectives of development plans." (Harding 1997:18).

2.1 General Housing

Housing has a defining role in the lifestyles of older people, due to the amount of time spent within the home. The relationship between the home and the surrounding environment is also very important (SEU/ODPM 2005). Hence, the increasing older population poses a challenge for future housing policy. There is a requirement for 3.8 million new households in England between 1996 and 2021 (DETR 1998) and given the increasing life expectancy and changing preferences of the 'baby boomer' generation, there is an expectation that a growing part of demand for new homes will be from the over 50's.

As these demographic and social changes take place, a move towards a more inclusive approach to housing for the older age groups is essential, ensuring that a wider range of choices are available so that they can lead an enjoyable life and fulfil their potential. This particular group will have different attitudes and preferences regarding accommodation (ODPM 2005c:18); with key concerns about being part of a safer community in a mixed-use environment (Chao 2004:1). Chao also states that most elderly people prefer to stay in general-need housing instead of sheltered accommodation and seek living environments with a greater vitality, and not be grouped in so-called 'Ghettos of the aged'. For many, the desire to remain near family or friends rather than move into more suitably designed accommodation is always going to be the deciding factor.

Unfortunately, little attention is paid to those who might choose to move within the general housing stock, perhaps to trade down or sideways to a more contemporary, thermally efficient, compact and easily managed house or bungalow (Appleton 2002:1).

2.2 Sheltered/Care Accommodation

Hanson states that society often tends to "think of housing for older people as housing for people with special needs" (Peace/Holland 2001:29). This is not the case as many older people lead independent, active lives. However, many older people, despite their income or wealth, are assigned to nursing homes. This will occur for a range of reasons. In certain instances, accommodation such as 'sheltered housing' is often viewed as an opportunity to provide companionship and with younger and more-able residents and staff giving assistance to older residents and helping them to sustain a more active life (Chao 2004:106; Peace/Holland 2001). Around 5 % of older people live in sheltered housing where they hope to achieve independence and security and can have assistance from a warden where and when necessary (Age Concern 2002) (Figure 4).

Figure 4. The residents in this sheltered housing development in Primrose Hill would much prefer general housing in the same area.

Source: Author's Photograph

Hanson believes that to avoid architectural discrimination, older people would be best suited to live in conveniently designed ordinary housing rather than 'special housing' (Peace/Holland 2001:38). In general terms, housing units that are smaller in size and subsequently easy to manage are popular amongst this group (Tinker 1997:116-121). Older people may also require single storey or ground floor accommodation to alleviate issues such as changes of level that may prevent them from fulfilling an autonomous and active lifestyle within their home. Features such as the absence of stairs may facilitate even a very frail person to carry on living independently. Jarvis et al. discuss the associated issues of "getting around the home" and maintain that "the hardest task [is] getting up and down stairs" (1996:33). In this respect, city centre apartment blocks may pose a problem if they do not have lifts. The preferences of older people have to be considered when developing new housing or refurbishing old stock (Peace/Holland 2001).

2.3 Independent Living

The current group of people in their sixties have very different life experiences to their parents; namely a greater expectation of living longer, more freedom of movement, more exposure to other cultures, fewer children, more working opportunities, better social benefits and care and higher disposable incomes. Unlike earlier generations, they typically encourage children to be independent and leave home when they grow up. Research shows that more people are now likely to delay their retirement due to a healthier and longer life. By continuing to work longer and with more savings, older people are less reliant on their children and are more likely to have their own accommodation (Chao 2004:95).

Several studies reveal a consistent commitment amongst older people to stay in their own home rather than move in with their children or into residential care (Grundy/Glaser 1999). Rhoden (1998) states that as well as the growing number of elderly households, there is also a growing trend for older people to live alone. This is the result of recent increases in the divorce rate and low remarriage rate of elderly divorced and widowed people. All of these factors imply that a major impact of the ageing population will be a significant increase in single person as well as two-person households.

Unfortunately current research suggests that older people that are living in rented accommodation endure some of the poorest housing conditions of any tenure (ODPM 2005c). Increases in rent by local authorities as well as registered social landlords and the private sector means that affordability is now an important issue for older people (Age Concern 2002). Sykes (1992) states that older people that are living alone are more likely to live in poor-quality housing than other age and social groups. Age Concern's 'Housing Policy Position Paper' states that there is an urgent need to improve housing conditions and provide better assistance with adaptations (Age Concern 2002). There are schemes such as 'Care and Repair' and 'Staying Put' that offer assistance, which often includes continuing support during the period when the work is being undertaken.

Williams suggests that the issue of single-person households is not merely one of accommodation, but of sustainability (2005). An increasing body of research links an increase in the number of small households with an increase in domestic resource consumption and waste production. Williams (2005) notes that in the UK one-person households consumed 23 % more electricity, 38 % more gas and 45 % more space than per person consumption in two-person households. Compared to per person consumption in four-person households, single-person households consumed 77 % more electricity, 54 % more gas and 65 % more space. This can be explained partly by the mismatch of the type and size of accommodation with the household size. The changing population profile indicates that this could be a growing problem if there is not significant re-focussing of the housing provision.

It has been suggested that 'co-housing' may be a model of accommodation that could offer high levels of social capital for older people and encourage pro-environmental behaviour (Williams 2005). This idea combines the autonomy of private dwellings with the positive aspects of community living. The residents have a more participative role in the development and can be involved in recruiting, development, and design of the community. This is a model that is being introduced in all new housing developments in Denmark, Holland and Sweden through a pro-active planning process and financial assistance from the government. Williams (2005) underlines the sustainability objectives of co-housing to be strong social networks and cohesion, general well-being, affordable lifestyles, pro-environmental behaviour and reduction in resource consumption. These advantages of co-housing would ensure benefits to the society as a whole and especially to the ageing population whose levels of income invariably fall over time and who require increasingly more support from social networks.

2.4 Residential Re-location

Re-location following retirement is a trend that has long influenced the distribution of older people across cities and between areas of the country. Many people feel that the need to be located near to work has tied them to suburban or inner urban locations, which ceases to be an issue in retirement. Appleton notes that, "the spur to migrate might come from the desire to have a smaller house, to realise a capital sum from the sale of a family dwelling and to be in a more congenial location… retirement or approaching retirement can be a time of mobility for a number of elderly people." (Appleton 2002:13).

However, Phillips and Bartlett emphasise the fact that most ageing does occur in-situ and the image of footloose pensioners is not altogether accurate (Phillips/Bartlett 1997:282-283). The idea of 'ageing in place' is seen to prevent the anxiety or stress associated with moving, with the majority of older people preferring not to move at this stage of their lives. This would seem to be the case as older people are said to be less likely to move than any other age group (Harris 1990:30). The Mulholland Research Associates reported that life in a cul-de-sac, secure private gardens and leafy vistas are more important to residents of suburban areas than the vicinity to shops and restaurants

(Biddulph 2001). However, the development industry is arguing that people's pre-dispositions are changing and that there is a growing demand from the over 50's for apartments and town-houses. J. Knight in the Times reports that empty nesters are reversing the trend by fleeing the peace of countryside for the buzz of the metropolis. According to the head of residential research at a national network of estate agents, research shows "the empty nesters are moving back into city centres in places like Bristol, Edinburgh and Southampton" (The Times 09/16/2005, 10/14/2005).

2.5 Transport and Mobility

The ageing population will have a significant impact on both public and private transport requirements and provision. Nearly half of households without a car are pensioner households. A recent ODPM report (2005c) notes that, "91 % of single pensioners and 53 % of pensioner couples do not own a car and depend on public transport". The financial status of the individuals is still likely to dictate car ownership. The ability to walk and have easy access to public transport will continue to be a major issue for many older people who cannot afford to own a car, or are no longer able to drive due to illness. In fact, recent research shows walking to have an extremely important role in the general health and well-being of older people. Pedestrian access to shops, doctors' surgeries, libraries and other local facilities can also have a key role in enabling older people to participate in their communities.

Mobility amongst older age groups is a significant concern. Only one third of those aged 65 to 70 have mobility problems but this increases to one half for those aged 75 to 80 and three quarters for those aged 85 and over (Age Concern 2002). This highlights the importance of improving the accessibility of public transport, as well as access to public and open spaces and other particular forums designed to cater for their social activities. It is noted that, "fear of crime and lack of accessible transport systems can unfairly disadvantage older people and restrict their possibilities" (Gordon et al. 1999; ODPM 2005c) leaving them isolated and depressed.

As well as the aspects of mobility, there are issues of safety that are apparent. Older pedestrians are below average in the likelihood of being involved in road accidents but have an above average likelihood of being killed. Only 14.6 % of pedestrian casualties are aged 60 or over, yet 46.6 % of these are fatalities (Age Concern 2002). Walking is often restricted by a fear of falling, brought about by concerns over accessibility and poor condition of pavements, especially coupled with winter conditions. Another concern is that older people are often apprehensive about using public transport due to fear of crime, discrimination, accessibility and affordability (ODPM 2005c).

An increasing ageing population will raise issues about the location of and link to services. Future land use planning must recognise the transport needs of this age group, particularly those who do not own a car. Ease of access to healthcare is a key concern amongst the older population and can have significant knock-on effects. Recent research shows that older people that do not have easy access to GP's do not visit them as frequently. If certain illnesses are detected and treated at an early stage then it often reduces the need for more expensive provision of residential care or hospitalisation. There could be similar benefits if local transport plans took into account the needs of older people to have easy access to other support services.

2.6 Economic Implications

The issue of transport and housing is only part of a much wider problem. The ageing population has predominantly been viewed as a threat to the future sustainability of health and social security systems. The economy will encounter the dilemma of the increasing number of early retirees and the increasing number of non-pensionable applicants in the labour market (Chao 2004:205). Frank Shaw identifies the potential issue of inter-generational transfer of resources that "an ageing society represents a troublesome claim on the resources of the productive generations of the future" (Centre for Future Studies 2002). There is a common belief that the ageing population could prove to have a damaging impact on general economic growth (Catalyst 2003).

Appleton highlights the concern that there will be an insufficient supply of younger people to meet the requirements of service industries, especially those providing care to people in advanced old age (Appleton 2002:5). Catalyst adds that some fear even worse consequences, with democratic society falling apart as inter-generational conflict becomes the new 'class war' (2003).

However, Japan, a country with the advanced world's most rapidly ageing population, has seen it's percentage of over 60-year olds rise from 9 % to 18 % within the space of a single generation without any dramatically adverse economic or social consequences (Centre for Future Studies 2002). This is an illustration of how demographic changes can be absorbed through sustained economic growth with equanimity. In the UK, research has suggested that even modest rates of economic growth will make public pension schemes manageable indefinitely.

Indeed, the findings in 'The Challenge of Longer Life: Economic Burden or Social Opportunity?' suggest that much of these concerns are greatly exaggerated. However, this is not to say that nothing needs to be done. Instead, it should be made possible for older people to lead active and independent lives longer, without the number of social and institutional barriers that currently restrict this (Catalyst 2003). Infact, Age

Concern's 'Age Discrimination Policy Position Paper' cites that the annual cost of age discrimination in employment to the UK economy is £ 31 billion. 'Better Government for Older People' suggest that "there is a strong economic argument for the employment of older people. Central and local government should demonstrate good employment practice. Central and local government should support education and training (including IT)" (BGOP 2000).

A study for the Equal Opportunities Commission (EOC 2005) notes that we need to consider flexible work options for the population aged over 50. In Spring 2004, 644,000 men and 1,650,000 women in this group worked part-time in their main jobs. This is due to a number of factors including gradual retirement, caring responsibility, health reasons, and importantly insufficient income in later life (EOC 2005). According to the ODPM (2005c), 21 % of older people are on low incomes. These studies further indicate the positive impact of employment on the health and economic well-being of the older population. Therefore, we need better informed approaches to employment, and the location of jobs. In France, 'Senior Actif Plus' is a new employment agency to provide opportunities for those over fifty.

2.7 Changing Lifestyles

The lifestyle choices that are made by older people need to be considered, alongside the established concerns for potential increases in dependence and frailty. The concerns over deteriorating health and diminishing functional capacity are considerable for people approaching old age, but focussing on these problems can promote a limited view of the experience of many older people, particularly of those in early or pre-old age and many of those in mid-old age. Retirement or change to part-time employment does not inherently create breakdowns in other social activities. Many people in the early years of old age will experience increased opportunities for travel, for study and informal learning, for increased participation in existing hobbies and perhaps the development of new interests. The 'University of the Third Age' is growing, as is general interest in lifelong learning, and this would suggest a desire among older people to view old age as an opportunity for continuing development rather than decline (Carlton/Soulsby 1999).

A new generation of grandmothers is redefining their role replacing the stereotypes of knitting by the fire with an altogether more dynamic image of globe-trotting, e-mailing and cappuccino-drinking. The grandmother of today feels 20 years younger than she is and does not believe she is truly old until she is at least 80 (The Times 10/12/2005). In discussing older age groups, people often think of nursing homes and sheltered housing, and ignore the fact that older people can be of good health and very active well into their 80's.

Klerk and Vijgen (1992) suggest that demand for both accommodation and activities are clearly affected by household structure, which is seen to be changing with the increasing aged population. People living in single-person households may go out frequently to make social contacts, in contrast to members of multi-person households, particularly those including children, who are more likely to engage in activities within their home. In terms of urban impacts, Williams suggests that 'social capital' is unlikely to be diminished by an increase in single-person households living in residential areas (Williams 2005) if they are socially networked. Opportunities for voluntary work as well as contact with family and friends and access to local services seem to be associated with good health (ODPM 2005c:31).

In the 'Environment and Identity in Later Life', the 'Theory of Reengagement' refers to a 'Life of Quality' being achieved when older people can, "…adopt specific strategies that allow attachment on their own terms to the social and material fabric of everyday life. People in the study used material, social and cognitive mediators to optimise the mix of 'self' and 'other' in their environments, and by a process of 'Option Recognition' they looked for ways to reinforce or recreate points of attachment to place. The significance of favourite spaces was enhanced by individuals' ability to be able to move away from them as part of their daily routine in order to return 'energised' by change. This 'journey' could be into or beyond the neighbourhood … and it had physical and psychological benefits related to the sense of self and mastery of environment, which could be compromised in more institutional settings." (Peace/Holland 2003).

Therefore, it could be argued that designing urban environments that facilitate social capital and enable the ageing population to lead more active lives needs to be a priority for planners and urban designers. Active, engaged and healthy older population should pay dividends to the society not only in terms of reducing the burden associated with ill health and loneliness but also gain from this group's contribution to their communities.

2.8 Needs of the Ageing Population

Older people, as with other social groups, will often have specialised requirements. These needs have to be identified and considered in order to allow them to live autonomously. It is often supposed that the costs of health and social care must increase significantly as people live longer and require greater care for a proportionately longer period of their lives (Centre for Future Studies 2002). The NHS and the Department of Health have envisaged that the increasing older population will require increasing social care services and certain Acts have been implemented with the aim of reducing the health service costs. Care packages that enable older people to remain at home are deemed more efficient and could benefit a wider range of people in need. Much of this legislation and guidance emphasises the importance of promoting independence (Chao 2004:95).

The built environment has a key role to play because the health of older people may be affected by the poor condition or location of their housing. Tinker states that the link between poor health and housing is becoming more apparent, particularly for less active people (Tinker 1997:110). Isolation can also have repercussions on health and mental well-being for older people that are living alone although this is something that is often difficult to 'engineer' (Age Concern 2002). Older people with specific needs will also need to be considered. For example, the number of people with dementia is rising as a consequence of the ageing population and is predicted to rise further, with the current UK figure of 750,000 sufferers estimated to increase to 1.2 million by 2040 (Mitchell et al. 2002:89). This underlines the need for the creation of legible neighbourhoods, enabling sufferers to use their immediate environments in the early stages of their illness.

2.9 Social Inclusion/ Social Exclusion and Ageism

In the urban environment, it is important to remain aware that the vast majority of older people are not institutionalised, but become less and less visible in the neighbourhoods in which they live (Phillips/Bartlett 1997:297). Research shows that older people on low incomes suffer more from social exclusion, disadvantage and poor health than any other group (ODPM 2005c). While progress has been made in tackling pensioner poverty, older people remain highly vulnerable in other ways. Victor and Scharf (quoted in ODPM 2005c) highlight that many older people are isolated from family, friends and neighbours. 30 % of those over 65 do not see any friends, over 30 % do not see family and one in ten do not see neighbours once a week. Hence, unfortunately one in six suffer from depression.

In terms of integration versus isolation in the urban environment, there needs to be an understanding of issues regarding access to public and spaces, including parks, designed to cater for their social activities and the social mix in those spaces (Figure 5). This also comes with a concern over the lack of adaptability of those spaces and affect on ability of older people to use and socialise in those spaces.

Figure 5. The Primrose Hill park used by all ages is overlooked by housing, it is safe as well as pleasant.

Source: Author's Photograph

Research also suggests that the characteristics of the UK's ethnic minority populations will ensure that the future pensioner population will comprise of significantly more Black and Minority Ethnic groups, particularly in terms of Afro-Caribbean and British Asian pensioners (Atkin 1998). This ageing profile provokes a number of increasingly key questions for policy-makers regarding how their needs can best be anticipated and met. (DWP 2004:8).

There is much to suggest that current attitudes towards the older generation could be vastly improved to prevent issues of social exclusion. Many people do not realise the key role that older people have in community and associative activities. This includes a role in 'local management' of their own neighbourhoods and Chao suggests that there is a need to recognise the contribution that older people can make to society and sustainable city centres (2004:206). Such positive contributions are made through their families, as well as caring and volunteer work through their communities. Ageing is a natural process and attitudes towards the aged in society are of fundamental importance.

2.10 Crime/Safety

Crime and the fear of crime can have a significant role in undermining the well-being of older people and can lead to the feeling of exclusion from the community they live in (Age Concern 2002; ODPM 2005c). Fear of crime can also prevent older people from actively participating in activities beyond the home. A third of people say fear of crime affects their quality of life. The 'Age Concern Crime Policy Position Paper' cites that 9 % of older men and 33 % of older women over 60 felt unsafe when out walking alone after dark. The likelihood of older people being actual victims of crime is much less than other groups because they put curfews on themselves hence they are less exposed to street crime. A further problem older people's experience is 'distraction burglary': 15,113 incidents were reported in 2003/04 in England (ODPM 2005c). The fear of crime leading to isolation in their homes can have negative consequences on people's health and general well-being. The consequences for those who do become the victims can be extremely traumatic. It is, therefore, essential to consider the security needs of older people in the design of the built environment, both in terms of the urban realm and the residential units. A number of older people reject mixed-use schemes as preferable accommodation despite its many advantages mainly due to fear of crime and discrimination, preferring segregation by means such as gated communities (Chao 2004:200).

Older people are also often the target for anti-social behaviour and despite various government measures; it would seem that it is the attitude towards the ageing population that needs to change, perhaps by promoting respect for the elderly through the education system (Chao 2004:200). Violent and non-violent crimes are cited as the two most important variables in people's assessments of their quality of life (Rogerson et al. 1989). Given this, attempts to reduce crime, or perhaps, more importantly, the fear of crime, are therefore essential to the creation of viable urban areas (Thomas/Bromley 2000).

3. Current Planning Policy

There is perhaps a lack of understanding of the needs and demands that the ageing population places on the environment (RTPI 2004). Given the likely financial implications for the taxpayer highlighted previously, the ageing population is perhaps understandably viewed more readily as a threat as opposed to an opportunity.

The government is aware of the need to carefully manage the social impact of the ageing population. The strategic goals of public policy for the ageing population have been summarised by a government think-tank group, "The first is to ensure that age does not become a social dividing line – that current concerns about social exclusion are broadened to encompass potential exclusion by age. The second is to ensure intergenerational fairness. The needs, rights and duties of today's older generation must be balanced against those of today's younger people, who will have to save more and to update their skills regularly throughout their longer lives. The third is to offer the highest possible quality of life for all as the UK's population ages" (Foresight 2000).

Due to its ability to deal with long-term change, town planning as a function is well-placed to address these goals (RTPI 2004:11). The British Town Planning system is undergoing a complete overhaul. The incoming Local Development Frameworks (LDFs), a portfolio of documents that incorporate more localised community-based Action Plans and a Statement of Community Involvement (SCI) that will set out how the local community will be involved in reviewing the LDF will provide the tools for "local authorities to exercise their discretion in a way that is both inclusive and accountable to older people" (Age Concern 2002:2). The 'grey vote' in local elections should ensure that the needs of this population are met in Local Plans. The Royal Town Planning Institute (RTPI) states that there is considerable inclusiveness built-in to the UK system but this is often more focused towards provision of services that address the 'special needs' of the elderly rather than the "differential land use consequences of the changing demographic structure" (2004:24).

It is reasonable to assert that the built environment preferences of the ageing population have not been at the forefront of local government thinking. The issue has also proved difficult to integrate into land use planning documents (RTPI 2004). However, there is much that can be done at the local level to directly and indirectly manage the impacts and make sure that older people can get the most out of urban areas. The new legislation gives councils powers to do anything that promotes or improves the economic, social or environmental well being of their areas.

This can be used to meet the needs of the ageing population as well as other vulnerable groups locally. The new community strategy framework offers a very useful mechanism for implementing the measures set out above. Local authority planners will ideally have a key role to play in developing and implementing elements of the community strategy.Working with health, social services and education authorities in particular, the changing needs of service providers arising from changes in the local population age structure can be identified and planned for. In many cases there will be land-use implications to the planning of future services. For example, there may be a need to change recreation provision to suit the elderly active rather than just the young. "The Local Development Framework should respond to the needs identified in the community strategy with appropriate planning policies and land-use allocations" (RTPI 2004).

The responsibility to provide for communities lies ultimately with officers of the local authorities and its elected representatives and service providers. The RTPI (2004:26) recommend that during the assessment of all planning policies and practices, consideration should be made of their suitability for people of all ages. They argue that age related issues should become 'mainstream' in the way issues of income, ethnicity, disability and more recently sustainability have become.

3.1 Sustainable Cities

The recent guidance in Planning Policy Statement 6 (PPS6), Planning for Town Centres aims to promote social inclusion: "ensuring that communities have access to a range of main town centre uses, and that deficiencies in provision in areas with poor access to facilities are remedied to deliver more sustainable patterns of development, ensuring that locations are fully exploited through high-density, mixed-use development and promoting sustainable transport choices, including reducing the need to travel and providing alternatives to car use." (ODPM 2005b).

National retail planning policy has made a significant impact upon reducing the number of out of town developments. However, much of the 'damage' has already been done, with supermarkets causing significant damage to traditional local and district retail areas, particularly in market towns (RTPI 2004). The elderly are often associated with 'food poverty' where there is insufficient access to local convenience retailers. Superstores often fail to address the needs of the less affluent and less mobile who do not live within the immediate vicinity of the store. Guidance in PPS6 (ODPM 2005b) recognises that people on low incomes may shop in a very different way to those with cars, making frequent trips on foot to a range of shops rather than doing a weekly car-based shop to a superstore. Those on lower incomes which include a growing number of the elderly are therefore particularly vulnerable to impacts upon local shopping provision (Centre for Future Studies 2002). While PPS6 represents a further strengthening of policy to protect local shopping facilities, the Department of Health's 'National Strategy for Neighbourhood Renewal' states that planning should be much more proactive in strengthening local retail centres and working with communities to develop locally generated solutions. This is not only beneficial for the poor and the elderly. Reducing transport needs would also make a positive contribution to the sustainable environments agenda.

Effective town centre management plays a crucial role in allowing all sectors of the community to get the most from urban areas. For example in recent years there has been a steady reduction in the number of public lavatory facilities in town and city centres (Gilroy 2004). This is due in part to the cost of maintaining them but also the fact that many department stores and all pubs offer toilets, however this may not appeal to older generations. This is just one example of how the public realm is becoming privatised. Another is outdoor seating areas of street cafés that are offered to those willing to pay for the privilege, public seating areas can be in short supply or designed to be attractive rather than functional. Small issues such as these have a huge implication for the way in which the elderly can use an urban area. Older people prefer peaceful places to sit and talk, this is often at odds with the idea of creating vibrant and bustling 24 hour cities (Gilroy 2004).

The Disability Discrimination Act 1995 came into full force in October 2004. This has some relevance to the aging population as it is reasonable to assume that escalating longevity will see a corresponding increase in mobility problems. The recent Planning Policy Statement 1 (PPS1), Delivering Sustainable Development restates the need for planning to include disabled and disadvantaged people. This legal duty to ensure rights of access for everyone may serve to break down another barrier to the elderly living in or visiting urban areas. Planners and town centre managers face a huge challenge in managing the competing interests of the 24 hour city. There are many conflicting demands when cities are increasingly dominated by consumption, by day in shops and by night through pubs and clubs (Gilroy 2004). The soon to be implemented policy of 24 hour opening for pubs and clubs is expected to have a negative impact on city centres and city living and may deter many over 50's from moving to the city centre as well as using them at night.

3.2 Housing

In terms of predicting future demand for new homes, much of the debate covers the numbers and location in which housing should be located rather than potential future occupiers. Beyond the provisions of social housing and 'affordable' housing targets, there is little that a local planning authority can do to determine future tenure in private developments. This leaves it to the market to provide homes to suit all sectors of the community. Planning can affect the level of attraction of an urban area by ensuring that the physical environment is enabling in terms of access and layout and that local facilities meet the needs of everyone, partly by securing developer contributions towards them (RTPI 2004). The real challenge of creating sustainable communities is to make them attractive places for everyone to live, acknowledging that different age groups place different demands and requirements upon a locality as well as their housing (Figure 6).

Figure 6. Lace Market in Nottingham which is enjoying a 'renaissance' as a mixed use quarter is extremely unattractive to anyone over 30! It is noisy, with unsafe streets and housing designed as vertical gated developments. Many buildings are not easily accessible for the elderly and the disabled. A missed opportunity.

Source: Author's Photograph

Currently the city centre building boom has resulted in a 140 % increase in residents in less than a decade in Manchester, Leeds, Newcastle and Liverpool. It is predicted that the current 20,000 residents will increase to 80,000 over the next decade in these cities. Unfortunately, the Local Authorities have so far allowed these areas to develop as ghettos for the young. As a recent editorial in The Times notes, "the regeneration of our city centres is a good thing but the balance of homes being built has to be carefully considered: a thriving city centre is not founded on a young, bar-going generation of one-bedroom apartment dwellers, but has to welcome families, older couples and the retired" (The Times 10/12/2005).

The preference for the re-use of brownfield land, together with the strength of the residential investment market are two reasons why there has been unprecedented numbers of homes built in town and city centres. The introduction of residential uses in town centres provides numerous benefits to the vitality of street life, with reduction in crime through increased 'eyes on the street' for example (Oc/Tiesdell 1997). Public policy faces numerous challenges in reducing inequality and creating environments that everyone can benefit from. The sustainability agenda and promotion of vibrant mixed-use urban areas will go some way if it ensures that no section of the community is disadvantaged by their local environment.

4. Conclusion

Older people in our society are making a diverse range of life choices. They are retiring at different ages, living in different locations and although some professionals would like them to go into retirement communities, there is a clear indication that people want to lead normal, independent lives in mixed communities for as long as possible. Residential care homes do not seem to be the choice of many, even the frailest. Those who move into these arrangements are often coerced into them. Current research and policy also tends to focus more on the needs of the poor elderly. The disadvantaged older people must be a focus because they have fewer choices. However, the needs of the middle class elderly must also be a focus although they can buy the housing and the services that they need, their choice is also limited because the market does not yet quite understand their need and government policy does not provide for their changing needs and demands. It must be stressed that in terms of the built environment the needs of both groups are very similar if not identical.

One demonstration of ageing which is not sufficiently researched is the experience of ethnic minority elderly. Ethnic minorities now constitute 8 % of the population in England and post-World War II immigrants are now in their 60's and 70's. It is wrongly assumed that the family networks would cater for their needs. Firstly, a number of the elderly, mainly Afro-Caribbean women, in this group were never partnered; secondly, the family support among the Asian groups is not as comprehensive as it is assumed. Although the Afro-Caribbean population are reasonably well equipped to navigate through the support systems available, the Asian elderly, especially Asian women are not, because many don't even speak the language. As seen above, there is significant concern about the economic implications of an ageing population, its consequences on our social security system and our health services. There is not adequate understanding in terms of the built environment's need to adapt. The re-configured built environment would not only provide a more inclusive environment for the ageing population but also for women, the very young and the disabled. The research into the economic impacts and research into the urban design facets of the built environment need to be considered together rather than independently. There is a need for further research into the design dimensions of individual residences using 'universal design' – creating buildings that are enabling for all, the young, the old, the pregnant and the disabled. Research into the use of the built environment by the ageing people within the agenda of sustainable cities would benefit the society as a whole.

What might be very effective is a greater political organisation of the elderly, similar to the 'Grey Vote' in the United States. Experience shows that when marginal groups like women or the ethnic minorities mobilise their political power, then policies which reflect their preferences are more likely to be explored and implemented. Society needs to see its changing age structure as an opportunity to develop more inclusive social and economic policies and environments, rather than viewing it as a burden. Cities that are to be inhabited by an ageing society must be sustainable environments that are more cohesive and more supportive to the needs and aspirations of the older citizens as well as other groups.

The 'Urban Renaissance' which is reshaping many British cities, driven by the sustainable cities agenda provides us with an opportunity. In restructuring our cities as high density agglomerations with good public transport supporting the new economy: policy and plans must take into consideration the needs of an ageing population. Our cities must enable the 55+'s to lead full and fulfilling lives in safe environments with employment opportunities and services that are easy to reach and easy to use. The public realm should be designed to enrich our lives through the various stages of our lives, including old age. We should build inclusive environments and avoid 'Ghettos of the elderly'.

References

AGE CONCERN ENGLAND (2002), *Age Concern's Policy Papers* ('Response to the Department of Transport, Local Government and the Regions Planning Green paper: Delivering a Fundamental Change', 'Transport Policy Position Paper', 'CapacityBuildingandCommunityDevelopment', 'Age Discrimination Policy Position Paper', The National Council on Ageing, Age Concern Policy Unit, London

APPLETON, N. (2002), "Planning for the Majority: The Needs and Aspirations of Older People", in: Joseph Rowntree Foundation (ed.), *General Housing*, York, York Publishing Services,

APPLETON, N. (2004), *Ready, Steady... But Not Quite Go: Older Home Owners and Equity Release: a Review*, York, Joseph Rowntree Foundation

BGOP (Better Government for older people), 2000, All Our Futures: The report of the Better Government for Older People steering committee, Wolverhampton.

CARLTON, S.,SOULSBY, J. (1999), Learning to Grow Older and Bolder: A Policy Discussion Paper on Learning, Leicester, NIACE

CATALYST (2003), *The Challenge of Longer Life: Economic Burden or Social Opportunity?*, the report of the Qorking Group on the Amplications of Demographic Change, London

CENTRE FOR FUTURE STUDIES (ed.) (2002), *Is the Ageing Population the Problem it's Made Out to Be?*, Canterbury

CHAO. T. Y. (2004), *City Living and Empty Nesters – Attitudes to Mixed-use Areas*, Nottingham, University of Nottingham, Ph.D. Thesis

DETR (Department of the Environment, Transport and the Regions) (1996), *English House Condition Survey*, www.detr.gov.uk, accessed Aug. 5, 2005

DETR (Department of the Environment, Transport and the Regions) (1998a), *Sustainable Development: Opportunities for Change*, Consultation Paper on a Revised UK Strategy (Consultation document)

DETR (Department of the Environment, Transport and the Regions) (1998b), *Planning for the Communities of the Future*, Stationery Office, London

DETR (Department of the Environment, Transport and the Regions) (2001), *Quality and Choice for Older People's Housing: A Strategic Framework*, www.housing.detr.gov.uk/information/hsc/older-people/index.htm, accessed August 5, 2005

DWP (Department for Work and Pensions) (2004), *Independent Living in Later Life*, www.dwp.gov.uk/asd/asd5/rports2003-2004/rport216/Main.pdf, London

EOC (Equal Opportunities Commission) (2005), *Older Workers and Options for Flexible Work*, Working Paper 31, www.eoc.org.uk/research, London

FORREST, R., LEATHER, P., PANTAZIS, C. (1997), *Home Ownership in Old Age: The Future of Owner Occupation in an Ageing Society*, www.anchor.org.uk/publications_pdfs/home-ownership.pdf, accessed August 5, 2005

GAD (Government Actuary's Department) (2003), *Projections database*, www.gad.gov.uk/Population/index.asp, accessed August 5, 2005

GILROY, R. (2004), "Making Cities Friendly to Older People", *Town and Country Planning*, No. 73, p. 254-256

GRUNDY, E., GLASER, K. (1999); "Gender, Migration and Household Change in Elderly Age Groups", in: Boyle, B., Halfacree, K. (eds.), *Migration and Gender in the Developed World*, London, Routledge, p. 280-293

HEA (Health Education Authority) (1997), *Promoting the Health of Older People: A Compendium*, London

JARVIS, C., HANCOCK, R., ASKHAM, J., TINKER, A. (1996), *Getting Around After 60: A Profile of Britain's Older Population*, London, HMSO (Her Majesty's Stationery Office)

KLERK, L. de, VIJGEN, J. (1992), "Inner Cities as a cultural and Public Arena: Plans and People in Amsterdam and Rotterdam", *Built Environment*, Vol. 18, No. 2, p. 100-110

MITCHELL, K. (2002), "Older People and Road Safety: Dispelling the Myths", *World Transport Policy & Practice*, No. 8/2002, p. 17-26

MITCHELL, I., BURTON, E., RAMAN, S. (2004), "Dementia-friendly Cities: Designing Intelligible Neighbourhoods", *Journal of Urban Design*, Vol. 9, Oxfordshire, Carfax Publishing

NATIONAL STATISTICS (2006), *Census 2001: The most comprehensive survey of the UK population*, www.statistics.gov.uk/census/default.asp, accessed Jan/10 2006

NOP WORLD RESEARCH (2005), *'Location, Location, Location', Survey Conducted on behalf of Halifax Estate Agents 8th May 2005*, www.hbosplc.com/media/pressreleases/articles/halifax/2005-06-04-01.asp

OC, T., CHAO, T. Y., (2004), Future City Centre Living and the Ageing Society – Attitudes to Mixviews Developments in the UK, www.uic.edu/cuppa/cityfutures/papers/session5_4/5_4futurecity.pdf, accessed August 5, 2005

OC, T., TIESDELL, S. (1997), *Safer City Centres: Reviving the Public Realm*, London, Paul Chapman/Sage

ODPM (Office of the Deputy Prime Minister) (2005a), *Planning Policy Statement 1: Delivering Sustainable Development*, London, HMSO

ODPM (Office of the Deputy Prime Minister) (2005b), *Planning Policy Statement 6 – Planning for Town Centres*, London, HMSO,

ODPM (Office of the Deputy Prime Minister) (2005c), *Excluded Older People: Social Exclusion Unit Interim Report*, www.info4local.gov.uk/searchreport.asp?id=23553&heading=e-mail+alert

ONS (Office for National Statistics) (2003), *Population Estimates*, www.statistics.gov.uk/cci/nugget.asp?id=6, accessed August 5, 2005

ONS (Office for National Statistics) (2004), *Annual Abstract of Statistics 2004*, Newport

PEACE, S. M., HOLLAND, C. (2001), *Inclusive Housing in an Ageing Society*, Bristol, *Policy Press*

PEACE, S. M., HOLLAND, C. (2003), "Environment and Identity in Later Life: A Cross-setting Study", in: ESRC (Economic and Social Research Council) (ed.) (2004), *Growing Older Programme: Project Summaries, Economic and Social Research Council*, Swindon.

PHILLIPS, D., BARTLETT, H. (1997), "Age", in: Pacione, M. (ed.), *Britain's Cities: Geographies of Division in Urban Britain*, London, Routledge

PHILLIPS, J. (1999), *Broadening our Vision of Housing and Community Care for Older People: Innovative Examples from Finland, Sweden and England*, Kidlington, Anchor Research

RHODEN, M. (1998), "Equal Opportunities in Housing", in: Balchin, P., Rhoden, M. (eds.), *Housing the Essential Foundations*, London, Routledge

ROGERSON, R., FINDLAY, A., MORRIS, A., COOMBES, M. (1989), "Indicators of Quality of Life: Some Methodological Issues", *Environment and Planning A*, Vol. 21, No. 12, p. 1655-1666

RTPI (Royal Town Planning Institute) (2004), Planning for an Ageing Population, www.rtpi.org.uk/resources/publications/ageing/

SYKES, R. (ed.) (1992), *Age, Care and Housing*, Oxford, Anchor Housing Trust

THOMAS, C., BROMLEY, R. (2000), "City Centre Revitalisation: Problems of Fragmentation and Fear in the Evening and Night-time City", *Urban Studies*, No. 37, p. 1403-29

TINKER, A. (1997), *Older People in Modern Society*, London, Longman

WILLIAMS, J. (2005), "Homes For The Future – A Sustainable Way to Accommodate One-person Households", *Town and Country Planning*, No. 4/2005, p. 138-142

LEISURE IN AN URBAN ENVIRONMENT

by David Camp

Introduction

I'm not a planner, what I deal with is numbers. This paper is going to talk about leisure from a market and an economic perspective and will try to give a bit of a flavour of how some of the leisure environments work. I want to debunk some of the myths about leisure and try to focus on facts and figures about the markets and their dynamics. I also want to give an insight on how we try to establish a balance between planners/designers who have great visions and aspirations and want to do noble things and make great landmarks, and developers who do not really care about all that but are interested in their monetary return from a project. To do that we have to try and juggle the balance between the developers and the ultimate landowners.

After defining some key aspects of leisure, the paper will look at some of the important markets and the ways the economics of leisure work. Some of the principles behind leisure are explored and how all they relate to development and planning. In the following section some of the life-style trends and aspects of socio-economic change impacting upon urban cores are covered. The final part of the paper is presenting some conclusions on how to put all that together and plan for the future.

One preliminary remark: Leisure is a tough business. Nevertheless, everybody in the world is an expert on leisure. Too many people seem to know better than Disney; too many times we see a project announced as being completely unique. On the contrary, leisure works in more or less the same ways all around the world. About 80 % of the things we do around the world are pretty similar. In Germany, Hong Kong, the US, South Africa, wherever you are, people are going out with friends, having a good time, socializing, spending time enjoying leisure activities. But there are important local factors – the final 20 %. For example if you open a restaurant in Minnesota and you plan to open at 9 pm. you will need to change plans quickly because at that time no one's out and all your would-be guests are home and gone to bed. In Madrid no one goes out before 9 pm. in the evening for a meal. Understanding these local nuances is vitally important. But that's the remaining 20 % of a project's details. The fundamental principles of what makes a good restaurant work apply around the world. I want to focus on the general dynamics that apply around the world and show how we look at it.

1. Types of Leisure in the Urban Context

When talking about leisure, a distinction can be made in between 'destination leisure' and 'regular leisure'. Retail can be found in the two of them but as a stand-alone category it shows patterns pretty similar to those of regular leisure.

Destination leisure covers everything from theme parks and fun fairs to historic houses and museums. Destination leisure is what you do on a day out or on a weekend break, things you don't just do by chance but explicitly go to, where there is a little planning involved. The EXPO for example was a destination leisure activity in Hanover. Depending on where you live, going there could be a day trip out while for others it is a luxurious holiday because they already have to go so far. Regular leisure is very different. It is by far more local. It's the cinemas, the clubs, bars and restaurants, the fitness centres and all those sorts of things. And retail is part of that as it is something you do frequently.

1.1 Destination Leisure

Destination fun – the theme parks and all sorts of big thrill activities – has a broad appeal. It draws people from many kilometres away, sometimes draws people overnight. You pay a high ticket price to go in. It can be profitable operationally but there is massive capital cost associated with it. And that's the big problem with theme parks: They don't make money. The common perspective on theme parks as money making machines is the first myth to be debunked. Many of the big developments like Disneyland Paris for example share similar problems.

Nowadays you cannot make money when you build a big new theme park, but you can make money when you grow over time. In Europe some fantastic theme parks have been around for 25-30 years now, they have grown gradually, used the money from the business to reinvest and gradually expanded. Such an approach is far less risky than to try and develop a new large sized theme park from scratch. You do not get a second chance with a 200 million Euro new theme park if the public does not like it.

Culture has a more narrow appeal and more of a niche character. Ticket prices are generally lower because people don't travel as far, and do not stay as long. In economic terms they are marginal operations at best and many require subsidies. Generally capital costs are lower here than at theme parks, although some of the big landmark icon projects are huge. The Guggenheim in Bilbao for example cost over 50 million Euros, although this is still modest compared to the 200 million Euros of Warner's in Bottrop.

1.2 Regular Leisure

Regular leisure has a local appeal. You generally do not go much further than 20 or 30 minutes from your home to do these activities, unless it is a meal out with friends in a particular location. Regular leisure is more neighbourhood based, so for developers it is local environments they have to work on. Here, a lower ticket price is profitable because capital costs are not that high. A great advantage of this market is that others fund your project. Increasingly, developers only build the shell, a framework and someone comes in and fits in a bar, a restaurant and those sorts of things. This method has proven to work pretty well in order to leverage other people's money.

2. Leisure Supply: Comparing Characteristics of Different Types of Businesses

Figure 1 shows different examples of leisure destinations and how they relate to certain characteristics such as the educational approach of a destination vis à vis the fun-approach of another. The graphic also indicates the different levels of excitement or 'wow-effect' these forms of leisure have.

The top right field of the figure indicates the biggest appeal. The theme parks clearly have the broadest appeal. They are the most fun and have the wildest big new rides, although the big thrill rides often aren't the most popular. The most ridden are the family water rides that grandma and the kids and everyone go on. Nevertheless the big ride still serves as a magnet for the park as a whole even if people only look at it to decide to take a smaller, less intimidating ride next to it. Moving across the diagram, you get a diminishment of appeal. As a broad generalisation we may say 5 % of a population within a range of one hour might be seen going to a museum or perhaps 10 % might do a wildlife attraction or a zoo, maybe 15 % might do a theme park. The diagonal line indicates operational viability. Projects above to the upper right of that line make profits on an operational basis. Capital cost is not considered here. Projects below to the left don't even cover their operating costs. That is the major issue especially with cultural and historic attractions and museums. You can't actually make money because you can't charge people ticket prices high enough to warrant the operating costs. In the middle of the diagram you find leisure projects such as heritage centres, science centres, wildlife attractions and zoos that all are on the margin of making operational profits. Sometimes they work very well, other times they plunge into deficit and struggle with funding problems and communities will have to decide whether and how to maintain them.

2.1 Business Characteristics of Destination Leisure

As an example for the dimensions of profits that can be made with leisure area, the table below shows figures for EBITDA (i.e. earnings before interest, tax, depreciation and amortisation) of selected theme parks. EBITDA basically indicates the operating profit of a business, the way that banks and funds focus on the operational business. For every Euro spent at Disney in Paris, 17 cents of profit are made. 83 cents go back out in costs. There are very few theme parks that make more than 40 % profits in EBITDA.

2.1.1 Theme Parks

Developers of any given theme park probably spend an equivalent of 100 Euros per visitor on capital cost. So a theme park for a million people would cost around 100 million Euros to build. They charge probably about 30 Euros per person as an entrance fee. It is a bit cheaper in Germany, a bit more expensive in the UK, but the average is about 30 Euros. If they can make approximately 33 % profit they are making 10 Euros profit per person on that 100 million Euros investment (Table 1).

Even more important is the problem of reinvestment. You must reinvest – just to stand still, not to move forward. In theme parks and attractions you reinvest just to keep your operating business going. And that investment makes up for probably about 10 % of your turnover. So that suggests may be only seven Euros profit per visitor left to fund 100 Euros capital cost, to pay the principal, to pay the interest, to pay the shareholders, to put aside for a rainy day – it really is a tough business. And that's why you see problems with new parks such as those in Spain because the investment level is too high to be borne by the business. And there's no way around it – at some point you have to write

Table 1. EBITDA of selected Theme Parks and Groups.

Cedar Fair group	32,1 %
Six Flags group	29,1 %
Parc Asterix, north of Paris	27,0 %
Disneyland Paris	17,1 %

Source: Author's compilation

Table 2. EBITDA of selected Wildlife Destinations.

Chester Zoo	30,3 %
Genoa Aquarium	10,0 %
New Jersey Aquarium	1,9 %
London Zoo	1,3 %

Source: Author's compilation

Figure 1. Breadth of appeal of different examples of leisure destinations.

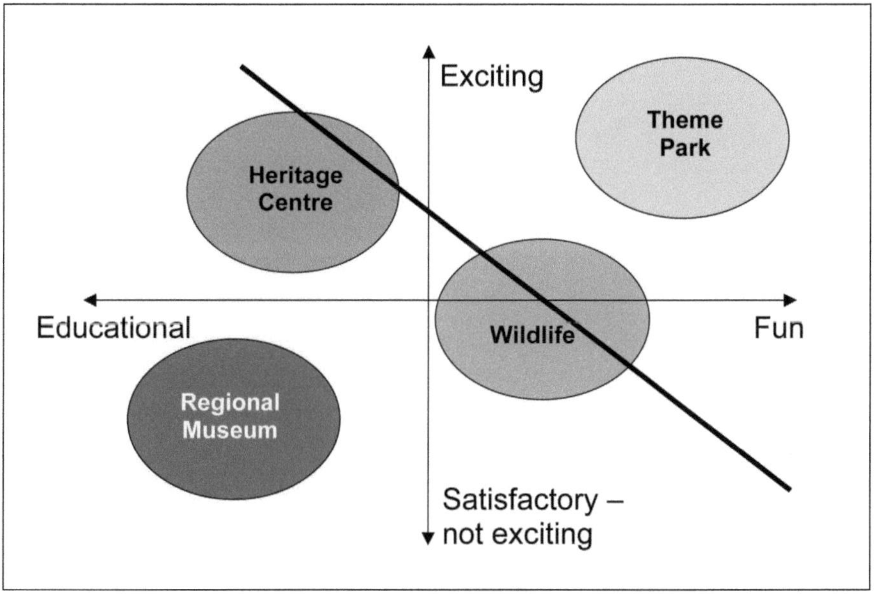

Source: Author's compilation

off the money. In fact what we see now is banks writing off massive chunks of money to get the asset bases down to a level where the business can support it.

When our company does business valuations on theme parks, we value it on a multiple of EBITDA. If a park is getting 10 million Euros EBITDA, then you have to multiply that maybe five, six, seven times to calculate the value of the business. Thus you may have a business that's worth 80-90 million Euros even though 200 million has been invested in its creation. The issue with the valuation of the business is that it is based on bodies per passing through it not the amount invested.

ERA is an American company and our founder did the first feasibility study of Disneyland in California. One of the early studies on the completed park found that with one dollar spent inside the theme park in Anaheim two dollars were spent outside on hotels, restaurants, lodging etc. The external economic effects of Disneyland were important. That's why when Disney went to Orlando, they built a complex on 10,000 hectares of land outside the city, to effectively control the full three dollars, not just one. Theme parks have a wide impact on the surrounding areas raising values, profile and awareness, and to assess a park purely on its internal business does not reflect these benefits.

2.1.2 Zoos and Wildlife Attractions

Wildlife is a business sector with very mixed results. Chester Zoo for example is a very well operated small zoo in the UK that gets a profit margin equivalent to some of the theme parks. Genoa Aquarium is a great aquarium down in the waterfront in Genoa that also runs very well. But there are many examples that just cannot do without subsidies. The Aquarium of New Jersey in the US for example makes only 1.9 % profits in EBITDA. And this number has significant subsidies included. If you remove the subsidies you end up with minus 44 % profit. Thus subsidies make up for almost half of the income in this case. This is a common occurrence with aquariums, they are massively subsidised. The aquarium of Monterey Bay makes about 30 % profit with the subsidies included; without the subsidies it has less than 10 % profit. This often makes it very hard to reinvest in new attractions once your spending depends on subsidies from outside. Subsidies can get cut as often as they increase (Table 2).

2.1.3 Museums

Looking at museums you generally do not look at profits, you look at subsidies. For every one of the 3 million visitors per year at the Louvre in Paris there are almost 30 Euros of subsidies paid by the French and Paris government. That makes up for 90 million Euros a year in subsidies for the Louvre alone. A big share of that is put to acquisitions and only partly to operations but it is still a massive subsidy. The Van Gogh Museum in Amsterdam as well as the Guggenheim in Bilbao both receive approximately five Euros per visitor in subsidies (Table 3). With around 1 million visitors to the Guggenheim at a subside of five Euros a head plus the 50 plus million Euros capital cost being paid for by the regional government adds up to a considerable investment. So why do local and national governments spend so much on a single museum? For an answer just consider what the image of Bilbao is like now compared to what it was like ten years ago. Tourism has grown, business conferences have grown as the image of Bilbao from being a run-down poor north Spanish industrial back lands has changed to being one of the most desirable European cities. This one development has transformed Bilbao and that is why it is a great investment for the city council. But for a private de-

Table 3. Subsidies per visitor in selected museums.

Louvre, Paris	29.57 Euro
National History Museum, London	18.95 Euro
Van Gogh, Amsterdam	5.15 Euro
Guggenheim, Bilbao	4.84 Euro

Source: Author's compilation

veloper or someone that is involved in a mixed use scheme, there is no return. So how to balance leisure with a private developer's aspiration is a very important and difficult question. The benefits of such investments do not go to the developer. Investments like Guggenheim in Bilbao benefit the wider city and benefit the region on a whole.

2.2 Business Characteristics of Regular Leisure

Generally EBITDA for a fitness centre, restaurant, bar or a cinema complex is between 10 % and 25 %. The operators of these venues pay rent to a landlord/developer but as they often do not give huge returns to the developer there are many schemes that are little more than sheds surrounding a car park.

A distinct concept is Heron City. UK developer Heron wanted to create coordinated entertainment centres with activities and events in multi-levelled schemes combining bars, restaurants, dining, and other leisure activities. The only trouble is: the extra capital costs that were required to create that were not sufficiently rewarded by the increasing rents. A leisure operator that would typically pay rents of maybe 100 or 150 Euros per square meter would not be prepared to pay 250 Euros just because it is in a nice pretty building unless their business levels were twice as strong. Tenants can only afford a certain level of rent. At in Heron City, the rent level was not high enough to cover the additional costs of the urban design. Heron has now stopped developing those schemes.

2.3 Business Principles in Leisure

Leisure's about bums on seats. Whether you look at a restaurant or a cinema – an empty seat does not make you any money. Leisure spending is linked to time and value. With an assumed ticket price for a cinema of about 7.50 Euros that makes about 3.50 to 4 Euros per hour. That is a pretty good measure of a value. In a theme park you stay for maybe eight hours and you are paying 30 Euros. Generally people do not rigidly say: "Right, my hour is worth four Euros" but in their mind they have a view of value. When you are trying to charge 20 Euros to go to a museum, which is a two hours' stay, the average customer will expect a high quality experience and if he does not get this he will tell his friends about it.

As I mentioned earlier, high capital costs and the need to reinvest are the biggest problems. The more locals you get going through an attraction, the more frequently you need to reinvest. If you're lucky enough to deal with tourists who come once every 10 years, you rely on the same concept drawing people for a number of years as the market will be regularly changing. Drawing local customers back requires there to be something new to see and do. If there is not, they won't revisit. Theme parks have got the broadest appeal and invest the most. Mature theme parks do not advertise the park they advertise this year's new ride. It is similar in established museums and galleries – they seek to attract people to come back through events, a special activity or a new exhibition.

3. Leisure as Part of Mixed-Use Developments

3.1 General Principles

When you decide to look at leisure as part of a mixed use scheme, you need to understand what you are doing it for. What are the driving forces behind the scheme as a whole? Leisure on its own is tough to make work. Leisure as part of a mixed use scheme creating a work-live-play environment is fantastic. But how do you mix it in with other uses when you know that it is probably not going to make enough money on its own? You're going to need to subsidise the construction and provide for reinvestment. You go to allow for the operators to put money back into the business. You cannot bleed them in terms of charging them high rents. So when looking at such a development ask some questions. What are you doing? What are you creating? Who are you creating it for? Importantly (and this is a rather obvious but under-asked question), who are the customers?

Sadly, most developers and most planners do not think of the end users as the customers. The customers for most developers are their investors or their tenants. But it is the people actually using the facilities who – if you do not do it right – will go somewhere else and your scheme will die. So when conceiving such a project it has to be clear whether you are looking at residents or tourists or a business market? Questions of time play a very important role too. A daytime environment is not necessarily a good night time environment and vice versa. While residential developments can bring in money, not everyone likes to live close to noisy bars, restaurants and clubs. Sports venues such as stadiums and arenas are used only occasionally. But when they are used, they are full of people and very noisy. And the surges of people in and out of the venue can be a transport nightmare. So they generally do not make for good neighbours.

3.2 Strategic Programming

A strategic look at target markets is very important. Who are the customers, the people who are going to be using it ultimately?

It is important to look at the gaps and the opportunities in the market-place. It is not enough to have a vision and to be willing to create something special. If your project is

actually five blocks from the downtown night time circuit and there is not enough density, not enough critical mass to make it work and there is no links between the two you are destined to struggle or fail because you're not close enough. In that situation you will have to ensure that there is enough critical mass within a project itself or to chose the location for your project in way that expands the centre.
The selection and arrangement of uses within a mixed-use scheme is vital. Developers need to determine what's going to drive a mixed use scheme commercially? Once the commercial drivers are set, they can then look at subsidised anchors that do not make profit on their own but attract people to the site. Generally, leisure, art and culture can be subsidised on the back of a commercially-driven scheme. In between the subsidised elements and the commercial drivers are those that are meant to operate on a break-even basis. Finally developers look at questions of community support and community needs they are required to provide for. In the end this process of strategic decision making hopefully leads to successful mix and phasing.

The biggest appeal once again is with theme parks and icon attractions like the London Eye (Figure 2). Over to the left are projects with a far more local appeal. On the top are profitable uses that could subsidise other functions. Down at the bottom are the cultural attractions, public assembly, art centres, museums and other cultural offers. Those are the ones that need money from other elements of the scheme.

Figure 2. Breadth of appeal of selected uses and functions and their profitability, their capability to work as a commercial driver of a mixed-use scheme.

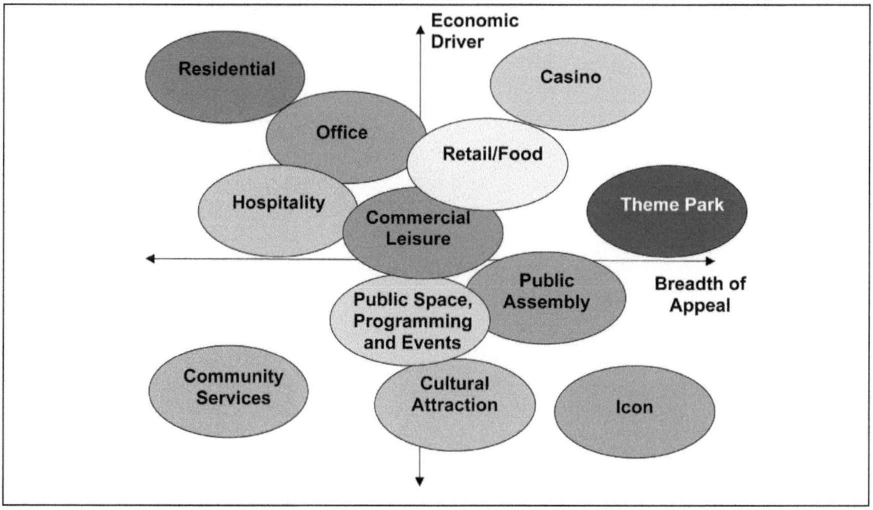

Source: Author's diagram

In the example of Gunwharf Keys in Portsmouth residential units are included which give a significant cash input to allow for a lot of other uses. Gunwharf Keys is adjacent to the town centre. As well as residential, the scheme includes office units, retail, food and beverage, a casino, a hotel, cinema, bingo and a bowling centre. And finally there is the Spinnaker Tower – a 110 meter high viewing tower and icon for the site. The scheme features a very good mix of uses, of daytime, night time activities, with people living there and people working there. The whole environment works very well.

As an example for an unbalanced scheme that did not work out so well one is the Old Port in Barcelona. When it opened, it was very popular. It is got a retail centre, entertainment, an aquarium and an IMAX cinema. But no one lives there and no one works there. In the day it is busy with tourists but in the evening when all the tourists go it is empty. The locals do not go shopping there because the shopping centre is focused on tourists. Some locals were using the bars and restaurants at the start but this has declined and they've gradually moved downmarket. The whole development is caught up in a downward spiral and it stems from a lack of balance between people living, working and enjoying themselves there to make it effective.

4. Demand-side Developments: Socio-economic Change and Lifestyle-trends

4.1 The Coming of Age

There are major changes occurring on the demand side of the leisure market result from the ageing of our societies. The 'Limbo Generation' of 60 plus year-olds are far more active and able to do far more than people of the same age were 20 years ago. No one considers himself old anymore. This changes more than just attitudes, and people want to do the things they were doing at 40 and now have more time and money to do it. The problem is that most people working in advertising and marketing are 20 somethings. They do not understand older people and how aging has changed. They focus on the young exciting people because they do not consider older people a market. But 50 % of discretionary income lies within this age profile. That is a massive market. When you go on an Easy Jet or an Air Berlin flight – who is the market? Students and 50 plus, they are the main groups. These flights are full of people who go on a trip in mid-week because they can go whenever they want to. They drive a massive part of the economy. They look for experiences, they look for multiple activities to do. They are very active but unfortunately people tend to put them down and think they cannot do anything anymore.

Three quarters of all baby boomers would rather spend their money than leave it for their kids. There was even a whole new term created for this attitude: SKINS – spending kids' inheritance now. People are spending and having fun. But they are not only spending on fun but on education too.

Another important development is the comeback of grandparents in childcare. The term for this is 'Granny nannies', grandparents who are available and want to spend time with their grandkids, particularly when they are not yet in school. But because granny nannies have a traditional view of what is appropriate and like to understand what they are doing they have a different view of the new leisure offers to their children. That is why the three-generation product is important as is how to communicate with this market. Grandparents, parents and children don't read the same magazines or watch the same TV programmes. The communication as well as the media used to communicate to be very different between these three markets.

Markets for kids and families are also changing because parents are having less children, are often older when they have kids than in previous years, and have more money but less time. So when their kids have playtime, they are going to value out of it. So leisure time is quality time. In addition, parents' aspirations have also changed. You cannot simply have fun as a kid anymore. You have to learn something; you have to get something out of it. Legoland for example has a far higher social profile of visitors than any other theme park because the parents see Lego as an instructional toy. You have your fun as well, but you can learn something.

4.2 Developments in Free-time Arrangements: Vacation

In many countries free-time and vacations are actually diminishing, particularly for highly qualified personnel. One third of professionals in the UK do not take all of their holidays. One third of managers in the US take only half of their holiday entitlement. People find it harder and harder to let go of their work. They take more and more work home at night or over the week-end and stay available in holidays. When people do have holidays they want to make sure it is perfect. They go on short breaks to places where there is everything to do in a short period of time. In mixed urban cores with a certain amount of attractions you get a lot of things in a very easily accessible pedestrian environment. That is why short breaks to smaller cities and regional cities work so well. You can get a new experience in two days and be back at work immediately. You missed no time at work but you have had a different cultural experience. So creating these places where people can do a lot of things in one go is important.

4.3 Developments in Free-time Arrangements: Lunch-breaks

Meal times are getting shorter and shorter. Today, lunch is most often nothing more than a sandwich at your desk or five minutes sitting outside in the sunshine then straight back in to finish off what you have been doing. The trend to shorten breaks has already changed our supermarkets. When you went into a supermarket ten years ago, there would not be a big rack of sandwiches, drinks, snacks and quick meals to take away. Today you find that in each and every supermarket and there are chain stores like Prêt-A-Manger on every corner of office and commercial areas. People are moving to grazing rather than dining. So will Starbucks be the death of the family meal? It could. But maybe it is an opportunity for city centres. Maybe only the big family meal at home is dying out and people prefer going out together. At home at least one family member will always be too distracted to come to dinner – one's on the computer, the kids are doing this, mum's watching that – you always end up with a tray on your lap, watching TV or whatever. But once you are out in town to have a family dinner, there is no turning back to your computer or the TV. People who want to make sure they enjoy their family meal will increasingly go out together even if it is only for some coffee and cake at a Starbucks. And that perhaps changes the dynamic in advantage for the city centres.

4.4 Healthcare and Fitness

In the UK – and it is probably similar in many other countries – a third of the population will be medically obese by 2020. As a consequence, the demand for healthcare is expected to triple and similarly the need for exercise and weight loss programmes is going to increase. What does that mean for urban environments? Obviously there will be growth in health and fitness centres but these issues are also linked to questions of healthy lifestyles and healthy urban living. In terms of design, a fitness centre with a bank full of mirrors for beautiful people to look at themselves is not going to be very appealing for people with weight problems. For this growing group of people, developers of fitness and wellness centres will have to design clubs in order to encourage them to go back on a regular basis. So creating the design environment that actually makes that work is very important.

Another development related to this issue is that designing for larger people will go hand in hand with charging those people more. Especially flight companies will have to deal with this. Planes in the US already tend to have a bit more room than they do in Europe, because there are more large people in the US. The challenge for companies like Easy Jet will be, how to fit in more and more passengers into their planes, while people actually get bigger and bigger and still be able to charge them more money to make more profits.

4.5 Cocacolaisation and McDisneyfication: Brandscapes

The retail and food & beverage sectors all over the world experience ever increasing levels of concentration and franchising. In consequence, city centres are looking more and more alike. When you travel to the centre of most European cities it is often hard to tell where you are as the retail centres and restaurants are all similar. People complain but the trouble is the customers want this. They want brands like GAP, MANGO and McDonald's and they are always going to go where they get those kinds of offers.

So how do you blend the customers' aspirations for brand-driven environments with the need to try and create something that is a bit different and gives you a flavour and a feel for an individual environment? It is a difficult problem. Public realm is very important: open spaces and other environmental measures as well as an innovative mix of uses can be used to differentiate your project. You can put the brands in, but the decisive question is how you mix those into an individual and distinctive location and then actually create a very good place.

5. Conclusions

What does it mean if you try to create a place and destination, what do you do? You have to start with vision. The vision is the key. You cannot succeed without a vision but you must also take account of markets and economics. The key is getting the balance right in being led by a vision and guided by the markets. This way you can create some fantastic environments and fantastic spaces and fantastic icons that work. And that is really where cities and developers alike want to be aiming.

APPENDIX

LIST OF AUTHORS

BROWN, NICHOLAS, BArch/DipArch
was research assistant at the Institute of Urban Planning, Nottingham University and currently works as practising architect.

CAMP, DAVID
is Associate Director in the London Office of ERA (Economic Research Associates). He specialises on consulting business in the leisure and entertainment industries throughout Europe and heads ERA's European attractions and entertainment team.

CAPELLO, ROBERTA, Prof.
teaches Urban and Regional Economics at Milan's Technical University. Roberta Capello is on the boards of both the Italian Regional Science Association AISRe (Associazione Italiana di Scienze Regionali) and the Regional Science Association International (RSAI). Her major fields of research are: Regional Endogenous Theories, Innovation and Regional Development, Urban Networks, Urban Rent and Urban Growth.

CARSTEN, STEFAN, Dr.
works as geographer and futurologist for DaimlerChrysler's Society and Technology Research Group (RMI/Y) in Berlin.

CHAO, TZU-YUAN, PhD
is currently working as an assistant professor in Taiwan. She acquired her PhD degree at Nottingham University where she worked on 'City Living and Baby Boomers – Attitudes to mixed use areas'.

CHRISTIAANSE, KEES, Prof.

is a practising architect with offices in The Netherlands and Germany and teaches Architecture and Urban Design at Zurich's Technical University (ETH). Kees Christiaanse worked for OMA (Office for Metropolitan Architecture) before founding his own offices KCAP and later ASTOC. He held a Visiting Professorship for Architecture and Urban Design at the Institute of Architecture at Berlin's Technical University.

GRAHAM, STEPHEN, Prof.

is Professor of Human Geography at the University of Durham. He was a Visiting Professor at the Department of Urban Studies and Planning at Massachusetts Institute of Technology (MIT), as well as at the Centre for Sustainable Urban and Regional Futures at Salford University and at Newcastle University's Global Urban Research Unit. Stephen Graham worked in planning and economic development at Sheffield City Council and co-founded the Centre for Urban Technology (CUT) at Newcastle University. Graham specialises in exploring the intersections of mobility, technology and urban life.

HENCKEL, DIETRICH, Prof.

worked as a researcher at the German Institute of Urban Affairs (Difu). He is now dean of the Institute of Urban and Regional Planning where he teaches Urban and Regional Economics and, Technical University of Berlin. Dietrich Henckel is member of several German and international research associations andon the executive board of the German Society for Time Policy (DGfZP). He specialises in Urban Structural Change, Time and the City, Knowledge and the Informational City, Urban and Regional Economic Development Policy.

HERKOMMER, BENJAMIN

studies Urban and Regional Planning at the Technical University Berlin. He was research assistant at the German Institute of Urban Affairs (Difu) and the Institute of Sociology, Technical University Berlin. Benjamin Herkommer is member of the German Society for Time Policy (DGfZP) and currently works as research assistant at the Institute of Urban and Regional Planning, Technical University Berlin.

KOCH, MICHAEL, Prof.

is member of several professional association in Germany and Switzerland and associate of Büro Z – Architektur, Städtebau, Planung, Zurich. He had several teaching assignments at different universities in Switzerland, was visiting professor at the Institute of Urban and Regional Planning, Technical University Berlin, then professor for Urban Design and dean of Wuppertal University's School of Architecture, Design and Art. Currently, Michael Koch is Professor for Urban Design and Management of Neighbourhoods and head of the Department for Urban Development, Town Planning and Management of Neighbourhoods and Projects at the HafenCity University Hamburg.

MARKUSEN, ANN, Prof.
teaches Urban Planning as well as Urban and Regional Economics at Minnesota University's Hubert Humphrey Institute of Public Affairs and is the director of the Institute's Project on Regional and Industrial Economics. Ann Markusen was State of New Jersey Professor of Urban Planning and Policy Development at Rutgers University and has held faculty positions at Northwestern University, the University of California at Berkeley and the University of Colorado. She presided the North American Regional Science Association and served as a member of the President's Commission on Offsets in International Trade.

OC, TANER, Prof.
teaches Urban Design, Urban Regeneration and Planning and is director of Nottingham University's Institute of Urban Planning. Taner Oc specialises in Ageing and City Living, Safer Cities and Ethnic Minorities and Planning.

PAHL-WEBER, ELKE, Prof.
is head of Urban Planning and Design Consultants BPW-Hamburg and teaches Urban Renewal and Planning at the Institute of Urban and Regional Planning, Technical University Berlin. Elke Pahl-Weber is member of the German Academy for Urban and Regional Planning DASL (Deutsche Akademie für Städtebau und Landesplanung DASL) and on the Institutional Board of the German Institute of Urban Affairs (Difu). She had several teaching assignments and held a Visiting Professorship at Kassel University's Institute of Architecture, Urban and Landscape Planning.

SANDER, HENRIK, Dipl.-Ing.
had teaching assignments at the Institute of Urban and Regional Planning, Technical University Berlin, at Wuppertal University's School of Architecture, Design and Art and at the Institute of Urban Design, HafenCity University Hamburg (HCU). Currently, he works as a research assistant of Prof. Michael Koch at the Institute of Urban Design and Management of Neighbourhoods, HCU. He also is associate of orange.edge, Office for Urban Research + Marketing, Essen.